UTILITY
OF
GAINS AND LOSSES:

Measurement-Theoretical
and Experimental Approaches

SCIENTIFIC PSYCHOLOGY SERIES

Stephen W. Link and James T. Townsend, Series Editors

MONOGRAPHS

R. Duncan Luce • Utility of Gains and Losses: Measurement-Theoretical and Experimental Approaches

William R. Uttal • The War Between Mentalism and Behaviorism: On the Accessibility of Mental Processes

William R. Uttal • Toward a New Behaviorism: The Case Against Perceptual Reductionism

Gordon M. Redding and Benjamin Wallace • Adaptive Spatial Alignment

John C. Baird • Sensation and Judgment: Complementarity Theory of Psychophysics

John A. Swets • Signal Detection Theory and ROC Analysis in Psychology and Diagnostics: Collected Papers

William R. Uttal • The Swimmer: An Integrated Computational Model of a Perceptual–Motor System

Stephen W. Link • The Wave Theory of Difference and Similarity

EDITED VOLUMES

Jonathan Grainger and Arthur M. Jacobs • Localist Connectionist Approaches to Human Cognition

Cornilia E. Dowling, Fred S. Roberts, and Peter Theuns • Recent Progress in Mathematical Psychology

F. Gregory Ashby • Multidimensional Models of Perception and Cognition

Hans-Georg Geissler, Stephen W. Link, and James T. Townsend • Cognition, Information Processing, and Psychophysics: Basic Issues

UTILITY
OF
GAINS AND LOSSES:

Measurement-Theoretical
and Experimental Approaches

R. Duncan Luce
University of California, Irvine

LAWRENCE ERLBAUM ASSOCIATES, PUBLISHERS
2000   Mahwah, New Jersey   London

Lawrence Erlbaum Associates, Inc., Publishers
10 Industrial Avenue
Mahwah, New Jersey 07430

Library of Congress Cataloging-in-Publication Data

Luce, R. Duncan (Robert Duncan)
    Utility of gains and losses : measurement-theoretical and experimental
        approaches / R. Duncan Luce.
      p. cm. – (Scientific psychology series)
    Includes bibliographical references and index.
    ISBN 0-8058-3460-5 (cloth : alk. paper)
    1. Utility theory–Mathematical models. 2. Cost effectiveness–Mathematical
    models. 3. Decision-making–Mathematical models. I. Title. II. Series.
    HB201.L83 2000
    332.67'9'019–dc21

                                      99-55910

Books published by Lawrence Erlbaum Associates are printed
on acid-free paper, and their bindings are chosen
for strength and durability.

Printed in the United States of America

10 9 8 7 6 5 4 3 2 1

To Carolyn and Aurora

To Carolyn and Aurora

Contents

Preface

This monograph brings together in one place my current understanding of the behavioral properties people either exhibit or should exhibit when they make selections among valued alternatives, and it investigates how these properties lead to numerical representations of these preferences. The entire field has been under development, both theoretically and empirically, since the 1947 publication of the second edition of von Neumann and Morgenstern's *The Theory of Games and Economic Behavior*, and by now the literature is enormous. For relevant reviews from a psychological perspective, see various volumes of the *Annual Review of Psychology*, in particular, the latest one that includes a chapter by Mellers, Schwartz, and Cooke (1998). For an economic perspective, the recent *Handbook of Utility Theory, Vol. I Principles* (Barberà, Hammond, & Seidel, 1998) covers much of the theoretical area.

I shall report on this literature very selectively, focusing on those papers that strike me as involving decisive steps toward our current theories of utility and subjective weighting functions. The selection is biased, no doubt, toward the ideas that I have worked on during the past 11 years, which is why this is best thought of as a monograph, not a survey. My contributions are scattered over a number of journals and are interrelated in fairly complex ways. It is unlikely that anyone other than me actually understands all of the connections and modifications that have taken place as my understanding has developed. I hope it will prove useful to organize the material in a coherent fashion.

In an effort to increase the accessibility both to psychologists, who frequently respond with some revulsion to pages of mathematics, and to economists, who although typically quite mathematical often have a preferred style (differential equations, matrix analysis, and topology) different from mine (algebra and functional equations), I have relegated all but the simplest proofs to sections so marked.

The material has been presented and discussed in various forms in several graduate seminars on utility (one co-taught with Professor L. Robin Keller) at the University of California, Irvine (UCI). The most recent version was during the fall of 1998 in which the penultimate draft of this volume served as text. I appreciate the several roles that students in these seminars have played: audience while I tried out ways of organizing the material, critics of ideas and formulations, spotters of errors, and sources of results and ideas that I had overlooked. In particular in the last seminar, three of the students, Rolf H. Johnson, Bethany R. Knapp, and Robert K. Plice, and a visitor, Dr. Thierry Marchant, made numerous very helpful suggestions for improvements and dug out several errors or misstatements.

Most important, of course, have been my collaborators and former graduate students (whose degree dates and current positions are shown) who have worked on related problems during the development of the work. They are, in alphabetical order, János Aczél (Professor Emeritus of Pure Mathematics, University of Waterloo), Alan Brothers (UCI Ph. D., 1990, Battelle Pacific Northwest Laboratories), Younghee Cho (Ph. D. UCI, 1995, Assistant Professor, California State University at Long Beach), Peter C. Fishburn (AT&T Laboratories-Research), Gerald R. Fisher (Ph. D. UCI, 1999), Robert Hamm (Ph. D. Harvard, 1979, Department of Family Medicine, University of Oklahoma), A. A. J. Marley (Ph. D. University of Pennsylvania, 1965, Professor, McGill University), Barbara A. Mellers (Professor, Ohio State

University), Robert Sneddon (Ph. D. UCI, 1999, Postdoctoral Fellow, California Institute of Technology), Detlof von Winterfeldt (Professor, University of Southern California), and Elke U. Weber (Ph. D. Harvard, 1985, Professor, Ohio State University). Their contributions are many and without them the work, especially the experimental aspects, would be far, far less complete than it now is—however incomplete it may still seem.

There are others whose contributions to my thinking have been very considerable even though in some cases we have not collaborated directly on these materials. Continual conversations and e-mail correspondence with Michael H. Birnbaum (Professor, California State University at Fullerton), including very detailed comments on the penultimate version of this monograph, have kept me sensitive to what, from my perspective, often seemed at first to be unpleasant empirical realities. The late Amos Tversky (Professor, Stanford University), often in collaboration with Daniel Kahneman (Professor, Princeton University), has clearly had a major impact over the past 30 years on the way all of us look at decision problems, and at a theoretical level our work is intertwined, as will be apparent from the text. Marley followed much of the work on joint receipts and urged me to explore the important fully associative case that is discussed in Chapter 7. Moreover, as a result of his reading the previous draft, he and I came to collaborate on several results that are reported in Chapter 3, and he has commented in great detail on the previous version and parts of the present one. Louis Narens (Professor, UCI) has been a singular force in the development of modern measurement theory, and I have been greatly influenced by his ideas. Even though we have not collaborated directly on utility theory, his influence is clearly there. Peter P. Wakker (Professor, University of Leiden) has, in detailed critiques of two drafts, repeatedly shown me connections with his work and that of others, questioned ambiguities and misinterpretations on my part, and urged me to make as clear as I can the ways in which my point of view differs significantly from that of mainstream economics. And Elke Weber, commenting on an earlier version, tried hard, but probably not very successfully from her perspective, to push me to toward increasing its accessibility to psychologists with limited mathematical experience. In addition, I greatly appreciate specific comments and suggestions of Drs. J. Aczél, J.-C. Falmagne, Reid Hastie, L. R. Keller, Stephen Link, Barbara A. Mellers, Robin Pope.

The monograph is much better for the efforts of all these scientists. Nonetheless, as hardly need be said, its faults and errors can be charged only to me.

All of my work in this area (and indeed in all of the areas on which I have worked) has been supported in part by National Science Foundation grants. During the preparation of the monograph, it was by grants SBR-9520107 and SBR-9808057 to the University of California, Irvine. I am deeply indebted to the Foundation for supporting my research for well over 40 years.

Finally, producing such a volume involves a somewhat prolonged gestation and more than a few hours of intense labor—a total of over two years in this case—that imposes in various ways on those who are personally close, especially my wife Carolyn. I greatly appreciate her forbearance and support during this, her fourth, encounter with the birth of a book. Would that I could guarantee to her that it will never happen again.

Irvine, CA, September 1999

Chapter 1
INTRODUCTION

This monograph focuses on choices between (and occasionally among) valued entities or alternatives, and the properties that these choices seem to satisfy (descriptive ones) or should satisfy (normative ones). To a lesser degree, it also focuses on evaluations assigned to single entities or alternatives as occur, for example, when a store sets prices on goods. At least one of these topics is of lively importance to most of us, although only a few of us—including, presumably, the reader—find fascinating the formal (mathematical) attempts to model such choices. Such modeling is both more intricate and more extensive than one might anticipate.

There are several options about how to begin, and some of these early decisions tend to be reasonably decisive for the nature of theory that evolves. My aim in this first chapter is to lay out some of these options and make clear which I follow and why; others will arise as we move along. For other general perspectives on these issues, Edwards (1992a), Marley (1997b), and Mellers, Schwartz, and Cooke (1998) are useful.

1.1 Certain, Uncertain, and Risky Alternatives

One surprising feature of the pre-1979 literature was the assumption that choices are among states of wealth, not increments or decrements of it. Of course, no one who ran experiments ever tried to phrase it that way. The gambles involved changes from the status quo, some desirable, some not. Moreover, most of us, without the opportunity to do some tallying, probably do not know our total wealth to better than about 10% accuracy, and typically we do not think of our choices in that way. For example, if one is purchasing a briefcase and the choice is down to two, one's wealth is a factor only to the extent of determining whether both alternatives are feasible, but otherwise it is a background variable common to both and they are evaluated on their own terms relative to the status quo. Although a few authors commented upon the lack of realism of the standard interpretation (Edwards, 1954a; Markowitz, 1952), the major break in that tradition was the famous "prospect theory" paper (Kahneman & Tversky, 1979) that showed vividly that "absolute" gains and losses behaved differently. This monograph is based upon such a distinction, which is elaborated below.

So in some sense, there is a status quo, which often refers to our current if only partially known situation, and each alternative is evaluated relative to the status quo as either effecting an incremental gain or loss from it. Often one can interpret the status quo as the current situation, but that may not be useful if, for example, the decision maker defines the effective status quo as some reference level different from the current situation. However defined, the distinction between gains and losses as modifications in the status quo that are seen as better

1

or worse, respectively, has a major impact on the nature of the theory one constructs, as we shall see in Chapters 6 and, especially, 7. For some contemporary views of economists about the role of the status quo, see Samuelson and Zeckhauser (1988).

1.1.1   Certain alternatives

A *certain alternative* or, more briefly, *consequence* is something that you value (positively or negatively) and which, if received, will be whatever it purports to be. Other commonly used terms are "riskless" and "pure" alternatives. Examples are most goods available in reputable stores. "Certainty" is, of course, an ideal concept. In various ways goods may fail to meet their specifications, and so there is uncertainty or risk involved in the sense that what you buy may fail to be what you thought it was: The car may be a lemon, the TV may be defective, the garment poorly made, the money counterfeit, and so on. Today in the developed countries many goods are made virtually riskless by various warranties and laws, and so the concept of certain alternatives is not vacuous. Nevertheless, certainty is an idealization because of the inconvenience when it fails to hold, even with warranties.

Typically, a domain of certain alternatives is modeled as a set C. It is useful to assume C includes money—both receipts and expenditures—as a special case, which is modeled as a subset $\mathcal{R}$ of the real numbers, $\mathbb{R}$. So $\mathcal{R} = C \cap \mathbb{R}$. Often, we assume $\mathcal{R} = \mathbb{R}$.

We assume that the set of certain consequences, i.e., changes from the status quo, includes a distinguished element, called *no change from the status quo.* Intuitively, this refers to a null consequence that does not alter the decision maker's current state. Rather than use 0 to represent no change from the status quo, which tempts one to think exclusively in monetary terms, I use e, which is often the symbol used in algebra for the analogue of an additive identify element. And, indeed, as we will see in Section 4.2.1, it is precisely that. It is a convenient abuse of terminology to speak of e just as "the status quo," without the modifying phrase "no change from."

The status quo plays two roles. Once we introduce the idea of preferences over consequences, it partitions C into *gains* and *losses,* where the former are consequences preferred to the status quo and the latter are consequences less preferred than the status quo. This distinction plays a crucial role in this monograph. The other use, as was mentioned, is as an identity element in the operation of joint receipt studied in Chapters 4, 6, and 7.

1.1.2   Uncertain alternatives

An *uncertain alternative* involves uncertainty about which consequence actually will be received, and that uncertainty is not resolved until some *chance experiment,* in the sense used in statistics, takes place. The outcome of the experiment determines which one of finitely many consequences from C one actually receives. (A formal definition is provided in Section 1.1.6.) The statistical use of the term "experiment" is considerably narrower than its use in the empirical sciences where experimental manipulations are key to the concept. Here it simply means carrying out some process whose outcomes have a random aspect. The context should make clear which use is intended. The limitation to finitely many consequences

is convenient and, for the most part, realistic. However, a good deal of the theoretical literature addresses infinite cases and replaces the sums we shall encounter with integrals. I do not
find these infinite idealizations particularly helpful.

One needs to distinguish carefully the use of the terms "outcome" and "consequence."
When the chance experiment of tossing a die is run, the outcome is the face that comes up,
usually identified by a symbol or number on the face. To each outcome, some consequence
may be attached, such as winning or losing an amount of money. Throughout the monograph
I use the term *outcome* to refer only to what happens in the experiment and the term *consequence* to refer to any valued good that is arbitrarily associated to an outcome. Consequences
can be from the set C of certain alternatives, in which case the resulting uncertain alternative is called *first order.* But sometimes the consequences are more complex objects, such as
sets of certain alternatives or other uncertain alternatives. This aspect is discussed more fully
below.

There can be various degrees of uncertainty in which the decision maker knows something about the likelihood of outcomes of the experiment but does not know a probability
distribution over them. Events occur, but the decision maker does not have an objective appraisal of how likely they are. This can happen when we are dealing with situations for which
repetitions of the experiment underlying the event are either impossible or are only very approximately possible. Most alternatives are of this character. Choosing among them is called
decision making under uncertainty. If one is contemplating investing in drilling for oil, one
does not have a firm probability distribution concerning the possible consequences of drilling
in particular locations. Our knowledge about estimating the location and extent of oil fields
simply is insufficient to reduce this to a probability. Or if one is thinking of setting up a business in Ukraine, there are many uncertainties that cannot be reduced to probabilities.

Of course, many examples of uncertain chance events are coupled with delayed resolution
of the uncertainty. This interesting but difficult problem of time delay is not addressed in this
monograph. For an introduction to such issues, see Loewenstein and Elster (1992) and Pope
(1983, 1985, 1996/7).

1.1.3   Risky alternatives

In this literature, the word "risky" has a double meaning, the one specific and objective, the
other vague and quite subjective. The specific meaning refers to an uncertain alternative for
which the probability is known (or given) for each chance outcome that can arise when the
experiment is performed. Such alternatives are called *risky.* The simplest *first-order risky
alternatives* involve only consequences that are certain. An example is a bet on the toss of a
fair die, with the consequences being a ticket to a ball game if either the 1 or the 6 face arises,
or two tickets to the same ball game if the 3 arises, or the loss of $10 otherwise. Given that
the die is fair, the probability of a 1 or 6, and so of the consequence of a ticket, is $\frac{1}{3}$; that of a
3, and so two tickets, is $\frac{1}{6}$; and that of the balance, and so a loss of $10, is $\frac{1}{2}$.

Given the concept of a first-order risky alternative, one can easily imagine more complex
risky alternatives in which one or more of the consequences are themselves risky alternatives.
When the probabilities are known at both levels, we speak of a *second-order risky alternative.*

3

A typical example is a state lottery in which winning on the first stage leads to an additional lottery, usually with a good deal of publicity for those who go to the second stage. Such *compound alternatives,* both risky and uncertain, are discussed in Section 1.1.6.5, and second-order gambles recur several times in the monograph.

The distinction between risky and uncertain alternatives dates at least to Knight (1921), and is reflected in the contrast between the theory of risk of von Neumann and Morgenstern (1947) and the theory of uncertainty of Savage (1954). See also the comments of Arrow (1951). It is a question of either having or not having known or constructible probabilities over the events. With Ellsberg (1961) the idea of ambiguity of probability—an urn with some fixed mix of white and red balls, but with no knowledge about the mix—began to play a role (§ 2.4.2). There is a small, growing literature concerning ambiguity and its avoidance (Curley, Yates, & Abrams, 1986; Fox & Tversky, 1995, 1997; Heath & Tversky, 1991). A relatively recent survey of uncertainty and ambiguity with more detailed references is Camerer and M. Weber (1992).

The other, subjective, meaning of "risky" is as an appraisal by either the theorist or by the decision maker that one alternative is "perceived as more or less risky" than another. The concept of "perceived riskiness" is treated as a primitive judgment on the part of the decision maker. Theorists have often tried to identify the riskiness of an alternative with one or another property that can be defined in terms of features of the alternatives. An example is the assumption that increasing the variance, while holding the mean of a money lottery fixed, increases the perceived risk. Several of these notions of risk manipulation and risk aversion are examined in Section 4.6. Other approaches, mine among them (Luce & Weber, 1986), have attempted to model judgments of relative risk, and Coombs (1975) developed an interesting theory of preferences based on trade-offs between risk and expected value. I do not attempt to cover this area, in part because of excellent review articles by Brachinger and M. Weber (1997), E. U. Weber (1997), and M. Weber and Camerer (1987).

1.1.4   Lotteries

A special, but important, class of risky alternatives is those whose consequences are all sums of money. I call them *lotteries.* The literature is not fully consistent on this language. Some authors treat the word "lottery" as interchangeable with the word "gamble," which term has, as we shall see, a far more general meaning in my lexicon. Examples of lotteries are many of the U. S. state lotteries [some of which are compound ones (see §1.1.6.5)], roulette, and any of the casino dice or card games. Because we are modeling money as a set (often idealized as an interval) of real numbers, it is possible, but not necessary, to view a first-order lottery as a probability distribution over that numerical set, i.e., as a *random variable.* Lotteries are often modeled in this fashion and, so far as I know, no difficulties are encountered provided one limits attention to first-order ones. But as we shall see (§§ 1.1.6.6, 2.3.1, and 2.4.3), extending this random variable formulation to second-order lotteries has very serious drawbacks, and as a result I strongly discourage using it in formulating general theories.

1.1.5   Gambles

The generic term *gamble* is used here to cover both risky and uncertain alternatives. Thus, a lottery is a special case of a gamble. [Other terms have been suggested: "act" (Savage, 1954) and "prospect" (Kahneman & Tversky, 1979) are the most common.] The set of gambles under consideration is denoted $\mathcal{G}$, sometimes with subscripts and/or superscripts to denote particular subclasses of gambles. It is convenient always to treat the set of certain consequences $\mathcal{C}$ under consideration as being a subset of $\mathcal{G}$. Ignoring timing differences about the resolution of gambles, as I do, the certain consequences can be viewed as arising either from degenerate gambles where the same consequence is attached to all outcomes of the chance experiment or from degenerate ones in which the consequence is assigned to the certain event, which of course occurs with probability 1 (see the first two definitions of § 2.1).

1.1.6   Alternative notations and representations of gambles

1.1.6.1   Savage's states of nature: Most economists today follow, more or less explicitly, the convention introduced by Savage (1954) that the uncertain or chance aspect of the situation is described as a universal set Ω, whose elements (or outcomes) are called *states of nature*. A gamble (he called it an *act*) is a function $g : \Omega \rightarrow \mathcal{C}$, where if Ω is infinite then g has *finite support*[1] in the sense that its image in $\mathcal{C}$ is a finite subset of $\mathcal{C}$. When Ω is finite, this formulation often is placed in matrix form where the columns are labeled by the states of nature $s_1, ..., s_j, ..., s_n$, the rows by the gambles $g_1, ..., g_i, ..., g_m$, and the i, j entry, which is denoted g_{ij}, is the consequence assigned to g_i when the state of nature turns out to be s_j:

$$
\begin{array}{cccccc}
 & s_1 & \cdots & s_j & \cdots & s_n \\
g_1 : & g_{11} & \cdots & g_{1j} & \cdots & g_{1n} \\
\vdots & \vdots & \vdots & \vdots & \vdots & \vdots \\
g_i : & g_{i1} & \cdots & g_{ij} & \cdots & g_{in} \\
\vdots & \vdots & \vdots & \vdots & \vdots & \vdots \\
g_m : & g_{m1} & \cdots & g_{mj} & \cdots & g_{mn}
\end{array}
$$

Although this notation is very compact and an elegant theory can be formulated in terms of it, it has three crucial drawbacks. The first is that Ω tends to be very large indeed because very often multiple chance experiments are involved in decisions. For example, if one is considering a trip from New York to Boston, there are a number of ways that one might go. Probably the primary ones that most of us would consider are, in alphabetical order, airplane, bus, car, and train. Each of these instances of travel can be thought of as a chance "experiment," and so there will be four different ones under consideration. And certainly when we run laboratory experiments to study how people behave when choosing among gambles, often a number of distinct chance experiments must be considered. In the travel example, let $A, B, C,$ and T denote, respectively, the spaces of possible outcomes of the airplane, bus, car,

---

[1]   Theories for infinitely many consequences are possible, but I do not focus on them.

and train trips from New York to Boston. In each case it is not difficult to think of several reasonable outcomes having to do with the success or not of the travel by that mode, and in the successful cases the time of arrival can be partitioned into some units, such as half hours, and in the unsuccessful ones into various aspects about the severity of the breakdown or crash. It is certainly not unreasonable to suppose that each mode of travel entails, as a bare minimum, at least 10 distinct outcomes. To place this simple decision situation in the Savage framework we must set $\Omega = A \times B \times C \times T$, and so there are at least 10,000 states of nature. Make the problem a bit more complex and it is easy to see that millions or billions of states must be contemplated. I think very few of us are able or willing to structure decisions in this fashion. Rather, we contemplate each of the alternatives as something unitary.

The second drawback with the Savage framework is that it has some difficulty in talking about experiments that might be carried out, but in fact are not. So, in the travel example, the experiments A, B, and T occur whether or not the decision maker decides to use one of these modes of travel, but in general that is not true for C, especially if he or she would be the driver. This control by the decision maker of what experiments are actually realized is somewhat awkward in the Savage framework, although it can be dealt with by careful definition of the acts. It is dealt with far more naturally in the scheme we shall use because the events of one experiment never appear in the formulation of a different experiment.

The third drawback is that it is difficult, although again not impossible, to talk about compound gambles, and these will play a role in, primarily, Chapter 3. Moreover, they are not uncommon in ordinary decisions. Consider, as I often do, travel from Santa Ana (SNA or more popularly Orange County or John Wayne Airport), California to the East Coast, say, Washington. Because it is usually most convenient for me to go into National Airport (DCA) and because both DCA and SNA have relatively short runways, the range of fully loaded aircraft originating at either field is limited and so a refueling stop (and usually a change of planes) is needed. The most common option is to make a connection somewhere in the middle of the country, such as Dallas-Forth Worth (DFW). Such a trip is then a compound gamble in which the first flight from SNA to DFW is a gamble, one of whose consequences—the desired and most likely one—is that one will connect to the intended flight from DFW to DCA. Note that once one considers compound gambles the number of columns of the Savage matrix grows even more. Indeed, the number will have to be countably infinite in order to describe elements of $\mathcal{G}$ as I have defined it.

So, I will attempt to introduce a different formulation, one designed to capture explicitly the unitary character of uncertain alternatives.

1.1.6.2   Chance experiments: Let $\mathcal{E}$ denote a set of chance experiments that will underlie the gambles under consideration. For example, one experiment might be the toss of a pair of coins, another the spinning of a roulette-like wheel, and the third the draw of a ball from an opaque urn having some unknown composition of red and white balls. Each chance experiment, $\mathbf{E} \in \mathcal{E}$, has its own (universal) set $\Omega_{\mathbf{E}}$ of its possible outcomes. So, for example, in the case of tossing the two coins it is the set of pairs $\{(H, H), (H, T), (T, H), (T, T)\}$, where H means a head occurs and T a tail and the order distinguishes the coins. In the spin of a roulette-like wheel it is the separately identified sectors. Or in the case of the travel example, the "experiments" would be trips of each of the four types mentioned.

To reduce the notation a bit, I will often write $E = \Omega_{\mathbf{E}}$, thus using the same letter for both the name of the experiment and the set of possible outcomes of a realization of the experiment, but place the former in bold face. Let $\mathcal{E}_{\mathbf{E}}$ denote a family of subsets of E, the set of possible outcomes of experiment **E**. We suppose $\mathcal{E}_{\mathbf{E}}$ exhibits the following basic properties:

(i) $E \in \mathcal{E}_{\mathbf{E}}$.

(ii)   If $C \in \mathcal{E}_{\mathbf{E}}$, then $\overline{C} \in \mathcal{E}_{\mathbf{E}}$, where $\overline{C} = E \backslash C$ is the complement of C relative to the set E.

(iii)   If $C, D \in \mathcal{E}_{\mathbf{E}}$, then $C \cup D \in \mathcal{E}_{\mathbf{E}}$.

Note that it follows immediately that $\emptyset = \overline{E} \in \mathcal{E}_{\mathbf{E}}$ and if $C, D \in \mathcal{E}_{\mathbf{E}}$, then $C \cap D = \overline{\overline{C} \cup \overline{D}} \in \mathcal{E}_{\mathbf{E}}$. Such a family of subsets of a set is called an *algebra of sets*.[2] When E is finite, there is no loss in generality in assuming $\mathcal{E}_{\mathbf{E}}$ to be the set of all subsets of E, which is called the power set of E and is denoted 2^{E}. The members of $\mathcal{E}_{\mathbf{E}}$, i.e., (some) subsets of E, are called *events*.

For much of this chapter and the next, it suffices to work with a single $\mathcal{E}_{\mathbf{E}}$. But beginning in Chapter 3 we will be considering how several experiments relate to one another. From a purely mathematical point of view, one can think of all the experiments we wish to consider as being imbedded in master experiment Ω, much as in the Savage approach. That is to say, there is a single set Ω of all possible outcomes, and each chance experiment **E** we wish to consider has as its set of outcomes $E \subset \Omega$. Thus, the decision maker's isolation of E for special consideration is a form of conditionalization.

One must, however, be very cautious in following this approach. For example, it is not plausible to think of the experimenter's selection of **E** for use in a laboratory experiment or a traveler's choice of going by aircraft, bus, car, or train as in any sense a chance event governed by some master statistical structure over $\mathcal{E}_{\Omega}$. A choice of when and how to travel differs deeply from the statistical risks entailed by that choice. The potential for confusion in trying to treat them in a unitary fashion is so great that I eschew this perhaps mathematically more elegant approach.

1.1.6.3   First-order gambles: Let C denote the set of certain consequences under consideration. For $\mathbf{E} \in \mathcal{E}$, let $\{E_1, ..., E_i, ..., E_n\}$ denote a partition of E $(= \Omega_{\mathbf{E}})$, i.e., for $i, j \in \{1, 2, ..., n\}$ with $i \neq j$, $E_i \in \mathcal{E}_{\mathbf{E}}$, $E_i \cap E_j = \emptyset$, and $\bigcup_{i=1}^{n} E_i = E$. Note that because the outcome of running **E** is exactly one outcome, i.e., one element of E, it follows that exactly one of the E_i occurs. I do not assume that, for each i, $E_i \neq \emptyset$ because on occasion such degeneracy is useful, e.g., Definition 2.1.2.

Suppose $\{E_1, ..., E_i, ..., E_n\}$ is a partition of the experiment **E**. Many authors treat a *first-order* (or *simple*) gamble g as an assignment of a consequence to each event in the partition, i.e., a function

$$g : \{E_1, ..., E_i, ..., E_n\} \rightarrow C. \tag{1.1}$$

---

[2]   For any countable set of elements $E_i \in \mathcal{E}_{\mathbf{E}}$, $i = 1, 2, ...$, if in addition we have the property that $\bigcup_{i=1}^{\infty} E_i \in \mathcal{E}_{\mathbf{E}}$, then one calls the algebra $\mathcal{E}_{\mathbf{E}}$ a σ-*algebra*. We do not need this concept in the present formulation.

Often it is convenient to denote $g(E_i) = g_i$. Frequently such functions are displayed explicitly in the following fashion. Let $g_i = f(E_i)$, and then the function is a collection of such pairs (g_i, E_i), i.e.,

$$\{(g_1, E_1), (g_2, E_2), ..., (g_n, E_n)\}. \tag{1.2}$$

This mathematical model of a gamble is mathematically neat, but it does not really work as the basis of a theory of behavior for a very simple reason. A function can be presented in very many different formats, but people do not always perceive these mathematically equivalent formats as equally valuable. During the 1980s, psychologists became increasingly aware of these problems, which go under the generic name of *framing effects* (Tversky & Kahneman, 1986). So we must use a notation for gambles that is helpful in letting us formulate when such framing effects occur and, importantly, when they do not. I refer to the class of properties that say certain framings do not matter as "accounting indifferences" (§2.1).

A notation that imposes an ordering of the pairs in Display (1.2) has turned out to be useful in formulating theories. Thus, the gamble is thought of as an array of n ordered pairs. The ordering we encounter repeatedly arises from the assumption, discussed in some detail in Section 1.2 and a great deal more in Chapter 2, that there is a preference ordering over the consequences of gambles. The convention often followed is that the subscripts increase with decreasing preference of the associated consequences, i.e.,

$$g_i \text{ is preferred to } g_j \iff i < j.$$

When emphasizing the order, typically we replace the commas between pairs by semicolons, drop the parentheses, and change from the set notation to an ordered n-tuple one, yielding

$$(g_1, E_1; ...; g_i, E_i; ...; g_n, E_n). \tag{1.3}$$

Although the notation of (1.3) is convenient for much of what we will be doing, one must recognize that it is different from the function of (1.1), because order plays no role in the concept of a function. No distinction exists between $\{E_1, E_2, E_3\}$ and, say, $\{E_2, E_1, E_3\}$, whereas in the ordered 3-tuple notation it is not automatic that

$$(g_1, E_1; g_2, E_2; g_3, E_3) \quad \text{and} \quad (g_2, E_2; g_1, E_1; g_3, E_3)$$

are perceived to be the same. We will introduce assumptions about preferences to the effect that the order is irrelevant for some of the simpler gambles while allowing it to be relevant for more complex ones.

Furthermore, issues of order arise in empirical studies because, necessarily, the several terms of a gamble must be presented in some ordered fashion. This aspect is discussed some in Section 1.1.7.

For risky alternatives, where there are known probabilities of the event occurring, and when it seems reasonable to assume that only these probabilities matter to the decision maker, then the notation is changed as follows. Let $p_i = \Pr(E_i)$ and Display (1.3) becomes

$$(g_1, p_1; ...; g_i, p_i; ...; g_n, p_n). \tag{1.4}$$

The notation for uncertain alternatives, Display (1.3), described above, which is what I will use in this monograph, is a variant on the notations first used by Herstein and Milnor (1953), von Neumann and Morgenstern (1947), and Pfanzagl (1959). It is substantially different from the one most commonly used by economists today, which was described in Section 1.1.6.1. It attempts to capture explicitly the fact that we deal with uncertain alternatives as unitary things contingent on the underlying chance experiment being carried out.

1.1.6.4   Binary gambles: In the case of first-order binary gambles, i.e., $n = 2$, with $x, y \in \mathcal{C}$, it is often convenient to drop the subscripts and to abbreviate the notation even further to $g_1 = x$, $g_2 = y$, $E_1 \doteq C$, and $E_2 = \overline{C} = E \backslash C$. So the first-order, binary gamble becomes in several alternate notations

$$(x, C; y, E \backslash C) \equiv (x, C; y, \overline{C}) \equiv (x, C; y). \tag{1.5}$$

Some authors abbreviate it even further by omitting all punctuation, so it reduces to

$$xCy, \tag{1.6}$$

where one thinks of the event as a (mixture) operation between the consequences x and y, much as with numbers α and β we write the operation of addition as $\alpha + \beta$. In the case of risk, for $p \in [0, 1]$, these brief notations become xpy.

Perhaps the least satisfactory notation is the initial one of von Neumann and Morgenstern (1947), who wrote the risky gamble as $px + (1-p)y$. The potential for misunderstanding both the $+$ and the "multiplication" px is simply too great, and so no one has used this notation subsequently except when treating consequences as random variables (see §1.1.6.6 below).

I use Display (1.5) in the binary case and Display (1.3) in the general case except for risky alternatives, in which case I use Display (1.4).

1.1.6.5   Compound gambles: Let $\mathcal{G}_0 = \mathcal{C}$ and let $\mathcal{G}_1$ denote the union of the set of first-order gambles and $\mathcal{G}_0$. We may define $\mathcal{G}_2$ as consisting of all assignments from an (ordered) finite event partition into $\mathcal{G}_1$. Thus, $\mathcal{G}_2 \supset \mathcal{G}_1$. Note that all of the experiments under consideration go into constructing these new gambles. One can continue this process recursively as follows: $\mathcal{G}_k$ is the set all assignments from an (ordered) finite event partition into $\mathcal{G}_{k-1}$. Of course, $\mathcal{G}_k \supset \mathcal{G}_{k-1}$. Any gamble in $\mathcal{G}_k \backslash \mathcal{G}_{k-1}$ is referred to as k^{th}-order gamble. Any gamble that is not a first-order one is called a *compound gamble*. For the most part we will confine our attention to first- and second-order gambles. Although all of the theories have formulations in terms just of certain alternatives and first-order gambles, it often becomes much simpler if second-order ones are admitted. An example will arise when we study separability in Section 3.4, Eq. (3.20).

Finally, let $\mathcal{G}_\infty$ denote the full countable recursion, i.e., $\bigcup_{k=0}^{\infty} \mathcal{G}_k$. From a purely mathematical perspective, for $\mathcal{G}_\infty$ one can omit explicit mention of the set $\mathcal{C}$ of certain consequences and simply begin with a set $\mathcal{G}$ of gambles and require that it be closed under the formation of gambles using elements of $\mathcal{G}$ as consequences. This was how von Neumann and Morgenstern (1947) formulated binary gambles. Because in this monograph, except for relatively incidental comments, we need only $\mathcal{G}_0 = \mathcal{C}$, $\mathcal{G}_1$, or $\mathcal{G}_2$, it is better to use the explicit inductive definition. The use of second-order gambles is similar to the modeling found in Anscombe and Aumann (1963) and Schmeidler (1989).

When dealing with compound gambles, the notation of Display (1.3) is used but with the g_i interpreted as gambles, not certain consequences.

In the case of binary gambles in $\mathcal{G}_\infty$, the operator aspect has sometimes been made more conspicuous by using a notation such as

$$g \otimes_C h, \tag{1.7}$$

where g and h are gambles. Since $g \otimes_C h$ is itself a gamble, this means $\otimes_C$ is a binary operation. I do not use this notation here. When the operation is defined only for $g, h \in \mathcal{G}_{k-1}$, then it is a partial operation.

For risky alternatives, such compounding of gambles at the level of the probabilities does not seem problematic. But for uncertain ones, it may be. The reason is that some of the properties we will examine depend upon compounding gambles based on independent replications of the same underlying experiment. Here "independent replications" is used as a primitive undefined concept; it cannot in general be formulated in probability terms because, by assumption, such probabilities are unknown. Indeed, replication many times is contrary to uncertainty because relative frequencies can be used to estimate probabilities, thus transforming the problem into one of risk. In practice, of course, even statistical independence, such as in selecting a random sample, is often based on procedures, such as repeated tosses of a coin, not on actual probability estimates. For example, in the utility literature, where experiments are realized by some device such as choosing one ball from an urn of balls of several different colors, independence is typically achieved by replacing the ball, re-randomizing by thoroughly shaking the urn, and drawing a second time.

But in many situations of uncertainty, such replication simply is not possible. For example, if the consequences of an investment in Ukraine vary as a function of whether or not the country is at war in the next 10 years, that uncertain event obviously cannot be replicated. So, to a degree, the assumption of compounding a particular uncertain experiment is at variance with the assumption of uncertainty. For example, as Peter Wakker has noted,[3] if one is confronted with a single toss of an unknown coin, it is plausible to assume that the faces are equally likely to arise, despite the fact one may feel great uncertainty about that hypothesis. However, after 1,000 tosses in which heads always comes up, one's hypothesis on the next toss is likely to be very different from what it was initially.

The problem of independent realizations of uncertain events is mitigated to a degree, but not entirely, by the fact that the only compounding that we will deal with is second order—those gambles whose consequences are either certain ones or first-order gambles.

1.1.6.6   Compound lotteries and random variables: As was noted earlier, many economists model lotteries, first-order and compound, as random variables, which are first-order by definition. This formulation has, depending upon how one views it, the advantage or dis-

---

[3]   Personal communication, April 13, 1998.

advantage of automatically reducing any compound lottery to an equivalent first-order one.

So, to model lotteries as random variables one must either (i) avoid compound gambles or (ii) assume a probability reduction to its equivalent first-order form. I take up both points.

(i) Some researchers may claim that they do not work with compound lotteries, but such claims tend to be violated regularly. Frequently, one sees decision trees of the sort described below in Section 1.1.7, and these can only be viewed as compound lotteries. And certainly the discussions of what is called the "independence axiom" (§ 2.3.1) implicitly require second-order lotteries. So, I do not believe it is realistic to assume that such compound lotteries can be avoided.

(ii) Assuming that some compound lotteries are involved, then modeling them as random variables introduces the following problem. Random variables are defined only in terms of a distribution over ultimate (in this case, money) consequences, so the compound lottery

$$((x, r; y), p; (z, s; w)),$$

where $p, r, s \in [0, 1]$, automatically reduces to its probabilistically equivalent first-order form

$$(x, pr; y, p(1 - r); z, (1 - p)s; w, (1 - p)(1 - s)).$$

Typically, the notation used in such a case is

$$
\begin{aligned}
p(x, r; y) + (1 - p)(z, s; w) &= p(rx + (1 - r)y) + (1 - p)(sz + (1 - s)w) \\
&= prx + p(1 - r)y + (1 - p)sz + (1 - p)(1 - s)w.
\end{aligned}
$$

To be more concrete,

$$(($100, .30; 0); .20; ($50, .60; -$20))$$

automatically reduces to:

$$($100, .06; $50, .48; 0; .14; -$20, .32),$$

where the consequences are listed in descending order.

However, it is by no means clear that people necessarily perceive these two descriptions of the situation as the same—indeed, we will see evidence strongly suggesting that, in general, they do not. Yet, modeling the domain as random variables simply precludes the option of the two descriptions being treated as non-equivalent. I much prefer to make such a reduction assumption explicit as an axiom rather than build it into the initial formulation of the decision situation. von Neumann and Morgenstern (1947) did exactly this. Such assumptions are called "reduction (of compound gambles) axioms." They are discussed below.

1.1.7   Empirical realizations of gambles

The possible mathematical notations for gambles are far fewer than the potential ways of describing gambles to people in experimental settings. I will mention only the most commonly used presentations.

- Present the gamble more or less explicitly as text:

  There is a 60% chance of gaining $50, a 30% chance of losing $10, and a 10% chance of losing $100.

- Or present it in one of the mathematical notations, e.g.:

$$(\$50, 0.60; -\$10, 0.30; -\$100, 0.10)$$

or

$$\begin{pmatrix} 0.60 & 0.30 & 0.10 \\ \$50 & -\$10 & -\$100 \end{pmatrix}$$

- Or as a tree diagram such as shown in Fig. 1.1:

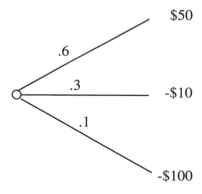

Figure 1.1. Representation of a gambles as a tree diagram.

- Or as a pie chart such as shown in Fig. 1.2:

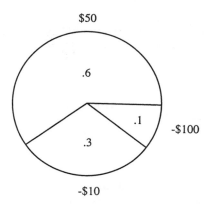

Figure 1.2. Representation of a gamble as a pie diagram.

- Or as a cumulative distribution function such as shown in Fig. 1.3:

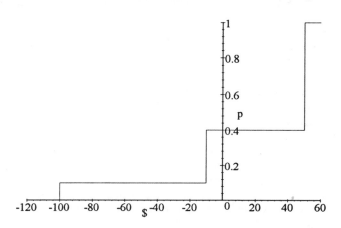

Figure 1.3. Representation of a lottery as a cumulative distribution function.

Many other modes are possible; see Keller (1985b) for a study in which several alternatives were examined in connection with her work on the hypothesis of the reduction of compound gambles (§ 3.4). In each of the presentation modes shown, several additional options exist, e.g., the order in which the outcomes are listed, the orientation of the display, color coding, etc. None of these things should matter, but probably they all do to some minor degree, as Keller found in her work. One of the realities of empirical behavioral research is that experimenters have not arrived at a consensus about how best to represent the gambles, and equally competent experimenters will disagree on procedural details. In describing experiments, I will usually mention the type of display used.

1.2   Preference and Its Determination

1.2.1   Choice and its problems

1.2.1.1   The algebraic view: Because we are presuming that the consequences and gambles under consideration are valued—either positively or negatively—by the decision maker, we can think of there being relative values between any two of them. If one gamble is seen as more valuable than another, it seems reasonable to assume that, in choosing between them, the more valued one will be selected, and conversely. In this literature, this is often thought of as an operational definition of *preference* or, as it is sometimes called, *revealed preference* (Samuelson, 1948; Kreps, 1990).

There is a subtle and complex philosophical literature on the meaning of preference; see, e.g., McClennen (1990). Here I treat it in a highly operational fashion; even so, as we shall see, ambiguity remains. When a person assigns numerical evaluations to gambles, we do not necessarily find that the ordering of the gambles induced by these numbers always agrees with the persons's ordering of them by choice (see § 2.2.5).

Let G be the set of gambles under consideration, usually G_2. So, if $g, h \in G$, then we assume that either g is seen as preferred to h, which we denote by $g \succ h$; or h is seen as preferred to g, denoted, of course, $h \succ g$ (or equally well by $g \prec h$); or g and h are seen as indifferent in preference, denoted $g \sim h$.

Often it is convenient to work with the relation[4] of "more or equally valued," i.e., $\succsim$ means either $\succ$ or $\sim$ holds, which relation is often called *weak preference*. Note that $\succsim$ is a *connected* or *complete relation* in the sense that for each $g, h \in G$ either $g \succsim h$ or $h \succsim g$ (or both, in which case $g \sim h$). This observation rests, of course, on the initial assumption that just one of the three possibilities, $g \succ h$, $h \succ g$, or $g \sim h$, occurs. Some authors have contemplated situations where for some pairs no response is, or can be, given to the question: Which of the pair do you prefer or are you indifferent? Such orderings are called "partial." Anand (1987) summarizes a number of the reasons for doubting that people always have existing or constructible preference orders among alternatives.

---

[4]   A mathematical, binary relation $\succsim$ on a set G is simply a subset of $G \times G = \{(g, h) : g, h \in G\}$. Rather than write $(g, h) \in \succsim$ to mean g is prefered or indifferent to h, we write $g \succsim h$, just as with numbers rather than $(x, y) \in \geq$ we write $x \geq y$. As we shall see, we will be interested in the special class of relations known as *orderings*. More about this later.

Mainly because the theory becomes appreciably more complex with partial orders, I will postulate only situations in which resolving the choice is always possible. Moreover, in most experiments respondents[5] are required to express preference or indifference and usually without providing a "no choice" option. Generalizations to theories with partial orders might well be useful for some applications where some consequences are seen as incomparable.

1.2.1.2   Are the respondents in experiments serious?   A question repeatedly raised, especially by economists, is: Do respondents in our experiments take seriously the many choices they are forced to make when we try to elicit $\succsim$ over a somewhat large set of gambles? They could, after all, simply respond randomly or always choose the right-hand display or the like. One line of evidence that tends to impress psychologists is that we can rather easily spot those respondents whose responses exhibit total consistency, such as always choosing one response key, or total chaos, for which the data are patternless. Usually such data, which are in fact rare, are dropped from further consideration. Other respondents typically exhibit patterns of behavior of the sort described in Chapter 2 and elsewhere, which seems to suggest that at least some thought has been given to their choices.

Some theorists have expressed the concern that some of the observed anomalies reported in Chapter 2 may result from insufficient attention, which they believe can be focused by introducing substantial monetary consequences to be won or lost by the respondents. The evidence is to the contrary.[6] For example, in connection with the preference reversal phenomenon (§ 2.2.5), two studies were aimed at getting rid of it by making the monetary outcomes serious. Perhaps the most striking was the study of Lichtenstein and Slovic (1973) in which the phenomenon was exhibited by ordinary gamblers in Las Vegas playing for high stakes. Grether and Plott (1979) carried out a series of systematic manipulations in an attempt to eliminate preference reversals, including increasing the monetary stakes, and again they found the phenomenon robust. Comparable robustness with the magnitude of consequences was reported by Kachelmeier and Shehata (1992) when they carried out studies in China using money amounts that, although modest by western standards, amounted to several months' salary for the Chinese respondent. [See also Hsee and Weber (1999) and Weber and Hsee (1998).] Camerer (1989) reported no significant difference between having respondents play some gambles at the end of the experiment and not doing so; however, the stakes involved were modest.

In many, but by no means all, of the empirical studies I shall mention, the experimenter randomly selected some of the choice pairs presented and then, after all choices were completed, ran off those gambles selected by the respondent. The outcomes of these chance experiments determined a financial payment beyond the respondent's assured hourly rate for participating in the experiment. Everyone agrees that any such running of gambles should be carried out

---

[5]   It is common to speak of the people from whom judgments and choices are solicited as "subjects." That term, it seems to me, makes sense when these people are subjected to experimental manipulations, such as number of trials of exposure to a stimulus in a memory experiment, but it is less appropriate when we are attempting to elicit some information about what the person feels or thinks. Better terms seem to be either "informant," "participant," or "respondent." I have elected to use the last term.

[6]   This comment applies to the anomalies discussed here and does not cover others in the literature. Some of the latter do seem to attenuate, and in some cases evaporate, when real payoffs are used.

after all of the choices have been made in order to avoid the possibility of varying endowment effects, of a changed sense of status quo from choice to choice.

1.2.1.3   Context inconsistencies: MacCrimmon, Stanbury, and Wehrung (1980) made a case against the assumption of consistent preferences. Their idea was simple: Devise two sets of five lotteries that have two lotteries in common and that each involves only changes in one of the variables. The sets they chose are shown in Table 1.1. Note that both subsets have the same first certain consequence and the same fourth lottery. The respondents, 40 middle-aged business executives, some presidents and CEOs and some mid-level executives of large companies, rank ordered each set by preference under a scenario, designed to capture their attention, involving stock market behavior. Thirteen of the 40 respondents had opposite orderings of the common alternatives, the first and the fourth, in contexts B and C. The specific pattern is shown in Table 1.2.

Table 1.1 Binary lotteries used by MacCrimmon, Stanbury, and Wehrung (1980) to show context effects. It is part of their Table 9.1. The probability of the worst outcome $= 1-$ probability of best outcome. Note that B1 = C1 and B4 = C4.

Lottery	Best Outcome	Probability of Best Outcome	Worst Outcome
B1	$ 5.00	1.0000	$ 5.00
B2	20.00	.0692	3.90
B3	20.00	.2752	-.70
B4	20.00	.6185	-19.30
B5	20.00	.9046	-137.00
C1	$ 5.00	1.0000	$ 5.00
C2	10.00	.6185	-3.10
C3	15.00	.6185	-11.20
C4	20.00	.6185	-19.30
C5	25.00	.6185	-27.40

Thus, for these respondents, apparently the context had partially controlled their preferences, which were otherwise quite coherent within each set. This finding, if the data were correctly interpreted, is disturbing. The issue, as we shall discuss in the next subsection, is that choices in this area are notoriously noisy, and no attempt was made to determine if that could explain the findings.

Although there is certainly reason for concern, I will act here as if the invariant preference approach makes sense at least for judgments between pairs of gambles.

Table 1.2. The numbers of respondents exhibiting each choice pattern in MacCrimmon et al. (1980).

		Context C		
		1>4	4>1	Total
Context	1>4	23	3	26
B	4>1	10	4	14
	Total	33	7	40

1.2.1.4   Inconsistent choices: A major difficulty with the algebraic formulation of preferences and choices is that the empirical world does not seem to be so simple. If, during the course of an experiment, we present a particular pair (g, h) several times, but each presentation is some tens of trials from its predecessor, we do not necessarily find that one gamble is consistently chosen over the other. Such inconsistency seems to occur even when experimenters go to great effort to keep the state of the respondent the same except, of course, for the fact that he or she will have encountered more total choices at the time of the later choice than the earlier one. Although this fact is unavoidable, it really should not matter.

Given that the observed choices are inconsistent, an obvious idea is to postulate not an algebraic relation $\succsim$ for choices but rather an underlying probability $P(g, h)$. There is a substantial literature on such probabilistic models of choice, and summaries of it may be found in Suppes, Luce, Krantz, and Tversky (1989, Ch. 17) and in the several articles of the issues of Volume 23, 1992, of *Mathematical Social Sciences*. That being so, why do I not use it here? The reason is simple if unfortunate. The stimuli, gambles in our case, are rather highly structured objects with components involving events and consequences, and our algebraic models will draw heavily on that structure. The difficulty is that no one has very successfully combined that type of structure with a probabilistic choice structure. Although there are continuing efforts in this direction (e.g., Marley, 1997a), the general lack of success is a major failing of the field—actually a failing with far broader implications than just for utility measurement. Given this failure, we have to adapt as best we can.

The following approach is taken by many experimentalists. Estimate $P(g, h)$ from repeated presentations of the pair (g, h) and then define

$$g \succsim h \iff P(g, h) \geq \frac{1}{2}. \tag{1.8}$$

As we shall see (§ 2.2.3), using this definition and checking properties of $\succsim$ in terms of it can be a fairly subtle matter, and significant mistakes appear to have been made in the literature.

1.2.2   Matching and its problems

If one is going to have to use Eq. (1.8) to determine $\succsim$, it clearly becomes expensive and demanding on the respondents to do so. Suppose the experiment involves m gambles, then $\frac{1}{2}m(m-1)$ pairs have to be examined. If, to estimate any one $P(g,h)$, we make k separate presentations, then a total of $\frac{1}{2}m(m-1)k$ observations are required. In other areas of psychology, such as psychophysics, k is rarely less than 100 and sometimes samples are as large as 1,000. If $m = 10$, which is actually a very modest stimulus set, and $k = 100$, we see that 4,500 observations are required. In the kinds of experimental procedures commonly used in decision making, a choice on average every 15 seconds is rather fast, i.e., 240 per hour, which comes to almost 19 hours as a minimum. That is a lot of sessions for what really is a very simple experiment. So one must seek more efficient methods. The basic idea is to select some one-dimensional subset and use that to evaluate the value of gambles.

1.2.2.1   Certainty equivalents: The most obvious idea for evaluating a gamble g is to establish its *certainty equivalent,* which is defined to be that amount of money, $CE(g) \in \mathcal{R} = \mathcal{C} \cap \mathbb{R}$, such that

$$CE(g) \sim g. \tag{1.9}$$

This is a "match" between money and the gamble. Because preference between CEs, i.e., money, is expected to agree with the numerical order, i.e.,

$$CE(g) \succsim CE(h) \Longleftrightarrow CE(g) \geq CE(h),$$

this device reduces the problem from determining $\frac{1}{2}m(m-1)$ to m values—in our example from 45 to 10. Of course, other one-dimensional valued attributes can be used instead of money.

Now, if we can also reduce k substantially, the whole issue of evaluating preferences becomes vastly simpler. The lower limit of replications, $k = 1$, is achieved very simply by having a respondent tell us just once his or her CE for each gamble, and such estimated CEs are called *judged certainty equivalents,* denoted JCEs. There are at least three difficulties with this solution.

- First, given the fact that choices are not stable, we can hardly expect JCEs to be. The only data that I know of on repeated judgments of CEs for the same gamble are the repeated pairs of judgments of von Winterfeldt, Chung, Luce, and Cho (1997) and Weber and Hsee (1998). As one would expect, they exhibit substantial variability. A systematic study of the distribution of such responses has not been conducted.[7]
- Second, and more subtle, is the fact that JCEs do not appear always to agree with estimates of CE based on at least some choice procedures or, for that matter, with choices themselves. The latter point is carefully explored by Tversky, Sattath, and Slovic (1988). Whichever procedure—judgments or choices—one believes provides basic preference information, the other must be considered to be biased. This difficulty is encountered later (§§ 2.2.5 and 2.3.5).

---

[7]   Clearly, the judgments about one gamble would have to be fairly widely separated by trials on which other gambles are presented so that the subject does not simply recall what he or she said earlier.

- Third, however CEs are estimated, comparing a gamble to an amount of money rather than to another gamble may induce a systematic effect because people respond very differently to certainty than to uncertainty, e.g., due to some utility of gambling. This, if correct, again may mean that CEs give biased estimates of the worth of gambles. I will deal with such bias issues as they come up. For now, it is sufficient to recognize that if CEs can be determined in some reasonably efficient way, they provide a very efficient way for indirectly evaluating choices.

1.2.2.2   Probability equivalents: Another method sometimes used is to hold the consequences (usually, amounts of money) x, y fixed, with y in the interval bounded by 0 and x, and to ask for a probability equivalent PE such that $y \sim (x, PE; 0)$. Depending upon whether the PE is a judged value or is determined by some sort of choice procedure, it is called a JPE or CPE. Note that PEs are not useful in ordering pre-chosen gambles in the way CEs are, but as we will see in Section 6.3.4, they can be very useful in other ways.

1.2.2.3   Consistency of certainty and probability equivalents: Hershey and Schoemaker (1985) raised the question whether judged certainty equivalents and judged probability equivalents are consistent in the following sense. Suppose one first determines $y = CE(x, p; 0)$ and then the PE such that $y \sim (x, PE; 0)$. The responses are called *consistent* if $PE = p$. Equally well, one can begin with a given $x > y > 0$ or $x < y < 0$ and ask for PE such that $y \sim (x, PE; 0)$ and follow that with a CE such that $CE \sim (x, PE; 0)$. Here consistency means $CE = y$.

To study this empirically they obtained judged responses from 147 undergraduate students who had been exposed to expected utility theory in a business course. Eighty-three answered questions involving gains, of which 41 were asked to make the judgments in the order CE-PE and 42 were given the order PE-CE. The other 64 respondents were split equally between the CE-PE and PE-CE versions for losses. The two types of judgments were made a week apart. The values of y were $100, $500, $1,000, and $5,000, with the corresponding values of $x = 2y$. The losses were the corresponding negative values. The questions were presented on paper with text descriptions of the gambles and task

The data exhibited two notable features. First, there were huge individual differences. In particular, estimated utility functions exhibited all four combinations of concavity and convexity for money gains and losses. Second, the consistency hypothesis—that the points fall on the diagonal—failed in systematic ways as shown in Fig. 1.4. Without going into detail, the authors considered six possible hypotheses about what might be causing the inconsistency. Among these, they suggest that perhaps the respondents tended to recast the judgments as follows. Suppose that when asked to report JPE such $y \sim (x, JPE; 0)$, the respondents actually did not make this judgment directly, but rather recast it as the judgment $0 \sim (x - y; JPE; -y)$. This account, if true, probably destroys any chance of consistency because, as we shall see, under certain reasonable assumptions to be introduced later, gambles of mixed gains and losses are evaluated differently from gambles of just gains (compare Chapters 4, 6, and 7). Indeed, this proposal is formally the same as treating y as a buying price as developed Sections 6.4 and 7.4, and as we shall see the resulting formulas are complex. In

19

the next subsection, other data will cast doubt on this explanation.

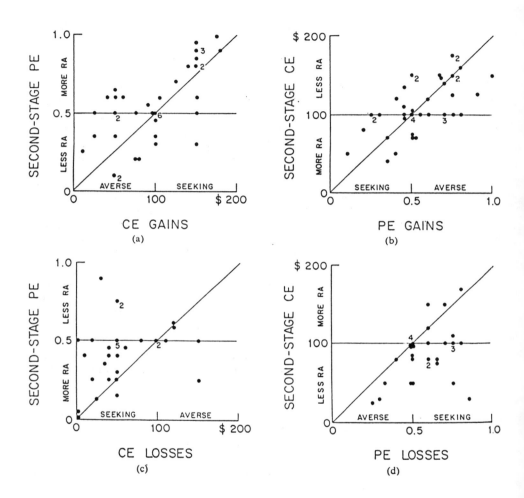

Figure 1.4. Failure of estimated CEs and PEs to be consistent. This is Fig. 1 of Hershey and Schoemaker (1985). Reprinted by permission, Hershey and Schoemaker, "Probability versus certainty equivalence methods in utility measurement: Are they equivalent?" *Management Science*, Volume 31, Number 10, October 1985, 1218. Copyright 1985, The Institute of Management Science (currently INFORMS), 901 Elkridge Landing Road, Suite 400, Linthicum, Maryland 21090-2909, USA.

Johnson and Schkade (1989) ran a somewhat similar study, which agreed with Hershey and Schoemaker (1985) for gains but obtained biases opposite to theirs for losses.

Something the latter authors did not comment upon directly, which in 1985 was not so widely recognized as it is now, is the inconsistency of choice and judged certainty equivalents (see §§ 2.2.5 and 2.3.4). Presumably, a similar inconsistency may exist between choice and judged probability equivalents, but I do not know of any data on this issue.

In any event, it would be interesting to know whether or not choice-determined CEs and PEs are consistent. However, the results of the next subsection do not make one sanguine and, according to Peter Wakker,[8] the conclusion among those studying medical decision making is that the PE estimates are too high. This was also found in Wakker and Deneffe (1996).

1.2.2.4   Lottery equivalents:

Many are uncomfortable about the asymmetry between a gamble and a certain sum of money involved in making CE and PE evaluations and have suggested that one should work only with lotteries. So, for example, one can be given p, q, x and ask for the solution LEO, which stands for lottery equivalent outcome, to the equivalence $(LEO, q; 0) \sim (x, p; 0)$, or given q, x, y one can ask for LEP, for lottery equivalent probability, to $(x, LEP; 0) \sim (y, q; 0)$. The LEO reduces to CE and LEP to PE when $q = 1$. The analogous consistency issue arises:

1. Find LEO and LEP, in that order, such that

$$(LEO, q; 0) \sim (x, p; 0) \quad \text{and} \quad (x, LEP; 0) \sim (LEO, q; 0),$$

then consistency means $LEP = p$.

2. Find LEP and LEO, in that order such that

$$(y, LEP; 0) \sim (x, p; 0) \quad \text{and} \quad (LEO, q; 0) \sim (y, LEP; 0),$$

then consistency means $LEO = x$.

The first study of such consistency was by McCord and de Neufville (1986), who used judged values and found inconsistencies. More persuasive is the very systematic study by Delquié (1993), who used a procedure that he described as a "converging sequence of choices." Presumably this is some variant of the PEST procedure described in the Appendix C. He ran five distinct experiments that involved between 10 and 47 MBA students except for one experiment with 38 engineering students. His conclusion was that they all "show, in matching objects $[X, Y]$, trading off X against Y is not equivalent to trading off Y against X" (p. 1390). The overall result is that in method 1 the LEP lies between p and q, rather than equaling p, and in method 2 the LEO lies between x and y, rather than equaling x.

Because these findings do not entail any certain consequences, they undermine Hershey and Schoemaker's (1985) explanation in terms of recoding the PE gamble into one of gains and losses. Moreover, in the domain of losses, the biases exhibited by Delquié's respondents agree, as noted earlier, with those of Johnson and Schkade and disagree with those of Hershey and Schoemaker. Delquié concludes that it is unlikely that a common explanation exists for both sets of biases. He discusses a number of possible sources for these effects, including a

---

[8]   Personal communication, April 13, 1998.

form of statistical error propagation, but rules each out as a single source explanation.

The unsatisfactory conclusion that I draw is that we do not understand these effects, but there is little doubt they exist.

1.3   Possible Additional Primitives

So far, the underlying preference structure to be studied is $\langle \mathcal{C}, \mathcal{E}, \mathcal{G}, \succsim, e \rangle$, where $\mathcal{C}$ is a set of riskless consequences, $\mathcal{E}$ is a set of chance experiments, $\mathcal{G}$ is the set of gambles under consideration (often $\mathcal{G}_2$), $\succsim$ is a binary (preference) relation on $\mathcal{G}$, and $e \in \mathcal{C}$ is the status quo. This, or a variant of it such as Savage's (1954) system, is the classic framework for studies of decision making under risk and uncertainty, and much of the well-developed theory has been limited to just these primitives.

Within this framework it is, however, difficult to study preferences over certain consequences $\mathcal{C}$ in any self-contained fashion independent of the complexities of the gambles. Yet preferences over $\mathcal{C}$ seem, in a sense, far more basic than preferences over $\mathcal{G}$. To study the certain consequences by themselves, some other basic primitive appears to be needed. I know of four distinct and independent approaches. Of these, I will use only one, joint receipts. For completeness, however, let me make explicit the other three.

The first, worked out in considerable detail by Keeney and Raiffa (1976) and which has led to an extensive subsequent literature under the name "multiattribute utility theory," is to suppose that the elements of $\mathcal{C}$ are multidimensional in the sense that they have several attributes that can be combined in various ways. Most goods have distinct attributes that are of pertinence to the decision maker. For example, cars vary on many dimensions—type, color, horsepower, amenities of various sorts, etc. Focusing on the attributes permits an analysis using the measurement theory methods of conjoint analysis (see Krantz, Luce, Suppes, & Tversky, 1971, Chs. 6 and 7; Luce, Krantz, Suppes, & Tversky, 1990, Chs. 19 and 20; Michell, 1990, 1999; and Appendix D). To some degree, the 2-attribute theory is similar to joint receipts.

A second approach is to introduce an additional ordering primitive, $\succsim^*$, defined over $\mathcal{G} \times \mathcal{G}$ rather than over $\mathcal{G}$. It is interpreted as follows: For $g, h, g', h' \in \mathcal{G}$, $(g, h) \succsim^* (g', h')$ means that the decision maker judges that the "preference distance" or "interval" in going from g to h is at least as large as that in going from g' to h'. Of course for $h = h'$, one assumes that $\succsim^*$ restricted to the first component coincides with the preference ordering $\succsim$ on these gambles. Examples of such theoretical work on judged "strength of preference" are Alt (1936/1971), Barron, von Winterfeldt, and Fischer (1984), Bouyssou and Vansnick (1988), Dyer and Sarin (1982), and Keller (1985c).

Such an approach of comparing pairs provides a good deal of extra mathematical structure (Suppes, Krantz, Luce, & Tversky, 1989, Ch. 14), and it has been widely used in psychological studies of stimulus similarity. Nonetheless, to me, it seems rather artificial in the context of uncertain alternatives. When and where in ordinary life do people make such judgments, that gamble g is "closer to" h than is g' to h'? It is true that if you ask respondents in the laboratory to make such judgments, they will; but that may be an experimental snare and delusion. People are surprisingly flexible about doing unusual things for an experimenter even though they have had no experience in life with such judgments. So I am skeptical about the value of this approach.

It is certainly the case that we do make judgments of strength of preference such as considering whether good g is worth the extra cost above that of a lesser good h. As we shall see, such judgments can be recast naturally in terms of the primitive, joint receipts, that we shall investigate.

Third, within economics a good deal of attention has been devoted to aspects of time discounting and attempts to use it to infer something about the nature of preferences. As it stands, I view this more as a challenge to incorporate into the kind of work represented here. Some additional comments are made about it in Section 1.4.5.

The fourth approach, the one I adopt here, is to introduce a binary operation into the situation. I call it *joint receipt* and denote it by $\oplus$. For $g, h \in \mathcal{G}$, $g \oplus h$ is interpreted to mean having or receiving both g and h. Certainly such an operation is totally familiar, we encounter it daily. The mail brings bills and checks, holidays bring multiple gifts, purchases in the store leads to the joint receipt of goods, etc. Often, as these examples make clear, joint receipt involves more than two things. For all gains or all losses, no problem seems to arise in extending the theory to any finite number of jointly received goods because associativity is satisfied. But as we shall see in Chapter 6, the most common utility models for gambles are not consistent with associativity, which generates a difficulty. However, recent studies suggest that these utility models are empirically incorrect in the mixed case. Chapter 7 approaches the issue by assuming associativity of joint receipts and derives what that must mean for the utility of gambles. These models appear to be more satisfactory for a substantial majority of respondents.

Strength of preference can be recoded in monetary differences using joint receipt. For example, suppose g is preferred to h, and that they cost, respectively, x and y. Then the question of strength of preference becomes one of deciding if $g \oplus (-x)$ is or is not preferred to $h \oplus (-y)$.

So Chapters 4, 6, and 7 investigate the joint-receipt, preference structure $\langle \mathcal{C}, \mathcal{E}, \mathcal{D}, \succsim, e, \oplus \rangle$, where $\oplus$ is a binary operation on $\mathcal{D}$, where $\mathcal{D}$ is the closure of the set of gambles being considered, $\mathcal{G}$, under $\oplus$. Thus, $\mathcal{D}$ includes not only compound gambles, but also the recursive formation of joint receipt of gambles. When $\mathcal{G}_2$ suffices within the domain of gambles, its closure under $\oplus$ is denoted $\mathcal{D}_2$. The main task is to understand how these primitives inter-relate—the putative behavioral laws holding among them—and to discover the degree to which the structure of preferences over gambles and their joint receipt can be summarized numerically. We turn to that general possibility next.

1.4   Numerical Representations

The concept of utility is a numerical one—the idea being that there is a strength of preference that in some sense can be measured in a way similar to the measurement of various physical attributes. Indeed, the aim of this monograph is to see just what numerical representations can be justified from (potentially) observable behavioral properties. So, a number of the assertions (theorems) will take the form: Given that some behavioral properties $P_1, P_2, ..., P_r$ are true in some fairly general context, then there exists a numerical function U over the domain of gambles (or pure consequences) such that for $g, h \in \mathcal{G}$,

$$g \succsim h \Longleftrightarrow U(g) \geq U(h), \tag{1.10}$$

and U also reflects numerically aspects of the structure of the gambles, their compounding, and their joint receipt. Several comments about such representations are needed.

1.4.1   What behavioral properties?

Behavioral properties are assertions about the nature of the behavior of the decision maker. They are to be distinguished from structural conditions that say something about the nature of the gambles involved, which is discussed in Subsection 1.4.3. One can often distinguish between behavioral and structural properties in terms of the logical quantifiers that are used. The behavioral ones often involve only universal quantifiers whereas as structural ones always involve existential ones as well. But sometimes, as in Section 4.4.7, a behavioral property entails the existence of something, so existential quantifiers are not a reliable way to tell them apart.

Certain combinations of behavioral and structural properties can be shown to have a numerical representation. When that happens, it is usual for the behavioral properties, whether descriptive or normative, to be *necessary conditions* of the representation. In general, the structural conditions are not necessary, but only sufficient for the representation. As an example of a necessary condition, any representation for which Eq. (1.10) holds, which is true of all the representations we consider, implies that the behavior must be transitive in the sense that:

$$\text{If } f \succsim g \text{ and } g \succsim h, \text{ then } f \succsim h. \tag{1.11}$$

This follows immediately from the Eq. (1.10) and the transitivity of real numbers.

1.4.2   Descriptive versus normative properties

The behavioral properties can be approached in either of two ways, corresponding very roughly to the approaches of psychologists and decision theorists. The one is whether or not the property seems to describe the behavior of fairly ordinary people. The other is whether or not the property is rational or desirable in some generally agreed upon sense. These properties are called descriptive and normative, respectively, and the two kinds of resulting theories have description or prescription of behavior as their goal.

Much attention will be paid to properties that are both normative and descriptive, and so are common to the resulting descriptive and normative theories. Great efforts have been made to decide whether certain fairly simple behavioral properties are both. Perhaps the simplest is transitivity of preference, Eq. (1.11). We will explore some of this literature in Section 2.2.

Of course, for there to be a real distinction there must be some properties that are descriptive and not normative—e.g., duplex decomposition (§ 6.2.2)—and others that are normative but not descriptive—e.g., the universal accounting indifferences (§ 3.2.2). It is equally important to know about these, for it is here where prescriptive training can come into play.

On the other hand, I consider it highly desirable for any descriptive theory to include the corresponding normative theory as a special case. It does not seem reasonable for the descriptive theory to exclude from its scope the, admittedly rare, rational decision maker. This view seems not to be widely accepted by psychologists, who often seem to feel that the two domains are quite distinct (Edwards, 1992b; Tversky & Kahneman, 1986).

1.4.3   Structural properties

In proving such representation theorems, typically we also invoke properties that do not follow from the representation, but that we find useful in the proof. For example, with risky gambles, we may find it useful to assume that any probability can arise in a gamble, so in the binary case if $p \in [0, 1]$ and $g, h \in \mathcal{G}_1$, then $(g, p; h) \in \mathcal{G}_2$. Such properties are referred to as *structural*. For example, in this example the underlying set of outcomes of the chance experiment is assumed to be what is called *nonatomic*. We like to invoke only structural properties that do not seem greatly at variance with what may be true of the situations to which the theory applies. We try as much as we can to reduce the structural assumptions, but the domain under consideration must be reasonably rich, like a continuum, or regular, like the integers, in order to get results.

1.4.4   Axiom systems

Because we can look at the behavioral and structural properties relating the underlying primitives as forming an axiomatic mathematical system, it is common to refer to the assumed properties—both behavioral and structural—as *axioms*. But it should never be forgotten that such systems are primarily proposed for their scientific, not their mathematical, interest. And they are scientifically interesting only if two conditions are met: First, the behavioral properties have either empirical or normative support. Second, the resulting theory is useful in making either predictions or prescriptions in one or another discipline.

As in any axiomatic system, many different sets of axioms can yield the same representation. This is illustrated in Chapters 3 and 5, which both provide several axiom systems for exactly the same representation. Which system to use is, to a considerable degree, a matter of mathematical taste and the empirical feasibility of evaluating the behavioral axioms. From time to time I will express personal judgments when comparing systems.

1.4.5   Who knows the axioms and the representation?

It is important at the outset to get straight the answer to this question. A number of people have seemed confused about it. For example, anyone who says that these theories of choice "*postulate* the maximization of utility" probably is confused. The representation theorems go in only one direction: from behavioral and structural properties to numerical representations. The behavioral properties embody the scientific information that we, as scientists, have about the decision maker. It is the scientist, not the decision maker, who formulates both the properties (axioms) and the representation. The decision maker exhibits the behavior which, presumably, arises from some fairly complex neuronal processes, but no one is saying that either the axioms or the representation are related in any direct way to these internal and largely unknown and currently unknowable processes.

An analogy may be useful. Consider tossing a sphere of some homogeneous material in a vacuum. A physical analysis of its trajectory is formulated as a differential equation in terms of several variables such as mass, time, displacement, velocity, acceleration, and gravitational force. Given some initial conditions, the solution to that equation describes the motion as a function of time and spatial location. Here we have no trouble recognizing that the variables, the differential equation, and the solution are all products of the scientist, not the sphere. They serve to describe its macroscopic behavior. They do not in any way describe what play of forces exists among the molecules, let alone atoms, composing the sphere. Moreover, it is possible to recast this physical phenomenon as one of minimizing a function, but no one will claim that the sphere is carrying out any explicit minimization calculations.

Likewise, we have absolutely no reason here either to impute to the decision maker any knowledge of the numerical utility function or to suppose that he or she is carrying out any maximization calculations.

1.4.6   Other modeling approaches

The approach to utility measurement we are taking is thus a very classical one—purely behavioral. Within the psychological, but not the economic, community, such behavioral approaches are decidedly out of fashion, and have been ever since the so-called "cognitive revolution." The fashionable models are of two other types.

One, called *information processing*, attempts to describe hypothesized internal processing that starts with input information provided by the situation (including the experimenter or his or her surrogate, the computer), passing through various stages of information processing (some in parallel, some serial) until a response is made. Frequently, the outlines of hypothetical processing architectures are presented as flow diagrams and then either systems of equations representing the postulated processes or computer simulations of them are developed to arrive at predictions of behavior. An example of such mathematical modeling in the decision making area is Busemeyer and Townsend (1993).

These information-processing models have one major advantage over the behavioral models now formulated in that they typically provide a fairly natural account of the time it takes to respond as well as characterizing the response made (Link, 1992; Luce, 1986; Newell, 1990; Townsend & Ashby, 1983). A major challenge facing behavioral decision theorists is to incorporate at least two temporal aspects into our work, namely, time to decision and the impact of delays in the resolution of decisions. Some work on the latter can be found in the psychological literature on operant procedures and some beginning fragments in the economic literature (Chew & Ho, 1994; Davison & McCarthy, 1988; Herrnstein, 1997; Loewenstein & Elster, 1992; and Pope, 1983, 1985). But so far, little rapprochement exists between that approach and the kind of utility theory I am reporting here.

On the other hand, the information processing models have two decided disadvantages.

First, it is exceedingly difficult to devise sensitive and isolated tests of the several underlying components. No one has figured out how to do this at the behavioral level (although W. H. Batchelder and his colleagues have made some progress, e.g. Batchelder and Riefer, 1990), and the level of processing being postulated seems, at present, to have little to do with the neuroimaging that can be done with EEG, PET, or fMRI techniques, let alone with results about firing patterns of single neurons, which data are, in any event, pretty much limited to animals.

Second, these models tend to proliferate numerous free parameters (or free programming choices) that often have to be estimated from the data that are to be explained. To be sure, if the data have many more degrees of freedom than there are parameters, the model can be tested for goodness of fit. But what the parameters mean is something else. And, typically, these estimated parameters do not seem to exhibit much invariance from situation to situation. Such invariance is needed if we are to be confident that we are onto something important, and it makes it possible to estimate them once and for all and to use them to predict in new situations. A similar charge can be made against behavioral utility theories as they are often formulated because they typically have unknown utility and weighting (over events) functions—both entailing a continuum of parameters. However, as we shall see, there are principled ways of adding behavioral properties that, on the one hand, can be studied empirically and, on the other hand, determine these functions up to a mathematical form with very few parameters. Examples limiting weighting functions are in Section 3.4.3.4 and utility functions in Sections 4.4.6 and 4.5.

Another class of popular models in psychology goes under the name of *connectionism* or *distributed processing*. Typically, these models involve the idea of input nodes, output nodes, and hidden nodes that are linked by weighted links to the other two classes of nodes. The model entails some learning mechanism that, with experience, alters the strengths of the links in such a way that the device responds not only to the inputs on which it has been trained but also to new stimuli. Such modeling of decision making is beginning to be developed by, e.g., Jerome Busemeyer at the University of Indiana and by members of Stephen Grossberg's group at Boston University.

1.5   Empirical Evaluation of Models

There are two extreme ways one can approach the testing of axiomatic models of the type we will be encountering. One can examine the axioms individually and ask in specifically designed experiments whether the observed behavior accords with them. The experiments one designs are highly focused on the individual properties, although often a single study will attempt to examine several axioms within the same overall design. Alternatively, one can ask how well the overall numerical representation accords with global preference data that are not selected with any specific property in mind. Here, the scope of the experiments should be broad in an attempt to encompass the full range of possible behaviors.

Studies that examine axioms usually are not concerned with choosing one axiom over another closely related one—although we will encounter that occasionally (e.g., §7.3)—but with a Yes-No decision on whether or not the axiom in question seems to be correct. Doing this is made difficult by the fact that choices appear to be in part statistical—or, at least, repeating the same choice does not always result in the same response (§1.2.1.4). Thus, one is confronted with devising or selecting some sort of statistical test, and very often it is unclear what it should be. We will encounter a number of ad hoc solutions that have been used, some of which have been demonstrated to lead to error (§2.2.3).

The great advantage of examining individual axioms is that in improving theories it helps to know which axioms appear valid and which are in need of change. Knowing that an entire representation fails to fit data usually fails to focus on what is wrong and may, indeed, lead theorists in the wrong direction.

When there are several competing theories, studies that focus on representations have the great advantage of pitting them against one another. Usually it is easier to decide that one theory fits data more closely than another than it is to evaluate how well a single theory fits data.

Often, however, there are difficulties that make this approach problematical. First, most of the theories are rather underdetermined in the sense of having numerical representations with unspecified utility and weighting functions—in some sense, infinite degrees of freedom. Of course, from finite data sets one can only estimate them approximately and often there are many combinations of functions that will account for the behavior. For example, much data on risk aversion can be explained either in terms of the form of the utility function or in terms of the weighting function or both. In my opinion, the existence of very unspecified functions simply means that the theory is not adequately characterized and is in need of a more complete behavioral analysis leading to additional axiomatic structure. The purported advantage of having relatively unspecified functions is the relative ease with which they can be adapted to different bodies of data.

The typical approach has been to select, often without much reason, particular families of functions with one to three free parameters that have to be estimated from the data. We will encounter numerous examples of this approach. This leads to the second problem of comparing theories, namely, how to deal with different numbers of parameters. Statistical correction procedures for estimated parameters have been suggested but, except for the simplest textbook models, they continue to be debated. (See, for example, a forthcoming issue of Volume 44 (2000) of the *Journal of Mathematical Psychology* where papers from a 1997 miniconference on general techniques of model evaluation will be published.) Moreover, for me at least, not all parameters are "equal." Consider three types: (i) Sometimes a data analysis estimates certain parameters to be approximately equal, and so the theorist "argues" for their equality and reestimates on that assumption. That is fine if explained, but sometimes it does not appear to be acknowledged. Should one receive any penalty for trying different parametric families and simply reporting the most parsimonious of the lot? (ii) The theory only partially specifies a function and the theorist picks, often out of the blue, a function with one or two parameters. (iii) A principled (axiomatic) argument leads to a function with one or two parameters. Are the fits to data using (ii) and (iii) to be thought of as being on a par scientifically? Of course, they are statistically.

The third issue is the nature of the probabilistic structure to be imposed. None of the theories considered here comes with a natural source of randomness. Thus, it is somewhat arbitrary what we assume about it. For example, Harless and Camerer (1994) postulated that each choice is a probabilistic mix of the algebraic model and what amounts to the toss of a coin, independent of whether the algebraic difference is large or small. In contrast, Hey and Orme (1994), at the same time and in the same journal, postulated a model in the spirit of the psychological tradition that began with L. L. Thurstone (1927, 1959) of assuming that if X and Y are the numerical values associated to two alternatives x and y, then the probability of choosing x over y is determined by whether $X - Y + \epsilon > 0$, where ϵ is some random variable. Note that the impact of the randomness varies greatly with the magnitude of $X - Y$. Carbone and Hey (1997) compared the two models and concluded that neither model is clearly correct, and I know of no principled reason for choosing either. Indeed, they concluded that there may well be individual differences underlying the probabilistic behavior. Thus, any attempt at an overall evaluation of theories is seriously confounded both with the choice of a statistical model and with the parametric specification of functions.

Which approach one takes depends somewhat upon one's goals. If they are scientific— trying to understand what is going on—then I think there is reasonable agreement that testing axioms individually is the way to go. There is a purposeful double meaning to what I just said: Each axiom should be tested in as much isolation as is possible, and it should be done in so far as possible for each person individually, not using group aggregations. Whenever we look, we find substantial individual differences, so aggregation must be done with a good deal of restraint and care. Thus, this monograph, which attempts to deal with scientific questions, focuses attention whenever possible on individual axioms tested on individual people. (Because the literature is often otherwise, it is not always possible to report individual data.)

If, on the other hand, one wants the theory primarily for purposes of prediction, either of behavior in new situations or as the grounding for microeconomic theory, then global testing of representations is the correct way to go. It tells one that with a particular representation coupled with a particular statistical add-on, one will do as well in predicting choices among uncertain alternatives as currently we know how to do. Because I will not be making use of this approach, it may be well to list some of the key references here. In addition to the two just mentioned above, there are: Carbone (1997), Carbone and Hey (1994, 1995), Daniels and Keller (1990, 1992), Hey (1995, 1997a, 1997b, 1997c), Hey and Carbone (1995), Loomes and Sugden (1995), Selten (1991), and a forthcoming (2000, Vol. 44) issue of the *Journal of Mathematical Psychology* on model evaluation.

Of course, the empirical world is rarely dealt with solely using one extreme approach or the other.

1.6   Outline

One might expect me to begin with the simplest case of certain alternatives and then move on to gambles. To do so encounters a difficulty. The behavioral linkages that seem to exist between certain consequences and gambles are such that for gains alone or losses alone one can have the mathematically simplest available numerical representation of preference either in the domain of certain consequences or in the domain of gambles, but they cannot both be simultaneously simple except in special cases. So one must choose which representation to make more complex, and when one knows the results it is reasonably clear that it is better to impose the greater complexity on the representation of certain alternatives. So, we take up gambles first.

Chapter 2 describes a series of fundamental, underlying properties that are common to the preference structures $\langle \mathcal{C}, \mathcal{E}, \mathcal{D}, \succsim, e, \oplus \rangle$, with or without $\oplus$, of rest of the monograph. These basic behavioral axioms, which are summarized in Section 2.7 (and also Appendix B), are postulated in almost all theories that have been proposed. One of these assumptions is that a gamble with three or more distinct consequences of both gains and losses is decomposed into an equivalent binary gamble whose consequence are two subgambles, the one being based on all of the events leading to gains, the other on all of those events leading to losses. The monograph is structured accordingly. The study of the gains subgamble is given in Chapters 3-5.

Chapter 3 focuses on a particular numerical representation of binary gambles of gains (or equally well, losses) relative to the status quo that are of the form $(x, C; y, E\backslash C)$. It explores two necessary trade-off relations—that between x and C with y fixed at the status quo e, and that between x and y with (C, E) held fixed—as well as a behavioral condition called event commutativity. Data on these are reported. This representation includes, as special cases, the classical (binary) theories of subjective expected and expected utility. Conditions characterizing these special cases are laid out, and it is made experimentally clear how the more general subjective expected utility representation fails descriptively. The mathematical forms of the weighting and utility functions that are estimated from data assuming the representation are discussed. Going the other way, each behavioral trade-off can be used to generate a numerical representation of the underlying preference order. From these, two axiomatizations of the representation are provided.

Chapter 4 introduces into the situation the additional primitive of the joint receipt of gambles and consequences. Some argument is given for supposing this operation on certain gains (and by symmetry, losses) satisfies properties akin to those of mass measurement, which therefore means it has an additive numerical representation. The major issue of the chapter is to work out the relation between this measure of value over the certain alternatives and the utility measure that was arrived at in Chapter 3 for binary gambles. A very simple and locally rational,[9] accounting indifference that links them is introduced. It leads to either a proportional or an exponential relation between the two measures. Ultimately, this provides us with an axiomatization of the binary rank-dependent representation of Chapter 3. A variety of empirical issues are explored in connection with this and the related linking laws.

Chapter 5 turns to general gambles of more than two gains consequences. The binary theory was studied in the previous two chapters, and so what remains is to understand how to generalize that theory. We explore one axiomatization based on properties holding for what are known as comonotonic gambles and two other axiomatizations that involve inductive behav-

---

[9]   The term "rational" is tricky to use in talking about aspects of models. Some scientists identify it with a very specific overall representation, whereas I want to be able to class some specific behavioral properties as rational in certain well-defined senses. I will speak of these as "locally rational."

ioral laws that begin with the binary representation of Chapter 3. At least one of the inductive principles, coalescing, is very compelling—so much so that some authors do not view it as even testable—although it is most likely not descriptive. All three axiomatizations lead to a representation that goes under various names, the most common being rank-dependent utility (RDU) and Choquet expected utility (CEU). The latter term arises from the fact that the weighting functions that arise are examples of Choquet's (1953) capacities. There is a fair amount of inconsistency in how these terms are used. Some authors use RDU for risk and CEU for uncertainty, but others use RDU for both. Here I will take RDU to apply to both risk and uncertainty. Various sets of data are described, some of which favor RDU and some of which cast it into considerable doubt. Some alternative and historically important ideas about the representation of general gambles of gains are described. The conclusion that I draw is the situation is very much in flux and there is no agreed upon satisfactory model for more than binary gambles.

Chapters 6 and 7 extend the study of gambles to the cases of mixed consequences. This is done by separating the gains from the losses and assuming that it can be reduced to the binary case of one gain and one loss. So the main focus is on the binary mixed case. Two fundamentally different approaches are considered that lead to substantially different representations. The first, in Chapter 6, assumes a simple additive utility representation for mixed joint receipts which, via either of two possible linking "laws," leads to familiar bilinear representations of mixed binary gambles. I call the resulting class of models "rank- and sign-dependent utility" (RSDU), and Tversky and Kahneman (1992) called it "cumulative prospect theory" (CPT). The major theoretical difficulty of this approach is to understand why the utility functions found in Chapters 3 and 5 agree with those found this way. The story, while fully understood mathematically, is not very intuitive. Moreover, some recent data cast into great doubt the kind of bilinear model that arises in this way. The other approach, in Chapter 7, follows the simplest possible extension from the gains and losses theory for joint receipts, which turns out to lead to a somewhat complex utility representation for mixed gambles. Despite its complexity, it appears to accord appreciably better with the data that reject the models of Chapter 6. Data analyses to discriminate further between the two approaches are also presented.

Chapter 8 provides a brief summary of the main theoretical ideas and lessons learned, and it lists some open problems. It also raises the possibility that perhaps we are on the wrong track in assuming choice is the basic primitive and that instead we should be concerned with how respondents establish reference levels for choice situations and then assume that the analysis is carried out on deviations from that reference level.

This is followed by five appendices concerning various matters. Appendix A summarizes the basic notations that were introduced in this Chapter. Appendix B summarizes the basic behavioral assumptions of Chapter 2. Appendix C describes the nature of the PEST procedure used by me and my colleagues to estimate certainty equivalents of gambles. Appendix D describes the measurement results concerning additive conjoint measurement that are first used in Chapter 3. And finally, Appendix E pulls together in alphabetic order all of the major definitions of the monograph.

Chapter 2
BASIC ASSUMPTIONS

This chapter formulates several assumptions that are common to the rest of the monograph and that are, in some sense, basic to the approach taken in much of utility theory. Some of these assumptions have been considered so transparent as to be virtually untestable, and they have not been tested empirically. Others, which are also basic to the approach and are highly rational, have been questioned empirically. I will attempt to summarize the major features of these tests and the conclusions that I have drawn from them.

Fundamentally, three distinct concepts of rationality are at play in this monograph which all ignore the experiment(s) that give rise to the consequences, ignore any utility of gambling. They are:

- *Two distinct framings of a gamble should be seen as the same and so be indifferent.* Specific cases of this principle when the framing concerns compounding and the order in which things are written are called *accounting indifferences.* As we shall see, descriptive theories do not satisfy this principle of rationality except in the simplest cases, which are taken up in Section 2.1.
- *Consider a set S of valued entities with none preferred to g ∈ S. If g' is created by replacing some aspect of g by something at least as preferred, all else fixed, then no entity in S is preferred to g'.* The implications of this principle are explored in Sections 2.2 and 2.3. Considerable controversy exits concerning their descriptive accuracy.
- *If the chance of receiving something that is valued is made more likely at the expense of something less valued, the modified alternative is preferred to the original one.* This principle is explored in Section 2.4 and is found wanting descriptively in one version and not in another.

Because the behavioral properties satisfying these requirements pertain to limited aspects of behavior, I shall refer to them as *locally rational,* reserving the unconditional word *rational* for overall models of behavior that are built up by assuming several locally rational conditions. The general consensus in the literature is that subjective expected utility theory and, in the case of known probabilities, expected utility is *the* rational theory. The major properties exhibited by expected utility that are said to characterize rationality are consequentialism, dynamic consistency, and reduction of compound gambles to equivalent first-order ones (Machina, 1989). We will come to see in Chapter 7 how a representation quite different from subjective expected utility arises from different, but entirely locally rational, conditions.

2.1   Elementary Accounting Indifferences

This section introduces three very simple indifferences that will be assumed without further ado in the rest of the monograph. They have never been tested empirically because many believe that if a decision maker understands the situation being described, then the equivalence of the two gambles is apparent and so the decision maker must be indifferent between them. By *equivalence* one means that both gambles give rise to the same consequences under the same circumstances. As we shall ultimately see, it is not clear exactly where among such pairs of equivalent gambles the dividing line falls between those that are so obvious as not to need empirical verification of indifference and those for which empirical study is needed. Researchers certainly differ in their belief about which equivalences need empirical study.

I will state all of these definitions at the level of second-order gambles $\mathcal{G}_2$ and leave implicit the definitions for those of order $n \neq 2$. In practice we will only use first- and second-order ones. The notational convention to be followed is that at the zeroth order, the elements are $x, y \in \mathcal{C} = \mathcal{G}_0$. At the first order, $g, h \in \mathcal{G}_1 \backslash \mathcal{G}_0$. And at the second order we write $(g, C; h)$.

Note that in numbering definitions I employ the following convention: $c.s.n$, where c is the chapter number, s the section number, and n the ordinal number of definitions within that section. The same convention is followed separately for lemmas, propositions, and theorems as a group. Thus, by looking for the section heading at the top of a page, the reader can often quickly find the item to which reference is made. In contrast, the equations are numbered consecutively within a chapter.

Definition 2.1.1.   The preference substructure of binary gambles from $\langle \mathcal{C}, \mathcal{E}, \mathcal{G}_2, \succsim \rangle$ exhibits *idempotence* if and only if for every $\mathbf{E} \in \mathcal{E}$, $C \in \mathcal{E}_{\mathbf{E}}$, and $g \in \mathcal{G}_1$,

$$(g, C; g) \sim g, \tag{2.1}$$

where it is implicit that the partition is $\{C, E \backslash C\}$.

Here we have a gamble, call it g', in which an experiment $\mathbf{E}$ is run and if $C(\subseteq E)$ occurs the outcome is g and, equally, if C fails to occur, the outcome is also g. The assertion is that the decision maker is indifferent between g' and g. Note that this is not a mathematical or conceptual triviality because $g' \in \mathcal{G}_2$ whereas $g \in \mathcal{G}_1$, so they cannot be equal. The only reason indifference might fail is if, in addition to valuing the consequence g, the decision maker also feels some pleasure or displeasure in seeing the experiment run, even though its outcome does not affect the consequence received. The assumption we make is that when the experiment has no impact on what is received, then running it has no inherent value itself to a decision maker.

When $x \in \mathcal{G}_0 = \mathcal{C}$, Eq. (2.1) becomes $(x, C; x) \sim x$, which is idempotence for first-order gambles. This assumption, which at first seems quite innocent, may well not be. What happens when it is dropped has recently been studied by Luce and Marley (1999b), and this seems to capture one aspect of what has informally been called the "utility of gambling." I do not take it up here. For another approach to the utility of gambling see Pope (1991, 1995, 1996/97, 1998).

Definition 2.1.2.   The substructure of binary gambles from $\langle \mathcal{C}, \mathcal{E}, \mathcal{G}_2, \succsim \rangle$ exhibits *certainty* if and only if for every $\mathbf{E} \in \mathcal{E}$, $g, h \in \mathcal{G}_1$

$$(g, E; h) \sim g. \tag{2.2}$$

Note that the assertion is independent of which experiment is used.

The arguments in favor of and against certainty are substantially those for idempotence: On both sides the decision maker receives g, the only difference being whether or not the (pointless) experiment is run.

Definition 2.1.3. The substructure of binary gambles from $\langle \mathcal{C}, \mathcal{E}, \mathcal{G}_2, \succsim \rangle$ exhibits *complementarity* if and only if for every $\mathbf{E} \in \mathcal{E}$, $C \in \mathcal{E}_\mathbf{E}$, $g, h \in \mathcal{G}_2$,

$$(g, C; h) \sim (h, \overline{C}; g), \tag{2.3}$$

where $\overline{C} = E \backslash C$.

Here the two sides say exactly the same thing except for the order of writing, and that really should not matter in such a simple situation. Indeed, were we to treat a gamble as a function rather than an ordered tuple, we would have $(g, C; h) \equiv (h, \overline{C}; g)$, but for ordered tuples all such equivalences must be explicit.

In experimental practice, the concern about the order in which things are presented is often less simple. For example, if a pie display (see Fig. 1.2) is used, there is a continuum of possibilities because the same gamble can be rotated to any angle from $0°$ to $360°$. Other types of displays have other equivalent alternatives. These experimental choices may have a (small) effect on a decision maker's decisions (Keller, 1985a; Moskowitz, 1974). The theory assumes none.

A famous empirical example in which complementarity appears to fail concerns the impact on behavior of how a mixed gamble is framed (Kahneman & Tversky, 1984; Tversky & Kahneman, 1981, 1986). The typical example is the "Asian disease" problem in which a vaccine is described in one frame as having a probability p of saving the lives of k people in a population of n and in the other as the probability $1 - p$ of losing $n - k$ lives in the same population. These are obviously the same gamble of mixed consequences, one a gain and one a loss. Yet in a number of studies of this and similar problems with different scenarios, respondents do not act as if they are the same gamble. The pattern among the various studies is complex, as is described by Schneider (1992). As we shall see in Chapters 6 and 7, one does not need to invoke complementarity in the mixed case, and as a result a fairly natural explanation of the framing effect exists.

2.2 Transitivity

The next four properties all involve the full preference relation $\succsim$ over $\mathcal{G}$, not just $\sim$ as in the first three. These are all subject to some descriptive doubt, so they have been explored empirically reasonably carefully.

Definition 2.2.1. A structure of gambles $\langle \mathcal{C}, \mathcal{E}, \mathcal{G}_2, \succsim \rangle$ exhibits *transitivity* if and only if for all $f, g, h \in \mathcal{G}_2$:

$$\text{If } f \succsim g \text{ and } g \succsim h, \text{ then } f \succsim h. \tag{2.4}$$

Transitivity is simply a special case of the second rationality principle in which $S = \{g, h\}$, with $\text{not}(h \succ g)$, i.e., $g \succsim h$, and the modification of g being $g' = f \succsim g$. The principle says that in addition to $f \succsim g$ we also know $\text{not}(h \succ f)$, i.e., $f \succsim h$.

Any theory with order-preserving numerical utilities assigned to gambles necessarily exhibits transitivity because the numerical order $\geq$ is transitive (§ 1.4). So if the data reject transitivity, they reject all such theories as being descriptive.

For a general discussion of all the issues surrounding transitivity, see van Acker (1990).

2.2.1   Normative strength of transitivity

Before turning to data, there is the issue of normativeness of transitivity. As was noted in Section 1.2.1.1, the issue of what behavior is postulated to reveal preference may affect considerably what we conclude. Many philosophers and economists have argued that, much as with logic, probability, and mathematics, theories of decision making based on the concept of preference can be interpreted as normative in the sense of telling one how one must behave so as to adhere to certain basic principles of "locally rational behavior," some of which were described informally at the beginning of the chapter. Should a rational person behave transitively, and do people who have violated transitivity feel they made an error?

Answering the purely normative question rests, therefore, upon how "rational behavior" is defined, and my impression of these discussions (e.g., Anand, 1987) is that often it is not sharply defined. For me, the underlying principle of preference rationality, which was stated just after Definition 2.2.1 and which I take as one aspect of the definition of "rational," makes transitivity an automatic consequence. Others seem to feel that it should be derived from some deeper principles, but they do not seem to me to make very clear what they are.

Various arguments have been made against its normativeness. One camp holds that for some respondents the running of the underlying experiment has itself positive or negative value in addition to that arising from the consequences assigned to its possible outcomes. These people cannot accept transitivity as a normative condition, at least when the three elements f, g, h are some mix of nontrivial gambles and certain consequences. The theory developed in this monograph simply does not take this into account.

In addition, Fishburn (1982, 1991) has argued against transitivity even normatively, and he has constructed a number of models in which transitivity fails to hold. I do not find his arguments against it particularly compelling, but I return to this issue again in Section 8.3.4.

For me, the strongest argument against normatively imposing transitivity arises if one feels that each decision problem is and should be, in some sense, the source of its own status quo relative to which the alternatives are evaluated. One example of this is Loomes and Sugden's (1982) regret theory. Although this may be an important direction, I do not follow it.

Most people, when queried, claim to want to abide by transitivity, arguing that they find it a normatively compelling principle. And when someone's choices violate transitivity, then on being shown the violation that person usually admits to an "error" and wants to change at least one of the choices. Although many who have taught decision theory have experienced examples of this with students, the most compelling published evidence is MacCrimmon (1968). Because he looked at a number of basic properties of decision making, I will refer to the study several times under different headings. The respondents were 38 "upper-middle-level" business executives at a University of California training program. "The [median] executive can be described as forty-two years of age, holding a college degree, and earning $25,000 a year as a division manager in a company of about 6,000 employees." (p. 4). (Note that the study was done in 1964 when the value of the dollar was about 10 times its present value.)

The design involved three major steps. First, business-like scenarios were described and choices made. Second, the respondents were asked to reflect on the property being tested after being provided with pro and con arguments. "[T]he decision problems were especially constructed so that the strongest possible counter-argument to each postulate could be made" (p. 4). And third, there were individual terminal interviews of about 30 minutes in which the respondents were shown aspects of their data that violated various postulates, and they were allowed to comment in an open ended fashion on the patterns actually exhibited by their choices.

For transitivity, the respondents responded to three sets of choices of 6 binary pairs formed from 4 alternatives and they also ranked all 4 alternatives. Among these choices, 8 of the 38 respondents exhibited intransitivities among the binary choices. In the interview, 6 of the 8 acknowledged "mistakes" whereas two persisted in arguing that they had focused on different dimensions of the choice (see § 2.2.3). Thirty of the respondents exhibited inconsistencies between choices and the ranking. When confronted with the difference, all wished to change their responses. A slight majority preferred to change their choices rather than their rankings. MacCrimmon's conclusion was that although there are behavioral violations of transitivity, they are generally viewed as mistakes. So, at least the normative aspect of the theory was sustained.

2.2.2   The slippery slope of coarse indifferences

One immediate consequence of transitivity of weak preference, Eq. (2.4), is that the indifference relation $\sim$ itself must also be transitive:

$$\text{If } f \sim g \text{ and } g \sim h, \text{ then } f \sim h. \tag{2.5}$$

It has long been recognized that the transitivity of indifference must be a considerable idealization in almost any area involving human judgment, especially if a long string of indifferences is involved. An hypothetical example suggested by Luce (1956) was a series of cups of coffee of increasing sugar content beginning at black and progressing a grain at a time to fully saturated. Because one simply cannot discriminate any difference involving a single granule of sugar, one must be indifferent between adjacent pairs. Yet few of us are indifferent between black coffee and coffee saturated with sugar.

This example strongly suggests that an idealization is involved in assuming transitivity, but there are ways to live with that. One is to model strict preferences as transitive and indifferences as not transitive, called *semiorders* (Luce, 1956), and weakened further to what

Fishburn (1985) called *interval orders*. Such orderings have been studied quite extensively in numerous subsequent papers; for summaries see Fishburn (1985) and Suppes, Krantz, Luce, and Tversky (1989, Ch. 16). When the stimuli are multidimensional, one can combine the idea of a semiorder with a trade-off between dimensions within the indifference span to form what has been called a *lexicographic semiorder.*

One simple feature of such models is that one can infer from the observed order an underlying ordering. For example, suppose we observe $f \sim g$, $h \sim f$, and $h \succ g$, then indirectly we conclude that f is really "greater than" g, i.e., $f \succsim' g$. Moreover, under the assumptions of a semiorder, one can show that $\succsim'$ is transitive. So, in a sense, there really is an underlying transitive ordering.

Thus, although there may be a problem in dealing directly with observed indifferences, one can refine them sufficiently to maintain the assumption of transitivity.

2.2.3   The slippery slope of smallish compensating changes

Tversky (1969) in a paper titled "Intransitivity of preferences" claimed to demonstrate intransitivity as follows. In five lotteries of the form $(\$x, p; 0)$ the value of x was decreased from \$5.00 to \$4.00 in \$0.25 steps while, in compensation, p was increased from 7/24 to 11/24 in steps of 1/24. The expected value rose from \$1.46 to \$1.83. Individual lotteries were presented as pie sector diagrams. All distinct pairs were presented as well as 10 pairs of five irrelevant lotteries designed to increase the separation of repeated presentations of the experimental lotteries. A session took place once a week for five weeks, and each of the 20 pairs was repeated 4 times within each session. Thus, each pair was judged 20 times. The respondents were 8 Harvard University undergraduates selected from a pool of 18 as those most likely to violate transitivity on the basis of a preliminary test.

The proportions of choice for each pair were reported. Using the notion that preponderance of choice defines an ordering from Eq. (1.6) where P is replaced by its estimate $\widehat{P}$, i.e.,

$$g \succsim h \iff \widehat{P}(g,h) \geq \frac{1}{2}.$$

Substituting Eq. (1.6) into Eq. (2.4) yields:

$$\text{If } P(f,g) \geq \frac{1}{2} \text{ and } P(g,h) \geq \frac{1}{2}, \text{ then } P(f,h) \geq \frac{1}{2},$$

which is called *weak stochastic transitivity* (WST). This was tested by replacing P by $\widehat{P}$ with the stimuli ordered as described above. Tversky's conclusion was that there were a number of statistically significant violations of weak stochastic transitivity.

Iverson and Falmagne (1985) pointed out a basic difficulty with Tversky's evaluation of WST. In a nutshell, the problem lies in two related facts: First, one cannot be sure that the experimental order of the stimuli is actually the best one for any individual and, second, one cannot be certain, from estimated data—especially those fairly near $\frac{1}{2}$—which way the corresponding underlying inequalities actually go. Tversky treated the data not really as estimates, but as true probabilities. Iverson and Falmagne worked out in detail the surprisingly complex statistical analysis that takes these uncertainties into account and that is needed to test WST statistically. They report their reanalysis in detail for one of the 8 respondents, and summarize it for the remainder. Their conclusion was that for only one of the 8 could WST be rejected at the 0.05 level of significance.

So, although Tversky's paper is often cited as demonstrating a failure of transitivity, the less read and cited Iverson and Falmagne paper places his conclusion and that of several replications, modifications, and extensions (Lindman & Lyons, 1978; Montgomery, 1977) into considerable doubt.

Another, in my opinion, flawed rejection of transitivity is Starmer (1999), which is taken up in Section 5.5.2.1.

Ranyard (1976, 1977) approached the problem differently. In the 1977 paper he elicited evidence from his 8 respondents in Experiment[1] 1 concerning their decision strategies and classed two of them as following a lexicographic semiorder rule: When a difference in one dimension was sufficiently large, the choice was based on that dimension alone. The analysis, which is described in the 1976 paper, involves finding the minimum number of changes in choices needed to be consistent with transitivity. The median was 23 for the two lexicographic respondents and 4 for the others. The difference of the two groups was significant by the Mann-Whitney U test at the 0.04 level. The conclusion that I draw from this is that some people—the sample size is simply too small to say with any accuracy what fraction—use a very simplified decision strategy that entails few trade-offs and that is far more consistent with some sort of locally lexicographic behavior that leads to non-transitive behavior. The others, however, seem consistent with transitivity.

Historically, the main empirical concern about transitivity has not been these two studies but the topic taken up in Section 2.2.5. Before that, however, we need to make explicit an assumption that we use regularly.

2.2.4   Preference for money

It is very widely taken for granted that, everything else equal, more money is preferred to less. Formally, if money is modeled as $\mathbb{R}$, then for all $\alpha, \beta \in \mathbb{R}$,

$$\alpha \succsim \beta \Longleftrightarrow \alpha \geq \beta. \tag{2.6}$$

If this is correct, then necessarily preference is transitive over money. It seems pointless to check this assumption empirically in isolation.

I believe that this is the only assertion about preferences found in the literature on utility that alleges the same particular choices for all people. As with transitivity, all other assumptions assert a preference that is conditional on certain other preferences holding.

2.2.5   Preference reversals with mixed response procedures

2.2.5.1   The phenomenon: The basic phenomenon of *preference reversals* is this: Pairs

---

[1]   Experiment 2 will be discussed in Section 3.1.3.2.

of lotteries of the form (x, p; $0) are used. One member of the pair, often called the "dollar gamble" and which I will denote $g(\$)$, has a comparatively large value of x and comparatively small value of p. The other member, called the "probability gamble," denoted $g(P)$, has a more moderate value of x and a comparatively larger value for p. The gambles of a pair have approximately the same expected value ($EV = xp$).

For a substantial fraction—close to 50%—of the respondents the empirical finding is that the probability gamble is chosen over the money one, but the judged certainty equivalent (§ 1.2.2.1) assigned to the money gamble is larger than that assigned to the probability one, i.e.,

$$g(P) \succ g(\$) \quad \text{but} \quad JCE[g(P)] < JCE[g(\$)].$$

Putting these two observations together with the assumption that $JCE[g(P)] \sim g(P)$ we have the following apparent violation of transitivity:

$$JCE[g(\$)] > JCE[g(P)] \sim g(P) \succ g(\$) \sim JCE[g(\$)]. \tag{2.7}$$

Lichtenstein and Slovic (1971), with an almost immediate replication[2] by Lindman (1971), were the first to demonstrate and explore preference reversals using college student respondents, and the phenomenon was replicated in Lichtenstein and Slovic (1973) for considerably larger sums of money using actual gamblers in Las Vegas. Subsequently, the phenomenon has been replicated many, many times. A good summary of the references up to 1990 is Tversky, Slovic, and Kahneman (1990) or Tversky and Thaler (1990).

This phenomenon is perhaps most vividly demonstrated in a parametric study by Mellers, Chang, Birnbaum, and Ordóñez (1992). They constructed 36 gambles of the form shown in Table 2.1 and another 36 in which the signs of the consequences were all changed to negative values. Notice that as one looks at the diagonals running from the lower left to the upper right, the EVs are nearly the same. In the following figures the focus is on these pairs having approximately the same EV.

Table 2.1. The gains lotteries and their expected values used by Mellers, Chang, Birnbaum, and Ordóñez (1992).

Probability	Amount					
	$3	$5.40	$9.70	$17.50	$31.50	$56.70
0.05	0.15	0.27	0.49	0.88	1.58	2.84
0.09	0.27	0.49	0.87	1.58	2.84	5.10
0.17	0.48	0.86	1.55	2.80	5.04	9.07
0.29	0.87	1.57	2.81	5.08	9.14	16.44
0.52	1.56	2.81	5.04	9.10	16.38	29.48
0.94	2.82	5.08	9.12	16.45	29.61	53.30

[2]   Lindman refers to a 1968 American Psychological Association abstract on preference reversals by Lichtenstein and Slovic, suggesting that his work is a replication and extension of their work.

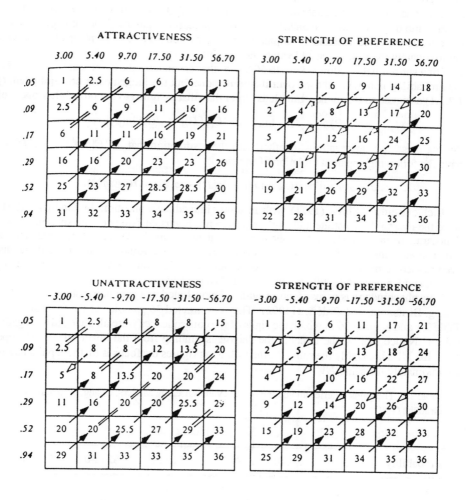

Figure 2.1. Attractiveness and strength of preference for gains and losses in the lotteries shown in Table 2.1. The numbers in the cells show rankings. The arrows indicate the ratings and the choice directions for lotteries with approximately the same expected values. Note the differences in direction in the upper right half. Adapted with permission from Figs. 4 and 7 of Mellers, Chang, Birnbaum, and Ordóñez (1992). Copyright © 1992 by the American Psychological Association.

Their respondents provided ratings of strength of preference (corresponding closely to choice), attractiveness (corresponding closely to JCE), and selling prices (another form of JCE, but not one that one would expect to be a very good estimate of the true CE). Figure 2.1 shows the patterns. Just comparing attractiveness and strength of preference we see a highly systematic reversal in the upper right half for both gains and losses, just as described above.

This robust apparent violation of transitivity attracted a great deal of attention including that of some economists who, despite the Las Vegas study, were initially concerned that the problem arose from respondents not taking the judgments and choices sufficiently seriously. The most systematic attempt to overcome these potential limitations was an empirical study by two economists, Grether and Plott (1979), who after experimenting with a number of variants concluded that the phenomenon is robust. And, indeed, it is.

But a question remained: What in fact does the phenomenon show? Many seemed to think it was evidence against transitivity, but this is only true if one assumes that

$$JCE(g) = CE(g) \sim g. \tag{2.8}$$

This assumption, which Tversky, Slovic, and Kahneman (1990) called the assumption of *procedure invariance,* is basic to the argument of Eq. (2.7). Independently, Bostic, Herrnstein, and Luce (1990) and Li (1994), taking different routes, arrived at the same conclusion, namely, that procedure invariance as embodied in Eq. (2.8) is false. The Tversky et al. (1990) and Bostic et al. (1990) approaches are sufficiently interesting to warrant description.

2.2.5.2   The Tversky, Slovic, and Kahneman (1990) study: The idea underlying Tversky et al. (1990) was to find, for those cases where the respondent reported $g(P) \succ g(\$)$, a sum of money X such that

$$JCE[g(\$)] > X > JCE[g(P)].$$

They then had the respondent make choices between $g(\$)$ and X and between $g(P)$ and X. Thus, there are four possible empirical outcomes:[3]

(1) *Intransitivity:* If $g(\$) \succ X$ and $X \succ g(P)$, then because $g(P) \succ g(\$)$ we have the clear intransitivity of choices, not of mixed choices and judgments:

$$X \succ g(P) \succ g(\$) \succ X.$$

(2) *Overpricing of $g(\$)$:* If $X \succ g(P)$ and $X \succ g(\$)$, then

$$JCE[g(\$)] \succ X \succ g(\$).$$

(3) *Underpricing of $g(P)$:* If $g(P) \succ X$ and $g(\$) \succ X$, then

$$g(P) \succ X \succ JCE[g(P)].$$

---

[3]   I have changed their notation to mine.

(4) *Both over- and underpricing:* If $g(P) \succ X$ and $X \succ g(\$)$, then

$$JCE[g(\$)] \succ X \succ g(\$) \text{ and } g(P) \succ X \succ JCE[g(P)].$$

Using monetary lotteries, 198 university students exhibited preference reversals on 45% of the opportunities to do so. For the values of X used there were a total of 620 cases that also met the condition that the selected X lay between the two judged CEs. Of these cases, according to the above classification 10% exhibited intransitivity, 65.5% overpricing of $g(\$)$, 6.1% under-pricing of $g(P)$, and 18.4% both overpricing and underpricing. Thus, in total, there was overpricing of $g(\$)$ 83.9% of the time.

Their conclusion was that they had little evidence against transitivity and considerable evidence that the money gambles are overpriced.

2.2.5.3   The Bostic, Herrnstein, and Luce (1990) study: This study was also based on the idea that there might be a substantial difference between judged and choice CEs. The authors opted to follow what amounted to a psychophysical procedure of having respondents make choices between various money amounts and each gamble for which a CE was needed. As noted in Section 1.2.2, this tends to be very expensive in observations. To try to reduce this cost—both in boredom for the respondents and in time and money for the experimenters— they adapted from psychophysics a sequential up-down procedure known as PEST (Parameter Estimation using Sequential Testing) to determine the 50% point on the psychometric function of the probability of choosing the money rather than the gamble as a function of money. The basic idea of PEST is that when the money is chosen, then on the next presentation of that particular gamble, the money amount is reduced; and when the gamble is chosen, the money amount is increased. The size of the decrement or increment is diminished each time a reversal occurs. The process is terminated when that size of the change is smaller than some preset criterion. The average of the last two values of money is taken as an estimate of CE, called the choice CE, or CCE. (The full details are outlined in Appendix C.)

I report their Experiment II, which improved on the PEST procedure used in Experiment I. Using the 6 stimuli of Lichtenstein and Slovic's (1971) Experiment 3, plus 2 more like them, they elicited from 21 students choices between the gamble pairs and $JCEs$ and $CCEs$ for individual gambles. As in other studies, they found preference reversals using $JCEs$: 81% when $g(P) \succ' g(\$)$ and 3% when $g(\$) \succ g(P)$ for an overall rate of 46%, which is very close to what Tversky et al. (1990) found. With $CCEs$ the corresponding percentages change to 51%, 22%, and 39%. More striking, a chi-square analysis shows a significant preference reversal for 7 of 8 cases using JCE and only 1 of 8 using CCE. The fact that the change in percentage is small but the number of significant violations drops from 7 to 1 reflects the relatively high noise levels of such estimates.

Figure 2.2 compares the average values of the $JCEs$ and the $CCEs$ for the two kinds of gamble pairs. We see that they are virtually the same for $g(P)$ but the former exceeds the latter by from \$1-\$2 for $g(\$)$. This is in agreement with the conclusion of Tversky et al. (1990) that the $g(\$)$ are overvalued in judgments as compared with choices. This conclusion is a special case of the general point made by Tversky, Sattath, and Slovic (1988) that matching and choice are very different phenomena, with the latter tending to focus more attention on the most conspicuous component of the stimuli.

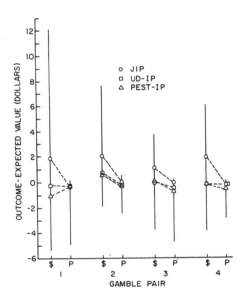

Figure 2.2. Judged and choice (PEST and UP-DOWN) monetary certainty equivalents (called "indifference points" in the figure) of the dollar and probability gambles of the standard preference reversal experiment. Note the differences for the money gambles and not for the probability ones. This is Fig. 1 of Bostic, Herrnstein, and Luce (1990), copyright 1990, which is reprinted by permission from Elsevier Science.

For a rather different interpretation see Hsee, Loewenstein, Blount, and Bazerman (1999).

2.2.6   Conclusions about transitivity, choices, and certainty equivalents

Transitivity, which was initially seriously questioned, seems reasonably secure, but the assumption that judged CEs are a fast way to estimate choice CEs, i.e., true choice indifference values, is very dubious. This conclusion, if accepted, has a major consequence which seems not yet to have had much impact on theorists: We need to develop distinct theories for choice and for judged values and to work out how they are related. This is of some social importance because, for example, store owners in developed countries set individual prices and customers typically make choices among priced items. The prices reflect, in part, a judgment on the part of the owner. It is entirely possible that both choices and judgments are basic, primitive human abilities, but it is also possible that the one somehow derives from the other. We simply do not know, and we do not have at this time as well worked out axiomatic theories of judgment as we do of choices. For the most part the monograph focuses on choice; however, one possible treatment of judged buying and selling prices in terms of choices is given later in Sections 6.4 and 7.4.

2.3   Monotonicity of Consequences

The following property is almost as fundamental as transitivity for theories of utility.

Definition 2.3.1.   A preference structure of gambles $\langle \mathcal{C}, \mathcal{E}, \mathcal{G}_2, \succsim \rangle$ exhibits *consequence monotonicity* if and only if for all $\mathbf{E} \in \mathcal{E}$, $i \in \{1, 2, ..., n\}$, $g_i, g_i' \in \mathcal{G}_1$, and nontrivial n-fold partitions $\{E_1, ..., E_i; ..., E_n\}$ of E, where $E_i \in \mathcal{E}_\mathbf{E}$,

$g_i' \succsim g_i$ if and only if

$$(g_1, E_1; ....; g_i', E_i; ...; g_n, E_n) \succsim (g_1, E_1; ....; g_i, E_i; ...; g_n, E_n). \tag{2.9}$$

In the binary case this becomes

$$g' \succsim g \Longleftrightarrow (g', C; h) \succsim (g, C; h).$$

Of course, using complementarity, Eq. (2.3), means it is unnecessary to state explicitly the monotonicity of the second consequence.

We see that, like transitivity, consequence monotonicity is the following special case of the second principle (stated for the binary case) in which $S = \{f\}$, where $f = (g, C; h)$, and $f' = (g', C; h)$ where $g' \succsim g$. The conclusion is that not$(f \succ f')$, i.e., $f' \succsim f$. The converse is trivial.

There is general agreement that consequence monotonicity is a major canon of rational behavior for first-order gambles, where all of the consequences are from $\mathcal{C}$ rather than gambles in $\mathcal{G}_1$. Nonetheless, one should not minimize how strong a condition it is. It is a form of "separability" in which the comparison between x_j' and x_j is unaffected by the rest of the gamble structure.

Concerns arise when one generalizes it to second- and higher-order gambles. And there it has been questioned empirically, as we shall see.

Before that, I note that if consequence monotonicity holds, then a violation of transitivity leads to a contradiction of sorts. Suppose we can find an intransitive triple of consequences (or gambles) $x \succ y$, $y \succ z$, $z \succ x$. Consider the following pair of risky alternatives:

	$\frac{1}{3}$	$\frac{1}{3}$	$\frac{1}{3}$
$f:$	x	y	z
$g:$	y	z	x

Observe, first, that f and g are exactly the same gamble: In each case, one receives each of the three consequences with probability $\frac{1}{3}$. This situation is sufficiently transparent that a person should be indifferent between them. But by consequence monotonicity and the assumed preference order, we see that f strictly dominates g in the sense that for each possible outcome of the experiment the person prefers what arises in the f gamble to what arises in the g gamble. So $f \succ g$, which is inconsistent with the fact that, ignoring the order in which the consequences are written, $f = g$ and so $f \sim g$.

2.3.1   Independence and the Allais paradox

Consider a family of lotteries and let them be treated as random variables. If f, g are two lotteries and p is a probability, the compound lottery $(f, p; g, 1 - p)$ is automatically reduced to the first-order lottery that arises from working out the probability distribution over consequences (§ 1.1.6.4). Thus, if in lottery f the consequence f_i arises with probability r_i then in the reduced gamble it arises with probability $r_i p$. Typically, the equivalent first-order gamble is written $fp + g(1 - p)$ to suggest the above calculation of probabilities. With that notation, then consequence monotonicity is written: for all $f, f', g \in \mathcal{G}$ and $p \in]0, 1[$,[4]

$$f' \succsim f \iff f'p + g(1 - p) \succsim fp + g(1 - p). \tag{2.10}$$

This property is commonly called *independence* in the economics literature. "Independence" is a word having multiple meanings in the mathematical sciences (e.g., Fishburn & Keeney, 1974) and care must be taken to ascertain the exact meaning intended in each usage. Usually the context is sufficient to tell.

   M. Allais (1953), a French Nobel Laureate in economics, early on posed the following choice situation as a challenge to the expected utility theories that had stemmed from von Neumann and Morgenstern's original theory (1947), all of which satisfied independence. It goes as follows.[5] In the first choice situation one selects between:

$$g_1 = \$1M \quad \text{and} \quad g_2 = (\$5M, 0.10; \$1M; 0.89; \$0, 0.01),$$

and many people say they prefer g_1 because, despite the attractiveness of a 10% chance at $\$5M$, that 1% chance of receiving nothing in g_2 makes many of us risk-averse types uneasy. In the second choice situation one selects between:

$$g_3 = (\$1M, 0.11; \$0, 0.89) \quad \text{and} \quad g_4 = (\$5M, 0.10; \$0, 0.90),$$

and here most of us select g_4 as being the better choice.

   This pattern of choice in fact violates independence. We may see this as follows: Define

$$f_1 = (\$1M, 1; \$0, 0) \quad \text{and} \quad f_2 = (\$5M, \frac{10}{11}; \$0, \frac{1}{11}).$$

Now observe that in random variable notation and carrying out the requisite probability cal-

---

[4]   I use the increasingly common notation $]a, b[$ for the open interval with end points $a < b$ rather than the earlier, widely used (a, b), saving the latter notation for an ordered pair. As always, the closed interval is $[a, b]$, and the two half-open ones are $]a, b]$ and $[a, b[$.
[5]   I have changed from francs to dollars, which makes no difference in the argument.

culations involved in the reduction of compound gambles to first-order ones,

$$g_1 \sim \$1M(0.89) + f_1(1 - 0.89) \quad \text{and} \quad g_2 \sim \$1M(0.89) + f_2(1 - 0.89)$$

and

$$g_3 \sim \$0(0.89) + f_1(1 - 0.89) \quad \text{and} \quad g_4 \sim \$0(0.89) + f_2(1 - 0.89).$$

So, if independence were satisfied, we should observe:

$$g_1 \succsim g_2 \iff f_1 \succsim f_2 \iff g_3 \succsim g_4,$$

which is contrary to the choices of a substantial proportion of people.

Such violations of independence have been verified empirically (for a summary see Keller, 1992; also see Allais & Hagen, 1979; Carlin, 1990; Conlisk, 1989; MacCrimmon & Larsson, 1979; Machina, 1987a,b; Starmer & Sugden, 1989), and one can readily illustrate the phenomenon in any class on decision making with sufficiently many students—I have found that with at least 15 the phenomenon is clear.

So, what is wrong? Some theorists (e.g., Chew, 1983; Chew, Epstein, & Segal, 1991; Machina, 1987a,b; Quiggin, 1982; Rubinstein, 1988; Weber & Camerer, 1987) have to a degree abandoned independence, but have continued to devise theories on the assumption that the lotteries are well modeled as random variables, and so they accept the (automatic) reduction of compound gambles. Others of us have interpreted the body of evidence as favoring consequence monotonicity and as making very dubious at a descriptive level the probability reduction principle built into the random variable notation (Kahneman & Tversky, 1979; Luce, 1990; Segal, 1988, 1990, 1992; Starmer & Sugden, 1991).

At least one author, Carlin (1990), provides evidence that the format of presenting probabilities may be at issue. His study involved 65 undergraduate students with the usual numerical display of probabilities, and he found that 42% exhibited the Allais violation and 3% exhibited the other inconsistency. When the problem was presented to another group of 142 students in terms of a roulette-like wheel with 100 slots, the two kinds of violations were 14% and 11%, respectively. Thus, with the wheel display, there is little evidence of a problem aside from a certain level of inconsistency. I do not understand the difference.

2.3.2   The sure-thing principle and the Allais paradox

There is an alternative way to think about the Allais paradox that does not entail compound gambles, but does involve another property that has been called various things: "combining" by Kahneman and Tversky (1979), "event splitting" by Starmer and Sugden (1993), and "coalescing" by Birnbaum (1997) and Luce (1998). This concept, which is explored more thoroughly in Section 5.3.2, is very transparent in the case of lotteries. Specifically, the probability assigned to a single consequence can be partitioned in convenient ways without affecting preferences. In particular, we may reformulate the four lotteries in question as

	0.10	0.01	0.89
g_1 :	\$1M	\$1M	\$1M
g_2 :	\$5M	\$0	\$1M
g_3 :	\$1M	\$1M	\$0
g_4 :	\$5M	\$0	\$0

One can readily see that by combining the probabilities that lead to the same consequence (or coalescing their underlying events) gives back the original gambles.

The *sure-thing principle* simply asserts that in making a choice one can ignore those parts of the gambles that give rise to exactly the same consequence. Thus, when comparing g_1 and g_2, the 0.89 chance of getting \$1M simply should not matter. Similarly, in g_3 and g_4 the 0.89 chance of getting \$0 also should not matter. In such a case, the decisions are identical. Savage's (1954) axiomatization stated what has come to be known as the sure-thing principle, his axiom P2, and consequence monotonicity, his axiom P3, and his Theorem 3 established that in the presence of transitivity and monotonicity, these assumptions yield the general cancellation of common terms. MacCrimmon (1968) called this general version the "irrelevance of identical outcomes," which is quite descriptive. This cancellation principle also follows from monotonicity and reduction of compound gambles, but it also seems totally plausible when stated purely for first-order gambles.

In three examples of choices presented in the Allais format, MacCrimmon (1968) found that about 40% of his business executives exhibited Allais' violation. During the second session arguments were presented pro and con, followed by the interview session. MacCrimmon reports (p. 10) that 75% accepted the sure-thing principle unconditionally, 11% did except when one alternative was a sure amount of money, and 14% remained in disagreement with the principle. "The reason most often given by these [respondents] was that the problem could not be decomposed as the postulate-based reason implied" (p. 11). As we will see in Section 5.3.2.2, this line of argument is not inconsistent with some evidence that coalescing may not be descriptive, no matter how reasonable it may seem.

2.3.3   Betweenness

The following property, which derives from several assumptions we are making, has received some attention on its own.

Proposition 2.3.1.   *Suppose that the binary substructure from $\langle \mathcal{C}, \mathcal{E}, \mathcal{G}_2, \succsim \rangle$ satisfies idempotence, Eq. (2.1), transitivity, Eq. (2.4), and consequence monotonicity, Eq. (2.9). Then it also satisfies the following* betweenness *property: For $\mathbf{E} \in \mathcal{E}, C \in \mathcal{E}_{\mathbf{E}}, g, h \in \mathcal{G}_1$ with $g \succsim h$,*

$$g \succsim (g, C; h) \succsim h. \tag{2.11}$$

Proof. Using the suppositions freely,

$$g \sim (g, C; g) \succsim (g, C; h) \succsim (h, C; h) \sim h. \quad \blacksquare$$

Although betweenness is implied by consequence monotonicity, under the conditions of the proposition the converse does not follow. For example, suppose the following indifferences and preferences hold plus all that follow using transitivity:

$$f \sim (f, C; f) \succ (g, C; g) \sim g \succ (g, C; h) \succ (f, C; h) \succ (h, C; h) \sim h.$$

We see that betweenness is met and consequence monotonicity is not because $f \succ g$ but $(g, C; h) \succ (f, C; h)$.

As with consequence monotonicity, for risky gambles and lotteries there is the reduced form of betweenness:

$$g \succ h \text{ implies } g \succsim pg + (1 - p)h \succsim h.$$

Clearly, this is a standard concept of "convexity," and that word might have been used rather than "betweenness." Probably because convexity was already widely used in connection with the shape of utility functions, a different term was chosen by utility theorists. In the measurement literature, the word "intern" has been used.

Camerer and Ho (1994, p. 176) summarized the findings of nine experimental papers that conducted tests of reduced betweenness. It was uniformly rejected in rather systematic ways. They then go to their own empirical study of both betweenness and independence in both reduced and compound forms. One of the triples they used was

$$
\begin{aligned}
g &= (\$20,000, 0.33; \$0), \\
h &= (\$30,000, 0.17; \$0) \\
\left(g, \frac{16}{17}; h\right) &= ((\$20,000, 0.33; \$0), \frac{16}{17}; (\$30,000, 0.17; \$0)) \\
\frac{16}{17}g + \frac{1}{17}h &= (\$30,000, 0.01; \$20,000, 0.31; \$0, 0.66)
\end{aligned}
$$

Their results are very clear. In reduced form, both betweenness and independence are clearly wrong. In compound form, neither is rejected. Thus, this extensive set of results is consistent with the hypotheses that consequence monotonicity is correct whereas the invoked reduction of compound gambles is not. "Both results add to indirect evidence that the reduction assumption is a surprisingly poor descriptive axiom" (p. 168)

2.3.4   Direct choices and consequence monotonicity

The few studies that tested monotonicity by presenting directly structured versions of the Allais paradox to respondents have found it sustained so long as the structure of the situation is completely transparent. Examples of this are Birnbaum and Sutton (1992, p. 207), Cho and Fisher (1999), Conlisk (1989), Diederich and Busemeyer (1999), and Kahneman and Tversky (1979). As an example of the finding, Conlisk presented the standard Allais situation to one group of 236 students and the compound gamble version of it to another set of 212 students. The pattern of violations found was:

	g_1, g_4	g_2, g_3
Standard Allais:	44%	7%
Compound version:	11%	17%

Conlisk provides two other variants that also show far fewer violations of the Allais type.

MacCrimmon (1968) studied monotonicity in its most transparent form, namely, *dominance*, which he called "admissibility." This is the case where each of the consequences of one alternative is preferred or indifferent to the corresponding one of the other, and at least one is strictly preferred. Of 37 respondents who completed this part of the study, 12 had at least one violation of dominance and 5 had two or more. In the interview session all violators admitted error, and changed their choices. So, once again, it is a principle that is imperfectly descriptive, but appears to be compelling normatively.

The most recent study of consequence monotonicity is Diederich and Busemeyer (1999). Their consequences were joint receipts[6] $x \oplus y$, where x was a sum of money (in DM) and y was a duration in seconds of a burst of 67 dB noise. The respondents received both. Clearly more money is preferred to less, and less duration is preferred to more. One example of their stimuli was condition 1:

	$p = \frac{1}{2}$	$1 - p = \frac{1}{2}$
A :	$0.10 \oplus 1$	$-0.05 \oplus 10$
B :	$-0.10 \oplus 15$	$0.05 \oplus 15$
C :	$0.05 \oplus 15$	$-0.10 \oplus 15$

By the assumed monotonicity of joint receipt,

$$0.10 \oplus 1 \;\succ\; 0.05 \oplus 15$$
$$-0.05 \oplus 10 \;\succ\; -0.10 \oplus 15,$$

so if the monotonicity of gambles holds, $A \succ C$. Moreover, if complementarity holds, then $B \sim C$.

The data were repeated observations on two respondents, analyzed individually, and single observations from each of 17 respondents, analyzed as a group. For this condition and two others similar to it, they found that, with almost no exceptions, A was chosen when the choice was between A and C. However, B was often chosen when the choice was between A and B. The conclusion seems to be that these respondents found it easy to see dominance when the stimuli were presented in a consistent (the authors called it correlated) fashion and not in

---

6   For a full discussion of this concept, see Chapters 4, 6, and 7.

cases (called negatively correlated) when a complementarity transformation was required in order to make the dominance transparent.

Conditions 4 and 5 were of the form

	p	$1-p$
A :	$0.10 \oplus 1$	$-0.05 \oplus 10$
B :	$-0.05 \oplus 15$	$0.10 \oplus 5$
C :	$0.10 \oplus 5$	$-0.05 \oplus 15$

with $p = 0.6$ and 0.7. Again, the dominance of A over C is obvious, and the respondents chose accordingly. That between A and B becomes transparent only by making both a complementarity transformation and a splitting of the probabilities as:

	$1-p$	$2p-1$	$1-p$
A :	$0.10 \oplus 1$	$0.10 \oplus 1$	$-0.05 \oplus 10$
B :	$0.10 \oplus 5$	$-0.05 \oplus 15$	$-0.05 \oplus 15$

Dominance clearly holds because $0.10 \oplus 1 \succ -0.05 \oplus 15$. Again, a substantial fraction of the choices showed that respondents failed to carry out these transformations. Later in Sections 5.3.2 and 5.4.2 we will see similar evidence suggesting that respondents do not usually arrive at dominance arguments of this sort.

2.3.5   Indirect choices via certainty equivalents

Despite the evidence sustaining monotonicity when it is tested without involving other assumptions, there are several studies that have been interpreted as challenging the empirical validity of consequence monotonicity itself. In several papers M. Birnbaum and colleagues (Birnbaum, 1992; Birnbaum, Coffey, Mellers, & Weiss, 1992; Birnbaum & Sutton, 1992; Mellers, Weiss, & Birnbaum, 1992) have argued that the property of consequence monotonicity can be systematically violated using certainty equivalents of one sort or another. Birnbaum (1997) provided a detailed general survey of his findings.

The type of lotteries evaluated (sometimes embedded among many other lotteries depending upon what else is involved in the study) are of the form $g_0(p) = (\$x, p; 0, 1 - p)$ and $g_y(p) = (\$x, p; \$y, 1 - p)$ where $\$x$ is much larger than $\$y > 0$. The typical finding is that $JCEs$[7] in both cases increase nearly linearly with p, starting at $y = JCE[g_y(0)] > JCE[g_0(0)] = 0$, respectively, and maintaining that inequality, as one would expect by con-

---

[7] Birnbaum (1992) actually provided his respondents with a list of money amounts from which they selected the one for which they were indifferent to a gamble. Tversky and Kahneman (1992) used a similar procedure. This strikes me—and Birnbaum (personal communication, December 15, 1998)—as closer to a judgment procedure than a choice one. Moreover, the behavior exhibited is like that from judged ones and different from PEST-determined choice ones.

sequence monotonicity, for increasing values of p except that somewhere in the neighborhood of 0.85 or 0.90 the inequality reverses. Put another way, the slope of the g_0 line exceeds that of g_y. An example of one of many similar plots is shown in Fig. 2.3, in which the judgment was according to selling price defined as the price "just preferred" to the gamble.

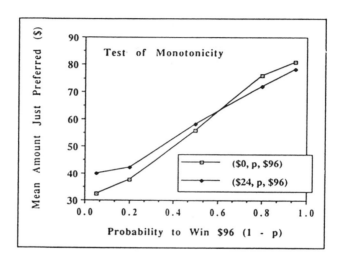

Figure 2.3. Typical judged certainty equivalent data showing violations of consequence monotonicity. This is Fig. 1 of Birnbaum (1992). Copyright © 1992 by Blackwell Publishers. Reprinted by permission.

I do not believe that there can be much, if any, doubt that consequence monotonicity is violated when using judged CEs, whether they are characterized as selling prices, buying prices, or some more neutral assessment. However, given what was seen with preference reversals and given that respondents do not appear to violate consequence monotonicity when direct choices are offered, one suspects that we are seeing once again a major difference between judgments and choices. To test that, von Winterfeldt, Chung, Luce, and Cho (1997) ran substantially the same experiment using both JCEs and CCEs. Their findings in the judged cases were essentially those of Birnbaum and his colleagues. For choices, there was far less evidence of violations of consequence monotonicity and what there was seemed attributable to the, unfortunately substantial, variability in the CCE estimates. Figure 2.4 shows both the JCE and PEST determined CCE data for a "real-life" scenario concerning lotteries involving student fees where the hypothetical amounts of money were substantial. Again the judged data exhibit a small reversal, but the choice data do not.

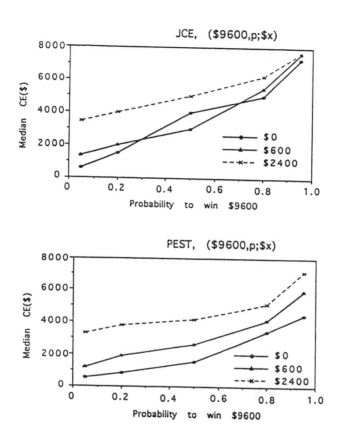

Figure 2.4. A comparison of judged and choice (PEST) determined certainty equivalents for stimuli similar to those of Birnbaum, but increased by a factor of 100 to makes sense of a real-life scenario. Adapted with permission from Fig. 6 of von Winterfeldt, Chung, Luce, and Cho (1997). Copyright © 1997 by the American Psychological Association.

2.3.6   Conclusions about monotonicity and independence

First, there seems little doubt that consequence monotonicity is sustained when people face it in a choice format that makes clear the dominance structure of the situation. They seem to view dominance as clearly dictating choice.

Second, consequence monotonicity is sometimes violated when judged CEs are used, but apparently not with choice ones.

Third, violations of consequence monotonicity and of reduced betweenness that rest also on one or another accounting indifferences (e.g., independence and the Allais paradox, complementarity, and probability splitting) suggest that these properties become seriously degraded. In particular, this happens when gambles are transformed as if they are random variables. Various authors (Camerer & Ho, 1994; Luce, 1990; Segal, 1990, 1992) have for this reason also cautioned against modeling lotteries as random variables.

Of course, as we shall see, the models of utility are built up of groups of assumptions such as consequence monotonicity and the elementary accounting indifferences, and some of these data cast doubt upon the descriptive accuracy of such models. Of course, that does not affect their normative status.

2.4   Monotonicity of Events

When we focus on events, there are two quite distinct forms of monotonicity to be considered. One of these looks at the kind of monotonicity that arises when one has a binary operation, in this case the partial operation of the union of disjoint events (§ 2.4.1). It is analogous to the numerical monotonicity of addition, which asserts that $\alpha \geq \beta$ if and only if $\alpha + \gamma \geq \beta + \gamma$. The other one is more directly analogous to consequence monotonicity (§ 2.4.5). Because we do not have an a priori ordering of events, stating the latter form of monotonicity is somewhat more subtle and requires the use of the concept of status quo. So we do the easier one first.

2.4.1   Event monotonicity

Definition 2.4.1.   A substructure of binary gambles from $\langle \mathcal{C}, \mathcal{E}, \mathcal{G}_2, \succsim \rangle$ exhibits *event monotonicity* if and only if for all $\mathbf{E} \in \mathcal{E}$, $A, B, C \in \mathcal{E}_{\mathbf{E}}$ with $A \cap C = B \cap C = \emptyset$, and $g, h \in \mathcal{G}_1$, with $g \succ h$,

$$(g, A; h) \succsim (g, B; h) \quad \text{iff} \quad (g, A \cup C; h) \succsim (g, B \cup C; h). \tag{2.12}$$

de Finetti (1931) first formulated this condition (called, in translation, "additivity in qualitative probability") as a central feature of his qualitative probability theory. See Fine (1973) and Fishburn (1986).

This condition is easily generalized to gambles of any order where the disjoint event C is adjoined to the event which gives rise to the most preferred consequence and is removed from the one giving rise to the least preferred one. Since I do not use this general property, I do not state it formally.

The rationality lying behind event monotonicity is clear; it is the third principle stated at the onset of the chapter. The decision maker prefers the gamble that makes g more likely to be the consequence than h. Therefore, from $(g, A; h) \succsim (g, B; h)$ one infers that the decision maker sees A as at least as likely as B to occur. But if that is true, then augmenting both by disjoint C should maintain that likelihood order and so $(g, A \cup C; h) \succsim (g, B \cup C; h)$ should occur. The converse argument involves removing a common amount.

Once again, it must be acknowledged that this is a mathematically strong condition and, as we shall see in the following subsection, it seems to be empirically wrong.

2.4.2 The Ellsberg paradox

Although this line of rational argument seems fairly compelling in the abstract, it loses its force in some concrete situations. Ellsberg (1961) suggested a decision situation in which many people violate event monotonicity. Suppose an opaque urn has 90 red, blue, and yellow balls that have been thoroughly mixed. There are 30 red ones, but the exact number of blue and the exact number of yellow ones is not known except that together they total 60. Although the partition of the 60 is unknown to the respondent, it is a fixed one that does not vary from one choice situation to the next. Let R, B, Y denote the events of a red, blue, or yellow ball, respectively, arising in a blind draw from the urn. Thus, $\Pr(R) = \frac{1}{3}$ and $\Pr(B) + \Pr(Y) = \Pr(B \cup Y) = \frac{2}{3}$, but the values of $\Pr(B)$ and $\Pr(Y)$ can be anything between 0 and $\frac{2}{3}$ so long as they sum to $\frac{2}{3}$. Consider first the choice

$$g_1 = \begin{pmatrix} R & B & Y \\ \$100 & \$0 & \$0 \end{pmatrix} \quad \text{and} \quad g_2 = \begin{pmatrix} R & B & Y \\ \$0 & \$100 & \$0 \end{pmatrix}.$$

A substantial majority of people choose g_1 over g_2. One line of argument for making this choice is that the former gives a firm $\frac{1}{3}$ chance of getting $\$100$, whereas the decision maker has no idea how likely the $\$100$ is in the latter—the proportion of blue balls might be very small.

Now, cover that choice situation over and consider

$$g_3 = \begin{pmatrix} R & B & Y \\ \$100 & \$0 & \$100 \end{pmatrix} \quad \text{and} \quad g_4 = \begin{pmatrix} R & B & Y \\ \$0 & \$100 & \$100 \end{pmatrix}.$$

A substantial fraction of people choose g_4 over g_3. Following the line of argument above, g_4 insures a $\frac{2}{3}$ chance of receiving $\$100$, whereas in g_3 one can only be certain of a $\frac{1}{3}$ chance of $\$100$ and the chance of a yellow ball being drawn may be very small. Of course, not both $\Pr(B)$ and $\Pr(Y)$ can be very small, but in each choice it seems conservative to assume that the relevant probability might be.

This behavior has been sustained empirically. For example, Slovic and Tversky (1974) ran 29 college students and found 19 exhibited the violation. Then they provided the argument for event monotonicity being rational to 49 respondents, and on testing them in an Ellsberg situation found that 38 exhibited the violation. MacCrimmon and Larsson (1979) varied the probability partition and found that changing it greatly above or below $\frac{1}{3}$ reduced the number of people exhibiting the paradox. Also, they found their respondents were, on average, more prone to the Ellsberg paradox than to the Allais one. For a comprehensive review of studies concerning ambiguity, of which the Ellsberg paradox is one type, see Camerer and Weber (1992, especially Table 3, p. 334).

Choosing g_1 over g_2 and g_4 over g_3 violates event monotonicity because these pairs of gambles can be rewritten[8]

$$g_1 \sim (\$100, R; \$0, B \cup Y) \succ g_2 \sim (\$100, B; \$0, R \cup Y)$$
$$g_3 \sim (\$100, R \cup Y; \$0, B) \prec g_4 \sim (\$100, B \cup Y; \$0, R).$$

Another way to look at the rational argument is to observe that in each pair of gambles the consequence assigned to Y is the same for both choices,

	$\Pr(R) = \frac{1}{3}$	$\Pr(B)$	$\Pr(Y)$
$g_1:$	\$100	\$0	\$0
$g_2:$	\$0	\$100	\$0
$g_3:$	\$100	\$0	\$100
$g_4:$	\$0	\$100	\$100

so by the sure-thing principle one should attend only to the assignments to R and B. And when one does that, one sees that the situations are identical.

The general conclusion of the field is that, unlike the other properties examined to this point, event monotonicity really is behaviorally false. Moreover, unlike violations of transitivity and consequence monotonicity, which most people view as errors, violations of event monotonicity are not so viewed. People defend their choices often using a worst-case scenario of the type mentioned above.

In effect, this conclusion rules out as descriptive theories, such as Savage's subjective expected utility, that represent the impact of uncertain events as subjective probabilities for which finite additivity holds.

2.4.3   First-order stochastic dominance

Within the framework of lotteries treated as random variables, a frequent assumption is that $g \succsim h$ should hold whenever the (cumulative) distribution describing g nowhere exceeds that describing h. This is called *first-order stochastic dominance*. A simple example illustrates the meaning. Suppose $g = (\$100, 0.4; \$75, 0.5; \$0, 0.1)$ and $h = (\$100, 0.3; \$50, 0.6; \$0, 0.1)$. Figure 2.5 shows the cumulative distributions, and we see that g does indeed stochastically dominate h, and so it should be preferred. Note, however, that formulating the concept in this way fails to distinguish between event and consequence monotonicity, which seem to be descriptively very different.

First-order stochastic dominance is irrelevant to the Ellsberg paradox because all the probabilities must be known for it to apply, which serves as another strike against modeling decision making in terms of random variables.

---

8   Here I am using a coalescing property of combining events with a common consequence. This is a stronger assumption than it might seem and is itself controversial. I return to it in Section 5.3.2.

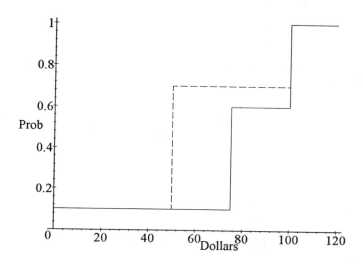

Figure 2.5. An example of cumulative distributions exhibiting first-order stochastic dominance. The solid distribution, corresponding to gamble g, dominates the dashed one, corresponding to gamble h.

2.4.4   Monotonicity of event inclusion

The following special case of event monotonicity will play a role later.

Definition 2.4.2.   The substructure of binary gambles from $\langle C, \mathcal{E}, \mathcal{G}_2, \succsim \rangle$ exhibits *monotonicity of event inclusion* if and only if for all $\mathbf{E} \in \mathcal{E}$, $C, D \in \mathcal{E}_\mathbf{E}$, and $g, h \in \mathcal{G}_1$,

$$g \succ h \text{ and } C \supset D \text{ imply } (g, C; h) \succ (g, D; h). \tag{2.13}$$

Proposition 2.4.1.   *Suppose idempotence, Eq. (2.1), certainty, Eq. (2.2), consequence monotonicity, Eq. (2.9), and transitivity, Eq. (2.4), hold in $\langle C, \mathcal{E}, \mathcal{G}_2, \succsim \rangle$. Then event monotonicity, Eq. (2.12), implies monotonicity of event inclusion, Eq. (2.13).*

Proof. Suppose $C \supset D$ and $g \succ h$ Thus, $A = C \backslash D$ is nonempty and invoking the suppositions freely,

$$(g, \emptyset; h) \sim (h; E; g) \sim h \sim (h, A; h) \prec (g, A; g).$$

57

So, adjoining D to both sides, by event monotonicity

$$(g, D; h) \prec (g; A \cup D; h) \sim (g, C; h),$$

which by transitivity implies monotonicity of event inclusion.   ∎

Note that if monotonicity of event inclusion were strengthened to an "if and only if" condition, then it would imply event monotonicity. But there is no reason to conclude from $(g, C; h) \succ (g, D; h)$ that $C \supset D$; indeed, any events such that neither $C \supset D$ nor $C \subset D$ will do because $\succsim$ is connected.

To the best of my knowledge, there are no empirical studies focused on monotonicity of event inclusion. It is, however, a feature of most theories of utility, and I shall assume it to be correct.

2.4.5   Order-independence of events

The last form of monotonicity involving events is the following:

Definition 2.4.3   The substructure of binary gambles from $\langle C, \mathcal{E}, \mathcal{G}_2, \succsim, e \rangle$, where e is the status quo, exhibits *order-independence of events* if and only if for all $E \in \mathcal{E}$, $C, D \in \mathcal{E}_\mathbf{E}$, $g, h \in \mathcal{G}_1$ with $g, h \succ e$

$$(g, C; e) \succsim (g, D; e) \iff (h, C; e) \succsim (h, D; e). \tag{2.14}$$

One could strengthen this condition to an arbitrary consequence z in place of e, but we do not need that.

Note that Eq. (2.14) allows one to define an induced order over events. The first-order version of this condition is Savage's (1954) axiom P4, which some call "independence of beliefs from tastes." In that language, consequence monotonicity becomes "independence of tastes from beliefs."

Order-independence of events for first-order gambles is certainly a locally rational and plausible property for the following reason. Because g is perceived as a gain, the first inequality makes sense only if C is judged to be more likely to occur than D, in which case since h is also a gain the second equality should hold. It is, of course, more problematic in the second-order version than in the first-order one. To the best of my knowledge, order-independence of events has not been subjected to experimental check.

2.5   Elementary Rational Structure

Because most of the following work invokes the same elementary assumptions, it is useful to pull them together in a formal, named definition:

Definition 2.5.1.   A structure of binary gambles $\langle \mathcal{B}_2, \succsim \rangle$ is said to be *elementary rational* if and only if it satisfies the following conditions: $\succsim$ is a weak order (transitive and connected), idempotence, certainty, complementarity, consequence monotonicity, monotonicity of event inclusion, and order-independence of events.

2.6   Decomposition into Gains and Losses Subgambles

As was emphasized in Section 1.1, the concepts of a status quo, gains, and losses play a substantial role in this monograph. Denote a general finite second-order gamble by

$$g = (g_1, E_1; g_2, E_2; ...; g_n, E_n), \quad E_i \cap E_j = \emptyset, i \neq j, \quad \bigcup_{i=1}^{n} E_i = E,$$

where the indices are chosen so that the consequences are rank ordered by preference, i.e.,

$$g_1 \succsim g_2 \succsim \cdots \succsim g_k \succsim e \succ g_{k+1} \succsim \cdots \succsim g_n$$

Thus, the first k consequences are perceived as gains (including possibly the status quo e) and those from $k + 1$ to n are perceived as losses, except of course for the limiting cases of all gains or all losses.

The hypothesis that we shall entertain is that people recast such a general gamble into a binary one composed of two subgambles. One subgamble consists of those events with consequences seen as gains or the status quo; the other consists only of events with consequences seen as losses. Formally, define

$$E(+) = \bigcup_{i=1}^{k} E_i, \quad \text{and} \quad E(-) = \bigcup_{i=k+1}^{n} E_i \quad (2.15)$$

and

$$g_+ = (g_1, E_1; ...; g_k, E_k), \quad g_- = (g_{k+1}, E_{k+1}; ...; g_n, E_n). \quad (2.16)$$

Observe that the subgamble g^+ is conditioned on the subevent $E(+)$ of E and g^- is conditional on $E(-)$.

Definition 2.6.1.   Suppose $\langle \mathcal{C}, \mathcal{E}, \mathcal{G}_2, \succsim, e \rangle$ is a second-order gambling structure with status quo. Then *gain-loss decomposition* is said to hold if for every $\mathbf{E} \in \mathcal{E}$ and $g \in \mathcal{G}_1$ with at least one gain and at least one loss consequence

$$g \sim (g_+, E(+); g_-, E(-)). \quad (2.17)$$

Note that $g \in \mathcal{G}_1$ whereas $(g_+, E(+); g_-, E(-)) \in \mathcal{G}_2$.

The prima facie reasonableness of assuming gambles are gain-loss decomposable lies in the fact that many people, including sophisticated decision makers, seem to think in terms of such a decomposition. For example, most of us deal with potential losses, such as fires and accidents, as very distinct from the gains associated with a house, possessions, and automobiles.

The mathematical power of assuming that gambles satisfy gain-loss decomposition is that it reduces a complex problem into three simpler ones, namely, the utility representations of binary mixed gambles and those for general gambles composed only of gains and those of only losses. The case for losses is formally the same as for gains and will in general not be written out separately. As it turns out, it is convenient to partition the gains case into the binary one, which is treated in the next chapter, and then the general one in Chapter 5. The reason for doing this is that three of the axiomatizations described in Chapters 5 are inductive, with the induction beginning with the binary case. The study of representations for mixed binary gambles is treated in two quite different ways in Chapters 6 and 7. The model examined in Chapter 7 is, on the one hand, very natural and reasonable and, on the other hand, surprising in that it leads to utility representations for gambles with both a gain and loss that cannot be expressed as a weighted linear expression in the utilities of the consequences.

Despite the importance of gain-loss decomposition, I know of no empirical study of it. This is a major empirical lacuna.

2.7   Summary

In the course of the chapter we have come up with nine properties—four pure indifferences and five "if...then" preference patterns—that will be assumed to hold throughout the rest of the monograph. I restate them here as a reminder (but for simplicity of statement I omit the universal quantifiers and the domains of the entities but assume $\mathbf{E} \in \mathcal{E}$, $C, D, E_i \in \mathcal{E}_{\mathbf{E}}$, and $f, g, h, g_i, g_i' \in \mathcal{G}_1$). They are also in Appendix B for easy reference.

Idempotence, Eq. (2.1):
$$(g, D; g) \sim g.$$

Certainty, Eq. (2.2):
$$(g, E; h) \sim g.$$

Complementarity, Eq. (2.3):
$$(g, D; h) \sim (g, \overline{D}; h).$$

Transitivity, Eq. (2.4):
$$\text{If } f \succsim g \text{ and } g \succsim h, \text{ then } f \succsim h.$$

Money Preference, Eq. (2.6): For $\alpha, \beta \in \mathbb{R} \cap C$,
$$\alpha \succsim \beta \Longleftrightarrow \alpha \geq \beta.$$

Consequence Monotonicity, Eq. (2.9): For $E_i \neq \emptyset$,
$$g_j' \succsim g_j \quad \text{if and only if}$$
$$(g_1, E_1; ....; g_j', E_j; ...; g_n, E_n) \succsim (g_1, E_1; ....; g_j, E_j; ...; g_n, E_n).$$

Monotonicity of Event Inclusion, Eq. (2.13):
$$\text{If } g \succ h \text{ and } C \supset D, \text{ then } (g, C; h) \succ (g, D; h).$$

Order-Independence of Events, Eq. (2.14) : If $g, h \succ e$, then

$$(g, C; e) \succsim (g, D; e) \iff (h, C; e) \succsim (h, D; e)$$

Gain-Loss Decomposition, Eq. (2.17): If $g \in \mathcal{G}_1$, then

$$g \sim (g_+, E(+); g_-, E(-)).$$

Note that although event monotonicity, Eq. (2.12), was discussed, it definitely is not assumed in the remainder of this monograph.

In addition to these nine assumptions, we reached two qualitative conclusions of some importance.

- Modeling lotteries as random variables is a bad idea—it simply presumes too much behavior that appears not to agree with observations.
- A theory of judged certainty equivalences is not automatically a special case of a choice theory because in general judged CEs are not the same as choice-based CEs. To mix choices and JCEs is a recipe for trouble.

Chapter 3
BINARY GAMBLES OF GAINS

This chapter begins to address questions involving properties of preferences over gambles that are more subtle than those embodied in the concept of an "elementary rational structure" (Def. 2.5.1). We will see how these additional properties can lead to a numerical representation, called utility, of preference. As was noted in the Introduction, the entire development is organized into five chapters beginning, here, with the binary case where both of the consequences are gains. The theory for binary gambles of just losses is formally identical provided one works with "dislike," i.e., the converse of the preference relation, as the ordering. The binary theory for gains is elaborated in Chapter 4 by adding the binary operation of joint receipt. This offers alternative ways of axiomatizing possible representations, and it provides considerably more detailed information about the mathematical form of the utility function. In Chapter 5 the binary theory of gains is extended to the nonbinary case, but data recently reported make clear that this generalization is descriptively unsatisfactory in crucial ways. Although there are various proposed representations that currently seem reasonably descriptive, the development of a descriptively acceptable axiomatic general theory remains open. The situation of binary mixed gains and losses, which is somewhat more complex than that of just binary gains (losses), is covered in Chapters 6 and 7.

As in all attempts to understand and measure attributes, we begin with a dependent variable —the to-be-measured attribute. This attribute defines an ordering $\succsim$. To get additional structure we explore trade-offs involving one or more independent variables that maintain invariance of the dependent variable.

In the case of binary gambles such as $(x, C; y, \overline{C})$, where $\overline{C} = E \backslash C$ and E is the universal set of the underlying experiment **E**. two trade-offs are the focus of attention. The first, which we take up in Section 3.1.3 and axiomatize in Section 3.5.2.3, is that between x and C for a fixed choice of **E** and y. For that purpose it is convenient to fix $y = e$, the status quo. This trade-off is called a *consequence-event trade-off.* The second, taken up in Sections 3.1.4 and axiomatized in Section 3.5.3, is the trade-off between x and y when the event pair (C, E) is held fixed, which is called a *consequence-consequence trade-off.*

As we shall see in Section 3.5, each trade-off when coupled with other somewhat plausible assumptions gives rise to a form of numerical measurement. At first glance, having several distinct numerical measures of preference, $\succsim$, based on different trade-offs seems an abundance of riches. But, because they all preserve the order $\succsim$, each pair of measures must relate by some strictly increasing numerical function from the image of the one measure to that of the other. Call a typical function of this type Φ.

The problem is how to constrain these Φs more precisely than mere monotonicity. To do so involves using various behavioral properties to establish numerical functional equations satisfied by the Φs and then solving these equations. We shall encounter this technique, which is typical of measurement, in several different contexts. Sometimes the resulting functional equation is easy to solve, sometimes not. The easy ones I solve explicitly, but for the more difficult ones I cite without proof the relevant mathematical literature. For excellent, standard introductions to functional equations see Aczél (1961/1966, 1987).

The two approaches followed in this chapter both lead ultimately to what is called the binary rank-dependent utility (RDU) representation (§§ 3.7 and 3.8). This representation, which is described shortly in Section 3.1.1, involves a utility function U that, for gains, maps the gambles and consequences into the nonnegative real numbers, and for each $\mathbf{E} \in \mathcal{E}$ a weighting function $W_{\mathbf{E}}$ that maps the events into the closed unit interval, $[0, 1]$, with $W_{\mathbf{E}}(\emptyset) = 0$, $W_{\mathbf{E}}(E) = 1$.

Even for fixed $\mathbf{E}$, such doubly infinite degrees of freedom are too generous if the theory is to reflect substantial constraints on behavior, and so a certain amount of subsequent work seeks additional behavioral properties designed to limit sharply the degrees of freedom. As we shall see in Chapter 4, powerful limitations on U arise quite naturally. The issue of limiting the form of $W_{\mathbf{E}}$, which is taken up in Section 3.4, has been controversial and simply cannot be viewed as yet settled. However, recent work, reported here, has led to a family of functions that appears to be very promising.

3.1   Binary Rank-Dependent Utility (RDU)

3.1.1   Definition

We proceed by first stating the representation whose properties will be explored and then will be ultimately justified axiomatically in terms of behavioral assumptions.

In what follows, we use more specific notations than those of Chapter 2 where, we recall, $\mathcal{B}_0 = \mathcal{C}$ is the set of certain alternatives, $\mathcal{B}_1$ the first-order gambles along with $\mathcal{B}_0$, and $\mathcal{B}_2$ the second-order gambles along with $\mathcal{B}_1$.

- $\mathcal{B}_0^+ = \mathcal{C}^+ = \{x : x \in \mathcal{C} \text{ and } x \succsim e\}$ is the set of certain gains, which, of course, includes the status quo e.
- $\mathcal{B}_i^+$ is the subset of $\mathcal{B}_i$ for all gambles that are generated inductively from $\mathcal{C}^+$ and $\mathcal{E}$.
- $\succsim$ is of course a preference order on $\mathcal{B}_2^+$.
- $\mathbb{B}_2^+ = \langle \mathcal{C}^+, e, \mathcal{E}, \mathcal{B}_2^+, \succsim \rangle$.
- When we deal with a subsystem, such as $\mathcal{B}_1^+$ or $\mathcal{B}_0^+$ and its ordering $\succsim$, we simply mean the restriction of the original $\succsim$ to the subsystem.

Definition 3.1.1. $\mathbb{B}_2^+$ is said to have a (binary) *rank-dependent utility (RDU)* representation if and only if there exists a mapping $U : \mathcal{B}_2^+ \to \mathbb{R}_+ = \{\alpha : \alpha \in \mathbb{R} \text{ and }$

$\alpha \geq 0\}$ and, for each $\mathbf{E} \in \mathcal{E}$, a mapping $W_{\mathbf{E}} : \mathcal{E}_{\mathbf{E}} \to [0, 1]$ with

$$W_{\mathbf{E}}(\emptyset) = 0, \quad W_{\mathbf{E}}(E) = 1, \tag{3.1}$$

such that U is order preserving in the sense that for $g, h \in \mathcal{B}_2^+$,

$$g \succsim h \Longleftrightarrow U(g) \geq U(h), \tag{3.2}$$

$$U(e) = 0, \tag{3.3}$$

and for $g, h \in \mathcal{B}_1^+$,

$$U(g, C; h, \overline{C}) = \begin{cases} U(g)W_{\mathbf{E}}(C) + U(h)[1 - W_{\mathbf{E}}(C)], & g \succ h \\ U(g), & g \sim h \\ U(g)[1 - W_{\mathbf{E}}(\overline{C})] + U(h)W_{\mathbf{E}}(\overline{C}), & g \prec h \end{cases} \tag{3.4}$$

The representation is said to be *dense in intervals* if the images of U and $W_{\mathbf{E}}$ are each dense in an interval, i.e., for r, s in the interval with $r < s$, there exists a t in the image of the function such that $r < t < s$. The representation is said to be *onto intervals* if and only if the image of U is onto a real interval including 0 and there is at least one experiment $\mathbf{K} \in \mathcal{E}$ with $W_{\mathbf{K}}$ onto $[0, 1]$.

Several comments are warranted.

- We confront a terminological dilemma. Certainly, this model is "rank-dependent" in the sense that the form used depends on whether $g \succsim h$ or $h \succsim g$. But, of course, it says much more than that. Each limb of the expression has a bilinear form like binary subjective expected utility. So, a more precise term would be "rank-dependent, subjective expected utility," which would be abbreviated RDSEU. Many authors prefer the shorter RDU and that use is fairly wide-spread in the literature. But if we ultimately develop models that are rank dependent, but different from Def. 3.1.1, we may rue that decision.

- If $W_{\mathbf{K}}$ were a probability measure, then the condition of being onto an interval could be formulated in terms of $\mathcal{E}_{\mathbf{E}}$ being a nonatomic sigma algebra [see, e.g., Rényi (1970)].

- We speak of U as a *utility function* and $W_{\mathbf{E}}$ as a *weighting function* (associated with experiment $\mathbf{E}$). In principle, we should distinguish between utility functions on $\mathcal{C}^+$ and on the first- and second-order gambles. However, given that idempotence (or, equally, certainty) is satisfied, the distinction is not really useful because the restriction of U on $\mathcal{B}_2^+$ to $\mathcal{B}_1^+$ and to $\mathcal{C}^+$ in Eq. (3.4) shows they are the same.

- Later when we are dealing with both gains and losses, it will be necessary to distinguish the weights derived from gains and those from losses, so we will write $W_{\mathbf{E}}^+$ and $W_{\mathbf{E}}^-$. In this chapter, we omit the $+$ sign.

- One sense in which the representation is rank dependent is our expectation that in general $W_{\mathbf{E}}$ will not be additive (§ 3.2.1), i.e., in particular over complementary events we do not necessarily have $W_{\mathbf{E}}(C) + W_{\mathbf{E}}(\overline{C}) = 1$. Were this to hold, the rank dependence disappears. Sometimes this property is called "symmetry" or "binary complementarity."

- Observe that the second line of Eq. (3.4) is an automatic consequence of idempotence, Eq. (2.1), and that the third line follows from the first line and complementarity, Eq. (2.3).
- The existence of a representation onto an interval, which is a kind of continuity condition, seems plausible if C^+ includes money and also if among the available experiments there is one in which any probability can be realized, e.g., a circle, partitioned into pie sectors, with a balanced spinner.

3.1.2   Canonical experiment

We first show that one feature of having an experiment with a representation onto an interval is that the evaluation of *all* binary gambles can be reduced to evaluating the binary gambles based on that experiment.

Definition 3.1.2.   In a structure $\mathbb{B}_2^+$ of binary gambles of gains, an experiment **K** is said to be *canonical* if and only if for any $E \in \mathcal{E}$ and $C \subseteq E$, there exists $D = D(C, E) \subseteq K$ such that for all $g, h \in \mathcal{B}_1^+$ with $g \succsim h$,

$$(g, C; h, E \backslash C) \sim (g, D; h, K \backslash D). \tag{3.5}$$

Note that here it could be misleading to use the brief notations $\overline{C}$ and $\overline{D}$ because they are complements relative to different universal sets, E and K, respectively.

Theorem 3.1.1.   *If $\mathbb{B}_2^+$ has an RDU representation and there is an experiment **K** for which $W_\mathbf{K}$ is onto $[0, 1]$, then **K** is canonical.*

Proof. Because $W_\mathbf{E}$ is into and $W_\mathbf{K}$ is onto $[0, 1]$, for any $C \subseteq E$ there must exist $D \subseteq K$ such that $W_\mathbf{K}(D) = W_\mathbf{E}(C)$. So by the RDU representation

$$\begin{aligned} U(g, C; h, E \backslash C) &= U(g)W_\mathbf{E}(C) + U(h)[1 - W_\mathbf{E}(C)] \\ &= U(g)W_\mathbf{K}(D) + U(h)[1 - W_\mathbf{K}(D)] \\ &= U(g, D; h, K \backslash D), \end{aligned}$$

and so by the fact U is order preserving, Eq. (3.5) holds.   ■

The existence of a canonical experiment will be important throughout the monograph. Although it is probably easiest to think of **K** as an experiment in which any numerical probability can arise, that may be too limiting. All that is actually required is that K have, in essence, a continuum of elements as outcomes.

3.1.3   Separable utility

In the remainder of this chapter we explore three necessary behavioral conditions that follow from the RDU representation and that will play major roles in axiomatizing it. The first is the event-consequence trade-off.

3.1.3.1   Definition of separability: Consider the gambles $(g, C; e, \overline{C})$ for fixed $\mathbf{E} \in \mathcal{E}$ and all $C \in \mathcal{E}_\mathbf{E}$ and all $g \in \mathcal{B}_1^+$. If the RDU representation holds with $U(e) = 0$, then

$\langle(\mathcal{B}_1^+\backslash\{e\})\times(\mathcal{E}_\mathbf{E}\backslash\{\emptyset\}),\succsim\rangle$ forms an additive conjoint structure with the positive multiplicative representation $U(g)W_\mathbf{E}(C)$ (see Appendix D on additive conjoint measurement). The multiplicative representation can, of course, be extended to include $x=e$ and $C=\emptyset$ because, by certainty, Eq. (2.2), and complementarity, Eq. (2.3), $(x,\emptyset;e,\overline{\emptyset})\sim e$. Also note, again by certainty, that $(x,E;e,\overline{E})\sim x$ and so $W_\mathbf{E}(E)=1$. However, it is clear that if $UW_\mathbf{E}$ is a representation, then for any $\beta>0$ so is $U^\beta(W_\mathbf{E})^\beta$, and we do not automatically know which one corresponds to the desired RDU representation. Working out this choice is a major task in Sections 3.6 and 3.7.

Definition 3.1.3   For each $\mathbf{E}\in\mathcal{E}$, the conjoint substructure $\mathbb{C}^+=\langle(\mathcal{B}_1^+\backslash\{e\})\times(\mathcal{E}_\mathbf{E}\backslash\{\emptyset\}),\succsim\rangle$ described above is said to have a *separable representation* if and only if there exist $U^*:\mathbb{C}^+\to\mathbb{R}_-$ and $W_\mathbf{E}^*:\mathcal{E}_\mathbf{E}\to[0,1]$ such that the product $U^*W_\mathbf{E}^*$ is order preserving, i.e.,

$$(x,C;e,\overline{C})\succsim(y,D;e,\overline{D})\iff U^*(x)W_\mathbf{E}^*(C)\geq U^*(y)W_\mathbf{E}^*(D)\qquad(3.6)$$

and $W_\mathbf{E}^*(E)=1$. The representation is said to be *onto* (or *dense*[1] *in*) *an interval* if in addition U^* is onto (dense in) a real interval containing 0 and also $W_\mathbf{E}^*$ is onto (dense in) $[0,1]$. In this case, $U^*(e)=0$ and $W_\mathbf{E}^*(\emptyset)=0$.

The term "separable" is widely used in economics to mean having an additive representation over factors, but under exponentials an additive representation becomes a multiplicative one on the positive real numbers. In other literatures, terms such as "multiplicative" and "factored" are more common.

3.1.3.2   Data on separable representations: Several studies have reported direct empirical tests of separability, and the overall summary is that it has been well sustained. A review of a number of early studies can be found in Shanteau (1975)—including a reanalysis of Slovic and Lichtenstein (1968), who had interpreted their data as rejecting separability—all of which provide support for it. Some of these studies were carried out within the framework of Anderson's method of "functional measurement" (Anderson, 1970, 1981, 1982, 1991a,b,c, 1996). Typically, that method involves each respondent providing some form of rating of the stimuli, in some cases gambles. The data are subjected to an analysis of variance either on the ratings themselves, when additivity is suspected, or on their logarithms, when, as in the case of separability, a multiplicative one is being tested. A good example where both models are studied is Shanteau (1974). (Some of those data are described in Section 4.1.3.) Separability is very well sustained in this study, as seen in Fig. 3.1. I am not aware of data that violate separability, although it is worth mentioning that it implies consequence monotonicity in the form $x\succsim y$ if and only if $(x,C;e,\overline{C})\succsim(y,C;e,\overline{C})$ provided that $W(C)<1$.

Komorita (1964) hypothesized that judgments of $CE(x,p)$ are of the form $\alpha x^\beta p^\gamma$. Taking logarithms of group data separately by gender (24 men and 30 women students for hypothetical stakes and 10 additional men for money stakes), a linear regression was fit. The model was not rejected, and the estimates of the parameters (β,γ) were $(0.994,0.755)$ for men and $(0.922,0.766)$ for women.

---

[1]   Definition 3.1.1.

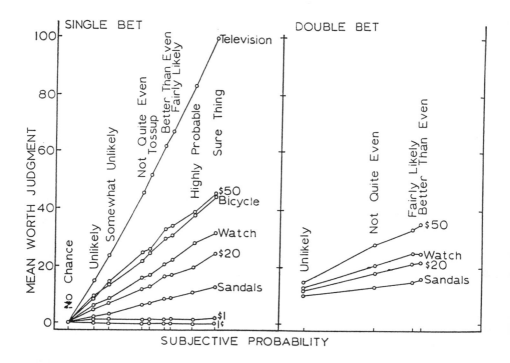

Figure 3.1. Fan-shaped evidence for separability in rating judgments of value. This is Fig. 1 of Shanteau (1974). Copyright © 1974 by the American Psychological Association. Reprinted with permission.

Birnbaum and Sutton (1992, pp. 209-210) also noted that if separability holds and U is a power function, then $\frac{CE(x,C)}{x}$ depends only on C, and they cited data in Mellers, Chang, Birnbaum, and Ordóñez (1992) as supportive; however, no alternative assumptions about utility were tested. M. H. Birnbaum (personal communication, December 15, 1998) reports that an analysis that he has done of the Preston and Baratta (1948) data, which are described more fully in Sec. 3.4.2.1, also exhibits a multiplicative fan structure similar to Fig. 3.1. Thus, these data are consistent with separability and possibly with power functions for utility.

Three of the early studies of separability were carried out within the framework of additive conjoint measurement theory (Appendix D): Coombs, Bezenbinder, and Good (1967) and Tversky (1967a, 1967b). All were unusual in using nonstudents as respondents. In Coombs et al. those of experiment I were 23 black working-class people and those of experiment II were 85 prisoners. In these analyses, 21 of 23 and 81 of 85 respondents satisfied separability. I go into the Tversky (1967a) study more fully. The respondents were 11 prisoners and the consequences were packs of cigarettes[2] or bags of candy, which both had the same price in the prison store. The chance device was a spinner with 10 possible outcomes. The experimental design involved four distinct sets of outcomes with a full factorial design in each:

Set	Stimuli	x packs	y bags	p	N
I	$(x, p; 0)$	1,2,3,4		0.2,0.4,0.6,0.8	16
II	$(y, p; 0)$		1,2,3,4	0.2,0.4,0.6,0.8	16
III	$x \oplus y$	1,2,3,4	1,2,3,4		16
IV	$(x \oplus y, p; 0)$	1,2,3	1,2,3	0.2,0.4,0.6,0.8	27

The notation $x \oplus y$ means that both x and y are received. So, for example, $3 \oplus 1$ denotes the consequence of receiving both 3 packs of cigarettes and 1 bag of candy. Chapters 4, 6, and 7 study the joint receipt operation $\oplus$ much more fully.

The 75 options were presented in some random order every other day in two-hour sessions for a total of three days. The prisoners were asked to state their lowest selling price for each alternative. Unknown to them, the experimenter had selected in advance three of the options to be played. They were told, and presumably believed, that the experimenter would attempt to take monetary advantage of their choices in deciding whether to pay the selling price stated or to run off the gamble. In reality, however, a number was randomly selected in the interval from one standard deviation below the expected value of the gamble to one standard deviation above it, and if the selling price was less than that random number, the experimenter paid that price and, otherwise, the gamble was run.

A plot of the mean selling price versus monetary value in set III exhibited virtually direct proportionality. For the three gambling cases the plots of prices versus expected monetary value were approximately linear with slopes slightly greater than 1.

The tests of separability for gambling sets I and II and of additivity over joint receipt for set III were carried out individually by applying an analysis of variance to the logarithm of selling prices. Only one significant (at the 0.10 level) interaction occurred in 33 cases, strongly confirming both separability of gambles and additivity over joint receipt.

Tversky (1967b) collected additional data on lotteries from 11 prisoners in which just separability could be examined. Assuming that utility is a power function of money, an analysis of variance was conducted for each respondent separately on the logarithm of buying prices. Very few interactions were found, thus sustaining separability. We will return to these data in Sections 3.4.1 and 3.4.2 where estimates of weights are discussed.

An interesting later study is Krzysztofowicz and Koch (1989). The basic idea was to transform the utility of gambles into that of money by replacing the gambles by their certainty equivalents. For simplicity, use the notation $(x, p) \equiv (x, p; 0, 1 - p)$. If one sets $U(x^*) = 1$

---

[2]   This study was carried out shortly before the Surgeon General issued the first report linking cigarette smoking to lung cancer disease and later to other diseases.

and if separability holds, then

$$\begin{aligned} U[CE(x^*,p)] &= U(x^*,p) \\ &= U(x^*)W(p) \\ &= W(p), \end{aligned}$$

and so

$$\begin{aligned} U[CE(x,p)] &= U(x,p) \\ &= U(x)W(p) \\ &= U[CE(x,1)]U[CE(x^*,p)]. \end{aligned}$$

Taking logarithms places this in additive form. The authors devised a linear programming method to fit their data.

Ten of their respondents were M.I.T. students and faculty in engineering and 44 were University of Virginia students in their fourth year who were majoring in systems engineering and had been exposed to decision theory. They used a factorial design involving 7 consequences ranging from \$2,000 to \$10,000 and 7 levels of probability ranging from $\frac{1}{8}$ to 1. The scenario involved probabilistic scholarships. The certainty equivalents were elicited by a bounding technique described by Farquhar (1984). The property of separability was well sustained. We return to these data in Section 3.3.1

A more recent study in which separability was sustained was Birnbaum, Coffey, Mellers, and Weiss (1992). They obtained judged certainty equivalents, JCEs, under three conditions of viewpoint: sellers, buyers, and neutral. The lotteries were of the form (x,p), and a full 3×9 factorial design with $x = \$24, 72$, and 96 and $p = 0.05, 0.10, 0.20, 0.40, 0.50, 0.60,$ 0.80, 0.90, 0.95 was used. The estimated utility was simply proportional to money.

A study closely related to separability is Ranyard (1977). In Experiment[3] 2 he explored the property of double cancellation, which is simply the Thomsen condition (Appendix D) with all of the $\sim$ symbols replaced by $\succsim$; it too is a necessary condition if a separable representation $U(x)W(p)$ holds (see § 3.5.2.2). He elicited information on respondents' decision strategies and concluded that 7 of 20 followed a pattern of lexicographic semiorder behavior in which one dimension dominated except when the values in that dimension were sufficiently close, in which case the decision shifted to the other dimension. The other respondents appeared to engage in some form of trade-off between consequences and probabilities. The analysis of Ranyard (1976) entails finding the minimum number of response changes required to meet the condition, in this case double cancellation. The median for the lexicographic group was 14, as against 4 for the others. The difference between the groups was significant by a Mann-Whitney U-test at less than 0.01. So, it appears that there are two classes of respondents, those who followed a simple decision rule in which trade-offs played little role and those for whom the trade-offs mattered. If so, the kind of theory developed here applies only to the latter.

In summary, a number of experimental studies have examined separability and found it sustained in a large majority of cases.

---

[3]   Experiment 1 was discussed in Section 2.2.3.

3.1.4   Rank-dependent additivity of consequences

The next necessary property of RDU formulates the nature of the consequence-consequence trade-off.

3.1.4.1   Definition: With $\mathbf{E}$ and $C \in \mathcal{E}_\mathbf{E}$ held fixed, the ordering $\succsim$ of the binary gambles can be viewed as imposing an ordering on $C^+ \times C^+$, which because of the role of $(C, \mathbf{E})$ is denoted $\succsim_{(C,\mathbf{E})}$. Formally:

Definition 3.1.4.   A structure $\mathbb{B}_1^+$ is said to have a *rank-dependent additive representation* (RDA) if and only if for each $\mathbf{E} \in \mathcal{E}$ there exists $U_{i,\mathbf{E}} : C^+ \times \mathcal{E}_\mathbf{E} \to \mathbb{R}$, $i = 1, 2$, such that the following additive order-preserving representation holds: For $x, x', y, y' \in C^+$ with $x \succsim y$ and $x' \succsim y'$, and $C \in \mathcal{E}$,

$$(x, C; y) \succsim (x', C; y')$$

if and only if

$$(x, y) \succsim_{(C,\mathbf{E})} (x', y')$$

if and only if

$$U_{1,\mathbf{E}}(x, C) + U_{2,\mathbf{E}}(y, C) \geq U_{1,\mathbf{E}}(x', C) + U_{2,\mathbf{E}}(y', C), \qquad (3.7)$$

and $U_{i,\mathbf{E}}(e, C) = 0$, $i = 1, 2$. A RDA representation is said to be *onto an interval* if and only if it is onto a real interval including 0.

It is convenient to define U over $\mathbb{B}_1^+$ as

$$U(x, C; y) = U_{1,\mathbf{E}}(x, C) + U_{2,\mathbf{E}}(y, C), \quad x \succsim y. \qquad (3.8)$$

The representation for $x \prec y$ follows from this and complementarity, namely,

$$U(x, C; y) = U(y, \overline{C}; x) = U_{1,\mathbf{E}}(y, \overline{C}) + U_{2,\mathbf{E}}(x, \overline{C}), \quad x \prec y.$$

The definition extends to $\mathbb{B}_2^+$ is the obvious way.

Although a behavioral, testable principle—comonotonic consistency (§ 3.7.3)—can be stated just in terms of $\succsim$ to arrive at rank dependence, i.e., that the evaluation differs between $x \succsim y$ and $x \precsim y$, I am not aware of any experiment testing it for binary gambles. And as we shall see in Section 3.2.2, ignoring the rank distinction certainly leads to incorrect behavioral predictions. Despite the lack of direct evidence, a number of authors have argued, based on strong intuition, that something at least as strong as ordinal rank-dependence should be involved.[4] The feeling is that we all deal differently with the best and worst consequences. This is especially vivid when thinking about large gains, as in a state lottery, and large losses, as in a home burning down. But even with all gains, the intuition is that the largest gain is handled differently from the least. Among psychologists, Birnbaum (1972), Lopes (1984,

---

[4]   The observations to be made about the intuitive basis of rank dependence come from a personal communication of Peter Wakker (April 13, 1998).

1987, 1990), Wakker (1990), Wakker and Tversky (1993), and Weber (1994) have made such arguments based on a mixture of intuitions about optimism/pessimism and on certain data in need of explanation. And among economists, Yaari (1987) and Schmeidler (1989) have made primarily intuitive arguments. A different argument for rank dependence is provided in Chapter 4.

The issue of which qualitative properties give rise to RDA and its degree of uniqueness is taken up in Section 3.5.3.

3.1.4.2   Empirical evidence: In the literature various studies, many discussed by Shanteau (1975), address the "additivity" of consequences. Most of these studies, however, concern the topic of joint receipt of two things—consequences or gambles—and will be discussed in Chapter 4. That is different from additivity within a gamble where one receives one or the other, but not both, consequence. The only study I am aware of that bears directly on this issue is Coombs and Komorita (1958).

Three male respondents each confronted four series of 8 lotteries of the form $(x, \frac{1}{2}; y, \frac{1}{2})$. Within each series the $EV = \frac{x+y}{2}$ was held constant. The first three series were used to estimate certain relations, to be explained, and the fourth served as a test of the additivity predictions. The method of triads was used in which triples of lotteries were judged for the best and worst alternative. This was found to yield a perfectly transitive order for each respondent in each of the first three series. Assuming $W(\frac{1}{2}) = \frac{1}{2}$, which as we will see below (§ 3.4) is a very dubious assumption, then with the RDU representation we have

$$(x, \frac{1}{2}; y) \succsim (x', \frac{1}{2}; y') \iff U(x) - U(x') \geq U(y') - U(y).$$

The fourth or test series had value pairs that could be estimated from the data series on the assumption of this model, and the authors reported that of 30 predictions made by the model, 29 were confirmed. Their conclusion was that consequence additivity was well sustained.

Data in Birnbaum et al. (1992), especially Fig. 5 (p. 337), and in Birnbaum and Sutton (1992) are consistent with the existence of an additive trade-off. Just how relevant they are to choice data is open to doubt. The respondents were asked to provide judgments of gambles from three perspectives: buying price, selling price, and worth. Although it is conceivable that each of these judgments orders the gambles in the same way as do the choices, there are ample reasons to be skeptical of that hypothesis. First, recall the data in Section 2.2.5.1 in which attractiveness judgments (and also in the paper, selling prices and avoidance prices for losses) were systematically inconsistent with choices. Second, as we know, judged evaluations exhibit violations of consequence monotonicity, whereas choices seem not to (§§ 2.3.4 and 2.3.5). And third, as we shall see when we develop a theory of buying and selling prices (§§ 6.4 and, especially, 7.4), agreement is not predicted to occur in general.

3.1.5   Event commutativity

3.1.5.1   Definition: Our third major necessary condition from RDU is not a trade-off, but rather a special accounting indifference involving compound gambles. It says that certain pairs of gambles that are equivalent from a "bottom line" perspective are also perceived as indifferent in preference.

Definition 3.1.5. A structure $\mathbb{B}_2^+$ satisfies *event commutativity* if for all $x, y \in \mathcal{C}^+$, $E, F \in \mathcal{E}$, $C \subseteq E$, and $D \subseteq F$,

$$((x, C; y, E\backslash C), D; y, F\backslash D) \sim ((x, D; y, F\backslash D), C; y, E\backslash C), \quad x, y \succsim e. \qquad (3.9)$$

When this holds just for $y = e$, i.e., restricted to $\mathbb{C}^+ = \langle \mathcal{B}_1^+ \times \mathcal{E}_E, \succsim \rangle$, we say that *status-quo event commutativity* holds.

The general property does not follow from the special one, but in Section 4.4.2 we examine an important case where it does.

This property is quite rational: Suppose, on running the two independent experiments $\mathbf{E}$ and $\mathbf{F}$, one receives x when both the subevent C occurs in $\mathbf{E}$ and D occurs in $\mathbf{F}$, and under the other three possible outcomes, the consequence is y. Then the condition asserts that the order in which the two experiments is carried out is immaterial to the decision maker.

It is easy to verify that if behavior is described by a RDU representation, then event commutativity holds: Suppose $x \succsim y$ and so $(x, C; y) \succsim y$,

$$
\begin{aligned}
U&((x, C; y, E\backslash C), D; y, F\backslash D) \\
&= U(x, C; y, C\backslash E)W_\mathbf{F}(D) + U(y)[1 - W_\mathbf{F}(D)] \\
&= U(x)W_\mathbf{E}(C)W_\mathbf{F}(D) + U(y)[1 - W_\mathbf{E}(C)]W(D) + U(y)[1 - W_\mathbf{F}(D)] \\
&= U(x)W_\mathbf{E}(C)W_\mathbf{F}(D) + U(y)[1 - W_\mathbf{E}(C)W_\mathbf{F}(D)],
\end{aligned}
$$

which is clearly symmetrical in the roles of $(C, \mathbf{E})$ and $(D, \mathbf{F})$.

The empirical status of event commutativity is discussed in the next subsection.

Several authors have used event commutativity in their work, and it has been called various things including "multi-symmetry." It bears a family resemblance to the measurement-theoretical concept of bisymmetry. For various uses of it, see Chew (1989), Chew and Epstein (1989), Luce (1988, 1990), Luce and Narens (1985), and Nakamura (1990, 1992, 1995).

In the case where $\mathbf{F} = \mathbf{E}$ and the same experiment is independently replicated, the condition can be put in simpler notation by suppressing[5] the complementary event, which makes its meaning very clear:

$$((x, C; y), D; y) \sim ((x, D; y), C; y). \qquad (3.10)$$

Note that the reduction of compound lotteries that underlies, for example, the Allais paradox (§ 2.3.1) can be generalized to the following reduction of compound gambles:

$$((x, C; y), D; y) \sim (x, C\&D; y). \qquad (3.11)$$

I do not make this assumption here, although a version of it is discussed briefly in Section 3.4.1. Note that $C\&D$ is not the same as $C \cap D$.

---

[5] I do this throughout the monograph when I do not think it will cause any confusion due to ambiguity.

3.1.5.2   Empirical evidence about event commutativity: The first study of this property of which I am aware is Ronen (1971, 1973).[6,7] In his first experiment 22 respondents made direct choices between 20 status-quo event commutativity pairs in which $x = \$0.40$ and the probabilities of C and D were varied. The lotteries were presented as trees of the form of Fig. 1.1. Following the choice, all lotteries were played. Three of the respondents always preferred the compound lottery for which the probability of going to the second stage was higher, and of the remaining 19 respondents 16 made a preponderance of such choices.

In a second experiment 96 business students considered scenarios involving business ventures in which x was described as "success" and the status quo e was described as no gain and no loss. Twenty-four pairs were used with varying probabilities and were presented in tree form. As before, he found that 70% of the respondents more often than not selected the gamble with the higher probability of advancing to the second stage.

The conclusion he drew from the two experiments was that status-quo event commutativity fails.

Because his experimental design forced choices, I do not believe that any such conclusion is justified. Consider a respondent who actually satisfies status-quo event commutativity and who faced the experimental instructions. What were his or her options for making a choice? One is to try to choose randomly, which appears to be what Ronen assumed would happen if status-quo event commutativity obtained. But a second, at least equally plausible, strategy is to seek some way to distinguish the two alternatives and to use that distinction to force a choice. After all, if the experimenter demands a choice, the respondent is likely to conclude that there must be some reasonable way to make one. Aside from the order in which the alternatives are presented either in space or time, the only distinction available is the order in which the two experiments are realized. If a majority of the time a majority of the respondents opt for choosing the one with the higher probability first, then they will exhibit this behavior even if, in fact, they are actually indifferent.

In an unpublished dissertation, Brothers (1990) explored event commutativity using three methods: direct choices, as in Ronen's method, judged certainty equivalents, and PEST-determined certainty equivalents (Appendix C). In the choice experiment, 30 student respondents compared on a strength of preference scale pairs of hypothetical gambles with consequences ranging from $-\$1,000$ to $+\$1,000$. His results were less sharp than Ronen's: 7 respondents appeared to be indifferent; 8 followed Ronen's pattern; and the remaining 15 showed considerable inconsistency. In the judged CE procedure respondents showed a tendency to assign a higher JCE to gambles having the lesser probability of winning at the first stage. This may be related to the "bias" of judgments relative to choices that was found in the preference reversal phenomenon (§ 2.2.5). Because PEST is quite time consuming, he obtained choice CEs for only four pairs of gambles. For these he found support for event commutativity, and he observed that JCEs were larger than CCEs for those gambles with a lower probability of going on to the second gamble.

Because of the critical importance of event commutativity to RDU, Chung, von Win-

---

6   The same data sets are reported in both papers.

7   There are several somewhat related studies in the accounting literature sparked by Ronen's work, but that bear on the much stronger property of reduction of compound gambles, Section 3.7.2, rather than event commutativity.

terfeldt, and Luce (1994) elected to study it again using the PEST procedure to determine certainty equivalents. They used a computer-generated display shown in Fig. 3.2. The respondents were 25 University of Southern California students. The stimuli were 6 gains pairs and 6 mixed gain and loss pairs. (The results for the latter stimuli are reported in Section 6.3.3.) The gambles were given a scenario involving a lawsuit based on an automobile accident about which two independent witnesses were to testify. Their probabilities of giving testimony favorable to the respondent were provided. If both testimonies were favorable, the respondent would "receive" $9,600. If either or both are unfavorable, y was received. The certain amount was an out-of-court settlement between the two drivers. In the gains case there were three probability pairs: $(0.50, 0.90)$, $(0.33, 0.75)$, and $(0.05, 0.90)$, and two values for y: $1,200 and $4,800. Figure 3.3 shows the scatter diagram of the median CCEs for gains.

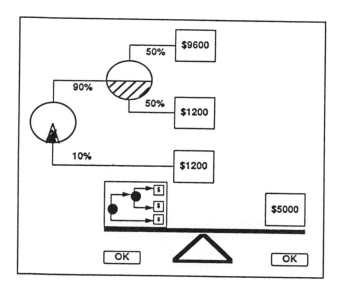

Figure 3.2. Typical display used in presenting a compound binary gamble in testing event commutativity. This is Fig. 2 of Chung, von Winterfeldt, and Luce (1994). Copyright 1994 by Blackwell Publishers, Malden, MA 02148. Reprinted by permission.

A detailed analysis of individual respondents revealed that 22 of them seemed to exhibit no systematic violations of event commutativity, but three did. For those respondents, their tendency to choose the order where the larger probability occurred first was 92%, 100%, and 83%. These three accord with Ronen's interpretation of his findings; however, the vast majority of respondents seem to satisfy event commutativity for gains.

So, although event commutativity does not seem always to hold, it does so sufficiently often that I believe it to be a viable property to assume. And certainly it is a rational one. The source of the failures is not known for certain. One can speculate that they may arise from a desire to increase the chance of going on to the second stage, but no empirical proof exists.

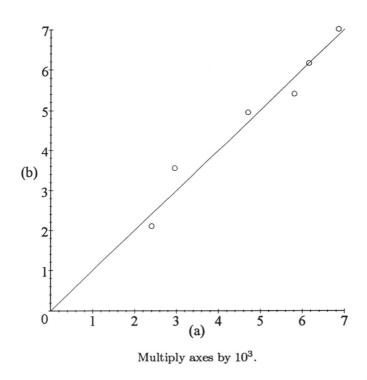

Multiply axes by 10^3.

Figure 3.3. Median certainty equivalents for the two sides, (a) and (b), of six event commutativity pairs for gains. Reading from upper right to lower left, the points correspond to gambles 1, 2, 3, 4, 5, and 8. Adapted from Fig. 3 of Chung, von Winterfeldt, and Luce (1994). Copyright 1994 by Blackwell Publishers, Malden, MA 02148. Reprinted by permission.

3.2   Distinguishing SEU and RDU

3.2.1   Additive weights for complementary events

The special case of RDU for which W_E is additive over complementary events, i.e., for each $\mathbf{E} \in \mathcal{E}$ and all $C \subseteq E$

$$W_E(C) + W_E(\overline{C}) = 1, \tag{3.12}$$

yields the representation

$$U(x, C; y) = U(x)W_E(C) + U(y)W_E(\overline{C}), \tag{3.13}$$

without any restriction on the preference order of x and y. This binary representation can be called *(binary) rank-independent utility* (RIU). The special case of RIU for which the weights are finitely additive, i.e., for each $\emptyset \subset C, D \subseteq E$ with $C \cap D = \emptyset$,

$$W_E(C \cup D) = W_E(C) + W_E(D), \tag{3.14}$$

is called *(binary) subjective expected utility* (SEU).

One way SEU follows from RIU is if the following reduction condition is satisfied:

Definition 3.2.1.   A structure $\langle \mathcal{C}^+, e, \mathcal{E}, \mathcal{B}_2^+, \succsim \rangle$ is said to satisfy *conditionalization* if and only if for $x \in \mathcal{C}^+$ and $C \subseteq D \subseteq E$,

$$((x, C; e, D \backslash C), D; e, E \backslash D) \sim (x, C; e, E \backslash C). \tag{3.15}$$

Proposition 3.2.1.   *The following statements hold:*

(i)   *Separability and conditionalization, Eq. (3.15), imply*

$$W_D(C)W_E(D) = W_E(C). \tag{3.16}$$

(ii)   *If, in addition, the weights are additive over complementary events, Eq. (3.12), then the weights are finitely additive.*

Proof. (i) The separability of RDU and Eq. (3.15) imply

$$
\begin{aligned}
U(x)W_E(C) &= U(x, C; e, E \backslash C) \\
&= U((x, C; e, D \backslash C), D; E \backslash D) \\
&= U(x, C; e, D \backslash C)W_E(D) \\
&= U(x)W_D(C)W_E(D),
\end{aligned}
$$

whence Eq. (3.16).

(ii) Now, suppose that $\{C, C'\}$ is a partition of D. Invoking the additivity of complementary events and the fact $W_{\mathbf{E}}(D) > 0$,

$$
\begin{aligned}
\frac{W_{\mathbf{E}}(D)}{W_{\mathbf{E}}(D)} &= 1 \\
&= W_{\mathbf{D}}(C) + W_{\mathbf{D}}(D \backslash C) \\
&= W_{\mathbf{D}}(C) + W_{\mathbf{D}}(C') \\
&= \frac{W_{\mathbf{E}}(C)}{W_{\mathbf{E}}(D)} + \frac{W_{\mathbf{E}}(C')}{W_{\mathbf{E}}(D)},
\end{aligned}
$$

whence Eq. (3.14). ∎

Thus, we see that RIU plus conditionalization implies SEU.

Equation (3.16) is the so-called choice axiom of Luce (1959). It simply says that the weights act somewhat like (subjective) conditional probabilities of the experiment **E**. This would be fully the case if also there were a universal set Ω that includes all experiments as subevents and on which there exists a function $W : \Omega \to [0, 1]$ such that

$$
W_E(C) = \frac{W(C)}{W(E)}.
$$

We do not search for this somewhat unrealistic ideal. It was, however, the model worked out by Savage (1954), who, as was noted (§ 1.1.6.1), assumed that all alternatives are defined over a single set of states of the world. He derived that the weighting function is additive over all finite sets of mutually disjoint events, not just complementary ones.

Binary SEU and its natural generalization to any gamble of finite order was the main focus of this area until the late 1970s. Various empirical drawbacks with this model led during the past 20 years to a variety of alternative suggestions including RDU .

One natural question is what behaviorally distinguishes RDU from SEU, to which we now turn.

3.2.2   Universal accounting indifferences

Consider two compound gambles of any degree of complexity that have the same "bottom line" in the following sense: Each has the same set of pure consequences and the conditions under which each arises are identical in the two gambles, except possibly for the order in which the underlying experiments are carried out. If all of the gambles involved are binary and SEU holds, then it follows that any such pair must be indifferent. The reasons underlying this assertion are: Because any given consequence arises via some combination of events occurring and because Eq. (3.13) is simply linear in the weights, the resulting overall weight for each consequence is the product of several component weights. Since products are commutative, the order in which they occur does not matter. We call this behavioral property (and its generalization to gambles of any order) *universal accounting indifferences*.[8] This postulate

---

[8]   This appears to have the same meaning as *consequentialism* which Hammond (1998a) described as requiring "...that actions should be evaluated purely on the basis of their consequences." See also Hammond (1988, 1998b,c)

greatly generalizes event commutativity and the three elementary accounting indifferences encountered in Chapter 2.

Universal accounting is a very strong set of properties. It is most unlikely that all will be satisfied empirically, as Luce (1992), Segal (1992), and Simon (1956) have emphasized. Indeed, anyone who has taught undergraduate decision theory knows that many students—most in my experience—have a difficult time seeing through any equivalences more complicated than status-quo event commutativity.

3.2.3   Autodistributivity

Consider, for example, an equivalence that is, in a sense, the next more complex one after event commutativity. It involves three consequences and the repetition of one experiment, whereas event commutativity has two consequences and two experiments.

Definition 3.2.2.   (Right[9]) *autodistributivity* is said to hold if and only if for each $E \in \mathcal{E}$, $C \subseteq E$, and $x, y, z \in C^+$,

$$((x, C'; y), C; z) \sim ((x, C'; z), C; (y, C''; z)), \tag{3.17}$$

where C', C'' are cases of C occurring on independent realizations of the underlying experiment **E**.

If we do a careful accounting on both sides we see that the three consequences arise under the following conditions (omitting the primes):

x :   if C occurs twice
y :   if $\overline{C}$ and C each occur once
z :   if $\overline{C}$ occurs on the left and $(C \& \overline{C})$ or $(\overline{C} \& \overline{C})$, i.e., $\overline{C}$ on the right

So a rational person should exhibit indifference between the two formulations.

Theorem 3.2.2.   *Suppose a structure with a binary RDU representation satisfies autodistributivity. Then Eq. (3.12), and so binary RIU, holds. If, in addition, conditionalization, Eq. (3.15), is satisfied, then SEU holds.*

The proof is in Section 3.9.1. My policy is to locate the longer, more complex proofs at the ends of chapters.

So if SEU is inadequate, we certainly do not expect to find autodistributivity holding experimentally. The only empirical study of autodistributivity that I know of is the unpublished dissertation of Brothers (1990), which unambiguously rejected it. Of course, other studies, such as the Allais paradox, make clear SEU is not descriptive. The present analysis, however, makes clear the behavioral nature of the breakdown.

---

[9]   Left autodistributivity is defined in the obvious way, but it need not be stated or investigated because it follows immediately from right autodistributivity, complementary, consequence monotonicity, and transitivity.

3.2.4   RDU and bounded rationality

Simon (1956) criticized theories leading to the SEU representation as being far too demand-ing in what amounts to computational power to provide a realistic description of behavior. Universal accounting is beyond the unaided capacity of most people. And so Simon urged, without providing a very precise meaning, the development of theories of *bounded rational-ity*. A primary form of boundedness is to state precisely which accounting indifferences hold and which do not. RDU is one theory that assigns a very precise meaning to the nature of the boundedness, namely, that only the simplest accounting indifferences hold: idempotence, certainty, complementarity, and event commutativity. Beyond that, as we have just seen, as-suming two additional accounting equivalence forces the unbounded rationality of SEU.

3.3   Utility Functions

3.3.1   Parametric estimates for money

Although RDU entails a number of empirical regularities, it nevertheless has a great deal of freedom in that two unspecified functions U and $W = W_K$ are involved. It is clear that it would be a far more useful theory if the forms for these functions were specified to within a parameter or two that had to be estimated for each decision maker. We explore in this section some of the ad hoc[10] proposals about U, but we will come to understand these issues better in Chapter 4. Section 3.4 concerns some of the proposals that have been made about W.

The special assumptions we explore limit us to lotteries with money consequences and events prescribed only as probabilities.

The two most common assumptions,[11] certainly by economists but also sometimes by psychologists, that have been made in the literature about U are the power form

$$U(x) = \begin{cases} \alpha x^\beta, & x \geq 0,\ \alpha, \beta > 0 \\ -\alpha'(-x)^{\beta'}, & x < 0,\ \alpha', \beta' > 0 \end{cases} \tag{3.18}$$

and for constants δ and κ the exponential family

$$U(x) = \frac{1 - e^{-\kappa x}}{\delta}, \quad \delta\kappa > 0. \tag{3.19}$$

The latter notation is slightly tricky in that $\delta\kappa > 0$ can come about in two ways: $\delta > 0$ and $\kappa > 0$ or $\delta < 0$ and $\kappa < 0$. In the latter case, it is more usual to write it as $\frac{e^{|\kappa||x|} - 1}{|\delta|}$.

Both functions have $U(0) = 0$.

The power function is strictly increasing and unbounded in x. For gains, it is concave if

---

10   The term "ad hoc" is used for any function—utility or weighting—for which no argument is given in terms of behavioral properties that can be studied in isolation. The forms are typically selected to exhibit qualitative features seen in numerical estimates.

11   For an exhaustive listing of proposals, see Bell and Fishburn (1999).

$0 < \beta < 1$, linear if $\beta = 1$, and convex if $\beta > 1$. The concave case is often described as diminishing marginal utility. For losses, replace α, β by α', β' and interchange concave and convex.

The exponential function with $\delta > 0$ and $\kappa > 0$ is strictly increasing, concave, and bounded by $1/\delta$. With $\delta < 0$ and $\kappa < 0$ it is strictly increasing, convex, and unbounded.

An argument, based on locally rational behavioral properties, is given in Sections 4.4.4, 4.5.3, and 4.5.4 that for money leads to either a power function or an exponential of a power function or a negative exponential of a power function.

Recall (§3.1.3.2) that Komorita (1964) tested separability assuming power transformations for utility and weights, and the joint assumptions were not rejected in the group data.

Fishburn and Kochenberger (1979) systematically fit power and exponential utility functions and estimated weighting functions to the data of 30 individual respondents gleaned from five studies. The results made clear that both the power and exponential do appreciably better than a linear function, and they were hardly distinguishable from one another in overall quality of fit. Krzysztofowicz and Koch (1989) collected individual data, as was described earlier in Section 3.1.3.2. Among the 54 respondents, they found five qualitatively different shapes for U of money gains: 20% linear, 35% concave, 19% convex, 17% concave and then convex, and 9% convex and then concave. (I will return to this observation in Section 4.5.3 where a theoretically plausible rationale is provided.) Restricting attention to the first three classes of functions, they fit to these data four parametric forms: linear, power, exponential, and logarithmic. The two poorest fits, on average, were linear and logarithmic; the two best were power and exponential, with power doing slightly better than exponential. As they noted, this was similar to what Fishburn and Kochenberger (1979) had reported earlier. Finally, they attempted to fit the original von Neumann-Morgenstern expected utility theory in which $W(p) = p$. They found that to do so required utility functions with a remarkably kinky shape, as van der Meer (1963) had earlier suggested would happen.

It is often said that, whatever the exact form may be, U appears to be concave for gains and convex for losses. For example, Kahneman and Tversky (1979) report (problems 13 and 13') that 82% of 66 respondents chose

$$(\$4,000, 0.25; \$2,000, 0.25; 0, 0.50) \text{ over } (\$6,000; 0.25; 0)$$

and that only 30% of 64 respondents chose

$$(-\$4,000, 0.25; -\$2,000, 0.25; 0, 0.50) \text{ over } (-\$6,000; 0.25; 0).$$

They assumed for a three-outcome gamble the following utility generalization (see Edwards, 1954a) of a binary gamble:

$$\begin{aligned}
U(\$4,&000, 0.25; \$2,000, 0.25; 0, 0.50) \\
&= U(\$4,000)W(0.25) + U(\$2,000)W(0.25) \\
&> U(\$6,000, 0.25; 0) \\
&= U(\$6,000)W(0.25),
\end{aligned}$$

whence $U(\$4,000) + U(\$2,000) > U(\$6,000)$, which is subadditive. Conjecturing that this holds generally, they concluded that U is subadditive for gains. By an analogous argument, U for losses is superadditive. Concavity implies subadditivity and convexity implies superadditivity.

Two comments are warranted.

- First, these data do not tell us anything about individual respondents, and they are certainly consistent with the assumption that respondents of all four combinations of concavity and convexity for gains and losses exist, which seems to be the case when individuals are examined separately.
- Second, the argument rests upon a generalization of the binary representation which subsequently has been rejected rather thoroughly, and in their cumulative prospect theory revision (Tversky & Kahneman, 1992) they abandoned it in favor of the general rank-dependent form (Chapter 4), which in this case says that

$$U(\$4,000, 0.25; \$2,000, 0.25; 0, 0.50)$$
$$= U(\$4,000)W(0.25) + U(\$2,000)[W(0.50) - W(0.25)],$$

and no simple inference follows from this. So even the average conclusion is no longer warranted.

Fishburn and Kochenberger (1979) in their examination of individual respondents found the following pattern of concavity and convexity:

	Concave gains	Convex gains
Convex losses	13	5
Concave losses	3	7

This makes clear that while concave gains coupled with convex losses is the most common pattern–46% of the cases–it is far from the exclusive one. We return to these data in Section 6.3.3, where we will see that to some degree what is found depends on the method of elicitation. Likewise, as was noted earlier, Krzysztofowicz and Koch (1989) reported that only 35% of their respondents were purely concave for gains.

Currim and Sarin (1989) compared Kahneman and Tversky's (1979) prospect theory with classical expected utility ($W(p) = p$) using responses of 37 MBA respondents. Their technique for expected utility was to ask the respondents to report their certainty equivalences for gambles of the form $(x^*, p; x_*)$ where x^* was the largest amount and x_* was the smallest amount considered. Setting $U(x^*) = 1$ and $U(x_*) = 0$, this yields for expected utility $U[CE(x^*, p; x_*)] = p$. For prospect theory, they estimated the "value" V of sure consequences by working with judgments of differences—I do not go into the details—and then with that known, they assumed $U = V$ and used them to determine the weights for gains from

$$W^+(p) = U[CE(x^*, p; 0)].$$

For losses the same formula was used with x^* replaced by x_*. They fit exponential functions to the data for value functions (see § 4.4.4). For the value function obtained by difference judgments, 26 of 34 respondents exhibited utility that was both concave for gains and convex for losses, the highest percentage by far of these three studies. Part of the reason may be the fact that the value functions were estimated in a different way from the utility functions.

Weber and Milliman (1997) report comparable data from an experiment concerning commuting times. Respondents were asked, among other things, to establish the probability that would make them indifferent between a train time that was 40 minutes faster (slower) than the status quo of 60 minutes and a gamble in which the arrival time was either 5, 10, 15, 20, or 30 minutes faster (slower) with probability 0.80 than the status quo. Assuming the expected utility model, they estimated the utility functions of individuals. Their summary (recoded in my terminology) of these estimates was:

		Concave	Convex	Gains Linear	Mixed	Totals
	Concave	5	7	2	5	19
Loss	Convex	3	6	2	3	14
	Linear	4	6	0	3	13
	Mixed	1	6	0	1	8
	Totals	13	25	4	12	54

Taken together, these studies provide sufficiently many examples of all four patterns that any overall generalization about the convexity or concavity of utility functions seems unwarranted. The most one can say is that concavity for gains and convexity for losses appears to be the most likely of the four patterns.

3.3.2   Nonparametric estimates

Wakker and Deneffe (1996) suggested that if one assumes binary RDU, then one can estimate utility functions using a familiar method from additive conjoint measurement based on standard sequences (Def. D.1). Specifically, fix three sums of money $x_0 > 0$ and $y_1 > y_0 > 0$ and a probability p. Then construct the sequence $x_1, ..., x_i, ...$ inductively so that the respondent satisfies the indifferences

$$(x_i, p; y_0) \sim (x_{i-1}, p; y_1).$$

83

If an RDU representation exists, then for all i for which x_i is constructed

$$U(x_i) - U(x_{i-1}) = [U(y_1) - U(y_0)] \left(\frac{1 - W(p)}{W(p)} \right).$$

Because the right side is independent of the x's, all of these utility differences are equal. The units of U may be chosen so that the common difference is 1.

Fennema and van Assen (1999) showed in several experiments that such functions can, indeed, be estimated in this fashion. The median function for gains was concave, and for losses, convex. These authors did not attempt to check how well any of the parametric forms fit their estimates.

3.4   Weighting Functions

Finding the form for weights has proved to be somewhat problematic, in part because a great many of the experimental analyses have looked only at group, not individual, data and in part because until very recently there has been no satisfactory theory for the form of the weighting function over probabilities. In addition, until very recently, most theories and experiments concerning weights were centered on the property of separability (Def. 3.1.3), which is entailed by RDU but is, of course, significantly weaker than that.

Observe that if one has the simplest first-order case of probabilistic reduction of compound gambles

$$((x, p; e), q; e) \sim (x, pq; e) \tag{3.20}$$

and separability, then the following variant of the Cauchy equation holds:

$$W(pq) = W(p)W(q), \quad p, q \in [0, 1].$$

By the monotonicity of event inclusion, Eq. (2.13), W is strictly increasing, and so by a well-known result of functional equations (Aczél, 1961/1966, Theorem 3, p. 48)

$$W(p) = p^\gamma, \quad \gamma > 0. \tag{3.21}$$

To the extent we think that the Allais paradox (§ 2.3.1) casts doubt upon the first-order reduction of compound gambles, Eq. (3.20), then that argument for the power function weight, Eq. (3.21), is undercut. This conclusion is confirmed by a series of fairly elaborate empirical studies in the accounting literature: Hirsch (1978), Lewis and Bell (1985), Moser, Birnberg, and Do (1994), and Snowball and Brown (1979). They varied the values of p and q so that one had either $pq = p'q'$ or $pq > p'q'$. With the equality holding, the question asked was: Did the respondents—somewhat advanced students—perceive the alternatives to be equivalent? And for the inequality holding: Did their choices agree with the direction of the joint probabilities? Both hypotheses were found wanting.

In addition, Keller (1985b) tested Eq. (3.20) and some more complex reduction indifferences using four different methods of depicting the gambles: written description, tubes containing 100 labeled balls, a matrix with column widths in proportion to probability and color-coded entries, and bar graphs. These presentations are illustrated in Fig. 3.4.

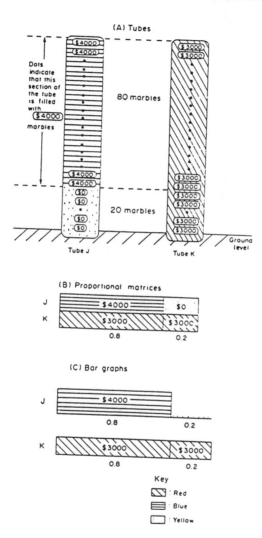

Figure 3.4. Three displays used in evaluating the impact of displays on the evaluations of lotteries. This is Fig. 1 of Keller (1985b). Reprinted from *OMEGA. The International Journal of Management Science, 13,* L. R. Keller, "Testing of the 'reduction of compound alternatives' principle, Volume 13, 349-358, Copyright 1985, with permission from Elsevier Science.

She found that the mode of presentation matters, with the tube one being the best and achieving a low of about 22% violations. Of course, this is still a substantial number. Moskowitz (1974) found a word presentation less prone to inconsistency than a tree or matrix one.

Kahneman and Tversky (1979), in their problems 7 and 8, used 66 respondents and found that 86% preferred ($3,000, 0.90; 0)$ to ($6,000, 0.45; 0$), whereas when the probabilities are reduced by a common factor of 0.0022 to 0.002 and 0.001, respectively, the direction changed with 73% preferring the latter gamble. Generalizing, if for $x > y > 0$, $(x, p; 0) \prec (y, q; 0)$ and $(x, rp; 0) \succ (y, rq; 0)$ for sufficiently small r, then we see that

$$\frac{W(p)}{W(q)} < \frac{U(y)}{U(x)} < \frac{W(rp)}{W(rq)}.$$

They call this property of the weights *subproportionality*. This, if true, completely rejects the power function form of Eq. (3.21). Note, however, that such group data may well be misleading. There is no report of how many of the respondents actually did make both judgments.

Other proposed mathematical forms for the weights are largely suggested by data analyses and, except for Prelec (1998) and Luce (1999) discussed in Section 3.4.3, do not have a behavioral property, similar in character to the first-order reduction of compound gambles, from which the form follows. As empirical background, the next two subsections report some empirical evidence about weights based on individual analyses. The results are quite consistently inconsistent: Depending upon how they have been estimated using binary gambles, one of two general patterns arises.

3.4.1   Data suggesting W is concave, linear, or convex

Edwards (1955) is an early study in which weights were explicitly estimated using a measurement procedure. He invoked a somewhat elaborate method to estimate U that is based upon the assumption that if g is a gamble and if $g^{(N)}$ denotes N repetitions of g—the joint receipt of N copies of g—then $U(g^{(N)}) = NU(g)$. This was neither defended nor did he appear to recognize that it virtually forces $U(x) = \alpha x$, $\alpha > 0$. The estimates obtained in this way were, indeed, nearly linear. Because, even in 1955, the money range involved, $\pm\$5.50$, was small, linearity probably is a good approximation to any plausible utility function.

If a is a fixed amount of money, p a fixed probability, and $x(a, p)$ is the lottery equivalent outcome (LEO, § 1.2.2.4) defined by $a \sim (x(a,p), p; 0)$, then because $U(x) = \alpha x$, $\alpha > 0$, separability yields

$$W(p) = \frac{U(a)}{U[x(a,p)]} = \frac{a}{x(a,p)}.$$

Five undergraduates served as respondents. The "chance device" was a pinball machine with 8 cells into which a ball could roll. In reality, the destination of the balls was predetermined by concealed electromagnets so that respondents ended up with a pay rate of $1 per hour. Seven probability levels from $\frac{1}{8}$ to $\frac{7}{8}$ were each paired with a certain gain and a certain loss of $0.55.

The $x(a, p)$ values were estimated by having each respondent choose between a and

$(x, p; 0)$, adjusting x in a way somewhat similar to the PEST procedure—except that in 1955 it was done by an experimenter recording responses and then writing in values on prepared cards that contained the remaining information for the next presentation of that lottery. Figure 3.5 shows the estimated probability functions. A reasonable summary is that for gains $W^+(p) > p$ and for losses $W^-(p) \simeq p$. The data are approximately consistent with the power function form, but they are clearly inconsistent with SEU because for gains, at least, the weights are not additive.

The paper also included additional data and attempted to fit them by models such as subjective weighted money. I do not go into this here

Returning to a study described in Section 3.1.3.2, Tversky (1967a) carried out overall fits to the data sets by estimating weighting functions under two assumptions:

Model 1: Additive weights as in SEU, i.e., Eq. (3.12)
Model 2: Risky $U =$ riskless U.

Model 1 was estimated from data sets I and II combined; Model 2 was estimated from the same data sets but using for the utility the nearly proportional riskless utilities from data set III. The resulting estimated weighting functions are shown in Fig. 3.6. These models, and two others to be described, were evaluated in terms of average absolute deviations using the data set IV. What he called the SEU model involved using the Model 1 weights and the riskless values obtained from Set III inserted into the separability formula. Expected value was, of course, just that. The overall results are that Models 1 and 2 do appreciably better—by a factor of more than 3 in average absolute deviations—than either SEU or EV, and Model 2 is better than Model 1 for 8 of the 11 respondents (but only one difference was significant at the 0.05 level). The estimated weights of Model 2 agree with those of Edwards (1955) in that with only one minor exception $W(p) > p$.

Currim and Sarin (1989), in the study mentioned earlier, estimated the weights for 9 probability values on three assumptions: separability; that the value function V, estimated from difference judgments, is exponential; and that $U = V$. They report that, at the 0.05 level of statistical significance, the hypothesis that $W^+ = W^-$ is rejected for 22 of their 37 respondents. Although they do not report the actual values for W^+ and W^-, they report general features of the shape. For example, for gains 10 respondents were convex, 5 concave, and 22 linear, whereas for losses 25 were convex, 1 concave, and 11 linear. This is surely different from the previously described data in which the majority of cases for gains were concave. One major difference of the Currim and Sarin study from others was their use of a difference method to determine the value function of money, which was then assumed that to be the same as the utility function that appears in such theories of risky behavior as prospect theory (in my terms, the assumption $U = V$). Without some empirically based argument, we have no particular reason to believe that this is valid. For further discussion of this concern, see Section 4.3.3.

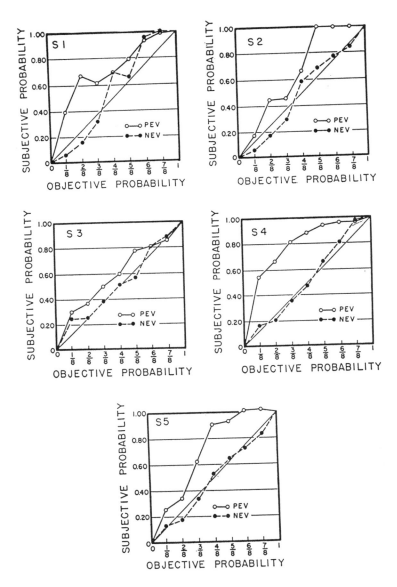

Figure 3.5. Weighting functions estimated for five respondents using direct measurement methods. The notation PEV means gains and NEV losses. This is Fig. 2 of Edwards (1955), which now is in the public domain.

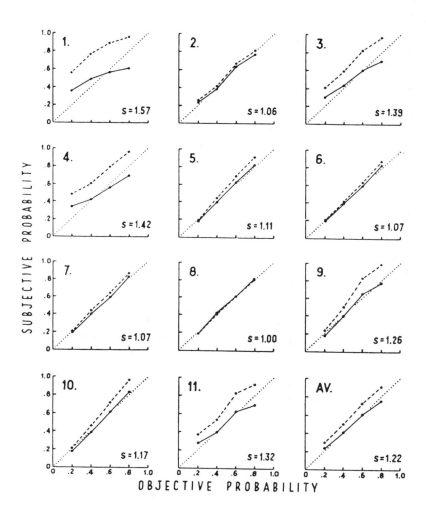

Figure 3.6. Estimated weighting functions. The solid line is for weights estimated from Model 1 in which the weights are additive as in SEU. The dotted line is for weights estimated from Model 2 for which riskless and risky utility functions are treated as identical. This is Fig. 10 of Tversky (1967a). Copyright 1967 by Academic Press, Orlando, FL 32887-6777. Permission granted.

3.4.2   Data suggesting W is inverse S-shaped

Three methods were used in the studies to be discussed in this subsection. The first involved indirect arguments, which I believe are in various ways suspect. The second involved estimating W from certainty equivalents on the assumption that U is a power function in the RDU representation, which, as will be argued later, appears to be too restrictive because the exponential seems more appropriate for some respondents (§4.4.6). The fact that both power and exponential functions fit the data about equally well suggests that there may be little change in conclusions in going from the power to the exponential study. But we do not know that for sure. The third involves two different nonparametric uses of RDU.

3.4.2.1   Separability and indirect arguments: The oldest study, Preston and Baratta (1948), used estimated CEs. The factorial design involved lotteries $(x, p; e)$ where $x = 5,$ $50, 100, 500, 1,000$ points and $p = 0.01, 0.05, 0.25, 0.50, 0.75, 0.95, 0.99$. The respondents were 5 pairs of undergraduate males, 5 of undergraduate females, 5 of (presumably male) faculty, and 5 sets of four undergraduates of unspecified sex. Each group participated in an auction in which each player was endowed with 4,000 points—about 67% of the total expected value of the 42 lotteries. Each lottery was played after the bidding. The highest bidder received the outcome of the lottery less the amount bid. The total remaining points at the end were converted in some fashion to a choice of candy, cigarettes, or cigars (then all socially acceptable prizes). The data were, of course, the bids.

They found something that has been repeatedly found: The bids for $p < 0.25$ were greater than the expected value $EV = xp$ and those for $p \geq 0.25$ were less than EV. The plot of $\frac{B(x,p;e)}{x}$ versus p is shown in Fig. 3.7. As one can see from the label on the ordinate, the authors interpreted this ratio as the subjective "probability" or weight. That makes sense if one assumes a separable representation in which utility is proportional to the points. The resulting weight can be described qualitatively as being an inverse S-shape in the sense that it crosses the main diagonal with a slope less than 1, i.e., there exists some value p_0 such that

$$W(p) \begin{cases} > p, & p < p_0 \\ = p_0, & p = p_0 \\ < p, & p > p_0 \end{cases} \tag{3.22}$$

and the curve is initially concave and at some point p_1 it become convex for all higher values of p. Clearly, these data, if interpreted as an estimate of the weights, are inconsistent with the data discussed in the previous subsection.

The next study of a similar character was Tversky (1967b), which was mentioned in connection with tests of separability. On the assumption that U is a power function, the estimates were very close to $W(p) = p$ and, to the degree that deviations occurred, they appeared to be inverse S-shaped.

Research on this issue continued in Kahneman and Tversky (1979). They based their conclusion that W is inverse S-shaped on two points:

(1) For small p, respondents are, on average, *risk seeking* for gains, i.e., $(x, p; 0) \succ xp = EV(x, p; 0)$, and *risk averse* for losses, i.e., $(-x, p; 0) \prec -xp$. From other group data, they

also concluded that on average U is concave for gains and convex for losses, which implies $U(xp) > pU(x)$ and $U(-xp) < pU(-x)$. Thus, assuming separability we have for gains

$$
\begin{aligned}
(x, p; 0) \succ xp \quad &\Longleftrightarrow \quad U(x, p; 0) > U(xp) \\
&\Longleftrightarrow \quad U(x)W^+(p) > U(xp) > pU(x) \\
&\Longleftrightarrow \quad W^+(p) > p.
\end{aligned}
\tag{3.23}
$$

A similar argument for losses leads to

$$
W^-(p) > p.
\tag{3.24}
$$

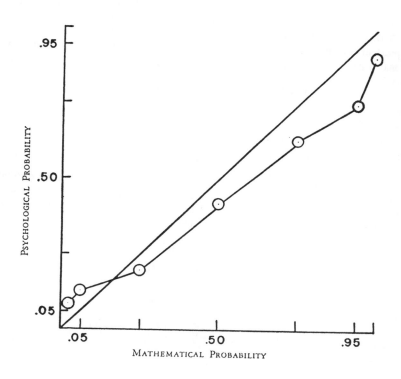

Figure 3.7. Mean weighting functions estimated by Preston and Baratta (1948, Fig. 1). From *American Journal of Psychology.* Copyright 1948 by the Board of Trustees of the University of Illinois. Used with the permission of the University of Illinois Press.

This part of the argument is fine, but by itself says nothing about the inequality reversing for large p.

(2) They also claim that

$$W^i(p) + W^i(1 - p) < W^i(p + 1 - p) = W^i(1) = 1, \qquad (3.25)$$

which is called *superadditivity* of weights. Before taking up the argument in support of Eq. (3.25), let me note that Eqs. (3.23) and (3.24) for small p together with Eq. (3.25) do indeed imply the S-shape of Eq. (3.22) for both gains and losses. So the key question is the accuracy of Eq. (3.25).

First, the earlier data analyses of Edwards (1955) and Tversky (1967a), based largely on the assumption (which was tested in the case of Tversky) of separability, definitely support subadditivity, not superadditivity, for gains; for losses the data appear to be approximately additive. These earlier studies appear to have been ignored; I do not know why.

Second, Kahneman and Tversky (1979, p. 281-282) made the following argument. Suppose the utility of a trinary lottery with one consequence 0 and $x > 0 > y$ is given by

$$U(x, p; y, q; 0, 1 - p - q) = U(x)W(p) + U(y)W(q). \qquad (3.26)$$

This formula was one of two proposed to be applied after a certain amount of preliminary "editing" was carried out (§ 4.4.1). And suppose that the Allais paradox occurs, for which ample data exist. They show that Eq. (3.25) follows.

So, the question comes down to the validity of Eq. (3.26). As they were aware (p. 283), it has two odd features. One is that if

$$(x, p; x, q; 0, 1 - p - q) \sim (x, p + q; 0, 1 - p - q),$$

which is a special case of what I call *coalescing* (see Section 5.3.2), then

$$W(p + q) = W(p) + W(q),$$

which is the Cauchy equation. Under monotonicity, it is well known to imply $W(p) = p$. The other is that dominance may be violated. They accept both that coalescing[12] occurs (others question it, as we shall see) and that dominated alternatives should not be chosen, and they bypass the problem with Eq. (3.26) by assuming that all possible coalescing and removal of dominated options are carried out in an editing phase prior to applying the theory.

Ultimately, however, other anomalies of Eq. (3.26) led them to change that form to a signed version of it in a revision and extension of prospect theory they called *cumulative prospect theory* (Tversky & Kahneman, 1992) and which others call a rank- and sign-dependent utility (RSDU) representation (see Chapters 4, 6, and 7). However, the above argument for superadditivity does not go through for the replacement formula.

3.4.2.2   RDU and U a power function: A wholly different approach to the inverse S-shaped function was used by Tversky and Kahneman (1992). They report CE data for se-

---

12   They spoke of "combining."

lected lotteries[13] obtained from 25 student respondents during three one-hour sessions for which each respondent received a total payment of $25. The method used to determine CEs involved a series of presentations on a computer screen of a lottery along with a display of a descending series of seven certain consequences equally spaced on a logarithm money scale between the maximum and minimum consequence of the lottery. Each respondent expressed a preference between each certain amount on the screen and the lottery. At the next presentation of that lottery, separated by many trials involving other gambles, a second series of seven certain consequences were equally spaced from 25% above the lowest value that had previously been accepted and 25% below the highest value rejected. The CE was taken to be the mid point of the separation between acceptance and rejection. Data were obtained for the following values of $p = 0.01, 0.05, 0.10, 0.25, 0.50, 0.75, 0.90, 0.95, 0.99$ selectively paired with three gain and loss values for x.

An analysis of individual respondents showed a highly consistent pattern of risk-seeking and risk-averse behavior. This is summarized in Table 3.1:

Table 3.1. Percent of choices exhibiting risk attitudes

	Gains		Losses	
	$p \le 0.1$	$p \ge 0.5$	$p \le 0.1$	$p \ge 0.5$
Risk-seeking	78	10	20	87
Risk-neutral	12	2	0	7
Risk-averse	10	88	80	6

Assuming that U is concave for gains and convex for losses, all one can derive from these data is that $W^i(p) > p$ for $p \le 0.1$. Nothing follows for $p \ge 0.5$, contrary to what the authors seem to suggest.

Suppose, however, that one makes the stronger assumption that U is a power function, Eq. (3.18), with exponents β and β' for gains and losses, respectively. Then the following conclusions can be drawn. Observe that because $U(x, p; 0) = U(x)W(p) = x^\beta W(p)$ and $U(xp) = x^\beta p^\beta$,

$$(x, p; 0) \succ (\prec) \; xp \quad \Longleftrightarrow \quad W^+(p) > (<) \, p^\beta$$
$$(-x, p; 0) \succ (\prec) \; -xp \quad \Longleftrightarrow \quad W^-(p) < (>) \, p^{\beta'}$$

So, from Table 3.1 and these properties, Table 3.2 shows how W^i relates to various powers of p.

Two things are noteworthy. First, this line of argument says absolutely nothing about whether or not the two Ws cross the 45° line. Second, it clearly rejects the hypothesis that

---

[13]   They spoke of "prospects."

$W^i(p)$, $i = +, -$, is a power function, and so also rejects the simple first-order reduction of compound gambles, Eq. (3.20).

Table 3.2 Relation of $W^i(p)$ to p

	$p \leq 0.1$	$p \geq 0.5$
Gains	$> p^\beta$	$< p^\beta$
Losses	$> p^{\beta'}$	$< p^{\beta'}$

Continuing for the moment to assume a power function for utility and assuming separability, Eq. (3.6), we see that

$$W^+(p) = \left(\frac{CE(x, p; 0)}{x} \right)^\beta$$

$$W^-(p) = \left(\frac{-CE(-x, p; 0)}{x} \right)^{\beta'}.$$

Plots of these dollar $\frac{CE}{x}$ ratios show a decidedly inverse S-shaped form, as shown in Figs. 3.8 and 3.9. Given estimates of α and β that are somewhat less than 1—they estimate both to be about 0.88—the shape is not greatly altered.[14] At the time, many felt that these data make the strongest case for the inverse S-shaped form.

Nevertheless, substantial reasons for doubt about the form of W^i remained. First, as is easily demonstrated by examples, averages of power functions with a variety of exponents on either side of 1 can exhibit an inverse S-shaped form (Luce, 1996a, p. 306). Second, within the context of cumulative prospect theory, a strong reason exists to think that an important form for U is exponential (§ 4.4.6). But with the exponential U, the expression for W is a function of $CE(x, p)$ and of x separately and not of their ratio. So we do not know how badly W may have been misestimated. Third, the method Tversky and Kahneman used to estimate CEs may have been, in fact, closer to $JCEs$ than to $CCEs$ despite the surface appearance of its being a choice method. It is entirely possible that, when confronted with the list of certain amounts to compare with the gamble, some respondents first establish a JCE, which is used to decide which certain amounts to choose over the lottery. If so, an unwanted bias may have entered that then affects the estimate of W. And finally, once again there are the subadditive findings of Edwards (1955) and Tversky (1967a).

Recall (§ 3.1.3.2) that the Birnbaum et al. (1992) study using $JCEs$ found utility to be proportional to money and so were able to plot the estimated weighting function as $\frac{JCE(x, p; 0)}{x}$. Between $p = 0.05$ and $p = 0.95$ the plot was nearly linear with a slope less than 1 and quite

---

[14]   The purported plots of $W^i(p)$ versus p in Tversky and Kahneman (1992) are actually of $\frac{CE(x, p; 0)}{x}$. The correct plot is shown in Tversky and Fox (1995).

symmetrical. So, it is consistent with the inverse S-form. No systematic attempt was made to try transformations of JCE to see if the fit could be improved.

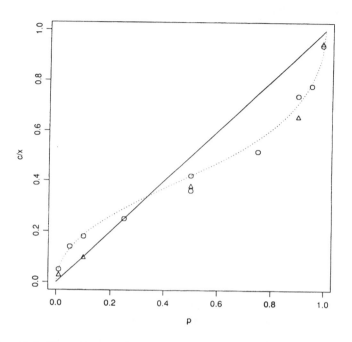

Figure 3.8. The median ratio $CE(x, p; 0)/x$ versus p for $x > 0$. A power of this is an estimate of W^+ if separability holds and U is a power function. This is Fig. 1 of Tversky and Kahneman (1992). Copyright 1992 by Kluwer Academic Publishers, Norwell, MA 02061. Reprinted by permission.

3.4.2.3   RDU and a nonparametric method:

In response to these considerations, Abdellaoui (1999), Bleichrodt and Pinto (1998b), and Wu and Gonzalez (1996, 1998) have independently devised ordinal analyses that do not require estimating any parameters. The first two analyses are described in this subsection, but because the argument underlying the third rests upon the form of rank dependence for gambles with three consequences, it is postponed to Section 5.5.

Abdellaoui (1999) and Bleichrodt and Pinto (1998b) adapted a nonparametric method proposed by Wakker and Deneffe (1996), which was described in Section 3.3.2, to estimate both the utility and weighting functions of 40 respondents. Recall that this rests on assuming binary RDU and estimating a standard sequence, $\{x_i\}$. Abdellaoui selected the largest x_i, say x_n, and had the respondent adjust p_i so that the following indifference holds:

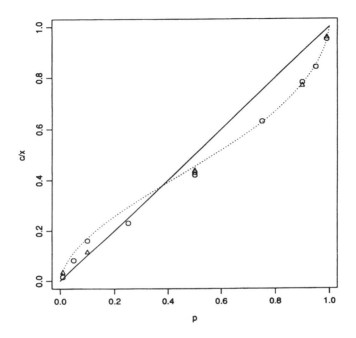

Figure 3.9. The median ratio $CE(x, p; 0)/x$ versus p for $x < 0$. A power of this is an estimate of W^- if separability holds and U is a power function. This is Fig. 2 of Tversky and Kahneman (1992). Copyright 1992 by Kluwer Academic Publishers, Norwell, MA 02061. Reprinted by permission.

$$(x_n, p_i; x_0) \sim (x_i, 1; x_0) \sim x_i, \quad i = 1, ..., n - 1.$$

Applying RDU , we see that

$$W(p_i) = \frac{U(x_i) - U(x_0)}{U(x_n) - U(x_0)} = \frac{i}{n}.$$

A potential weakness of this method is the accumulation of error. If, for example, the estimate of x_1 overestimates the true value, then on average this error is likely to propagate through the entire sequence of estimates. One can, however, make various checks about the severity of the problem. For example if one estimates probabilities r and s such that

$$x_3 \sim (x_6, r; x_0) \text{ and } x_3 \sim (x_4, s; x_2),$$

then from the RDU model one has $W(r) = \frac{1}{2} = W(s)$, yielding the qualitative prediction

96

that $r = s$. This was done (see below).

The 40 respondents were a mix of undergraduate and graduate students in economics. They received payments from a randomly selected gains gamble. The utility function was determined using $x_0 = FF1000$, $y_0 = 0$, $y_1 = FF500$, and $p = \frac{2}{3}$. Both Abdellaoui and Bleichrodt and Pinto took to heart the earlier work suggesting that judged indifference values might be biased from choice-based ones, and so they used a choice procedure somewhat like PEST, but different. Beginning with $\Delta = FF5000$, Abdellaoui selected the midpoint of the interval $[x_0, x_0 + \Delta] = [FF1000, FF6000]$, i.e., $FF3500$. The respondent was offered the choice between

$$(FF3500, \frac{2}{3}; 0) \text{ and } (FF1000, \frac{2}{3}; 500).$$

If the former were chosen, then the next midpoint was that of

$$[FF1000, FF3,500],$$

namely $FF2250$, and the next choice was between

$$(FF2250, \frac{2}{3}; 0) \text{ and the reference lottery } (FF1000, \frac{2}{3}; FF500).$$

If, however, the reference gamble were chosen, then the second midpoint was that of

$$[FF3500, FF6000]$$

and so the choice was between $(FF4750, \frac{2}{3}; 0)$ and the reference lottery. This process continued through 6 iterations, yielding an estimate for x_1 whose accuracy is approximately $\frac{\Delta}{2^6} = FF78.125$.

In like manner, the probabilities were approximated via a comparable series of choices.

The consistency of the results was checked using x_3, and no problem surfaced for gains but the results for losses were not consistent. So it is by no means clear that cumulative error was not a problem.

The shapes of utility and weighting functions were determined qualitatively in terms of successive spacings of the x_i's and p_j's. For example, if $x_3 - x_2 > x_2 - x_1$, that piece of the utility function is concave. The results are shown in Tables 3.3 and 3.4. Once again the predominant pattern is for U to be concave for gains and convex for losses, but this is far from exclusively true. For W^+, the dominant pattern was inverse S, but with a substantial number of linear or convex ($W^+(p) < p$ for all $p \in]0, 1[$) ones as well. The relation between the shape of U and W^+ appears to be that the dominant patterns go together in the sense that for gains 40% have both concave U and inverse S for W^+. For losses, slightly less than 40% are convex U and inverse S for W^-.

Note the substantial number—30%—of convex weighting functions found in this study. These respondents have $W(p) < p$ for all p. Somewhat similar findings were reported by Allais (1988) (1 of 4 respondents) and Lattimore, Baker, and Witte (1992) (5 of 114 respondents).

Table 3.3. Pattern of shapes of U and W for gains found by Abdellaoui (1999, personal communication June 19, 1998).

Utility	Weight Inverse S	Convex	Linear	Totals
Concave	16	4	1	21
Linear	3	4	0	7
Convex	4	1	3	8
Mixed	1	3	0	4
Totals	24	12	4	40

Table 3.4. Pattern of shapes of U and W for losses found by Abdellaoui (1999).

Utility	Weight Inverse S	Convex	Linear	Totals
Concave	3	3	2	8
Linear	5	4	1	10
Convex	15	2	0	17
Mixed	2	3	0	5
Totals	25	12	3	40

The Bleichrodt and Pinto (1998b) study is similar in general character to that of Abdellaoui (1999) except that it uses states of health as consequences. They found that the modal respondent is concave in years of survival and has inverse S-shaped weighting functions.

3.4.2.4   RDU and a second nonparametric method: Gonzalez and Wu (1999) took the following approach. Assume that the binary RDU representation holds, and collect certainty equivalents for many gambles with the same consequences and probabilities appearing in several different gambles. Specifically, they had 8 consequences from which they formed 15 lottery frames $(x, p; y)$. These were crossed with 11 probabilities generating 165 gambles. Nine of these gambles were chosen at random and repeated thus providing a crude estimate of the noise level of the experiment. The certainty equivalents of all 165+9 were determined using the method of Tversky and Kahneman (1992) in which a list of sure amounts spanning the interval $[y, x]$ was used to get a first cut on the location of the CE. Then a second list spanning the range of that cut was presented to get a more refined estimate of the CE, which was taken to the midpoint of the second cut.

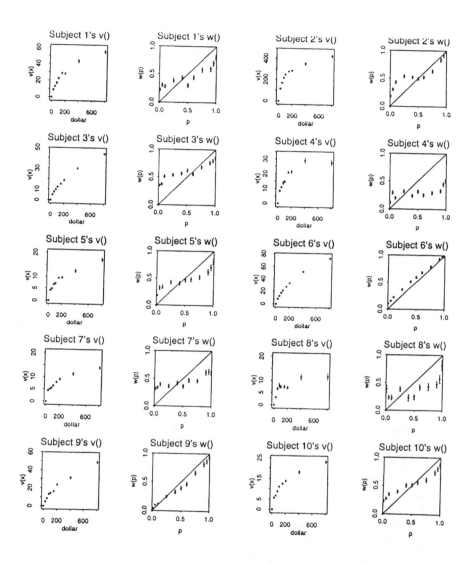

Figure 3.10. For each of 10 respondents, the estimated utilities and weights using the alternating least-squares iterative method described in the text. This is Fig. 6 of Gonzalez and Wu (1999). Copyright 1999 by Academic Press. Reproduced by permission.

The data analysis involved assuming binary RDU and using an alternating least squares algorithm (De Leeuw, Young, & Takane, 1976) as follows. Starting with the 165 CEs as initial estimates of $U(CE)$, the authors found the least squares solution for the 8 unknown $U(x)$ and 11 unknown $W(p)$. There is, of course, some error in the fit. Then, accepting these values as correct, calculate a new estimate of the $U(x, p; y)$. Nothing guaranteed monotonicity. This was imposed by using a linear interpolation technique. Accepting these new estimates of $U(x, p; y)$, then redo the least squares fit finding new estimates of $U(x)$ and $W(p)$. Keep iterating until the error change drops to 10^{-4}. The median number of iterations was 6. The empirical estimates of the utilities and weights for each of 10 respondents are shown in Fig. 3.10. Clearly, all of the utility functions are concave and, except perhaps for respondent 6, all of the weights are inverse S-shaped. Respondent 6 may be inverse S with the crossing point over 0.9, much higher than for other respondents' data, or may simply be concave.

3.4.2.5   Conclusion: From all of the data in this section, I think one must conclude that the inverse S-shaped pattern for weights describes a majority of people. I remain perplexed about why so much of the earlier data failed to detect this.

3.4.3   Prelec's unifying theory for W(p)[15]

3.4.3.1   Background: Until recently, there were three major suggested parametric forms for the weighting function plus some data-based analysis of properties that the function should exhibit:

- One is the power function, which is based on the simple first-order reduction of compound gambles, Eq. (3.20),

$$W(p) = p^\gamma, \tag{3.27}$$

where $\gamma > 0$, which is widely rejected by data and certainly does not encompass the inverse S-shaped form for individuals.

- A second is an ad hoc, i.e., not behaviorally axiomatized, asymmetric form:

$$W(p) = \frac{\eta p^\gamma}{\eta p^\gamma + (1-p)^\gamma}, \quad \gamma, \eta > 0, \tag{3.28}$$

which generalizes the symmetric form $\eta = 1$ proposed by Karmarkar (1978, 1979). This has been used by Birnbaum and McIntosh (1996), Gonzalez and Wu (1999), Kilka and Weber (1998), Lattimore, Baker, and Witte (1992), and Tversky and Fox (1995). It has an interesting odds formulation:

$$\frac{W(p)}{1 - W(p)} = \eta \left(\frac{p}{1-p}\right)^\gamma, \quad \gamma, \eta > 0. \tag{3.29}$$

---

[15] I will state everything for gains, but the formulas hold equally well for losses with, however, different parameters which I denote by the same symbol with a prime. This is less cumbersome than using either γ^+, γ^- or $\gamma(+), \gamma(-)$.

So far, no one has arrived at a qualitative axiomatization of this form.

- A third is a different modification of Karmarkar's form due to Tversky and Kahneman (1992),

$$W(p) = \frac{p^\gamma}{[p^\gamma + (1 - p^\gamma)]^{1/\gamma}}, \quad \eta > 0. \tag{3.30}$$

Also, no qualitative axiomatization of this has been provided.

- And fourth is a series of qualitative properties of weights over probabilities and/or events designed to capture some of the features of the data and corresponding qualitative preference patterns (Tversky & Wakker, 1995). Lopes (1987, 1990) coined some phrases for the several possible shapes:

    (i)   *Security-minded* for $W(p) < p$ and convex.
    (ii)   *Potential-minded* for $W(p) > p$ and concave.
    (iii)   *Cautiously hopeful* for inverse S-shaped.

Although the second and third ad hoc formulas both fit the empirical estimates reasonably well, they have the decided drawback that they do not include the power function as a special case. Thus, should one find a (possibly trained) respondent who actually reduces simple compound lotteries according to Eq. (3.20), his or her data could not be fit by these ad hoc proposals. Something more theoretically based is needed.

3.4.3.2   Prelec's formula: Fortunately, Prelec (1998) has overcome these limitations by providing an axiomatic theory leading to three possible expressions, of which, in my opinion, the most important is:

$$W(p) = \exp\left[-\gamma(-\ln p)^\eta\right], \quad \gamma, \eta > 0. \tag{3.31}$$

Note that this family of functions includes the family of power functions [$\eta = 1$].

For $\eta < 1$ the function closely approximates both Eq. (3.28) and the Tversky and Kahneman function Eq. (3.30) which in turn closely approximates the inverse-S data. The reason for this can be found by asking whether for $\eta \neq 1$ there exists a fixed point p_0, i.e., $W(p_0) = p_0$, and if so examining the slope of W at p_0. The fixed point condition yields immediately that

$$(-\ln p_0)^{\eta-1} = \frac{1}{\gamma} \iff p_0 = \exp\left[-\gamma^{\frac{1}{1-\eta}}\right]. \tag{3.32}$$

Taking the derivative of Eq. (3.31) and evaluating it at p_0 yields

$$\left.\frac{dW(p)}{dp}\right|_{p=p_0} = \eta.$$

Thus, for $\eta \neq 1$ there exists a single fixed point and the slope at that point is less than 1 if and only if $\eta < 1$, in which case the curve is inverse S-shaped.

3.4.3.3   Linear regressions: It is worth noting that there is an easy way to estimate α and γ for Eq. (3.31) once one has estimates of $W(p)$ for several values of p. Take the logarithm of Eq. (3.31) twice and we see

$$\ln[-\ln W(p)] = \ln \gamma + \eta \ln(-\ln p). \tag{3.33}$$

Thus, a simple linear regression gives both estimates of γ and η, and so of p_0, and a measure of the quality of the fit.

Likewise, taking the logarithm of Eq. (3.29), which is the odds version of Eq. (3.28), we have

$$\ln\left(\frac{1-W}{W}\right) = \ln \eta + \gamma \ln\left(\frac{1-p}{p}\right). \tag{3.34}$$

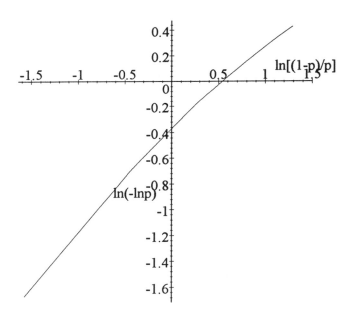

Figure 3.11. Plot of $\ln(-\ln p)$ versus $\ln \frac{1-p}{p}$ with p varying from 0.01 to 0.99.

So an empirical attempt to decide between the two forms amounts to deciding which of these two linear regressions provides a better fit to the data. Although the two terms $\ln(-\ln p)$ and $\ln\left(\frac{1-p}{p}\right)$ are distinct functions of p, their relation to one another, shown in Fig. 3.11, is fairly close to linear. Such an approximately linear relation suggests that the two models are very similar in their predictions. And, indeed, Gonzalez and Wu (1999) were not able to discriminate them using their data. The common fit is shown in Fig. 3.12.

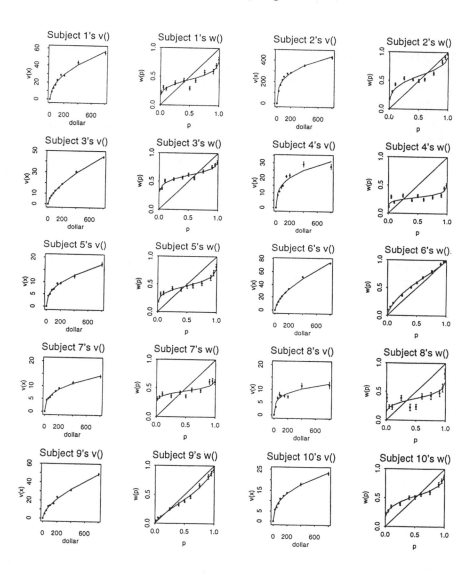

Figure 3.12. The data of Fig. 3.10 fit by the essentially equivalent Eqs. (3.28) and (3.31). This is Fig. 8 of Gonzalez and Wu (1999). Copyright 1999 by Academic Press. Reproduced by permission.

3.4.3.4   Compound and reduction invariance: We turn next to the question of what qualitative properties underlie the Prelec weighting function. It should be understood from the outset that what is derived here concerns only weights for the case of binary gambles. The issue about the form of the weights for gambles with more than two consequences is, as we shall see in Chapter 5, somewhat complex.

The key qualitative property underling Eq. (3.31) derives from the simple fact that for any real number $\lambda > 0$

$$
\begin{aligned}
W(p^\lambda) &= \exp\left[-\gamma(-\ln p^\lambda)^\eta\right] \\
&= \exp\left[-\gamma\lambda^\alpha(-\ln p)^\eta\right] \\
&= \left(\exp\left[-\gamma(-\ln p)^\alpha\right]\right)^{\lambda^\eta} \\
&= W(p)^{\lambda^\eta}.
\end{aligned}
\tag{3.35}
$$

Throughout the rest of this section (and the corresponding proofs) the focus will be on binary gambles of the form $(x, p; e)$. It is convenient to abbreviate this notation to (x, p). Assuming separability and Eq. (3.35), the following property must hold:

Definition 3.4.1.   (Prelec, 1998) Let N be a natural number. Then, N-*compound invariance* is said to hold if and only if for some $x, y, x', y' \in C^+$ and $p, q, r, s \in]0, 1[$, with $q < p, r < s$, if

$$
(x, p) \sim (y, q), \ (x, r) \sim (y, s), \text{ and } (x', p^N) \sim (y', q^N) \tag{3.36}
$$

implies

$$
(x', r^N) \sim (y', s^N). \tag{3.37}
$$

Assuming a separable representation, N-compound invariance follows for each integer N because by Eqs. (3.35) and (3.36),

$$
(x, p) \sim (y, q) \quad \text{and} \quad (x, r) \sim (y, s) \iff \frac{U(x)}{U(y)} = \frac{W(q)}{W(p)} = \frac{W(s)}{W(r)},
$$

and

$$
(x', p^N) \sim (y', q^N) \iff \frac{U(x')}{U(y')} = \frac{W(q^N)}{W(p^N)}.
$$

So,

$$
\frac{U(x')}{U(y')} = \left[\frac{W(q)}{W(p)}\right]^{N^\eta} = \left[\frac{W(s)}{W(r)}\right]^{N^\eta} = \frac{W(s^N)}{W(r^N)},
$$

which implies $(x', r^N) \sim (y', s^N)$, which is the conclusion of compound invariance.

Prelec formulated compound invariance as applying to all $x, y, x', y' \in C$ without distinguishing gains and losses. In a 1996 draft of his paper, he did make the distinction, and I believe that it is useful to maintain it. Later, I state explicitly the impact of including mixed consequences.

If one is willing to work with second-order compound gambles, then a simpler formulation is possible.

Definition 3.4.2.   (Luce, 1999) Let N be a natural number. Then, N-*reduction invariance* is said to hold if and only if, for $x \in C^+$ and $p, q, r \in]0, 1[$,

$$((x, p), q) \sim (x, r) \tag{3.38}$$

implies

$$((x, p^N), q^N) \sim (x, r^N) \tag{3.39}$$

Note that the simple first-order reduction of compound gambles, Eq. (3.20), for which $r = pq$ implies this condition, but not conversely.

Reduction invariance clearly is somewhat simpler to check empirically than is compound invariance. For the former, one fixes x, p, and q and then estimates r in Eq. (3.38) and then for arbitrary choices of N checks Eq. (3.39). For the latter, one fixes, say, x, x', y, p, r in Eq. (3.36) and then estimates q, s, y' and uses these to test Eq. (3.37) for arbitrary choices of N. Note that the estimate of y' depends not only on the fixed values but the prior estimate of q. The potential for trouble from errors of estimates is considerable.

Theorem 3.4.1.   *Suppose that a structure of lotteries in* $\mathbb{B}_2^+$ *satisfies: transitivity, Eq. (2.4); consequence monotonicity, Eq. (2.10); for any* $p, q \in]0, 1[$ *there exist* $x, y \in C^i$ *such that* $(x, p) \sim (y, q)$; *and the structure has a separable representation* UW^+ *with* $W^+ : [0, 1] \xrightarrow{onto} [0, 1]$ *and is strictly increasing in* p. *Then, the following statements are equivalent:*

(i) W^+ *satisfies Eq. (3.31).*

(ii) N-*Compound invariance holds for* $N = 2, 3$.

(iii) N-*Reduction invariance holds for* $N = 2, 3$.

The equivalence of (i) and (ii) when N-compound invariance holds for all integers N is established in Prelec (1998), and that of (i) and (iii) as well as of (ii) restricted to $N = 2, 3$ is in Luce (1999).

This certainly is an interesting theoretical result. However, unlike some other conditions we have encountered, I do not see a normative argument for either compound invariance or even the simpler reduction invariance. They may have to be defended empirically. However, I also offer a meta-theoretical argument below for using Prelec's function, Eq. (3.31).

3.4.3.5   Subproportionality: Prelec (1998) also examined other related properties. I focus on only one, which Kahneman and Tversky (1979) called "subproportionality" and for which there is substantial empirical support (see the beginning of § 3.4). It says that reducing two probabilities by a common factor has a differential impact on the decision maker. Specifically, the smaller one becomes more significant.

Definition 3.4.3.   Suppose $p, q, r \in]0, 1[$, $p \neq q$, and for some $x, y \in C$, $(x, p) \sim (y, q)$. Then, *subproportionality* is said to hold if and only if for $y > x > 0$, $(y, rq) \succ (x, rp)$, and for $0 > x > y$, $(y, rq) \prec (x, rp)$.

Assuming separability and continuing to omit the superscript +, it is easy to see that subproportionality is equivalent to saying that $\frac{W(rp)}{W(p)}$ decreases as p increases. Assuming Eq. (3.31) holds, we show now that subproportionality is equivalent to $\eta < 1$. Because Eq. (3.31) is clearly differentiable, the condition is equivalent to $\frac{\partial}{\partial p}\left(\frac{W(rp)}{Wp)}\right) < 0$. A routine calculation shows that

$$\frac{\partial}{\partial p}\left(\frac{W(rp)}{W(p)}\right) = \left(\frac{W(rp)}{W(p)}\right)\left(r\frac{W'(rp)}{W(rp)} - \frac{W'(p)}{W(p)}\right).$$

And another routine calculation on Eq. (3.31) shows that

$$\frac{W'(p)}{W(p)} = \frac{\gamma\eta(-\ln p)^{\eta-1}}{p},$$

hence

$$\frac{\partial}{\partial p}\left(\frac{W(rp)}{W(p)}\right) = \frac{W(rp)}{W(p)}\frac{\gamma\eta}{p}\left[(-\ln p - \ln r)^{\eta-1} - (-\ln p)^{\eta-1}\right].$$

Because $-\ln p - \ln r > -\ln p$, it follows that this is negative if and only if $\alpha < 1$. We incorporate this fact into the following result of Prelec (1998), to which I refer the reader for a proof.

Theorem 3.4.2.   *Suppose the conditions and conclusions of Theorem 3.4.1 hold. Then*

(i)   *Subproportionality (Def. 3.4.3) holds if and only if $\eta < 1$ in Eq. (3.31).*

(ii)   *Suppose the conditions of Theorem 3.4.1 are satisfied for any binary mixture of gains and losses, then $\eta' = \eta$, where η' is the corresponding parameter for losses.*

3.4.3.6 φ-Compound and φ-reduction invariance: Because it is difficult to see an a priori argument for focusing just on the transformations $p \to p^N$, the purpose of the next development is to consider other, more general families of transformations. The general idea is to consider invariance under the transformations $p \to \varphi(p, \lambda)$ for some family $\varphi(\cdot, \lambda)$, where λ is a parameter. We see that Prelec's case of either compound or reduction invariance is the family of transformations $p \to \varphi(p, N) = p^N$.

Some constraints need to be imposed so that the family is structured in a coherent fashion and is not just an unrelated set of transformations, one for each λ. One such formulation is:

Definition 3.4.4.   Suppose that for an open interval I of real numbers $\varphi :]0, 1[\times I \xrightarrow{onto}]0, 1[$ is a function that is strictly increasing in the first variable and strictly monotonic in the second. The family φ is said to be *permutable* if and only if for all $p \in]0, 1[$ and $\lambda, \mu \in I$,

$$\varphi[\varphi(p, \lambda), \mu] = \varphi[\varphi(p, \mu), \lambda], \tag{3.40}$$

and it is said to be *transitive* if and only if for each $p, q \in]0, 1[$ there is some $\lambda \in I$ such that

$$\varphi(p, \lambda) = q. \tag{3.41}$$

According to Aczél (1961/1966, p. 273), Eqs. (3.40) and (3.41) imply that there exist a strictly decreasing function $f :]0, 1[\xrightarrow{onto}]0, \infty[$ and a strictly monotonic function $g : I \xrightarrow{onto}]0, \infty[$ such that

$$\varphi(p, \lambda) = f^{-1}[f(p)g(\lambda)]. \tag{3.42}$$

The reason g is onto $]0, \infty[$ is that Eq. (3.41) requires that for any p, q there is a λ such that $g(\lambda) = \frac{f(p)}{f(q)}$, which can be any positive real.

Definition 3.4.5.   Suppose φ is a permutable and transitive family of functions. Then, *φ-compound invariance* is said to hold if and only if for consequences $x, y, x', y' \in C^+$, and probabilities $p, q, r, s \in]0, 1[$, with $q < p, r < s$, if

$$(x, p) \sim (y, q), \ (x, r) \sim (y, s), \ \text{and} \ (x', \varphi(p, \lambda)) \sim (y', \varphi(q, \lambda)) \tag{3.43}$$

then

$$(x', \varphi(r, \lambda)) \sim (y', \varphi(s, \lambda)). \tag{3.44}$$

Definition 3.4.6.   Suppose φ is a permutable and transitive family of functions. Then, *φ-reduction invariance* is said to hold if and only if for all $x \in C^i, p \in]0, 1[$, and $\lambda \in I$,

$$((x, p), q) \sim (x, r) \iff ((x, \varphi(p, \lambda)), \varphi(q, \lambda)) \sim (x, \varphi(r, \lambda)). \tag{3.45}$$

Although setting $\varphi(p, N) = p^N$ in these definitions yields Defs. (3.4.1) and (3.4.2), the fact is that Eq. (3.41) does not hold for these discrete transformations. Indeed, part of the proof of Theorem 3.4.1 is to show that from either compound or reduction invariance that compound or reduction invariance, respectively, holds for p^λ, where λ is any positive real number.

Theorem 3.4.3.   *Suppose that a structure of binary lotteries is weakly ordered in preference, has a separable representation UW^+ with $W^+ : [0, 1] \xrightarrow{onto} [0, 1]$, where W^+ is strictly increasing in p, and φ is a regular function with the representation of Eq. (3.42). Then the following three statements are equivalent:*

(i)   *φ-Compound invariance (Def. 3.4.5) holds.*

(ii)   *φ-Reduction invariance (Def. 3.4.6) holds.*

(iii)   *There are positive constants γ^*, η^* such that for f in Eq. (3.42),*

$$W^+(p) = \exp[-\gamma^* f(p)^{\eta^*}], \quad \gamma^*, \eta^* > 0. \tag{3.46}$$

For a proof, which is quite similar to Theorem 3.4.1, see Luce (1999). Observe that $f(p) = -\ln p$ is Prelec's case.

3.4.3.7   An argument for Prelec's function: The last result seems an overabundance of riches. For some examples of f and some choices for γ^* and η^*, it is easy to show that W can exhibit the variation needed to mimic the data, namely, either W wholly above the diagonal $W(p) = p$, or wholly below it, or crossing it from above to below. Specifically, Luce (1999) provided for $f(p) = \frac{1-p}{p}$ numerical examples of all three behaviors. Thus, it probably will be difficult to decide empirically on which function f to use.

However, there is a principled argument for selecting $f(p) = -\ln p$. As a meta-theoretical principle, I hold that any descriptive theory of decision making should always include as special cases any locally rational theory for the same topic. Here the relevant special case is weights that are powers, Eq. (3.27), that follows from separability and the accounting indifference

$$((x,p),q) \sim (x, pq),$$

which is a simple, first-order reduction of compound gambles.

Proposition 3.4.4.   *Of the families of weights W given by Eq. (3.46), the only one that includes the power functions of Eq.(3.27) is*

$$f(p)^{\eta^*} = -\frac{\gamma}{\gamma^*} \ln p,$$

i.e., the Prelec function, Eq. (3.31).

The proof of this is trivial: Simply equate Eq. (3.46) to $p^{\beta(i)}$ and take logarithms.

3.4.3.8   Conclusions about weights: Prelec's function Eq. (3.31) and its generalization Eq. (3.46) are too recent to have received much serious attention, so I think it is safe to conclude that, despite considerable progress in the past decade, the issues about the exact forms for W remain unsettled. On the positive side, however, is how well the Prelec weighting function fits the data of Gonzalez and Wu (1999) (Figs. 3.9 and 3.10). Also, in Section 7.3.5 we will encounter individual data analyses of 144 respondents, and in a large percentage of cases the Prelec function fits better than any of the suggested alternatives. This apparent success in fitting the Prelec function invites careful empirical examination of the underlying behavioral property of N-reduction invariance.

It is important that work continue in an attempt to clarify the form of weighting functions more fully. In particular, little has been done concerning the form of W for events not having known probabilities. One would like conditions stated in terms of uncertain alternatives that can play the role of compound and reduction invariance. Presumably a suitable theory would show how to construct a probability measure over events in terms of which the weights would be of the form of Eq. (3.46). The trick will be to see how to do this without simply passing through SEU on the way.

3.5   Separability and Rank-Dependent Additivity (RDA)

3.5.1   Strategy of finding conditions underlying RDU

Our next goal is to understand how the RDU representation onto an interval comes about from behavioral properties that we can observe. The approach involves examining some combinations of four major features implied by the RDU representation: separability, RDA, event commutativity, and that the same utility function over consequences is used for all experiments—it does not vary from experiment to experiment.

I divide the problem as follows. First, we examine in this section the behavioral conditions that give rise to separability and RDA. Event commutativity is, of course, itself behavioral. Then in Section 3.6 separability and another necessary condition not yet encountered, called "gains partition," are used with suitable structural conditions to arrive at RDU. This is, perhaps, the most efficient approach; however, it suffers from the fact that gains partition, while necessary, is not particularly intuitive.

A second approach—historically earlier and in one variant or another more thoroughly explored—assumes separability, RDA, and event commutativity. These conditions, along with suitable structural conditions, are shown in Section 3.7 to give rise to a new representation of which RDU is a special case. Two different necessary properties are added that limit this representation to RDU. In Section 4.4.5 a third, and to my mind more intuitive, property based on joint receipt is introduced that does the same thing. I include both approaches because some theorists feel it is better to limit the number of primitives, if at all possible.

3.5.2   Separability

A qualitative basis for a separable representation of the structure $\langle C^+ \times \mathcal{E}_K, \succsim \rangle$ is obviously based on the conjoint measurement axioms C1-C6 of Appendix D. First, we note that the Archimedean and restricted solvability axioms (C4 and C6) are not really empirically testable. Archimedeaness appears to make a behavioral claim, but because it is a second-order axiom in the sense of logic, it cannot be rejected directly using any finite data set. On the other hand, as is discussed both in Krantz et al. (1971, § 9.1) and Luce et al. (1990, §21.7), the Archimedean axiom is usually, although not always, fairly innocent.

The axioms of essentialness (C5) and restricted solvability impose restrictions on the domain, not on the behavior as such. Essentialness insures that there is something to study. What is far less clear is the power and implications of the kind of continuity built into restricted solvability. It entails not only the high density of consequences, achieved for example by including money gains among them, but also a high density of event-experiment pairs. That is no limitation for the canonical experiment K in which, by definition, any weight can be realized (Def. 3.1.2). It may be less likely to hold when we deal with uncertain events, some of which do not seem to be densely nested. For example, a decision based on whether or not two states are at war does not seem to have a continuum of degrees. Basically experiment K must be one for which the outcomes form a continuum. In experimental practice, this probably means something for which probabilities are known. The mathematical nature of real-world uncertainty is far from clear.

Of the other axioms, transitivity (C1) has been discussed. So this leaves us with order independence (C2) and the Thomsen condition (C3). I take them up in that order.

3.5.2.1   Order independence in the consequence-event trade-off: It is not difficult to see that when order independence is limited to the gambling context, it amounts to the following two conditions: For $x, y \in \mathcal{B}_0^+$, $C \in \mathcal{E}_\mathbf{E}$, and $D \in \mathcal{E}_\mathbf{F}$,

$$(x, C; e, E \backslash C) \succsim (x, D; e, F \backslash D) \iff (y, C; e, E \backslash C) \succsim (y, D; e, F \backslash D), \qquad (3.47)$$

and for $B, C \in \mathcal{E}_\mathbf{E} \backslash \{\emptyset\}$

$$(x, B; e, E \backslash B) \succsim (y, B; e, E \backslash B) \iff (x, C; e, E \backslash C) \succsim (y, C; e, E \backslash C). \qquad (3.48)$$

Note that Eq. (3.47) was discussed and assumed in Chapter 2, where it was labeled event independence, Eq. (2.14). Equation (3.48) follows from consequence monotonicity, Eq. (2.10), since each term is equivalent to $x \succsim y$. So there is nothing new here.

3.5.2.2   Event commutativity and the Thomsen condition: A key property underlying such additivity is the Thomsen condition (Appendix D, Axiom C3). One can, of course, simply write the Thomsen condition for gambles,

$$\text{if } (x, B; e) \sim (z, D; e) \text{ and } (z, C; e) \sim (y, B; e), \text{ then } (x, C; e) \sim (y, D; e), \qquad (3.49)$$

but this does not seem very compelling intuitively. Fortunately, there is a far better way to deal with it, which is given by the following fairly simple proposition (Luce, 1996a):

Proposition 3.5.1.   *Suppose the binary gambles $\mathbb{C}^+ = \langle \mathcal{B}_1^+ \times \mathcal{E}_\mathbf{E}, \succsim \rangle$ satisfy transitivity, Eq. (2.4), consequence monotonicity, Eq. (2.9), and status-quo event commutativity, Eq. (3.9). Then the Thomsen condition holds.*

Proof. Suppose $B, C, D \subseteq E$, $(x, B; e) \sim (z, D; e)$ and $(z, C; e) \sim (y, B; e)$. Using the assumptions of status-quo event commutativity and consequence monotonicity freely:

$$
\begin{aligned}
((x, C; e), B; e) &\sim ((x, B; e), C; e) \\
&\sim ((z, D; e), C; e) \\
&\sim ((z, C; e), D; e) \\
&\sim ((y, B; e), D; e) \\
&\sim ((y, D; e), B; e),
\end{aligned}
$$

whence by transitivity and consequence monotonicity, $(x, C; e) \sim (y, D; e)$, which establishes the Thomsen condition. ∎

3.5.2.3   The existence of a separable representation: Assuming an elementary rational structure $\langle \mathcal{B}_2^+, \succsim \rangle$, which we recall means that $\succsim$ is a weak order for which idempotence, certainty, complementarity, consequence monotonicity, and order independence of events hold

(Def. 2.5.1), we introduce two structural conditions and another necessary one.

Definition 3.5.1.   An ordering $\succsim$ is *nontrivial* if and only if there exist elements x, y in the domain such that $x \succ y$. It is *dense* if and only if whenever $x \succ y$, there exists z in the domain such that $x \succ z \succ y$.

Definition 3.5.2.   *Restricted solvability* is said to hold if and only if, for all $x, x^*, x_*, y, z \in \mathcal{B}_1^+$ and $C, C^*, C_*, D \in \mathcal{E}_{\mathbf{E}}$,

$$\text{if } (x^*, C; y) \;\succsim\; (z, D; y) \succsim (x_*, C; y),$$
$$\text{then there exists } x \;\in\; \mathcal{B}_0 \text{ such that } (x, C; y) \sim (z, D; y), \tag{3.50}$$
$$\text{if } (x, C^*; y) \;\succsim\; (z, D; y) \succsim (x, C_*; y),$$
$$\text{then there exists } C \;\in\; \mathcal{E} \text{ such that } (x, C; y) \sim (z, D; y). \tag{3.51}$$

Proposition 3.5.2.   *Suppose $\langle \mathcal{B}_2, \succsim \rangle$ is an elementary rational structure that satisfies restricted solvability. Then for any gamble $(x, C; y) \in \mathcal{B}_2$, $x \succsim y$, there exists $CE(x, C; y) \in \mathcal{B}_0$ such that*

$$CE(x, C; y) \sim (x, C; y). \tag{3.52}$$

The elementary proof is left as an exercise. Observe that this result means that any compound gamble is indifferent to a first-order one.

Definition 3.5.3.   Sequences $\{x_i\}$ from $\mathcal{B}_1^+$ and $\{E_j\}$ from $\mathcal{E}$ are said to form *standard sequences* if and only if

$$(x_i, C; z) \sim (x_{i+1}, D; z), \quad C \succ_{\mathcal{E}} D$$
$$(x, C_i; z) \sim (y, C_{i+1}; z), \quad x \succ y, \tag{3.53}$$

where $\succ_{\mathcal{E}}$ denotes the ordering induced by the assumption of order independence of events.

Definition 3.5.4.   The structure is said to be *Archimedean* if and only if every bounded standard sequence is finite.

Let $\mathcal{B}_1^{+*} = \{g : g = (x, C; e) \text{ where } x \in \mathcal{B}_0^+\}$.

Theorem 3.5.3.   *Suppose an elementary rational structure of binary gambles satisfies:*

(i)   *The orderings over $\mathcal{B}_2^+$ and $\mathcal{E}_{\mathbf{E}}$ are both dense and nontrivial.*
(ii)   *Restricted solvability holds.*
(iii)   *Archimedeanness holds.*
(iv)   *Status-quo event commutativity holds.*

Then there exists a set I that is dense in an interval $[0, a[$, $a \succ 0$, such that $U^* : \mathcal{B}_1^{+*} \xrightarrow{onto} I$, and a set J that is dense in $[0, 1]$ such that $W^* : \mathcal{E}_{\mathbf{E}} \xrightarrow{onto} J$ and $U^* W^*$ is a separable order preserving representation of $\langle \mathcal{B}_1^{+*}, \succsim \rangle$.

Proof. By Proposition 3.5.1 the Thomsen condition holds for the trade-off structure of consequences and events, which with Assumptions (i)-(iii) yields a multiplicative representa-

111

tion (Appendix D) of what may be called the proper part of $\mathcal{B}_1^{+*}$, excluding those $x \sim e$ and those $C \sim_E \emptyset$. The extension of that representation to include these elements is obvious. The density of the order insures that the image is dense in an interval $[0, a[$, where $a = \sup\{u(g) : g \in \mathcal{B}_2^*\}$. ■

Corollary. *Suppose that monotonicity of event inclusion is satisfied. Then, for events* $C, D,$

$$C \supseteq D \Rightarrow W(C) \geq W(D).$$

The proof is trivial.

3.5.3   The qualitative consequence-consequence trade-off

Our next concern is what gives rise to the RDA form. Obviously, it is very close to additive conjoint measurement (Appendix D) over the consequences, but that theory does not have the restriction $x \succsim y$. So those assumptions must be modified to take this restriction into account. The problem of carrying out this generalization is somewhat more subtle than it first seems, and Wakker (1993) notes some incorrect arguments in the literature. Indeed, he was the first to carry one out successfully. Wakker (1991a) does so in an algebraic context like ours, and Wakker (1993) does so in a topological context. Although the topological approach tends to be congenial to economists, Wakker (1988) provides reasons for preferring the algebraic one.

For the binary case, the major change introduced into the axioms of additive conjoint measurement is to restrict attention to the rank-ordered subdomain of the Cartesian product of C^+ with itself (not two sets), i.e., to

$$\mathcal{A}^+ = \{(x, y) : x, y \in C^+, x \succsim y\}.$$

Then one can proceed in either of two ways. The simplest to use for binary gambles is the Thomsen condition, i.e., for a fixed event C, whose notation is suppressed, and consequence pairs in $\mathcal{A}^+$:

If $(x, u) \sim (v, w)$ and $(v, y) \sim (z, u)$, then $(x, y) \sim (z, w)$,

or its generalization to $\succsim$, called double cancellation, again restricted to the domain $\mathcal{A}^+$. The other approach, a generalization of which is needed when one extends the representation to gambles with three or more consequences, is a somewhat more complex condition having three antecedent inequalities:

Definition 3.5.5.   *Triple cancellation* is said to hold if and only if, for each pair of elements lying in $\mathcal{A}^+$, where the fixed event C is again suppressed in the notation,

$$(x, r) \succsim (y, s), (t, s) \succsim (w, r), \text{ and } (w, u) \succsim (t, v) \Longrightarrow (x, u) \succsim (y, v). \tag{3.54}$$

Note that triple cancellation is also a necessary property of RDA.

In the theory of webs and with no order restriction on the variables, RC3 with $\succsim$ replaced by $\sim$ is known as the Reidemeister condition.

Theorem 3.5.4.   *Suppose a rank-ordered conjoint structure on $\mathcal{A}^+$ satisfies either the axioms of additive conjoint measurement (§ 9.4) or those with the Thomsen condition replaced by triple cancellation, RC3, and it has neither a maximal nor a minimal element. Then it has a numerical, additive, order-preserving representation $\phi_1 + \phi_2$. If $\phi_1(e) = \phi_2(e) = 0$, then the representation is unique up to multiplication by positive numbers.*

A proof of Theorem 3.5.4 is given by Wakker (1991a).

The empirical question is the degree to which the properties underlying Eq. (3.8) hold. In Chapter 2 we discussed the evidence for transitivity and for order independence, which in the gambling context is easily seen to be equivalent to consequence monotonicity. Neither the Thomsen condition nor triple cancellation, RC3, is particularly intuitive in the context of gambles, and I do not know of more natural properties that imply either—something comparable to the way status-quo event commutativity implies the Thomsen condition in the consequence-event trade-off. To my knowledge, no one has empirically studied either in this context in a direct fashion. However, the method of Wakker and Deneffe (1996) does provide an indirect test of these properties. As noted earlier, the Archimedean condition cannot be studied directly although sometimes it can be indirectly. The essentialness condition is certainly satisfied if we have more than one valued object. The restricted solvability condition is, in essence, a continuity requirement, which if, as we have assumed, money is included in the consequence set seems to be a decent idealization.

3.6   First Axiomatization of RDU

3.6.1   Gains partition

Only one new necessary property is needed at this point to get the RDU representation.

Definition 3.6.1.   *Gains partition* is said to hold provided that there exists a 1-1 function $M : \mathcal{E} \xrightarrow{onto} \mathcal{E}$ that inverts the order $\succsim_{\mathcal{E}}$ and for $x, x', y, y' \in B_0^+$, with $x \succsim y$, $x' \succsim y'$, and $C, C' \in \mathcal{E}$,

$$(x, C; e) \sim (x', C'; e) \quad \text{and} \quad (y, M(C); e) \sim (y', M(C'); e),$$

imply

$$(x, C; y) \sim (x', C'; y').$$

Although this assumption may seem at first almost tautological, it is not. For example, in Chapter 7 we will study certain models for binary gambles of mixed gains and losses for which the obvious extension of gains partition to mixed gains and losses fails. The correct expression for some of the models requires one to know not just the products $U(g)W^+(E)$ and $U(h)W^-(\overline{E})$, which are involved in the gains partition, but also the separate values of $U(g)$, $U(h)$, $W^+(E)$, and $W^-(\overline{E})$.

3.6.2   Separability, event commutativity, and gains partition

The first major result on the RDU representation that I shall state is due to Marley and Luce (1999).

Theorem 3.6.1.   *The following statements hold for the structure* $\langle \mathcal{B}_2^+, \succsim \rangle$:

(i)   *If* $\langle \mathcal{B}_2^+, \succsim \rangle$ *has a RDU representation, then it is an Archimedean elementary rational structure (Def. 2.5.1) that satisfies event commutativity and gains partition.*

(ii) $\langle \mathcal{B}_2^+, \succsim \rangle$ *has a RDU representation that is dense in intervals (Def. 3.2.3) if and only if* $\langle \mathcal{B}_2^+, \succsim \rangle$ *is an elementary rational structure that has a separable representation dense in intervals (Theorem 3.5.3) and satisfies both event commutativity and gains partition.*

Corollary.   *Under the conditions of the Theorem 3.6.1, W and M are related by:*

$$W[M(C)] = 1 - W(C).$$

Note that in the special case of $M(C) = \overline{C}$, we have $W(C) + W(\overline{C}) = 1$, which means that rank dependence is not exhibited.

A proof of the theorem as stated can be found in Marley and Luce (1999). A proof of the slightly simpler case where the separable representation U^*W^* has U^* onto an interval and W^* onto $[0, 1]$ is provided in Section 3.9.3.

Because separability and event commutativity have been carefully examined experimentally and appear to hold, the issue of the existence of a binary RDU representation devolves to the correctness of gains partition. At present, no data exist about the latter. Studying it promises to be difficult in that one really has to construct the function M empirically.

3.7   Second Axiomatization of RDU

Our second approach arises from dissatisfaction with the behavioral property of gains partition, which does not seem very natural. Let us instead consider three properties we know are implied by RDU: separability, RDA, and event commutativity. The question to be considered is whether these three properties are, in essence, sufficient. Luce (1998) claimed to prove RDU using just the first two, but A. A. J. Marley pointed out an error in the proof that makes it valid only for RIU where the rank order of the consequences is immaterial. The most prominent example of that case is, of course, subjective expected utility, SEU. When that error is eliminated, as it is in this section, it leads to a more complex functional equation and representation which then requires something additional to reduce it to RDU. We explore this equation first.

3.7.1   Functional equation from RDA and separability

Assume the axioms underlying RDA, Eq. (3.8), hold. Then setting $y = e$, we see that $U(x, C; e) = U_{1,\text{E}}(x, C)$ represents $\succsim$ restricted to gambles of the form $(x, C; e, E \backslash C)$. And

114

assuming the axioms that underlie separability (Theorem 3.5.3), we know that a representation of the form $U^*(x)W_{\mathbf{E}}^*(C)$ also preserves $\succsim$ on $(x, C; e, E\backslash C)$. We assume that all of the representations are onto intervals.

Because these representations preserve the same order, there exists a strictly increasing function Φ with $\Phi(0) = 0$ such that $U_{1,\mathbf{E}} = \Phi[U^*(x)W_{\mathbf{E}}^*(C)]$, so we have axiomatically justified a representation of the form: For $x \succsim y \succsim e$,

$$U(x, C; y) = \Phi[U^*(x)W_{\mathbf{E}}^*(C)] + U_{2,\mathbf{E}}(y, C).$$

Further, setting $C = E$ and $y = e$ and using both the certainty axiom and $U_{2,\mathbf{E}}(e, C) = 0$ yields

$$U(x) = \Phi[U^*(x)]. \tag{3.55}$$

Our assumptions also justify the existence of certainty equivalents $CE(x, C; y) \sim (x, C; y)$, where CE is a mapping from binary gambles into sure consequences (Proposition 3.5.2). So we can write

$$U(x, C; y) = \Phi\left(U^*[CE(x, C; y]\right) = \Phi[U^*(x, C; y)].$$

Thus, the axiomatically justified representation is

$$\Phi[U^*(x, C; y)] = \Phi[U^*(x)W_{\mathbf{E}}^*(C)] + U_{2,\mathbf{E}}(y, C), \tag{3.56}$$

where $\Phi(0) = 0$, $U_{2,\mathbf{E}}(e, C) = 0$, and Φ is strictly increasing.[16]

Setting $C = E$ and using the certainty axiom in Eq. (3.56), we get

$$\Phi[U^*(x)] = \Phi[U^*(x)] + U_{2,\mathbf{E}}(y, E),$$

and so $U_{2,\mathbf{E}}(y, E) = 0$. Similarly, assuming the idempotence axiom and setting $y = x$ in Eq. (3.56), we get

$$\Phi[U^*(y)] - \Phi[U^*(y)W_{\mathbf{E}}^*(C)] = U_{2,\mathbf{E}}(y, C).$$

Substituting this back into Eq. (3.56) yields: for $x \succsim y \succsim e$,

$$\Phi[U^*(x, C; y)] = \Phi[U^*(x)W_{\mathbf{E}}^*(C)] + \Phi[U^*(y)] - \Phi[U^*(y)W_{\mathbf{E}}^*(C)], \tag{3.57}$$

i.e.,

$$U^*(x, C; y) = \Phi^{-1}\left(\Phi[U^*(x)W_{\mathbf{E}}^*(C)] + \Phi[U^*(y)] - \Phi[U^*(y)W_{\mathbf{E}}^*(C)]\right). \tag{3.58}$$

---

[16]   Because of the rank dependence constraint that $x \succsim y$, we cannot make a similar argument to show that the $U_{2,\mathbf{E}}$ term has a separable representation. Luce (1998) claimed otherwise, but I was in error. My "proof," which is based on a functional equation solved by Aczél, Ger, and Járai (1999), only justifies a binary rank independent representation. Luce and Marley (1999a) explored the unaxiomatized assumption that $U_{2,\mathbf{E}}(y, C)$ is a function of a separable representation $U^{**}(x)W_{\mathbf{E}}^{**}(C)$. This led to a related, but more complex functional equation, which was solved by Aczél, Maksa, Ng, and Páles, (1999), and that has same solutions as those given below for the general axiomatized case.

Since Eq. (3.58) gives a general representation of $U^*(x, C; y, E \backslash C)$ in terms of $\Phi, U^*(x), U^*(y)$, and $W_E^*(C)$, further conditions are required to restrict the form of Φ.

3.7.2   Ratio rank-dependent utility from separability, RDA, and event commutativity

Although we used status-quo event commutativity in arriving at the representation in Eq. (3.58), we did not assume the more general property of *event commutativity* (Def. 3.1.5), namely, that for each $x, y, x \succsim y \succsim e$, and events C, D,

$$((x, C; y), D; y) \sim ((x, D; y), C; y).$$

So we now impose event commutativity, which has empirical support (§ 3.2.6)

Theorem 3.7.1.   *Assume that Eq. (3.57) and event commutativity both hold, and that* Φ *is twice differentiable. Suppose the image of* U^* *is the real interval* $[0, k[$ *and* W_E^* *is onto* $[0, 1]$. *Letting* $U = (U^*)^q$ *and* $W = (W_E^*)^q$, *then for some real constant* $\mu > -\frac{1}{k^q}$,

$$U(x, C; y) = \begin{cases} \frac{U(x)W(C) + U(y)[1 - W(C)] + \mu U(x) U(y) W(C)}{1 + \mu U(y) W(C)}, & \text{if } x \succ y \succsim e \\ U(x), & \text{if } x \sim y \succsim e \\ \frac{U(x)[1 - W(\overline{C})] + U(y) W(\overline{C}) + \mu U(x) U(y) W(\overline{C})}{1 + \mu U(x) W(\overline{C})} & \text{if } y \succ x \succsim e \end{cases} . \quad (3.59)$$

The case of $\mu = 0$ *is the standard rank-dependent utility model.*

The unit of μ is the inverse of the unit of U.

I anticipate that eventually the same results will be shown under only the assumption that Φ is strictly increasing, rather than that plus the fairly strong, non-axiomatized condition that it is also second-order differentiable.

So far as I know, this representation with $\mu \neq 0$ was first derived by Luce and Marley (1999a). This new representation of Eq. (3.59) is called *ratio rank-dependent utility*, RRDU, because of its being the ratio of two polynomials. (Such functions are called "rational" in the mathematical literature, but to speak of "rational rank-dependent utility" invites a confusion with the more familiar meaning of "rational" in the present area.)

Although event commutativity, Eq. (3.9), is used in deriving the RRDU representation, it is well to verify that it is satisfied, which is certainly not immediately obvious. I leave it to the reader to verify the following:

Proposition 3.7.2.   *RRDU satisfies event commutativity.*

3.7.3   Two conditions that force RRDU to be RDU

Luce and Marley explored three conditions that reduce RRDU to be RDU. Two of these involve only properties of $\succsim$, and so we report them here. The other involving joint receipt will be presented in Section 4.4.5. Of the three, the last one is the best tested and the most natural.

The first of these, called *comonotonic consistency*, was suggested and used in deriving the RDU representation by Wakker (1989), and Wakker and Tversky (1993). Consider any eight gambles of the form

$$
\begin{aligned}
\mathbf{f} &= (f, C; y), & \mathbf{f'} &= (f', C; y)\\
\mathbf{g} &= (g, C; z), & \mathbf{g'} &= (g', C; z)\\
\mathbf{h} &= (f, C; u), & \mathbf{h'} &= (f', C; u)\\
\mathbf{k} &= (g, C; v), & \mathbf{k'} &= (g', C; v),
\end{aligned}
$$

where in each the first consequence $\succsim$ the second consequence. Then *comonotonic trade-off consistency* holds if and only if not both $\{\mathbf{f} \succsim \mathbf{g}, \mathbf{f'} \prec \mathbf{g'}\}$ and $\{\mathbf{h} \prec \mathbf{k}, \mathbf{h'} \succsim \mathbf{k'}\}$.

Although with proper discussion of the assumptions, one can see that the property makes sense, no one seems to have an "of course" reaction to this postulate. It is routine to verify the RDU implies the property, and with RRDU Luce and Marley (1999a) show that it forces $\mu = 0$. The idea of the proof is simply to construct a counter example to comonotonic consistency when $\mu \neq 0$.

A second behavioral property is called *rank-dependent bisymmetry* because of its close mathematical relation to the well-studied property of bisymmetry (Aczél, 1961/1966) Consider consequences $x \succsim y \succsim s \succsim e$, $x \succsim r \succsim s \succsim e$ and events C, C', and C'' which are the event C on three independent replications of the underlying experiment $\mathbf{E}$. Then

$$
((x, C'; y), C; (r, C''; s)) \sim ((x, C'; r), C; (y, C''; s)). \tag{3.60}
$$

Note that the assumed conditions on the consequences, plus consequence monotonicity and complementarity, imply

$$
(x, C'; y) \succsim (r, C''; s), \quad (x, C'; r) \succsim (y, C''; s).
$$

Rank-dependent bisymmetry seems locally rational in the sense that the two sides of Eq. (3.60) have the same bottom line; however, there does not seem to be any a priori reason for imposing rank dependence. Nakamura (1990, 1992) used this property in his treatment of RDU.

Theorem 3.7.3.   *Suppose the RRDU representation of Eq. (3.59) holds with the image of U a real interval $[0, B[$ and W onto $[0, 1]$. Then the following are equivalent:*

(i) $\mu = 0$, i.e., RDU.

(ii)   *Comonotonic trade-off consistency holds.*

(iii)   *Rank-dependent bisymmetry holds.*

For a proof of this result, which involves counter examples of comonotonic consistency and rank-dependent bisymmetry when $\mu \neq 0$, see Luce and Marley (1999a). A better result is given as Theorem 4.4.3.

3.8   Summary

The chapter had four main topics. The first, covered in Sections 3.1-3.2, stated the binary rank-dependent utility representation of Eq. (3.4) and an explored three of its major necessary properties. They are: the consequence-event trade-off of separability, Eq. (3.6); the consequence-consequence trade-off of rank-dependent additivity, Eq. (3.7); and the behavioral property of event commutativity, Eq. (3.9). In each case empirical studies focussed on these properties were explored. The overall conclusion is that they are sustained for a substantial majority of respondents.

The special case of RDU called subjective expected utility (SEU) was then examined. The relation between binary SEU and binary RDU simply is whether the weighting function is additive or not over disjoint events. If it is, then SEU obtains and for compound binary gambles all accounting indifferences hold. If the weights are not additive, then SEU fails and no accounting indifferences hold that are (nontrivially) more complex than event commutativity.

The next part, Section 3.3, was devoted to possible constraints on the utility function of RDU. The power and exponential functions seem to do about equally well and both do better than linear or logarithmic functions. Theoretical reasons will be provided in Section 4.4.6 about why we might expect power and exponential function utility functions. Fitting either power or exponential functions to the data on an individual basis gives rise to all four combinations of concavity/convexity crossed with gains/losses, with concave gains and convex losses being the modal combination. There are some data not fit by such simple forms, and we will return to why this might be so in Section 4.5.3.

Third, Section 3.4 took up the form of the weighting function. Here the situation seems somewhat less settled. Most of the studies agree that the weights for gains differ from those for losses. But they do not agree about the form of the function. Many of the earlier studies suggested that they are either concave, convex, or linear. But one of the earlier studies and all of the later ones suggest an inverse S-shaped form that intersects the 45° line at some p_0 and that is initially concave and then becomes convex. There is some variation in estimates of p_0, but it mostly appears to be about 0.3. However, all but three of these studies involved group data, which, if there are substantial individual differences as there seem to be, could be misleading. A mixed population of concave and convex weighting functions will, when treated as average data, automatically look inverse S-shaped. The most recent nonparametric studies seem to show that a majority of, but far from all, individuals do exhibit the inverse S-form.

The discussion of weights ended on an upbeat note in that a nice axiomatic development has just appeared leading to a family for W that includes both the power and inverse S-shapes. Neither its main qualitative properties, compound or reduction invariance, nor the family itself, Eq. (3.31), have received a great deal of empirical study.

The fourth and final part, Sections 3.5-3.7, was concerned with behavioral conditions that give rise to RDU. It began by working out axiomatizations of separability and RDA. For the former, the important Thomsen condition was shown to follow from status-quo event commutativity. With those properties understood behaviorally, we turned to two ways to get RDU.

Under the assumptions of Chapter 2 and of the existence of a canonical experiment, the first showed that binary RDU for all gains (or all losses) is equivalent to separability, event commutativity, and gains partition (Def. 3.6.1). No empirical study of gains partition has yet been carried out, and it does not seem to be an especially intuitively natural condition. The second, more intuitive theory showed that separability, RDA, and event commutativity result in a representation, called ratio rank-dependent utility, that is more general than RDU (Theorem 3.7.1). To reduce it to RDU something else must added. Either of two necessary conditions do the job: comonotonic consistency or rank-dependent bisymmetry. But neither is especially compelling behaviorally. In Section 4.4.5 another, more easily defended, condition will be shown to do the same job.

3.9   Proofs

3.9.1   Theorem 3.2.2

Choose $x \succsim (x, C; y) \succsim z \succsim y$. Then the RDU of the left side of Eq. (3.17) is

$$
\begin{aligned}
U((x, C'; y), C; z) &= U(x, C'; y)W_{\mathbf{E}}(C) + U(z)[1 - W_{\mathbf{E}}(C)] \\
&= U(x)W_{\mathbf{E}}(C)^2 + U(y)W_{\mathbf{E}}(C)[1 - W_{\mathbf{E}}(C)] + U(z)[1 - W_{\mathbf{E}}(C)],
\end{aligned}
$$

where we take note that $W_{\mathbf{E}}(C') = W_{\mathbf{E}}(C)$. The right side is

$$
\begin{aligned}
U((x, C'; z), C; (y, C''; z)) &= U(x, C'; z)W_{\mathbf{E}}(C) + U(y, C''; z)[1 - W_{\mathbf{E}}(C)] \\
&= U(x)W_{\mathbf{E}}(C)^2 + U(z)[1 - W_{\mathbf{E}}(C)] \\
&\quad + U(y)[1 - W_{\mathbf{E}}(\overline{C})][1 - W_{\mathbf{E}}(C)] \\
&\quad + U(z)[1 - W_{\mathbf{E}}(C)]W_{\mathbf{E}}(\overline{C}).
\end{aligned}
$$

Equating these expressions and noting that the consequences can be varied, we see that Eq. (3.12) holds. ■

3.9.2   Theorem 3.4.1

We assume separability, transitivity, and consequence monotonicity. We prove the result only for gains and drop the superscript $+$ throughout.

(i) $\Rightarrow$ (ii). Proved in the text.

(ii) $\Rightarrow$ (iii). Fix $x, p, q, N = 2, 3$ and suppose $((x, p), q) \sim (x, r)$. By the solvability assumption, find consequences y, y' and probability r such that

$$
(x, p) \sim (y, 1), \quad (x, r) \sim (y, q), \quad (x, p^N) \sim (y', 1).
$$

Then in Eq. (3.36) set $q = 1, s = q$, and note that $y' \sim (y', 1)$, so N-compound invariance and consequence monotonicity yields

$$
\begin{aligned}
(x, r^N) &\sim (y', q^N) \\
&\sim ((y', 1), q^N) \\
&\sim ((x, p^N), q^N).
\end{aligned}
$$

(iii) $\Rightarrow$ (i). To show this result, our basic strategy is to show that N-reduction invariance, which is stated only for $N = 2, 3$, holds for any positive real number λ. First, by induction it clearly holds for $N = 2^n, 3^n$, where n is a natural number. Next, we show it for $\frac{1}{2^n}$. Suppose $((x, p^{\frac{1}{2^n}}), q^{\frac{1}{2^n}}) \sim (x, r^{\frac{1}{2^n}})$, then applying N-reduction invariance using $N = 2^n$ we see that $((x, p), q) \sim (x, r)$. So, by monotonicity of W with p and the fact W is onto $[0, 1]$, the converse must hold as well. Applying reduction invariance with $N = 3^m$ to $((x, p^{\frac{1}{2^n}}), q^{\frac{1}{2^n}}) \sim (x, r^{\frac{1}{2^n}})$ yields for $N = \frac{3^m}{2^n}$ that $((x, p^N), q^N) \sim (x, r^N)$. So by separability we have

$$W(p)W(q) = W(r) \iff W(p^N)W(q^N) = W(r^N), \ N = \frac{3^m}{2^n}$$

Because $\frac{3^m}{2^n}$ is dense in the positive real numbers and W is strictly increasing and onto, limits exist and so it follows that for $\lambda \in]0, \infty[$,

$$W(p)W(q) = W(r) \iff W(p^\lambda)W(q^\lambda) = W(r^\lambda)$$

Thus,

$$\left(W^{-1}[W(p)W(q)]\right)^\lambda = r^\lambda = W^{-1}[W(p^\lambda)W(q^\lambda)].$$

Setting $G(P) = -\ln W(e^{-P})$, $P = -\ln p$, and $Q = -\ln q$, this equation becomes

$$\lambda G^{-1}[G(P) + G(Q)] = G^{-1}[G(\lambda P) + G(\lambda Q)]. \tag{3.61}$$

This functional equation is similar[17] to, but appreciably simpler than, one solved by Aczél, Luce, and Maksa (1996). Following their strategy, for fixed λ, define

$$H(Z) = G(\lambda Z), \tag{3.62}$$

and then Eq. (3.61) can be rewritten as

$$G^{-1}[G(P) + G(Q)] = H^{-1}[H(P) + H(Q)]. \tag{3.63}$$

Now, let

$$f(V) = HG^{-1}(V) \tag{3.64}$$

and set $S = G(P)$ and $T = G(Q)$. Then, Eq. (3.63) becomes the Cauchy equation

$$f(S + T) = f(S) + f(T), \quad S, T \in]0, \infty[. \tag{3.65}$$

Because G is strictly increasing, so is f, and the solution to Eq. (3.65) is well known (Aczél, 1991/1966, p. 34) to be of the form $f(S) = AS$, $A > 0$. So from Eqs. (3.62) and (3.64),

$$G(\lambda P) = H(P) = fG(P) = AG(P).$$

---

[17]   The major difference is that Q was negative and bounded in their problem whereas here it is positive and unbounded.

Now treating λ as a variable, then $A = A(\lambda)$. Setting $P = 1$, we see $G(\lambda) = A(\lambda)\gamma$, where $\gamma = G(1)$, whence

$$G(\lambda P) = \frac{G(\lambda)G(P)}{\gamma}. \tag{3.66}$$

It is well known (Aczél, 1991/1966, p. 39) that the strictly increasing solutions to Eq. (3.66) are

$$G(P) = \gamma P^{\eta}, \quad \gamma > 0, \eta > 0. \tag{3.67}$$

Substituting Eq. (3.67) back into the definition of G and solving for W yields Eq. (3.31).
■

3.9.3   Theorem 3.6.1

(i) and (ii) are trivial.

(iii) To simplify notation a bit, we use u and w for U^* and W^* in the separable representation. As noted in the text, we prove the result under the added assumption that u is onto an interval $I = [0, a[$ and w is onto $[0, 1]$. The more general case of dense in intervals is treated by Marley and Luce (1999).

Let

$$A = \{(X, Y) : \exists x, y \in \mathcal{B}_0, C \in \mathcal{E} \text{ such that } X = u(x)w(C), Y = u(y)w[M(C)]\}.$$

Lemma 3.9.1.   *Suppose assumption (iii) holds and that uw is a separable representation with images an interval I and $[0, 1]$, respectively (Def. 3.1.3). Then, for $x, y \in \mathcal{B}_0$ with $x \succsim y$, there exists a function $R : A \xrightarrow{onto} I$ such that*

$$u(x, C; y) = R\left(u(x)w(C), u(y)w[M(C)]\right), \tag{3.68}$$
$$R(X, 0) = X, \quad X \in I, \tag{3.69}$$
$$R(0, Y) = Y, \quad Y \in I. \tag{3.70}$$

Proof.   We first extend u to $\mathcal{B}_1$ by setting $u(x, C; y) = u[CE(x, C; y)]$. Then for real X, Y, Z in the range of u define $R(X, Y) = Z$ if there exist $x, y \in \mathcal{B}_0, C \in \mathcal{E}$ with $X = u(x)w(C), Y = u(y)w[M(C)]$, and $Z = u(x, C; y)$. R is clearly order preserving by consequence monotonicity, Theorem 3.5.3, and the fact that u is order preserving of CEs. Observe that assumption of gains partition insures that R is well defined. So Eq. (3.68) holds.

We need to show R is onto I. That is obvious once we establish Eq. (3.69). To that end, by monotonicity of event inclusion, Eq. (2.13), note that $\emptyset$ is a lower bound and E is an upper bound under $\succsim_{\mathcal{E}}$. Thus, because w is onto $[0, 1]$, then $w(\emptyset) = 0, w(\bar{\emptyset}) = w(E) = 1$. Choosing $X = 0 = u(x)w(\emptyset), Y = 0 = u(y)w(\emptyset) = u(y)w[M(E)]$, and using certainty, Eq. (2.2), and complementarity, Eq. (2.3),

$$R(X, 0) = R\left(u(x)w(E), u(y)w[M(E)]\right)$$

$$
\begin{aligned}
&= \; u(x, E; y) \\
&= \; u(y; \emptyset; x) \\
&= \; u(x) \\
&= \; u(x)w(E) \\
&= \; X.
\end{aligned}
$$

The proof that $R(0, Y) = Y$ is similar. ∎

By Proposition 3.5.2 and Lemma 3.9.1, $u(x, C; y) = R[u(x)P, u(y)\pi(P)]$ is order preserving in each of $u(x)$, $u(y)$, and P.

It is convenient to work with open intervals and to introduce the notations

$$
\begin{aligned}
P &= \; w(C), \quad P \in]0, 1[\\
Z &= \; \frac{u(y)}{u(x)}, \quad Z \in]0, 1[\text{ if } x \succsim y \\
\pi(P) &= \; w(M[w^{-1}(P)]) = w[M(C)], \\
\gamma(P) &= \; \frac{\pi(P)}{P}, \quad \gamma :]0, 1[\to]1, \infty[.
\end{aligned}
$$

Observe that $\pi : [0, 1] \to [0, 1]$ is a well-defined strictly decreasing function for if $C, C' \in \mathcal{E}$ are such that $P = w(C) = w(C')$, then the fact that both w and M preserve equivalence with respect to the order $\succsim_{\mathcal{E}}$ gives that $C \sim_{\mathcal{E}} C'$ and $w[M(C)] = w[M(C')]$. Moreover, π is strictly decreasing because M inverts the order $\succsim_{\mathcal{E}}$. Because π is strictly decreasing in P, so is γ, and both are continuous on $]0, 1[$.

Lemma 3.9.2.   *Suppose assumption (ii) holds. Then, for $x \succsim y$,*

$$
u(x, C; y) = \begin{cases} \dfrac{u(x)P}{\gamma^{-1}[Z\gamma(P)]}, & \text{if } u(x)P > 0 \\ u(y)\pi(P), & \text{if } u(x)P = 0 \end{cases}. \tag{3.71}
$$

Proof. For $u(x)P = 0$,

$$
u(x, C; y) = R[u(x)P, u(y)\pi(P)] = R[0, u(y)\pi(P)] = u(y)\pi(P).
$$

So assume $u(x)P > 0$. By Proposition 3.5.2, let $v = CE(x, C; y)$. Let $Q = \frac{u(x)}{u(v)}P$, where $Q \in]0, 1[$ because by consequence monotonicity and Eq. (3.70),

$$
\begin{aligned}
u(v) &= \; u(x, C; y) \geq u(x, C; e) = R\left(u(x)w(C), u(e)w[M(C)]\right) \\
&= \; R[u(x)w(C), 0] = u(x)w(C) = u(x)P.
\end{aligned}
$$

So, using Lemma 3.10.1 and certainty,

$$
\begin{aligned}
R[u(x)P, u(y)\pi(P)] &= \; u(x, C; y) \\
&= \; u(v)
\end{aligned}
$$

$$
\begin{aligned}
&= u(v, D; v) \\
&= R(u(v)w(D), u(v)w[M(D)]) \\
&= R[u(v)Q, u(v)\pi(Q)] \\
&= R[u(x)P, u(v)\pi(Q)].
\end{aligned}
\tag{3.72}
$$

Using this we next show that $u(y)\pi(P) = u(v)\pi(Q)$. Assume the contrary. If $u(y)\pi(P) > u(v)\pi(Q)$, then choose z so that $u(y)\pi(P) > u(v)\pi(Q) = u(z)\pi(P)$, and so $u(y) > u(z)$. By the monotonicity of R with respect to u and Eq. (3.72) we have

$$
R[u(x)P, u(y)\pi(P)] > R[u(x)P, u(z)\pi(P)] = R[u(x)P, u(y)\pi(P)],
$$

a contradiction. The proof is similar for $u(y)\pi(P) < u(v)\pi(Q)$.
    On eliminating $u(v)$ we obtain

$$
\gamma(Q) = \frac{\pi(Q)}{Q} = \frac{u(y)}{u(x)}\frac{\pi(P)}{P} = Z\gamma(P).
$$

Therefore,

$$
u(x, C; y) = u(v) = \frac{u(x)P}{Q} = \frac{u(x)P}{\gamma^{-1}[Z\gamma(P)]}. \qquad \blacksquare
$$

By monotonicity of consequences and idempotence it follows immediately that the structure is *intern* in the sense that for all $x \succsim y$ and $C \in \mathcal{E}$,

$$
x \succsim (x, C; y) \succsim y.
\tag{3.73}
$$

Thus, from Eqs. (3.71) and (3.73) we see that

$$
P \le \gamma^{-1}[Z\gamma(P)] \le \frac{P}{Z}.
\tag{3.74}
$$

For the next result it is convenient to introduce two notations:

$$
\begin{aligned}
F(Z, P) &= \gamma^{-1}[Z\gamma(P)], \text{ where } F :]0, 1[\times]0, 1[\longrightarrow]0, \infty[, \tag{3.75} \\
G(Z, P) &= \frac{Z}{P}F(Z, P), \text{ where } Z, P \in]0, 1[, \tag{3.76}
\end{aligned}
$$

where we use the continuous extension of γ. From Eq. (3.74) we have the following bounds on F and G:

$$
P \le F(Z, P) \le \frac{P}{Z}, \quad Z \le G(Z, P) \le 1.
\tag{3.77}
$$

We introduce two additional concepts about G that will be used. First, the iteration of G is defined for $i \ge 1$,

$$
\begin{aligned}
G^1(Z, P) &= G(Z, P) \\
G^i(Z, P) &= G[G^{i-1}(Z, P), P].
\end{aligned}
$$

Lemma 3.9.3.   *Under the assumptions of the theorem, G has the following properties:*
(i)   *G is strictly increasing in the first variable and strictly decreasing in the second.*
(ii)   *For all $Z, P, Q \in]0, 1[$,*

$$G[G(Z, P), Q] = G[G(Z, Q), P]. \tag{3.78}$$

(iii)   *G is Archimedean in the first variable in the sense that for each $Y, Z, P \in]0, 1[$, there exists a positive integer m such that $G^m(Z, P) \geq Y$.*
(iv)   *G is solvable in the sense that, for Y, Z, P in $]0, 1[$, if there exists a nonnegative integer n with*

$$G^{n+1}(Z, P) \geq Y > G^n(Z, P), \tag{3.79}$$

then there exist Q in $]0, 1[$ with $Y = G[G^n(Z, P), Q]$..

Proof. (i) First, we show monotonicity for the first variable. Consider $P, Y, Z \in]0, 1[$ with $Y < Z = \frac{u(y)}{u(x)}$. Select x' such that $Y = \frac{u(y)}{u(x')}$. Thus,

$$
\begin{aligned}
Y < Z \iff &\; u(x') > u(x) \\
\iff &\; u(x', C; y) > u(x, C; y) \\
\iff &\; \frac{u(y)}{u(x', C; y)} < \frac{u(y)}{u(x, C; y)} \\
\iff &\; \frac{u(y)}{u(x')P} \gamma^{-1}[\frac{u(y)}{u(x')}\gamma(P)] < \frac{u(y)}{u(x)P}\gamma^{-1}[\frac{u(y)}{u(x)}\gamma(P)] \\
\iff &\; \frac{Y}{P}F(Y, P) < \frac{Z}{P}F(Z, P) \\
\iff &\; G(Y, P) < G(Z, P).
\end{aligned}
$$

Next, we show monotonicity for the second variable. Fix $Z = \frac{u(y)}{u(x)}$, and consider $C, D \in \mathcal{E}$ with $P = w(C), Q = w(D)$. Then

$$
\begin{aligned}
P > Q \iff &\; w(C) > w(D) \\
\iff &\; u(x, C; y) > u(x, D; y) \\
\iff &\; \frac{u(y)}{u(x, C; y)} < \frac{u(y)}{u(x, D; y)} \\
\iff &\; \frac{u(y)}{u(x)P}\gamma^{-1}\left(\frac{u(y)}{u(x)}\gamma(P)\right) < \frac{u(y)}{u(x)Q}\gamma^{-1}\left(\frac{u(y)}{u(x)}\gamma(Q)\right) \\
\iff &\; \frac{Z}{P}F(Z, P) < \frac{Z}{Q}F(Z, Q) \\
\iff &\; G(Z, P) < G(Z, Q).
\end{aligned}
$$

(ii) From Eq. (3.71),

$$
\begin{aligned}
u[((x,C;y),D;y)] &= u[(CE(x,C;y),D;y)] \\
&= \frac{u[CE(x,C;y)]w(D)}{\gamma^{-1}\left(\frac{u(y)}{u[CE(x,C;y)]}\gamma\,[w(D)]\right)} \\
&= \frac{u(x,C;y)w(D)}{\gamma^{-1}\left(\frac{u(y)}{u(x,C;y)}\gamma\,[w(D)]\right)} \\
&= \frac{u(x)w(C)w(D)}{\gamma^{-1}\left(\frac{u(y)}{u(x)}\gamma[w(C)]\right)\gamma^{-1}\left[\frac{u(y)}{u(x)w(C)}\gamma^{-1}\left(\frac{u(y)}{u(x)}\gamma[w(C)]\right)\gamma[w(D)]\right]} \\
&= \frac{u(x)PQ}{F(Z,P)F\left[\frac{Z}{P}F(Z,P),Q\right]}.
\end{aligned}
$$

So, assuming event commutativity, Eq. (3.9), we have

$$
F(Z,P)F\left[\frac{Z}{P}F(Z,P),Q\right] = F(Z,Q)F\left[\frac{Z}{Q}F(Z,Q),P\right].
$$

Multiply this equation by $\frac{Z}{PQ}$ and then rewrite it in terms of G to yield the functional equation (3.78).

(iii) Because G is strictly increasing in the first variable, the only way the Archimedean property can fail is for G^m to approach a limit $L < 1$. If L is a limit, then we have from Eqs. (3.75) and (3.76)

$$
L = G(L,P) = \frac{L}{P}\gamma^{-1}[L\gamma(P)],
$$

whence $\gamma(P) = L\gamma(P)$. So $L = 1$ since $\gamma(P) > 0$ for $P \in\,]0,1[$.

(iv) Turning to solvability, because $G(Z,P)$ is strictly monotonically decreasing in P, Eq. (3.79) with $G(Z,1) = 1$ yields

$$
G[G^n(Z,P),0] \geq G[G^n(Z,P),P] = G^{n+1}(Z,P) \geq Y > G^n(Z,P) = G[G^n(Z,P),1].
$$

The continuity of G in the second variable yields Q such that $Y = G[G^n(Z,P),Q]$.

Observe that because G is Archimedean and $Y < G(Z,P)$, the condition Eq. (3.79) is always satisfied and so under solvability Q always exists. ∎

We turn now to the proof of the theorem itself.

Equation (3.78) is the well-known commutativity functional equation studied by Luce (1964) and Marley (1967), who adapted results from Aczél (1961/1966). Specifically, Marley has shown that there exist functions $\varphi :]0,1[\rightarrow]0,\infty[$ and $\psi :]0,1[\rightarrow]1,\infty[$ such that

$$
G(Z,P) = \varphi^{-1}[\varphi(Z)\psi(P)] \tag{3.80}
$$

provided the following conditions are met: commutativity, strict monotonicity in Z, G is

Archimedean in iterations on the first variable, and it is restrictedly solvable. Lemma 9.1.3 established these conditions. [Because $G(Z, P) \geq Z$ for all $P > 0$, we only need consider the second parts of Definitions 9 and 10 of Marley (1967).]

Because G is strictly increasing in Z, φ is strictly increasing; and because G is strictly decreasing in P, ψ is strictly decreasing. From Eq. (3.77) we see

$$1 \leq \psi(P) \leq \frac{\varphi(1)}{\varphi(Z)}.$$

Putting together Eqs. (3.75), (3.76), and (3.80) yields

$$
\begin{aligned}
\frac{Z}{P}\gamma^{-1}[Z\gamma(P))] &= \frac{Z}{P}F(X, Z) \\
&= G(Z, P) \\
&= \varphi^{-1}[\varphi(Z)\psi(P)].
\end{aligned}
\tag{3.81}
$$

The task thus devolves to solving this functional equation in the three unknown functions γ, φ, and ψ. Aczél, Maksa, and Páles (1999b) have done so—which is not easy—yielding, for some constants $A > 0, k > 0, c < 0$,

$$
\begin{aligned}
\gamma(P) &= \frac{(1 - P^k)^{\frac{1}{k}}}{P}, \\
\varphi(Z) &= A\left(\frac{1 - Z^k}{Z^k}\right)^c, \\
\psi(P) &= P^{kc}.
\end{aligned}
$$

Thus,

$$\pi(P) = P\gamma(P) = \left(1 - P^k\right)^{\frac{1}{k}},$$

and

$$\varphi(Z)\psi(P) = \varphi\left(\frac{Z}{[(1 - P^k)Z^k + P^k]^{\frac{1}{k}}}\right). \tag{3.82}$$

Now, consider the expression for $u(x, E; y)$, $x \succsim y$:

$$
\begin{aligned}
u(x, C; y) &= \frac{u(x)w(C)}{F\left(\frac{u(y)}{u(x)}, \gamma[w(C)]\right)} \\
&= \frac{u(x)P}{\frac{P}{Z}G(Z, P)} \qquad \text{[Def. of } G\text{]} \\
&= \frac{u(y)}{G(Z, P)}
\end{aligned}
$$

$$= \frac{u(y)}{\varphi^{-1}[\varphi(Z)\psi(P)]} \qquad \text{[Eq. (3.80)]}$$

$$= \frac{u(y)}{\varphi^{-1}\left[\varphi\left(\frac{Z}{[(1-P^k)Z^k+P^k]^{\frac{1}{k}}}\right)\right]} \qquad \text{[Eq. (3.82)]}$$

$$= \frac{u(y)[(1-P^k)Z^k+P^k]^{\frac{1}{k}}}{Z}.$$

So, setting $U = u^k$ and $W = w^k$, we have

$$U(x,C;y) = U(x)W(C) + U(y)[1 - W(C)],$$

which is the binary rank-dependent form for $x \succsim y$. Complementarity, Eq. (2.3), yields the case where $x \precsim y$. ∎

3.9.4   Theorem 3.7.1

Proposition 3.9.4.   Assume that Φ satisfies Eq. (3.57) and that event commutativity holds. Let $A = \limsup u_1$. Then Φ satisfies the functional equation for $A > X \geq Y \geq 0$ and $W, Z \in [0,1]$,

$$\Phi\left(\Phi^{-1}[\Phi(XW) + \Phi(Y) - \Phi(YW)]Z\right) - \Phi(YZ)$$
$$= \Phi\left(\Phi^{-1}[\Phi(XZ) + \Phi(Y) - \Phi(YZ)]W\right) - \Phi(YW). \qquad (3.83)$$

Proof: Let

$$X = U^*(x), Y = U^*(y), W = W^*(C), Z = W^*(D), A = \limsup U^*$$

then for all X, Y, W, Z such that $A > X \geq Y \geq 0$ and $W, Z \in [0,1]$ Eqs. (3.55) and (3.58) yield

$$U\left((x,C;y), D; y\right)$$
$$= \Phi[U^*(x,C;y)W^*(D)] + \Phi[U^*(y)] - \Phi[U^*(y)w_1(D)]$$
$$= \Phi[\Phi^{-1}[u(x,C;y)]W^*(D)] + \Phi[U^*(y)] - \Phi[U^*(y)W^*(D)]$$
$$= \Phi\left(\Phi^{-1}[\Phi[U^*(x)W^*(C)] + \Phi[U^*(y)] - \Phi[U^*(y)W^*(C)]]W^*(D)\right)$$
$$\quad + \Phi[U^*(y)] - \Phi[U^*(y)W^*(D)]$$
$$= \Phi\left(\Phi^{-1}[\Phi(XW) + \Phi(Y) - \Phi(YW)]Z\right) + \Phi(Y) - \Phi(YZ).$$

So event commutativity, Eq. (3.9), imposes Eq. (3.83). ∎

Aczél, Maksa, Ng, and Páles (1999) have solved this equation under the assumption that the domains and ranges are intervals and Φ is twice differentiable. Their four solutions are

127

for some constants α, β, γ, q

$$\Phi(v) = \frac{1}{\beta q} \ln(\alpha + \beta v^q) + \gamma, \tag{3.84}$$

$$\Phi(v) = \frac{1}{\alpha q} v^q + \gamma, \tag{3.85}$$

$$\Phi(v) = \frac{1}{\alpha} \ln(-\alpha \ln v + \beta) + \gamma, \tag{3.86}$$

$$\Phi(v) = -\alpha \ln v + \beta. \tag{3.87}$$

Imposing the two requirements on Φ that $\Phi(0) = 0$ and that Φ is strictly increasing for each of Eqs. (3.84)-(3.87) in turn yields:

(i) From Eq. (3.84) and $\Phi(0) = 0$, we have $\gamma = -\frac{1}{\beta q} \ln \alpha$. Thus, $\alpha > 0$. Setting $\mu = \frac{\beta}{\alpha}$, Eq. (3.84) becomes

$$\Phi(v) = \frac{1}{\beta q} \ln(1 + \mu v^q). \tag{3.88}$$

Because Φ is strictly increasing and $\alpha > 0$, we see from $\Phi'(v) > 0$ that $\mu \beta > 0$. Also, because Φ is well defined, we must have $1 + \mu v^q > 0$. For $\mu > 0$ this imposes no restriction, but for $\mu < 0$, it means that $v^q < \frac{1}{|\mu|}$.

(ii) From Eq. (3.85) and $\Phi(0) = 0$, we see that $\gamma = 0$, and so the second case is

$$\Phi(v) = \frac{1}{\alpha q} v^q. \tag{3.89}$$

Because Φ is strictly increasing, $\alpha > 0$.

(iii) and (iv) Equations (3.86) and (3.87) are ruled out by the condition $\Phi(0) = 0$ because either $\Phi(v) \equiv 0$, which violates the strict monotonicity of Φ, or it fails because $\ln 0 = -\infty$.

So we need only see what Eqs. (3.88) and (3.89) imply.

Substituting Eq. (3.88) into Eq. (3.57) and using $U = (U^*)^q$, $W = (W_E^*)^q$, and recalling that $\beta \mu > 0$ and $1 + \mu u_1^q > 0$,

$$
\begin{aligned}
\frac{1}{\beta q} \ln[1 + \mu U(x, C; y)] &= \frac{1}{\beta q} \ln[1 + \mu U(x) W(C)] \\
&\quad + \frac{1}{\beta q} \ln[1 + \mu U(y)] - \frac{1}{\beta q} \ln[1 + \mu U(y) W(C)] \\
&= \frac{1}{\beta q} \ln\left(\frac{[1 + \mu U(x) W(C)][1 + \mu U(y)]}{[1 + \mu U(y) W(C)]}\right),
\end{aligned}
$$

whence

$$[1 + \mu U(x, C; y)] = \frac{[1 + \mu U(x) W(C)][1 + \mu U(y)]}{1 + \mu U(y) W(C)},$$

and so

$$U(x, C; y) = \frac{U(x)W(C) + U(y)[1 - W(C)] + \mu U(x)U(y)W(C)}{1 + \mu U(y)W(C)}.$$

The case $e \precsim x \precsim y$ is obtained from the complementarity axiom. The condition $1 + \mu u_1^q > 0$ implies that for $\mu < 0$, $U(x) < \frac{1}{|\mu|}$.

From Eq. (3.89) we see that with the same substitutions,

$$\frac{1}{\alpha q}U(x, C; y) = \frac{1}{\alpha q}U(x)W(C) + \frac{1}{\alpha q}U(y) - \frac{1}{\alpha q}U(y)W(C),$$

whence

$$U(x, C; y) = U(x)W(C) + U(y)[1 - W(C)],$$

which of course is the standard RDU model. ∎

Chapter 4
JOINT RECEIPT OF GAINS

This chapter and Chapters 6 and 7 deviate considerably from what has been mainstream utility theory in that they introduce another primitive beyond gambles and preferences over them. As we shall see, doing so has a number of advantages. First of all, the primitive is extremely natural and from time to time has been used somewhat informally in the literature, e.g., we have already encountered informal uses by Kahneman and Tversky (1979) and Tversky (1967a). Second, it imposes a strong constraint on the possible utility functions. Third, it allows one to develop new approaches to the case of binary mixed gambles, which, in my opinion, have not been handled very effectively in the traditional literature.

4.1 Joint Receipt

4.1.1 The intuitive concept

If two objects are each valued, i.e., seen as something for which questions of preference are relevant, then having both of them is, in general, also valued. In particular, if each is a gain, then together they are a gain. Or if each is seen as a loss, then together they are a loss. In the mixed case, the two together can be valued either as a gain, a loss, or indifferent to the status quo. We call this having two things their *joint receipt*.

Joint receipt is ubiquitous in much of our economic life. We encounter it in the daily mail, in shopping, in ordering from catalogues, in all forms of trade, etc. That being so, one might expect that it would be well studied. It has been somewhat empirically, but not much investigated theoretically until the early 1990s.

The earliest example of its experimental and theoretical use of which I am aware[1] is Gulliksen (1956b), who used the notation "x and y" and spoke of "composite stimuli." The next use, mentioned in Section 3.1.3.2, was Tversky's (1967a) study of the separability of gambles. Other empirical studies in which it has played a significant role are Cho and Fisher (1999), Cho and Luce (1995), Cho, Luce, and von Winterfeldt (1994), Fisher (1999), Linville and Fisher (1991), Payne and Braunstein (1971), Slovic and Lichtenstein (1968), Shanteau (1974, 1975), Thaler (1985), Thaler and Johnson (1990), and Tversky (1967b).

The theoretical studies of joint receipt as an operation are sparse and will be cited as they

---

[1] I thank Dr. C. Seidl for bringing this reference to my attention. So far as I know, it was not followed up by later studies.

arise. This is not to say that theorists, mainly economists, have actually ignored something of such importance, but only that they did not model it as a binary operation. Rather, they typically treat such composite alternatives as vectors in an n-dimensional numerical space whose dimensions are different commodities or goods. The numerical values of the vector components represent amounts of the corresponding commodity. Such a vector is called a *commodity bundle*. This leads them quickly to matrix equations and a particular style of theorizing typical of economics.

Another approach, related to commodity bundles, is to think of the commodities as forming a conjoint structure. This was suggested by Adams and Fagot (1959) prior to the formal development of additive conjoint measurement (Appendix D). They derived a number of the necessary conditions on the assumption of an additive representation of preference, but they did not prove any form of a converse. Within the conjoint framework, however, it is quite difficult to formulate some of the basic properties we shall invoke below.

Approaching the concept of joint receipt as a binary operation is likely to lead one to think more in measurement terms. In particular, the formalism is one of abstract algebra, not of vector or conjoint spaces. If the domain $\mathcal{D}$ is under consideration and if $g, h \in \mathcal{D}$, then the joint receipt of the two is denoted $g \oplus h$, and we assume that $g \oplus h \in \mathcal{D}$. That is, we assume that the domain under consideration is closed under joint receipt. Typically, we will assume that if $\mathcal{B}$ is the set of binary gambles generated from a set of consequences $\mathcal{C}$ and a set of experiments $\mathcal{E}$, then $\mathcal{B} \subset \mathcal{D}$. Indeed, $\mathcal{D}$ can be taken to be the closure of $\mathcal{B}$ under the operation $\oplus$. The same is true for restrictions on the set of gambles, e.g., $\mathcal{D}_2^+$ is the closure of $\mathcal{B}_2^+$ under $\oplus$.

4.1.2   Objections to joint receipt

I am aware of four objections to such an approach.

Complementary goods: One possible problem is that under some circumstances each object has no value except when both are held. Examples: Suppose one is in the wilderness without food. If one has a gun with the appropriate bullets, then the two together are certainly valuable. But either alone in that situation is not, and indeed may be discarded as being only extra weight of no value. A more commonplace version for most of us is that a single shoe is of no value; individual shoes only become valued as matched pairs. (Anyone who has raised a child is all too aware of the issue.) Such special cases can usually be dealt with easily on an ad hoc basis and are not in my opinion much of an objection. This is discussed further in Section 4.2.1 in connection with the monotonicity assumption.

Here a distinction must be made about who is establishing the sense of value. The manufacturer of shoes or the seller of guns and ammunition is far less concerned about complementarity in valuing objects than is the parent holding a single shoe or the person who finds herself on her own in the wilderness. Clearly, the interpretation of an elementary good differs by one's role: For some roles, pairs of things are unitary, and for others, each element of a normally paired set is unitary.

Conflicting goods: The concern here is the opposite of the one above, namely, that each of the individual items is valued but together they lack value or become totally transformed.

An example is two chemicals which when placed in close proximity produce an undesirable reaction. Again this can usually be handled by care in defining what constitute suitable stimuli, just as one would do in the theory of mass measurement when considering the placement of two objects on the same pan of an equal-arm pan balance.

Neither of these objections has any force if, for example, one is dealing with gambles with monetary consequences.

Why only pairs of goods? Since we often receive or purchase more than two things, why do we only model the special binary case? Certainly, economists embody the general case in the concept of a commodity bundle. The answer, fully described in the next subsection, is the property of associativity, which, if it holds, as in mass or length measurement, reduces the general case to the special one.

The wrong representation: I believe that the most telling objection to joint receipt has been the recognition that the resulting additive value representation of preference over joint receipt of sums of money does not exhibit a property known to hold for subjective measures of utility, namely, nonlinearity. So, it is argued, something must be wrong in assessing utility via joint receipts.

A major aspect of the present chapter is to demonstrate that the last objection to joint receipts simply is wrong, that it incorrectly assumes that the additive representation of $\oplus$ and the utility representation derived from gambles are the same. Their actual relationship is explored in the next three sections. But first, let us examine the empirical evidence about whether or not joint receipts have an additive representation.

4.1.3   Nonadditivity of the "utility" of joint receipts

Shanteau (1974, 1975), using the functional measurement method of Anderson (1970) in which respondents provide ratings of a stimulus attribute, in this case preference, on some numerical scale, examined the issue of additivity of joint receipt. For example, in the 1974 paper he ran what he called single bets of the form $(x, p; e)$ and double bets of the form $(x, p; e) \oplus (y, q; e)$ in a factorial design. Respondents evaluated the alternatives by placing a marker on a linear scale that was uncalibrated except for the end points, which were "worthless" and "a television set." Lengths were measured by the experimenter. The data for single bets showed nice evidence of separability, thus suggesting that the ratings R made by the respondent were probably close to some power of their utility functions, $R = U^\beta$. The additivity R was tested by simply predicting the ratings of the double bets from the ratings of the single bets by adding them. These predictions systematically overestimated the actual settings as seen in Fig. 4.1, i.e., subadditivity was found,

$$R(f \oplus g) < R(f) + R(g). \tag{4.1}$$

Of course, we cannot be sure whether additivity would have been rejected if power transformations of R had been tried.

Shanteau also examined a number of other studies, in some cases reanalyzing data that had not in his opinion been properly analyzed, and in all cases concluded that the claims of additivity were not supported and that subadditivity actually held in the usual utility measure

133

U. One task is to account for such findings.

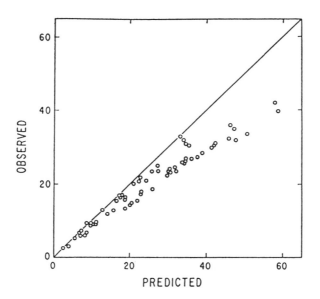

Figure 4.1. Evidence that joint receipt is subadditive in terms of estimated rating R. The ordinate is the observed value of $R(x, y)$ and the abscissa is the sum $R(x) + R(y)$ as estimated by Shanteau (1974). This is Fig. 3 of Shanteau (1974). Copyright © 1974 by the American Psychological Association.. Reprinted with permission.

4.2   Elementary Behavioral Properties

4.2.1   Joint-receipt preference structure

Consider the structure $\langle \mathcal{D}, e, \succsim, \oplus \rangle$, where $\mathcal{D}$ is the domain of joint receipts of gambles generated from the set $\mathcal{C}$ of consequences and experiments $\mathcal{E}$, $e \in \mathcal{C}$ is the status quo, $\succsim$ is a binary preference relation on $\mathcal{D}$, and $\oplus$ is a binary joint receipt operation $\oplus$ over $\mathcal{D}$.

In the following definition, each term is prefixed by the word "weak." The reason is that in mathematics each of these terms, except for "weak order," is usually defined in terms of equality, e.g., commutativity is $f \oplus g = g \oplus f$, but, in the context of preference, equality is far too strong. We need the conditions to hold under indifference, $\sim$. So replacing $=$ by $\sim$ invites some adjective, and taking the lead of weak order, I use "weak" as that adjective.

However, I often omit the adjective when doing so does appear to be misleading.

Definition 4.2.1. $\langle \mathcal{D}, e, \succsim, \oplus \rangle$ is said to form a *joint-receipt preference structure* if and only if for all $f, g, h \in \mathcal{D}$:

Axiom JR1. Weak Order:

$$\succsim \text{ is transitive and connected.}$$

Axiom JR2. Weak Commutativity:

$$f \oplus g \sim g \oplus f. \tag{4.2}$$

Axiom JR3. Weak Associativity:

$$f \oplus (g \oplus h) \sim (f \oplus g) \oplus h. \tag{4.3}$$

Axiom JR4. Weak Monotonicity:

$$f \succsim g \Longleftrightarrow f \oplus h \succsim g \oplus h. \tag{4.4}$$

Axiom JR5. Weak Identity:

$$f \oplus e \sim f \tag{4.5}$$

Proposition 4.2.1.   *A joint-receipt preference structure is* **positive** *in the sense that*

$$f \succ e \Longrightarrow f \oplus g \succ g. \tag{4.6}$$

Proof. By monotonicity, commutativity, and identity,

$$f \oplus g \succ e \oplus g \sim g \oplus e \sim g,$$

and the result follows by transitivity. ∎

Within the context of valued goods, all of these properties seem to be of a highly rational character.

Transitivity is defended as before.

Weak commutativity says that whatever the order means in writing the operation, it should not affect preferences. Depending upon the empirical interpretation of joint receipt, that order can mean various things—the order in which they are represented when talking about them, the order in which they are placed in a bag or box, the order in which bills and checks are opened in the mail, etc.—but none of that should matter in terms of overall preference for the goods themselves.

Similarly, weak associativity says that the binary groupings should not matter with respect to preference. Again, whatever the interpretation is of the binary concept, how the grouping is carried out, should be irrelevant to preference. (Of course, sometimes packaging can matter for other reasons such as the distribution of the weight of goods being carried.) If associativity is correct, then the parentheses can be omitted and we can just write $f \oplus g \oplus h$ for the common expression. It is in this sense that one does not need to consider receiving more than two things at a time. Whether or not associativity holds empirically is discussed in Section 4.2.2.

Weak monotonicity presumably holds for the same reason as it does for gambles: Replacing something by something preferable, all else held fixed, results in an alternative that is preferred to the original one. This too has been studied empirically and the results are summarized in Section 4.2.3. The most vivid hypothetical counter examples to it involve issues of complementarity of goods. For example, suppose f is a cup of black coffee, g is a cup of black tea, and h is a slice of lemon. I, at least, prefer f to g, but if one interprets $f \oplus h$ to mean that the lemon is squeezed into the coffee and $g \oplus h$ that the lemon is squeezed into the tea, then my preference reverses. If either the squeezing does not automatically occur or if one is thinking of f, g, and h as store items, then I remain monotonic. These examples mean that, as with any mathematical system, some care must be taken in empirical realizations so as to avoid trivial failures.

The idea that receiving the status quo along with a valued alternative has no impact on preference is, in a sense, a formal way to define no change from the status quo.

So, these all seem to be plausible assumptions from a rational perspective.

4.2.2   An indirect evaluation of associativity

Consider a paired-comparisons study involving single stimuli and all possible joint receipts of them, but excluding cases of the form $x \oplus x$. One can then attempt to construct a numerical representation[2] T over stimuli and their joint receipt by using the resulting relative frequencies and a statistical model within the standard Thurstonian framework (see, e.g., Bock & Jones, 1968, or Torgerson, 1958). Gulliksen (1956b) raised the question of whether when this is done there is a transformation Φ such that $V = \Phi^{-1}(T)$ is additive.

He used as stimuli five entrees: beef, lamb, pork, steak, and tongue, plus the 10 joint receipt pairs. The respondents were instructed to interpret both x and y as full portions when considering $x \oplus y$, which to some degree confounded food and amount preferences. Ninety-two college students judged all possible pairs according to preference. He then subjected the resulting proportions to a least squares scaling analysis using the method described in Gulliksen (1956a) to obtain the scale T. However, the zero point of the scale had to be inferred from the fact that some foods seemed relatively negative. For example, the scale value of tongue and lamb was 0.270 whereas lamb alone was 1.043. He examined four choices for Φ, namely,

logarithmic:	$k \log v/v_0$
square root:	$\sqrt{k(v - v_0)}$
negative exponential:	$k[1 - e^{-(v-v_0)}]$
linear:	$k(v - v_0)$

For each function he chose parameters to yield the best least squares fit to additivity over joint receipt. The negative exponential did the best, with linear a close second and the other two

---

[2] I use T rather than U to make clear this is a Thurstonian scale, not a utility derived from gambles.

less satisfactory. But he warned the reader that the data really were not adequate to tell for sure which function gave the best additive fit.

Later the negative exponential transformation will arise quite naturally as one of three possible relations between the additive V on joint receipts and a standard representation U based on gambles. However, I know of no principled reason why Gulliksen's scale based on least squares of paired comparisons among consequences and the utility arising from gambles should be the same. Moreover, as we shall see very clearly, there are considerable individual differences in preference patterns among people, so the preference proportions over a population of respondents are probably not very useful data.

To my knowledge, there is no direct empirical test of associativity. In Section 7.1.2 we will encounter an empirical study of the weak associativity of mixed alternatives in the sense that at least one is a gain and at least one is a loss. As we will see, it is not easy to do such a study.

4.2.3   Empirical evaluations of monotonicity

4.2.3.1   An indirect test: The only tests that I know of concerning the monotonicity of joint receipt are Cho and Fisher (1999), Cho and Luce (1995), and Fisher (1999). The 1995 study was based on a simple theoretical result of Luce (1995) which shows that if CEs are order preserving, CEs satisfy their defining property

$$g \sim CE(g) \text{ and } f \oplus g \sim CE(f \oplus g), \tag{4.7}$$

and $\oplus$ restricted to $\mathbb{R}_+ \times \mathbb{R}_+$ is commutative and monotonic, then general weak monotonicity of joint receipt is equivalent to

$$CE(f \oplus g) = CE(f) \oplus CE(g). \tag{4.8}$$

For the special case $x \in \mathbb{R}$, Eq. (4.7) implies $CE(x) = x$, so monotonicity becomes testable in terms of CEs,

$$CE(f \oplus g) = CE[CE(f) \oplus CE(g)]. \tag{4.9}$$

Using 40 student respondents, data were collected by Cho and Luce (1995) using the PEST procedure (§ 9.2) to estimate CEs for three (f, g) pairs of mixed gain/loss gambles.[3] The data analysis involved looking at the distribution over respondents of the CE estimates, denoted $\widehat{CE}$, of the numerical differences:

$$\widehat{CE}(f \oplus g) - \widehat{CE}[\widehat{CE}(f) \oplus \widehat{CE}(g)].$$

Despite the noise in estimating CEs, this difference should be symmetrical about 0 if Eq. (4.9)

---

[3]   A number of other things were examined in this study, and they will be reported when we come to the relevant properties (§§ 4.2.4 and 4.4.3).

is correct and the estimate is unbiased in the sense

$$E[\widehat{CE}] = CE. \tag{4.10}$$

They also looked at the difference

$$\widehat{CE}(f \oplus g) - \widehat{CE}(f) - \widehat{CE}(g).$$

Both hypotheses were rejected, and the tendency was for subadditivity to hold for gains in the sense

$$\widehat{CE}(f \oplus g) \; < \; \widehat{CE}[\widehat{CE}(f) \oplus \widehat{CE}(g)] \tag{4.11}$$

$$\widehat{CE}(f \oplus g) \; < \; \widehat{CE}(f) + \widehat{CE}(g). \tag{4.12}$$

For losses, the inequality was reversed. We will return in Section 4.4.4 to this subadditivity in connection with another, related experiment.

The conclusion Cho and Luce drew was that either monotonicity of joint receipt is false or our estimates of CEs for, at least, joint receipts are not order preserving. Actually, a more precise inference would be either of these two possibilities or that the estimates $\widehat{CE}$ are biased. My ultimate conclusion will be that it is the latter.

4.2.3.2   A direct test of weak monotonicity: Based on this inference, Cho and Fisher (1999) ran another study in which they attempted to explore monotonicity directly without estimating CEs, Fisher (1999) with Cho investigated whether the estimated CEs are order preserving, and Sneddon (1999b) approached the latter question in a different, novel way.

The design used to test monotonicity involved presenting comparison pairs, such as (f, g) and $(f \oplus h, g \oplus h)$, each 8 times. Successive presentations of the same pair were well separated by a number of other choices. The question was the degree to which the choice patterns for the pair agreed. In addition, CEs were estimated for the same gambles. The study was partitioned into two experiments and the latter had five distinct subparts. The numbers of respondents varied from 11 to 14 in each part for a total of 73. The experimental setup was that used by Cho in her other studies (§ 3.1.5.2). The data pattern was clear: Monotonicity of joint receipt was not rejected, yet the data were sufficiently sensitive to reject another somewhat related hypothesis (§4.2.3.4).

4.2.3.3   A direct test of CE being order preserving: The evidence concerning whether CEs are order preserving was ambiguous in Fisher (1999). Sneddon (1999a) noted that the way PEST had been implemented, which prohibited any certain amounts falling outside the range of consequences within a gamble, does produce a small bias for highly skewed gambles even assuming that the underlying psychometric function is symmetric, and the bias can be somewhat worse for appropriately skewed psychometric functions. However, compared to the variability of the estimates, the bias is really quite small. Variability may be the significant factor. It simply blurs things rather badly when the CEs of two gambles are fairly close.

Indeed, Fisher's (1999) experimental attempt to decide whether CEs are order preserving was inconclusive primarily for the following reasons. It is clear that if one gamble is sufficiently better than another, monotonicity will hold trivially. So to have a sensitive test the experimenters must select gamble pairs (g, h) that are valued quite similarly. But then we know from extensive experience that the choice will be probabilistic, governed by some unknown value $P(g, h)$. Equally, when $CE(g)$ and $CE(h)$ are estimated, these estimates are only approximately indifferent to g and h, respectively, i.e., the estimated values varying according to an unknown probability distribution. The problem is to tell within the noise level of the experiment whether or not CEs are order preserving.

One can, of course, make parametric assumptions and attempt to estimate these unknown probabilities. That usually is not very elegant nor, to my mind, very convincing. The following idea occurred to Sneddon. Suppose one can find a large number of stimulus pairs whose value of $P(g, h)$ is identical and known. Then, if we determine for each respondent and each (g, h) pair (for that respondent) their estimated $CE(g)$ and $CE(h)$, we can count the proportion of times $CE(g) \geq CE(h)$. The sample size is the number of respondents times the number of pairs, which can be sizable. The question is whether the noise level of the choices and that of the estimated CEs are basically the same. This was carried out by adapting the PEST procedure so as to generate gamble pairs with $P(g, h) = 0.84$ for all respondent/pairs. For each of 18 respondents, 6 gamble pairs were generated in this way; however, several respondents failed to complete the experiment, resulting in a total of 102 sets rather than 108. The overall proportion of times that $CE(g) \geq CE(h)$ turned out to be 0.81, reasonably close to the constructed choice probability. Thus, the conclusion is that the PEST-determined CEs are order preserving within the noise level of the experiment.

Taken together, these studies seem to establish that when examined directly, monotonicity is sustained and PEST-determined CEs are satisfactory for deciding the preference ordering. At the same time, we know that something went wrong when Eq. (4.9) was tested. So my tentative conclusion is that monotonicity of joint receipt is a reasonable assumption, but that under some conditions, of which Eq. (4.9) is an example, something can go wrong with the PEST estimates of CEs. I return to this issue and propose a possible explanation in Section 4.4.4.

4.2.3.4   An unworkable experimental idea:

One difficulty in collecting direct choice data is the fact that repeated choices are inconsistent, so, if one is to estimate the tendency of the choice to occur, one has to repeat each choice pair (f, g) a number of times. There is considerable concern that, after a while, the respondent recalls the previous response to the pair and does not appraise them anew. Thus, it would be nice if one could, in effect, obtain the information about replications without actually repeating anything. One suggestion to achieve this, which I first heard from Louis Narens but later realized was mentioned by Tversky and Kahneman (1992), is to change the consequences by a common factor. Suppose $f = (x_1, E_1; ...; x_n, E_n)$ is a monetary gamble. If $\alpha > 0$, let $\alpha f = (\alpha x_1, E_1; ...; \alpha x_n, E_n)$. Following Lopes and Oden (1999), αf is called a *scaled version of* f. Then the proposed hypothesis of *scale invariance* is

$$f \succsim g \iff \alpha f \succsim \alpha g. \tag{4.13}$$

Clearly, if this were true, one could get the equivalent of n replications of (f, g) by using

n distinct values of α and no repetitions. Cho and Fisher (1999) examined the scale invariance hypothesis experimentally in which the ratio of the largest to the smallest α was 15, as well as the monotonicity of joint receipt (§ 4.2.3.2), and they did not find it sustained whereas monotonicity was. [The latter remark is relevant because it provides evidence that the experimental method probably is not the reason for trouble with Eq. (4.13).]

There may be a good reason for the failure. As Tversky and Kahneman (1992) state without proof and as shown in Cho and Fisher (1999), Eq. (4.13) implies that U must be a power function of money. Birnbaum and Sutton (1992, pp. 210–211) also discuss this relation. But as we saw in Section 3.6, and as is vivid in Fig. 4.2 below, this form is too restrictive to be descriptive. Moreover, Theorem 4.4.3 and Proposition 4.5.2 make clear that, within the assumptions of this chapter, that assumption is excessively restrictive. I do not seen any implications that can be drawn about U from the nature of the failure of scale invariance that was found.

4.2.4   Is joint receipt of lotteries just convolution?

Assuming that $x \oplus y \sim x + y$, then from a purely statistical perspective joint receipt and convolution of lotteries[4] are formally identical because all convolution does is enumerate all the possible combinations of consequences and their probabilities of arising (assuming independence). In particular, if

$$g = (x_1, p_1; ...; x_i, p_i; ...; x_m, p_m) \quad \text{and} \quad h = (y_1, q_1; ...; y_j, q_j; ...; y_n, q_n),$$

where all the consequences are money and the probabilities in each gamble sum to 1, then their convolution is given by

$$g * h = (x_1 + y_1, p_1 q_1; ...; x_i + y_j, p_i q_j; ....; x_m + y_n, p_m q_n).$$

Of course, this formal identity does not mean that they are necessarily perceived as indifferent in preference, i.e.,

$$g \oplus h \sim g * h. \tag{4.14}$$

Although this chapter is focused on gains, the issue of whether Eq. (4.14) holds is most vividly raised in the context of mixed gains and losses. So for the moment we will look at that more general case, but our excursion does not involve knowing anything about the utility representations of joint receipts or of mixed gambles.

The first authors to study this question were Slovic and Lichtenstein (1968), who presented in their Experiment II what they called "parallel duplex" and "complex" gambles, which in our terms are joint receipt and the corresponding convolution. The data exhibited individual differences, with some respondents clearly not assigning the same bids to $g \oplus h$ and $g * h$ and others doing so. Payne and Braunstein (1971) followed up on this aspect of the earlier study in the following fashion. Their respondents chose between joint receipt pairs $g \oplus h$ and $g' \oplus h'$

---

4   Recall that a lottery means a gamble with money consequences and prescribed probabilities.

Section 4.2   Elementary Behavioral Properties

for which $g * h = g' * h'$. An example is:

$$g = (\$40, 0.6; 0), \quad h = (-\$40, 0.5; 0),$$
$$g' = (\$40, 0.5; 0), \quad h' = (-\$40, 0.4; 0)$$

with the common[5] convolution

$$(0, 0.3; \$40, 0.3; -\$40, 0.2; 0, 0.2).$$

Using 9 such pairs, they showed that the 40 respondents were not, on average, indifferent between joint receipts with a common convolution. So, according to this study, the answer to the question of the section heading—"Is joint receipt of lotteries just convolution?"—is *No*.

The next line of study somewhat refines that answer. Samuelson (1963) and Broome (1991) both noted that it is unlikely that both monotonicity of joint receipt and Eq. (4.14) hold for a good many people. Luce (1995) cast it in the following way. Millions of people buy state lottery tickets, say g, at some price c. The situation has the following features. Let h denote the lottery less its cost (= buying price) subtracted from each possible consequence,[6] and let $EV(h) = EV(g) - c$ be its expected value. Given that the person chooses to purchase the lottery and the state surely sells them at a profit, then

$$h \succ e \quad \text{and} \quad EV(h) < 0.$$

Now, assuming the monotonicity and associativity of joint receipts of gains,

$$h(n, \oplus) = \overbrace{h \oplus \cdots \oplus h}^{n \text{ times}} \succ e. \tag{4.15}$$

Let $h(n, *)$ denote the convolution of n copies of h, then we know two things. First, by induction on Eq. (4.14),

$$h(n, \oplus) \sim h(n, *). \tag{4.16}$$

Second, by well-known properties of convolution,

$$EV[h(n, *)] = nEV(h) \quad \text{and} \quad STD[h(n, *)] = \sqrt{n}STD(h).$$

Thus,

$$\frac{STD[h(n, *)]}{EV[h(n, *)]} = \frac{STD(h)}{\sqrt{n}EV(h)}.$$

One suspects that for n sufficiently large, the single shot gamble $h(n, *)$ ultimately becomes unacceptable, i.e.,

$$h(n, *) \prec e. \tag{4.17}$$

---

[5]   This rests upon the assumption that permuting the first and last term does not affect matters.
[6]   For more detail on buying prices see Sections 6.4 and 7.4.

141

Assuming transitivity, the three statements of Eqs. (4.15), (4.16), and (4.17) are inconsistent. Thus, for such people at least one of the following assumptions is wrong: transitivity of preference, monotonicity of joint receipt, or the indifference of joint receipt and convolution.

To explore these issues empirically, Cho and Luce (1995) classed their 40 respondents according to their behavior on 10 screening gambles all of which had EVs of about −$2. They defined as "moderate gamblers" those respondents whose PEST-estimated CEs were positive for 7 or more of these screening gambles. By this definition, 14 respondents were "moderate gamblers" and 26 were "nongamblers." The data were analyzed separately for these two groups, which by the above argument one might expect to behave differently.

The experiment simply involved estimating CEs for the joint receipts of five pairs of lotteries and for their corresponding convolutions. At the 0.01 level of significance, "gamblers" appeared to be indifferent between joint receipt and convolution, but monotonicity of joint receipt failed in the sense that

$$\widehat{CE}(g \oplus h) \cong \widehat{CE}(g * h) > \widehat{CE}(g) + \widehat{CE}(h).$$

For "nongamblers," joint receipt was seen as less valuable than convolution, and monotonicity of joint receipt appeared to hold in the sense that

$$\widehat{CE}(x \oplus y) < \widehat{CE}(x * y) \cong \widehat{CE}(g) + \widehat{CE}(h)$$

In retrospect, given the presumably greater experience "gamblers" may have had with gambling, it is not surprising that they realize joint receipts are the same as the equivalent convolution, in which case monotonicity must fail if they are to avoid total disaster. And it is equally plausible that the presumably less experienced "nongamblers" fail to see that joint receipt and convolution are equally valuable. So the answer to the question of the subsection is not a simple *Yes* or *No*; it depends on the respondent's type.

Although these results are suggestive, the issue is not yet adequately explored to be fully confident about what is true. In particular, there has been no study of all gains and of all losses and whether or not the gambler/nongambler distinction matters in these cases. And there remains the issue of whether the PEST-determined CEs maybe a source of sometimes misleading bias. We return to this issue in Section 4.4.4.

4.3   Representation of Joint Receipt of Gains

4.3.1   The Archimedean property

Let $\mathcal{D}^{++} = \{g : g \in \mathcal{D} \text{ and } g \succ e\}$. Substituting $\mathcal{D}^{++}$ for $\mathcal{D}$ in Definition 4.2.1, these properties are those used to model such physical attributes as mass or length when $\succsim$ is determined by concatenating masses on the pans of an equal-arm balance or by lengths juxtaposed along a straight line. The only missing property is an Archimedean one, which I will assume has the following form:

For $f \in \mathcal{D}$ and n an integer, let[7] $f(n)$ denote the joint receipt of n copies of f. Formally,

$$f(1) = f,$$
$$f(n) = f(n-1) \oplus f.$$

Axiom JR6. Archimedean: For all $f, g, h, h' \in \mathcal{D}^+$ with $f \succ g$, there exists an integer n such that

$$f(n) \oplus h \succsim g(n) \oplus h'. \tag{4.18}$$

The more usual definition in physical contexts has been to assume that for each $f, g \in \mathcal{D}^+$ there exists an integer n such that $g(n) \succsim f$. The advantage of the present formulation over that one is that it eliminates the need for an additional structural axiom such as: if $f \succ g$, then there exists $h \in \mathcal{D}^+$ such that $f \succsim g \oplus h$.

The intuition behind Axiom JR6 is this: No matter how much better h' is than h, sufficiently many copies of f coupled with h will be sufficient to overcome the h' advantage when combined with the same number of copies of g. This intuition may be rephrased by assuming that commutativity, associativity, and solvability hold and considering the defined operation of subtraction:

Definition 4.3.1.   For $f, g, k \in \mathcal{D}$ with $f \succsim g$, define

$$f \ominus g \sim k \Longleftrightarrow f \sim k \oplus g. \tag{4.19}$$

Proposition 4.3.1.   *Suppose* $\langle \mathcal{D}, \succsim, \oplus, e \rangle$ *is a joint receipt preference structure. Then, for all* $f, f', g, g' \in \mathcal{D}$ *with* $f \succsim g \succsim h, f' \succsim g'$

$$(f \ominus g) \oplus g \sim f, \tag{4.20}$$
$$f \ominus (g \ominus h) \sim (f \ominus g) \oplus h, \tag{4.21}$$
$$(f \oplus f') \ominus (g \oplus g') \sim (f \ominus g) \oplus (f' \ominus g'), \tag{4.22}$$
$$(f \oplus f') \ominus (g \ominus g') \sim (f \ominus g) \oplus f' \oplus g', \tag{4.23}$$
$$(f \ominus g)(n) \sim f(n) \ominus g(n). \tag{4.24}$$

Corollary.   *The Archimedean condition* Eq. (4.18) *is equivalent to:*

$$(f \ominus g)(n) \succsim h' \ominus h. \tag{4.25}$$

So in terms of this defined subtraction, we see that Archimedeaness amounts to the assertion that every bounded standard sequence of differences is finite.

For a general discussion of Archimedeaness in measurement structures, see Luce and Narens (1992).

---

[7]   The fuller notation $f(n, \oplus)$ is abbreviated to $f(n)$ because $\oplus$ is not varied in the discussion.

4.3.2   The additive representation of joint receipt

Such an Archimedean, joint-receipt preference structure on $\mathcal{D}^{++}$ (i.e., one satisfying Axioms JR1-6 for gains not including e) is an example of what is called an *extensive structure* in the representational theory of measurement. Of course, it is readily extended to e, and we do so. The following representation, which is basically due to Hölder (1901) but in this particular version was first formulated and proved by Roberts and Luce (1968), is well known; see, for example, Krantz et al. (1971, p. 74).

Theorem 4.3.2.   *Suppose $\langle \mathcal{D}^+, e, \succsim, \oplus \rangle$ is an Archimedean, joint-receipt preference structure, then there is a representation $V : \mathcal{D}^+ \to \mathbb{R}_+$ such that for all $f, g \in \mathcal{D}^+$*

$$f \succsim g \iff V(f) \geq V(g), \tag{4.26}$$

$$V(f \oplus g) = V(f) + V(g), \tag{4.27}$$

$$V(e) = 0. \tag{4.28}$$

This representation is unique up to multiplication by a positive constant, i.e., it forms a ratio scale.

It is convenient to have a name for this class of representations. Because I definitely do not want to assume V is the same thing as the utility function U of Chapter 3, I call V a *value function* or *value representation*. This needs amplification.

4.3.3   Why V is not in general U

Many have conjectured informally, and Tversky and Kahneman (1992) in writing, that if $x, y \in \mathbb{R}_+$ are sums of money, then $\oplus$ is simply addition, i.e.,

$$x \oplus y = x + y. \tag{4.29}$$

Certainly, this seems rational, and in Section 4.5.1 we will discuss the empirical evidence for it.

If we assume both the conclusion of Theorem 4.3.2 and Eq. (4.29) then we have the functional equation for all $x, y \in \mathbb{R}_+$,

$$V(x + y) = V(x) + V(y). \tag{4.30}$$

This is the well-known Cauchy equation. Because the value representation V is order preserving, then by Eq. (2.6) it must be strictly increasing, and because it is defined on $\mathbb{R}_+$, it is well known that for some $\alpha > 0$ and for all $x \in \mathbb{R}_+$,

$$V(x) = \alpha x. \tag{4.31}$$

So, the assertion is that when joint receipt of money is additive then the value of money is proportional to money. More general possibilities are explored in Sections 4.5.2-4.5.4.

Clearly, this linear value function does not exhibit the nonlinearities found in many estimates of the utility function U (§ 3.3). Three stances are possible. One is to question whether joint receipt of money is simply additive, i.e., whether Eq. (4.29) holds. The second is to suppose the axioms for joint receipt are in error. And the third is to assume everything is fine with the assumptions about joint receipt in general and about joint receipt of money and to focus on how U and V may be nonlinearly related. Because the Axioms JR1-6 are both plausible and to some extent confirmed empirically (§§ 2.2, 4.2.2, and 4.2.3), we explore the latter possibility, which is interesting independently of whether or not Eq. (4.29) is correct.

4.3.4   Alternative representations

The utility function U arising in RDU (Ch. 3) and the value function V arising from the assumptions of Theorem 4.3.2 both measure the same attribute over the binary gambles in $\mathcal{G}_1^+$ in the sense that both preserve the order $\succsim$. Thus for some strictly increasing function Φ,

$$U(g) = \Phi[V(g)], \quad g \in \mathcal{B}_1^+ \subseteq \mathcal{D}_1^+. \tag{4.32}$$

The task is to find some behavioral property relating joint receipt and binary gambles that tells us what Φ must be. Note that once we have done this we will be saying that U is a nonadditive representation of the Archimedean, joint-receipt preference structure.

The situation we are confronting is not uncommon in physical measurement. For example, in measuring mass one can study two distinct trade-offs using a pan balance. The one—the usual additive ratio measure m—is based on the so-called extensive structure of concatenating masses, which is a binary operation like $\oplus$. The other is the conjoint structure formed from volumes containing homogeneous substances. That leads to a multiplicative conjoint representation $m^* = V^* \rho^*$, where V^* is a mass-determined measure of volume and ρ^* a mass-determined measure of the substance, i.e., a form of density. And, of course, there is the usual measure of volume V based on lengths. One question that has been addressed is the conditions linking these three structures so that one can show, for some constant $\beta > 0$, $m = (m^*)^\beta$ and $V = (V^*)^\beta$. It is usual to refer to $(\rho^*)^\beta = \rho$ as density. (For details, see Krantz et al., 1971, Ch. 10, and Luce et al., 1990, Ch. 22.)

A second situation from physics is the case of relativistic velocity, which, it turns out, resembles our situation more closely than does mass. Consider frames of reference moving in the same direction at constant velocities relative to one another. Within a single frame, one can measure the velocity of another frame in terms of the time duration t required for an object to traverse a distance s. One shows that this forms an additive conjoint structure with the representation $s = vt$, where v is the usual measure of velocity. One can also look at the concatenation of frames of reference: A with respect both to B and to C, and B with respect to C. Within the theory of relativity one shows that the AB comparison concatenated with the BC comparison to give the AC comparison forms an extensive structure, and so the concatenation o of moving frames has an additive representation which is called "rapidity." Let v be the usual velocity measure of A relative to B and u that of B relative to C, and $u \circ v$ of A relative to C. In classical physics, rapidity and velocity are the same (or proportional) measures and so $u \circ v = u + v$. However, in the theory of special relativity rapidity and velocity are nonlinearly related and

$$u \circ v = \frac{u + v}{1 + \frac{uv}{c^2}},$$

where c is the velocity of light in the same units as u and v.

An interesting observation is that this representation is invariant under changes of unit: $u^* = \alpha u$ yields

$$u^* \circ v^* = \alpha u \circ \alpha v = \frac{\alpha u + \alpha v}{1 + \frac{\alpha u \alpha v}{(\alpha c)^2}} = \alpha(u \circ v) = (u \circ v)^*.$$

This change of unit corresponds to changes in units of either length or time or both. In turn these changes in the conjoint structure correspond to underlying symmetries (i.e., automorphisms = "self" isomorphisms) of that conjoint structure. Similarly, a change in the unit of the rapidity measure of concatenation corresponds to a symmetry of that underlying concatenation structure, but no such interpretation can be given to a change in the unit of velocity because velocity is nonlinearly related to rapidity. Many scientists seem not to have fully appreciated and understood the possibility of nonlinearly related measures that both exhibit ratio scale units but of which only one unit corresponds to symmetries (automorphisms) of the underlying concatenation structure. I believe the distinction is important. For example, invariance of physical laws under scale transformations is taken as one of their defining characteristics in dimensional analysis—this is the usual definition of the concept of dimensional invariance. A good justification can be offered for the concept when these scale changes correspond to automorphisms, but none otherwise. So it is essential to keep straight the two kinds of transformations if one is not to become confused. (See Luce et al., 1990, Ch. 22.)

A similar situation has been already encountered in utility measurement (§§ 3.3 and 3.4.3.4). It was explicitly dealt with by Dyer and Sarin (1982). We now turn to it in theoretical detail for joint receipts and gambles.

4.4 Linking Joint Receipts and Binary Gambles

4.4.1 Binary segregation

The property that I shall postulate as linking the gambling structure to the joint receipt structure was stated informally and named "segregation" by Kahneman and Tversky (1979, p. 274):[8]

"*Segregation:* Some prospects contain a riskless component that is segregated from the risky component in the editing phase. For example, the prospect (300,.80;200,.20) is naturally decomposed into a sure gain of 200 and the risky prospect (100,.80). Similarly, the prospect (-400,.40;-100,.60) is readily seen to consist of a sure loss of 100 and the prospect (-300,.40)."

---

[8] Earlier, Pfanzagl (1959) invoked a stronger version of segregation—too strong for our purposes because it forces U and the corresponding weights to form a SEU representation.

Kahneman and Tversky treated segregation as one of six "editing" rules which they claimed decision makers invoke prior to evaluating the edited gambles.[9] By invoking segregation as "pre-editing," they did not try to incorporate it into their representation for gambles. This was done later by Luce (1991) and Luce and Fishburn (1991, 1995), and I give a version of their results below. First, we provide a formal definition and examine data concerning segregation.

Definition 4.4.1.   Suppose $\mathcal{B}_1^+$ is a family of first-order, binary gambles of gains generated from the set $\mathcal{C}^+$ of consequences and the set of experiments $\mathcal{E}$. Let $\mathcal{D}_1^+$ be the closure of $\mathcal{B}_1^+$ under the binary operation $\oplus$ and $\succsim$ a binary preference order over $\mathcal{D}_1^+$. Then *(binary) segregation* is said to hold if and only if for all $f, g \in \mathcal{B}_1^+$,

$$(f \oplus g, C; g) \sim (f, C; e) \oplus g. \tag{4.33}$$

Five observations:

- By assuming that $\ominus$ is defined (Def. 4.3.1), it is easy to verify that segregation, Eq. (4.19), is equivalent to for $f \succsim g \succsim e$:

$$(f, C; g) \sim (f \ominus g, C; e) \oplus g. \tag{4.34}$$

If we restrict attention to money and assume that Eq. (4.29) holds, then it is easy to verify for $x \geq y > 0$ that $x \ominus y = x - y$, and so Eq. (4.34) becomes:

$$(x, C; y) \sim (x - y, C; 0) \oplus y,$$

which was the Kahneman and Tversky (1979) formulation.
- If g is taken to be one's current wealth, segregation asserts that it is immaterial whether g is added to the consequences f and e to form the gamble on the left or added on the right to the gamble $(f, C; e)$. Thus, the analysis of stimuli treated as states of total wealth devolves to the analysis of gambles of increments and of joint receipt.
- Note the highly rational character of segregation. On each side, one receives $f \oplus g$ if event C occurs and g otherwise. It is thus in the spirit of, and as compelling as, the several elementary accounting indifferences examined in Chapter 2.
- The formulation of segregation in the subtractive form, Eq. (4.34), shows why rank dependence is likely to arise in this approach. It is built into the condition of segregation, because one subtracts the smaller consequence so as to be sure both to subtract a gain and to continue to end up with a gamble involving only a gain and e. Maintaining all the

---

[9]   Two other of their editing rules were "the removal of dominated gambles" and the "coalescing of events" that result in the same consequence. Both of these turn out to be automatic consequences of the general rank-dependent theory (Ch. 5). A third editing rule they proposed, "the dropping of common consequences" in a pair of gambles, is only partially consistent with RDU. And its use in advance of evaluation may make the data appear to sustain SEU (§ 5.5.1.4). The last two are "simplification" in which what are described as nonessential diffferences are neglected, which is not incorporated in the RDU models, and that "all editing precede any evaluation." As Stevenson, Busemeyer, and Naylor (1991) pointed out, they do not specify the order of application of the editing principles, and that order affects the results.

components as perceived gains is important because, as we shall see in Chapters 6 and 7, the case of mixed joint receipts is more complicated.
- The formulation of segregation for losses is identical to Eq. (4.33) but with $f, g \precsim e$. The analogy to Eq. (4.34) is the same except that the condition is $f \precsim g \precsim e$, i.e., one segregates the smaller loss.

4.4.2   Event commutativity and segregation

The following observation is of interest in connection with the results of Chapter 3. It says that when we add segregation to the structure we can weaken any assumption involving event commutativity (Def. 3.1.5), i.e.,

$$((f, C; g), D; g) \sim ((f, D; g), C; g),$$

to status-quo event commutativity, i.e., the special case of $g = e$.

Proposition 4.4.1.   *(Luce & Marley, 1999a) Suppose $\mathcal{D}_2^+$ is the closure of $\mathcal{B}_2^+$ and suppose that for $f \succsim g$, there exists h such that $f \sim g \oplus h$. Then status-quo event commutativity and segregation imply event commutativity.*

Proof. For $f \succsim g$, define $\ominus$ by Eq. (4.19). Then, freely using segregation and status-quo event commutativity,

$$
\begin{aligned}
((f, C; g), D; g) &\sim ((f \ominus g, C; e) \oplus g, D; g) \\
&\sim ((f \ominus g, C; e), D; e) \oplus g \\
&\sim ((f \ominus g, D; e), C; e) \oplus g \\
&\sim ((f \ominus g, D; e) \oplus g, C; g) \\
&\sim ((f, D; g), C; g). \quad \blacksquare
\end{aligned}
$$

4.4.3   Empirical evidence about binary segregation

Segregation has been investigated in two experimental studies, Cho and Luce (1995) and Cho, Luce, and von Winterfeldt (1994). Indeed, because at the time they assumed

$$x \oplus y \sim x + y, \tag{4.35}$$

these studies looked at certainty equivalents of segregation and of three variants:

$$
\begin{aligned}
CE(x \oplus y, p; y) &= CE[(x, p; 0) \oplus y], & (4.36) \\
CE(x + y, p; y) &= CE[(x, p; 0) \oplus y], & (4.37) \\
CE[(x, p; 0) \oplus y] &= CE(x, p; 0) + y, & (4.38) \\
CE(x + y, p; y) &= CE(x, p; 0) + y. & (4.39)
\end{aligned}
$$

This limitation of these tests of modified versions of segregation is important because, as we shall see (§ 4.5.1), there is some reason to question whether joint receipt of money is simply additive. We may refer to these three variants as, respectively, IA-segregation (for internal additive), EA-segregation (for external additive), and A-segregation (for additive). The 1994 study explored, among other things, IA and EA-segregation,[10] Eqs. (4.37) and (4.38), and to that end the authors estimated the following types of CEs:

$$CE(x, p; 0), \ CE(x + y, p; y), \ CE[(x, p; 0) \oplus y],$$

with $(x, y) = (\$96, 70), \ (-\$96, -\$70)$ and $p = 0.2, 0.5, 0.9$. Cho and Luce (1995) tested both segregation and A-segregation, Eqs. (4.36) and (4.39)

Cho et al. (1994) obtained judged CEs from 91 respondents and choice ones from 144 using the PEST procedure described in Appendix C. I will discuss only the choice data. The display was in each case a pie chart of the sort shown in Fig. 1.2 displayed on a computer terminal. Medians were plotted and compared using a median test. For both $p = 0.2, 0.5$, IA- and EA-segregation were sustained, but for $p = 0.9$ both were rejected. The combined data showed IA sustained, i.e.,

$$\widehat{CE}(x + y, p; y) \cong \widehat{CE}[(x, p; 0) \oplus y], \tag{4.40}$$

and EA-segregation rejected in the following direction

$$\widehat{CE}[(x, p; 0) \oplus y] < \widehat{CE}(x, p; 0) + y \tag{4.41}$$

In the same study where monotonicity of joint receipt was examined, again Cho and Luce (1995) studied segregation and A-segregation, Eqs. (4.36) and (4.39), and independently using CEs they tested the additivity of joint receipt for money, Eq. (4.35). This time PEST data were collected from 40 subjects. The results sustained segregation, i.e.,

$$\widehat{CE}(x \oplus y, p; y) \cong \widehat{CE}[(x, p; 0) \oplus y] \tag{4.42}$$

but Eq. (4.39) fails because empirically

$$\widehat{CE}(x + y, p; y) < \widehat{CE}(x, p; 0) + y. \tag{4.43}$$

For money, the additivity of money was apparently sustained, i.e.,

$$\widehat{CE}(x \oplus y) \cong x + y. \tag{4.44}$$

We will soon question whether this means Eq. (4.35) is correct.

These various results exhibit some internal consistency. In particular, Eq. (4.41) is a special case of Eq. (4.12), i.e.,

$$\widehat{CE}(f \oplus g) < \widehat{CE}(f) + \widehat{CE}(g),$$

---

[10]   They called this "additivity of CEs."

which was noted earlier in the study of monotonicity. And either of these together with Eq. (4.40) "implies"[11] Eq. (4.43).

Thus, the major conclusion is that segregation appears to be descriptively accurate up to the noise level of these experiments, but that assuming $x \oplus y \sim x + y$ is probably unjustified. We explore the latter observation more fully in the next subsection and further in 4.5.1.

4.4.4 Bias in PEST and the relation of $x \oplus y$ to $x + y$

If we assume that $\widehat{CE}$ is an unbiased estimate of CE, then Eq. (4.44) strongly suggests joint receipt of money is additive, i.e., Eq. (4.35), since

$$x \oplus y \sim CE(x \oplus y) \cong \widehat{CE}(x \oplus y) \cong x + y.$$

But, as is discussed in Appendix C, we have reasons to suspect that the PEST procedure used in these experiments included a feature that resulted in a small bias in the estimates. To be specific, using simulations and assuming a symmetric psychometric function, Sneddon (1999a) has shown for gambles $(x, p; 0)$ with $p > \frac{1}{2}$, that $\widehat{CE}(x, p; 0) < CE(x, p; 0)$, where CE is defined to be the median of the psychometric function and $\widehat{CE}$ is the PEST-determined estimate. The magnitude of the effect grows with p. By symmetry, $\widehat{CE} > CE$ for $p < \frac{1}{2}$. In the Cho and Luce (1995) experiment, three values of p were used: 0.2, 0.5, 0.9, but they were paired with different values of x. So the effects reported by Sneddon go in opposite directions, and it is not possible to predict with any certainty the average direction of the bias. However, assuming symmetry of the psychometric function, we expect the bias for 0.9 to exceed somewhat that of 0.2 and to be virtually nonexistent for 0.5. So, on average there should be some bias in the direction $\widehat{CE} < CE$. The next observation tells us how the bias and the inference about how $x \oplus y$ relates to $x + y$ interact.

Observation 4.4.2. If CE is order preserving, $CE(x) = x$, and Eq. (4.44) holds, then

$$x \oplus y \prec (\succ) x + y \Longleftrightarrow \widehat{CE} > (<) CE.$$

"Proof": Suppose $x \oplus y \prec x + y$, then $CE(x \oplus y) < CE(x + y) = x + y$. If $\widehat{CE} < CE$, then we would conclude $\widehat{CE}(x \oplus y) < CE(x + y) = x + y$, which contradicts the empirical finding Eq. (4.44). Conversely, if $\widehat{CE} > CE$, and $x \oplus y \succ x + y$, then we have $\widehat{CE}(x \oplus y) > CE(x + y) = x + y$, again a contradiction. The other cases are similar. ■

So, if the argument is accepted that the direction of the bias should be $\widehat{CE} < CE$, then we conclude that $x \oplus y \succ x + y$. We will return to the issue of how $x \oplus y$ and $x + y$ relate in Section 4.5.1.

If there really is bias in the estimates of CEs, what does this do to our interpretation of these studies that have used? Should we simply throw them out? In principle, one should redo them with the modified PEST; however, in a number of cases I do not think this is actually necessary. Consider any indifference in which a $\widehat{CE}$ appears on both sides, then it is plausible

---

11   I put the word implies in quotes because the argument assumes that $\cong$ behaves as $=$.

that both estimates are biased about equally, and so the error roughly cancels. This applies to all of the variants of segregation. It does not, however, apply, as we just saw, in the case of Eq. (4.44).

4.4.5   First linking theorem: Ratio rank-dependent utility and binary segregation

In connection with forcing RDU when RRDU holds (Theorem 3.7.3), we promised a third, more natural property than comonotonic consistency or rank-dependent bisymmetry. It is simply segregation.

Theorem 4.4.3.   *(Luce & Marley, 1999) Suppose that $\langle \mathcal{D}_2^+, e, \succsim, \oplus \rangle$ is a joint-receipt structure for which $\mathcal{D}_2^+$ is the closure under $\oplus$ of the set B_2^+ of second-order, binary gambles of gains that are generated from C^+ and $\mathcal{E}$. If segregation and the RRDU representation, Eq. (3.59), with U onto an interval and W onto $[0,1]$, both hold, then $\mu = 0$.*

The proof is given in Section 4.8.2.

Corollary.   *Assume the conditions of Theorem 4.4.3. Then separability onto intervals, RDA, and segregation imply RDU.*

Proof of the corollary: Separability means that status-quo event commutativity holds and so, by Proposition 4.4.1, event commutativity also holds. So by Theorems 3.7.1 and 4.4.3 we conclude RDU.

4.4.6   Second linking theorem: Binary segregation, binary RDU , and additive joint receipt

Our next result is of considerable importance because it shows that an extremely tight interlock exists between binary RDU and additive joint receipts.

Theorem 4.4.4.   *(Luce, 1991; Luce & Fishburn, 1991) Suppose that $\langle \mathcal{D}_1^+, e, \succsim, \oplus \rangle$ is a joint-receipt structure for which*

(i) $\mathcal{D}_1^+$ *is the closure under $\oplus$ of the set B_1^+ of first-order, binary gambles that are generated from C^+ and $\mathcal{E}$, where $\mathbb{R}_+ \subseteq C^+$, $e \in C^+$ (so, by Eq. (2.6), if $x \in \mathbb{R}_+$, then $x \succsim e$).*

(ii)   *Axioms JR1 weak order, JR2 weak commutativity[12], JR4 weak monotonicity, and JR5 weak identity all hold.*

In the following statements $U : \mathcal{D}_1^+ \xrightarrow{onto} [0, a[$ preserves the order $\succsim$, and for $\mathbf{E} \in \mathcal{E}$, $W_\mathbf{E} : \mathcal{E}_\mathbf{E} \to [0,1]$. Then, any two of the following statements imply the third:

1.   *Binary segregation, Eq. (4.33), holds.*
2.   *$(U, W_\mathbf{E})$ forms a binary RDU representation over B_1^+.*

---

[12]   Dr. Thierry Marchant has noted that the result holds if weak commutativity is replaced by weak associativity.

3.   *For some real constant δ that has the unit[13] of $1/U$,*

$$U(f \oplus g) = U(f) + U(g) - \delta U(f)U(g), \tag{4.45}$$

and for some experiment $\mathbf{K}$ with $W_{\mathbf{K}}$ onto $[0,1]$, $(U, W_{\mathbf{K}})$ forms a separable representation of the gambles $(x, C; e, K \backslash C)$, $x \in C$.

Three observations about this theorem:

- I call the representation of Eq. (4.45) *polynomial-additive* or, for short, *p-additive*. According to Aczél (1961/1966, p. 61, Theorem 1), it is the only polynomial form that can be transformed into an additive form with $U(e) = 0$ (see the first observation following the corollary below). This term and the supporting reasoning is due to A. A. J. Marley.
- In the context of numerical attributes, Keeney (1973) arrived at the p-additive form by assuming that each of the variables, x and y, is risk independent of the other. He defined x to be risk independent of y if and only if

$$r_x(x,y) = -\frac{\partial^2}{\partial x^2} u(x,y) \left/ \frac{\partial}{\partial x} u(x,y) \right.$$

is independent of y. It is easy to verify that a p-additive form has both x risk independent of y and y risk independent of x. He proved the converse also holds.
- Although Theorem 4.4.4 provides a very tight relationship among the three concepts of segregation, binary RDU, and the representation of U of joint receipt, Eq. (4.45), Part 3 of the theorem has one major gap that must be addressed. How do we know that it is possible both for U to be separable and to satisfy Eq. (4.45)? We turn to this issue in the next subsection, but first a corollary of the theorem.

Corollary.   *If conditions 1-3 of Theorem 4.4.4 hold, then*

1. $\langle \mathcal{D}_1^+, e, \succsim, \oplus \rangle$ *has an additive representation V, and so the structure also satisfies associativity, JR3, and Archimedeaness, JR6 .*

2.   *If $\delta = 0$, then for some $\alpha > 0$,*

$$U = \alpha V. \tag{4.46}$$

3.   *If $\delta > 0$, then U is subadditive, i.e., $U(f \oplus g) < U(f) + U(g)$, is bounded by $1/\delta$, and for some $\kappa > 0$*

$$\delta U(f) = 1 - e^{-\kappa V(f)}, \quad \delta, \kappa > 0. \tag{4.47}$$

4.   *If $\delta < 0$, then U is superadditive, unbounded, and for some $\kappa > 0$*

$$|\delta| U(f) = e^{\kappa V(f)} - 1, \quad -\delta, \kappa > 0. \tag{4.48}$$

A proof can also be found in Section 4.8.3.

---

13   The term "unit" is used in the sense of ratio scale measurement, which is the case here.

Seven observations about the corollary:

- Keeney and Raiffa (1976, p. 238) noted the existence of the additive form V when U is p-additive, and of course Aczél (1961/1966) was aware of it also.
- In many places, especially in Chapters 6 and 7, for $\delta \neq 0$ it simplifies matters to work with the dimensionless forms

$$U_+(f) = |\delta| \, U(f) = \begin{cases} 1 - e^{-\kappa V(f)}, & \delta > 0 \\ e^{\kappa V(f)} - 1, & \delta < 0 \end{cases} \qquad f \succsim e, \qquad (4.49)$$

rather than U itself.

- When Eq. (4.46) holds, U is said to be *proportional in* V; when Eq. (4.47) holds, U is said to be *negative exponential in* V; and when Eq. (4.47) holds, U is said to be *exponential in* V.
- These relations between U and V do not say how U depends on money because that depends on what function V is of money (see § 4.5).
- By taking the second derivative of the U expressions relative to V, it is easy to see in the case of the negative exponential, Eq. (4.47), that U is always concave relative to V, and in the case of the exponential, Eq. (4.48), that it is always convex. This does not yet say anything about the concavity or convexity of U relative to money (see § 4.5). Also, U is bounded from above by $1/\delta$ in the concave case and is unbounded in the convex one.
- The general consensus (§ 4.1.2) of the field is that, for gains, U is concave with money (diminishing marginal utility), but as we saw in Section 3.3.1 this generalization is, at best, an oversimplification true for only a fraction of respondents. For losses, where a parallel theorem holds, the consensus is that U is convex in money, again an oversimplification that is only partially true.
- The entire theory can be duplicated for losses but with different constants δ' and κ'. Note that U is unbounded in V in the concave case and bounded from below by $1/\delta'$ in the convex case.

4.4.7   Third linking theorem: p-additive and separable

Presumably, the assumption that U both has the p-additive form and, at least for the canonical experiment K, is separable imposes some additional constraint on the structure that we have not yet encountered. We formulate the constraint as follows.

Definition 4.4.2.   The structure described in Theorem 4.4.3 is said to be *joint-receipt decomposable* if and only if for each $f \in \mathcal{D}_1^+$ and $C \in \mathcal{E}_K$, there exists an event $D = D(f, C) \in \mathcal{E}_K$ such that for all $g \in \mathcal{D}_1^+$,

$$(f \oplus g, C; e) \sim (f, C; e) \oplus (g, D; e). \qquad (4.50)$$

The first result establishes that this indifference indeed follows from the assumptions that there is a U that is both separable and p-additive, and it also shows exactly how D depends on f and C.

Theorem 4.4.5.   *Suppose the structure of binary gambles of gains under joint receipt has a p-additive representation U, Eq. (4.45), and that for the experiment $\mathbf{K}$ there is a weighting function $W_{\mathbf{K}}$ such that $UW_{\mathbf{K}}$ is a separable representation. Then joint-receipt decomposition, Eq. (4.50), is satisfied with*

$$W_{\mathbf{K}}(D) = W_{\mathbf{K}}(C)\frac{1 - \delta U(f)}{1 - \delta U(f)W_{\mathbf{K}}(C)}. \tag{4.51}$$

A proof is given in Section 4.8.4.

The deeper question is whether, for the canonical experiment, joint-receipt decomposability forces the existence of a representation that both is separable and p-additive. If we assume an Archimedean, joint-receipt preference structure, we know that there is always a p-additive representation, say $U^{(1)}$. We also know that the assumptions of Chapter 2 together with solvability, Archimedeaness, and status-quo event commutativity are enough to insure a separable representation for experiment $\mathbf{K}$, say $U^{(2)}W_{\mathbf{K}}^{(2)}$ (§ 3.5.3). One might anticipate our showing, under the assumption of joint receipt decomposability, that indeed $U^{(2)} = \alpha U^{(1)}$. But this is not necessarily true; rather, we show from these three assumptions that there exists a representation $(U, W_{\mathbf{K}})$ that is separable and U is p-additive.

Theorem 4.4.6.   *Suppose the structure $\langle \mathcal{D}_1^+, e, \succsim, \oplus \rangle$ satisfies joint receipt decomposability, Eq. (4.50), that $U^{(1)}$ is p-additive, Eq. (4.45), and that $U^{(2)}W_{\mathbf{K}}^{(2)}$ is a separable representation of the gambles $(f, C; e, K\backslash C)$ such that $W_{\mathbf{K}}^{(2)}$ is onto $[0,1]$. Then there exists $\beta > 0$ such that both $U = (U^{(2)})^{\beta}$ is p-additive and $(U, W_{\mathbf{K}})$, where $W_{\mathbf{K}} = (W_{\mathbf{K}}^{(2)})^{\beta}$, is separable.*

A proof is in Section 4.8.5. Let Ψ be defined by $U^{(1)} = \Psi\left(U^{(2)}\right)$. The theorem was first proved by the joint efforts of Luce (1996a) and Aczél, Luce, and Maksa (1996) under the assumption that both Ψ and Ψ^{-1} are differentiable. Because this additional smoothness beyond Ψ being strictly increasing did not seem intrinsic to the problem, efforts of several mathematicians over two years have gone into removing it. Success was achieved in the late spring of 1998 by Aczél, Maksa, and Páles (1999a).

I know of no empirical evidence one way or another about the property of joint-receipt decomposability. Typically, it is difficult to verify or refute such existential statements by direct experimentation, but an effort needs to be made.

4.5   Dependence of Utility on Money

4.5.1   Does $x \oplus y = x + y$?

We argue that the answer to this question is *No* and that, indeed, the best data we have suggest

$$x \oplus y \succ x + y. \tag{4.52}$$

Recall (§ 4.4.4) we argued for this hypothesis using two ideas. First, based on simulations we believe that, for $p > \frac{1}{2}$, $\widehat{CE}$ is a biased estimate of CE with $\widehat{CE} < CE$. Second, we argued that

$$x \oplus y \prec (\succ) x + y \Leftrightarrow \widehat{CE} > (<)CE.$$

Thus, Eq. (4.52). This argument, of course, is quite indirect, so direct evidence is desirable.

The only relevant work on the relation of $x \oplus y$ to $x + y$ is Thaler's (1985) classroom study involving judgments about scenarios of the following type:

> Mr. A was given tickets to lotteries involving the World Series. He won $50 in one lottery and $25 in the other.
> Mr. B was given a ticket to a single, larger World Series lottery. He won $75.
> Who was happier. ___A   ___B   ___no difference

Other scenarios entailed mixed gains and losses and all losses.

For gains, a substantial majority of respondents said A would be happier than B, which suggests that Eq. (4.52) is true, so we may conclude there is bias in the direction $\widehat{CE} < CE$. Thaler spoke of this as people preferring to "segregate" gains, which is an entirely different meaning of segregation than our use of it. For losses, the data led Thaler to the opposite conclusion, namely, that for $x \prec e, y \prec e$, then $x \oplus y \prec x + y$. He spoke of people preferring to "integrate" losses. The case of mixed consequences is addressed in Section 7.2.4.

There is, however, some ambiguity about what Thaler's data mean vis-à-vis the certainty equivalence data. Thaler's instructions asked each respondent to make what amounts to an interpersonal comparison of utility, and it is unclear that if a respondent were to think of $A = B =$ self, then the response would be the same. We do not have any relevant data on this point. Also, as M. H. Birnbaum[14] noted, the results may be colored by there being two "wins" in one case versus one "win" in the other, and the mere act of winning may be desirable independent of the amount won. If so, the empirical finding may reflect that fact more than any aspect of joint receipt. He suggested an alternative scenario in which a waiter compares getting tips from two tables versus the same amount from one table. In any event, I do not consider the conclusion of Eq. (4.52) yet as firm as one would like.

Note that if both Eqs. (4.52) and (4.45) for the concave case, $\delta > 0$, hold, then U is subadditive, i.e.,

$$U(x + y) < U(x \oplus y) = U(x) + U(y) - \delta U(x) U(y) < U(x) + U(y), \tag{4.53}$$

which was what Thaler concluded directly without an argument.

4.5.2   An invariance condition on $\oplus$

This last discussion, although far from conclusive, suggests that it may be wise to consider "addition" rules different from $x \oplus y \sim x + y$. So, what might they be? A very reasonable

---

[14]   Personal communication, December 15, 1998

constraint to impose on $\oplus$ for money is that it be invariant under changes of units of money, i.e., for real $r > 0$,

$$rx \oplus ry = r(x \oplus y). \tag{4.54}$$

It is easy to see that if we let $r = \frac{1}{y}$ and set $\varphi(z) = z \oplus 1$, then

$$x \oplus y = y\varphi(\frac{x}{y}), \tag{4.55}$$

where by the monotonicity of $\oplus$, JR4, both $\varphi(z)$ is strictly increasing with z and $\frac{\varphi(z)}{z}$ is strictly decreasing with z. The latter two conditions follow from the monotonicity of $\oplus$.

Note that setting $y = 1$ in Eq. (4.55) yields

$$\varphi(x) = x \oplus 1.$$

Thus, assuming an additive representation V of $\oplus$, we see that V and φ are related as

$$\varphi(x) = V^{-1}[V(x) + V(1)]. \tag{4.56}$$

4.5.3 V a power of money

Indeed, the existence of an additive representation V of $\oplus$ plus invariance, Eq. (4.54), places a strong constraint on V and so on the form of $\oplus$. J. Aczél[15] pointed out the following:

Proposition 4.5.1.   *Assume $\oplus$ is invariant and has an additive representation V. Then, there are positive constants α, α', and β such that*

$$V(x) = \begin{cases} \alpha x^\beta, & x \geq 0 \\ -\alpha' \mid x \mid^\beta, & x < 0 \end{cases}. \tag{4.57}$$

and

$$|x \oplus y|^\beta = \begin{cases} x^\beta + y^\beta, & x \geq 0, y \geq 0 \\ x^\beta - \frac{\alpha'}{\beta} \mid y \mid^\beta, & x \geq 0 > y, x \oplus y \succsim 0 \\ -\frac{\alpha}{\alpha'}x^\beta + \mid y \mid^\beta, & x \geq 0 > y, x \oplus y \prec 0 \\ \mid x \mid^\beta + \mid y \mid^\beta, & x \leq 0, y \leq 0 \end{cases}. \tag{4.58}$$

A proof is in Section 4.8.6. It is really a special case of a more general result given by Aczél (1955).

Note that for gains, Eq. (4.58) implies that $x \oplus y \succ x + y$ is equivalent to $\beta < 1$.

The net conclusion is that if we assume:

(i)   for money, $\oplus$ is invariant,
(ii)   binary RDU theory, and
(iii)   segregation,

---

[15]   Personal communication, March 1998

then there are three possible forms for U as a function of money: a power function, an exponential of a power function, or a negative exponential of a power function.

Now assuming Eq. (4.57), consider the case of gains where U is concave relative to V, then for $x \geq 0$

$$
\begin{aligned}
U_+(x) &= 1 - e^{-\kappa V(x)} \\
&= 1 - e^{-\kappa \alpha x^\beta}.
\end{aligned}
$$

Taking the second derivative of U with respect to x yields

$$
U_+''(x) = \alpha \beta \kappa e^{-\kappa \alpha x^\beta} x^{\beta-2}(\beta - 1 - \alpha \beta \kappa x^\beta).
$$

Since the terms to the left of the parentheses are always positive, the sign of U_+'' is determined by that of the term in the parentheses. In particular,

$$
U_+''(x) \gtreqless 0 \iff 1 - \frac{1}{\beta} \gtreqless \alpha \kappa x^\beta,
$$

so for $\beta \leq 1$, U_+'' is always negative and so U_+ is everywhere concave. For $\beta > 1$, U_+ is at first convex and then concave. In the case where U_+ is convex relative to V, a similar analysis shows that U_+ is always convex relative to x if $\beta \geq 1$, and for $\beta < 1$ it is initially concave and then convex.

Thus, the added flexibility of Eq. (4.57) allows a reasonable range of possible dependencies of U on money. This may be useful for the following reasons.

- There are some experiments in which some, usually student, respondents seem to have convex utility functions for small amounts of money, and yet in real-world situations involving much larger sums one suspects they would appear to have concave functions.
- Recall (§ 3.3.1) that some estimates of utility functions for individuals do exhibit such patterns. For example, Krzysztofowicz and Koch (1989) reported that for gains 17% of their 54 respondents were first concave and then convex and 9% were first convex and then concave. Examples are shown in Figure 4.2.
- Also, there are well-known, financially successful people whose utility for large amounts of money seems—I know of no hard evidence on this—almost insatiable, suggesting U may be convex and unbounded. It would be interesting to know if, when such people were dealing with smaller amounts early in their careers, they seemed to have utility functions that, like those of most us, were concave for these "small" amounts. Only later when they were dealing with some sufficiently large amounts they began to seem insatiably interested in money. Or, perhaps all of us are initially concave and then convex for sufficiently large sums—we just never get to experience the convex region!

4.5.4 U a power of money

Given that researchers have often assumed that U itself is a power function of money, it is worth asking to what property of joint receipts of money, $x \oplus y$, this corresponds. The following somewhat negative result is worth noting.

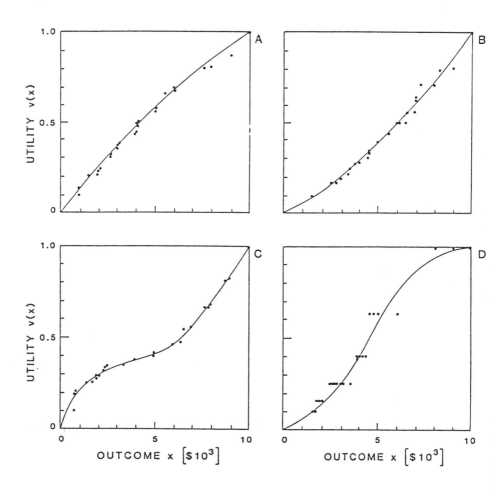

Figure 4.2. Examples of utility functions estimated by Krzysztofowicz and Koch (1989), Fig. 2, using the estimation procedure described in Section 3.3.1. Copyright by Baltzer Science Publishers BV, The Netherlands. Reprinted by permission.

Proposition 4.5.2. *Suppose that Theorem 4.4.3 holds. There does not exist any invariant operation $\oplus$ with an additive representation for which $U(x) = \alpha x^\beta$ except* *when $U = \alpha V, \alpha > 0$.*

This is an immediate consequence of Proposition 4.5.1.

This observation reinforces my concern about invoking the power function assumption for U when estimating the weighting function W (§ 3.4.2). Although U being a power function certainly is one possibility, it is equally certain that it is not the only possibility. Thus, except in special cases, the estimate of W will depend on the form assumed for U.

4.6   Aversions to Risk

Economists have noted various stylized behaviors which collectively go under the name of aversion to some aspect of the risk of lotteries or gambles. These conditions impose some constraints on the form of the utility function and/or weighting function. In this section we formulate some and ask what they mean when we assume that there is a binary RDU representation of the lotteries and joint receipt satisfies segregation. So the RDU utility function U forms a p-additive representation of $\oplus$ (Theorem 4.4.4).

The following types of risk aversion are well known. I have followed closely the listing of Chew and Tan (1999), who examined what these types imply for Chew's weighted utility (§ 5.5.2.2), except that attention is confined here to binary lotteries and for the first two concepts numerical addition of money consequences is replaced by the joint receipt of consequences. The last three concepts are restricted to money.

4.6.1   Aversion to mean-preserving increases in risk

The first of these conditions is *aversion to mean-preserving increases in risk* (Rothschild & Stiglitz, 1970), which in the case of binary lotteries says that for all $x \succsim y, \varepsilon \succsim e, y \ominus \varepsilon \succsim e$,

$$\left(x, \frac{1}{2}; y\right) \succsim \left(x \oplus \varepsilon, \frac{1}{2}; y \ominus \varepsilon\right), \tag{4.59}$$

where $\ominus$ is defined by Eq. (4.19). This reduces to their condition when the consequences are money and $\oplus = +$ and so $\ominus = -$.

Proposition 4.6.1.   *Suppose $\langle \mathcal{D}_1^+, e, \succsim, \oplus \rangle$ is a joint receipt preference structure over binary gambles of gains for which segregation holds and that has a binary rank-dependent representation. Then, Eq. (4.59) is equivalent to for all x, y, ε, $x \succsim y \succsim e, \varepsilon \succsim e$:*

$$W\left(\frac{1}{2}\right) \le \frac{1}{1 + \frac{[1 - \delta U(\varepsilon)][1 - \delta U(x)]}{1 - \delta U(y)}}.$$

Corollary.

(i)   *Assuming idempotence, the special case of $x = y$, which is called* aversion to even-chance gambles, *i.e.,*

$$x \succsim \left(x \oplus \varepsilon, \frac{1}{2}; x \ominus \varepsilon\right). \tag{4.60}$$

is equivalent to

$$W(\tfrac{1}{2}) \le \frac{1}{2 - \delta U(\varepsilon)}.$$

(ii)   *The special case $\varepsilon = y$, i.e., which may be called* aversion to an even chance of all-or-nothing,

$$(x, \tfrac{1}{2}; y) \succsim (x \oplus y, \tfrac{1}{2}; e), \tag{4.61}$$

is equivalent to

$$W(\tfrac{1}{2}) \le \frac{1}{2 - \delta U(x)}.$$

Aversion to even-chance lotteries, Case (i), simply requires that what amounts to the $\oplus$ analogue of expected value of the lottery be preferred to the lottery.

In the context of political science, B. O'Neill (1998) has suggested Case (ii), aversion to an even chance of all-or-nothing, Eq. (4.61), as way to evaluate risk aversion in such settings without assuming numerical measures. An alternative proposed measure is to determine the value p for which

$$(x, p; y) \sim (x \oplus y, p; e).$$

If A and B are two decision makers, A is said to be more risk averse than B for x and y if and only if $p_A > p_B$.

Note that for $\delta \le 0$, the convex case, and $z \succsim e$, we have $-\delta U(z) \ge 0$, which together with $U(x) \ge U(y)$ means that $1 + \frac{[1 - \delta U(\varepsilon)][1 - \delta U(x)]}{1 - \delta U(y)} \ge 2$, and so $W\left(\tfrac{1}{2}\right) \le \tfrac{1}{2}$, which appears to be empirically correct.

From either of the special cases, we see that

$$W(\tfrac{1}{2}) \ge \tfrac{1}{2} \implies \delta \ge 0,$$

which is the concave case. In the special case of expected utility, $W(\tfrac{1}{2}) = \tfrac{1}{2}$, Case (ii) is equivalent to $\delta \ge 0$.

4.6.2   Global risk aversion

Let g denote a gamble. The *risk premium at wealth* y of g is defined to be the sum of money $\pi(g, y)$ such that

$$y \ominus \pi(g, y) \sim y \oplus g. \tag{4.62}$$

Constant absolute risk attitude holds if and only if $\pi(g, y)$ is independent of y. *Global risk aversion* is said to hold if and only if for $g \precsim e$,

$$\pi(g, y) \succsim e.$$

These conditions are often stated on the assumption that the mean of g is zero, but the results reported here do not depend on that assumption. Note that for such lotteries with zero mean, the assumption $g \precsim e$ of pointwise risk aversion seems to hold for many people. Of course, this places us outside the domain of gains. However, assuming that $\oplus$ is both monotonic and associative for mixed gambles (Chapter 7), then by the definition of $\ominus$ and using the associativity of $\oplus$, it is shown in Section 4.8.8 that:

Proposition 4.6.2.   *Suppose* $\langle B, e, \succsim, \oplus \rangle$ *is a joint-receipt preference structure of binary gambles of gains and losses for which* $\oplus$ *is monotonic and associative. For any gamble, both constant absolute risk attitude and global risk aversion hold.*

4.6.3   Aversion to small probability hazards

For this and the next two subsections, the concepts are restricted to money lotteries and $e = 0$.

Chew and Tan (1999) formulate[16] the condition of *aversion to small probability hazards* as: For sufficiently small p,

$$y \ominus pl \succsim (y \ominus l, p; y) \sim (y, 1 - p; y \ominus l). \tag{4.63}$$

This amounts to the observation that many people prefer, for some values of p, paying pl to be rid of the lottery involving the loss of l.[17]

Proposition 4.6.3.   *Suppose* $\langle \mathcal{D}_1^+, 0, \succsim, \oplus \rangle$ *is a joint receipt preference structure of binary lotteries of gains for which segregation holds and that has a binary RDU representation. Then, for sufficiently small p for which it obtains, Eq. (4.63) is equivalent to:*

$$W(1 - p) \leq \frac{1 - \frac{U(pl)}{U(l)}}{1 - \delta U(pl)}.$$

For $\delta = 0$, $W(1-p) \leq 1 - \frac{U(pl)}{U(l)}$, which may or may not hold. For example, if $V(x) = x^\beta$, then the condition is $W(1 - p) \leq 1 - p^\beta$. Clearly, the condition is complex for $\delta \neq 0$, but for small p it implies that $W(1 - p)$ not approach 1 too fast.

4.6.4   Preference for long shots

The idea of *preference for a long shot* is that one is willing to bet on a lottery with a very low probability of a very large return, i.e., when y is sufficiently large and p is sufficiently small,

$$(y \oplus w, p; w) \succsim w \oplus py. \tag{4.64}$$

---

[16] They use $-$ instead of $\ominus$; however the present formulation seems to capture better the intuitive idea than does simple subtraction.

[17] In Chapters 6 and 7 we discuss selling and buying prices. This definition and the next one might better be phrased in those terms, although as we shall see the resulting equations are complex.

Assuming segregation, commutativity, and monotonicity of $\oplus$, Eq. (4.64) is equivalent to

$$(y, p; 0) \succsim py.$$

Because $U(y) > 0$, a routine calculation shows that:

Proposition 4.6.4.   *Suppose $\langle \mathcal{D}_1^+, 0, \succsim, \oplus \rangle$ is a joint receipt preference structure of binary lotteries of gains for which segregation holds and has a separable representation UW over lotteries of the form $(y, p; 0)$. Then, when Eq. (4.64) holds (small p and large y), it is equivalent to:*

$$W(p) \geq \frac{U(py)}{U(y)}.$$

Assuming that U is p-additive with parameter δ, for $\delta = 0$ the condition may or may not hold. For example, if V is a power function, then $W(p) \geq p^\beta$, which depending upon the form of W and the size of β may hold. Normalizing U, V so that the constants are 1, then for the exponential case, $\delta < 0$, and y large, the right side approaches $e^{-[V(y)-V(py)]}$, which in turn approaches 0 provided that $V(y) - V(py) \to \infty$ as $y \to \infty$, and so this case imposes no constraint. For the negative exponential case, $\delta > 0$, the right side approaches $1 - e^{-V(py)}$, which cannot be satisfied unless $p \to c/y$, i.e., the lotteries have constant expected value. This last observation strongly suggests that Eq. (4.64) may not correctly formulate the intuition lying behind it. In Chapter 6 we will suggest an alternative definition, which in the case of the long shot would be

$$(y \ominus py, p; -py) \succsim 0,$$

which depending upon the model we accept for mixed gambles leads to different constraints.

4.6.5   The Arrow-Pratt measure of absolute risk aversion

In connection with expected utility and assuming the consequences are money and that the first and second derivatives of U exist, Arrow (1971) and Pratt (1964) introduced the following well-known *measure of absolute risk aversion:*

$$A(x) = -\frac{U''(x)}{U'(x)}.$$

Although its justification centers on the special model of expected utility, we can, nonetheless, examine its properties for other models, in particular those of the p-additive form.

Assume U is p-additive. If $\delta = 0$ and if $V(x) = x^\beta$, then $A(x) > 0$ if and only if $\beta < 1$. Recall that we argued earlier (§ 4.5.3) from $x \oplus y \succ x + y$ that $\beta < 1$.

By normalizing U and V appropriately, the two exponential expressions can be written as:

$$U_+(x) = j\left(e^{jV(x)} - 1\right), \tag{4.65}$$

where $j = 1$ when $\delta < 0$ and $j = -1$ when $\delta > 0$. It is easy to verify that

$$A(x) = -\left[\frac{V''(x)}{V'(x)} + jV'(x)\right].$$

Thus, $A(x) > 0$ if and only if

$$V''(x) < -j[V'(x)]^2.$$

For $j = -1$, the condition is clearly satisfied provided V is concave in x and so $V''(x) < 0$. For $j = +1$, there is no reason to expect the condition to hold in general. Indeed, for the case where $V = x^\beta$, it is easy to see that it is false for $\beta > 1$.

4.7   Summary

The major idea of this chapter was to add to the structure of gambles, either $\mathcal{B}_1^+$ or $\mathcal{B}_2^+$, as the case may be, a binary operation $\oplus$ of joint receipt, and extend the preference order $\succsim$ to the closure under $\oplus$ of the gambling structure. We then examined the implications of two reasonable assumptions: (1) that the resulting joint receipt structure satisfies axioms that give rise to an additive value representation V (§§ 4.2 and 4.3), and (2) that the joint receipt and gambling structures be related by segregation, Eq. (4.33), i.e., for $f, g \succsim e$,

$$(f \oplus g, C; g) \sim (f, C; e) \oplus g.$$

Data concerning these assumptions were examined, and although they were not 100% supportive, the preponderance of the evidence seemed favorable.

The most important implications were three.

First, Theorem 4.4.3 established that segregation coupled with separability and RDA imply RDU. This conclusion rested on Theorem 3.7.1 that arrived at the RRDU representation and two additional facts. One is that, under segregation, status-quo event commutativity forces event commutativity. The other is that status-quo event commutativity follows from separability.

Second, Theorem 4.4.4 combined RDU and segregation to show that U forms a p-additive representation of $\oplus$, Eq. (4.45), so there is an additive representation, V, as well. The possible connections were shown in the corollary to be either proportional, exponential, or negative exponential.

Also the theorem asserted a converse result, which affords a fairly simple axiomatization of RDU: If there exist U and W such that UW_K is a separable representation and U is p-additive and binary segregation holds, then (U, W_K) forms an RDU representation of binary gambles.

Third, the previous result is not really satisfactory in the form just stated. We know what behavioral conditions give rise to separable representations and those that give rise to p-additive ones, but why should the same U be involved? Theorems 4.4.5 and 4.4.6 showed that a necessary and sufficient condition for that to be so is the property called joint receipt decomposition (Def. 4.4.2). There are currently no data on this property.

An analysis of how U depends on money came up with two findings. In Proposition 4.5.1, we saw that V being a power function corresponds to a family of "addition" rules for the joint receipt of money, Eq. (4.58). In the subsequent discussion we saw that combining the expressions arrived at in Theorem 4.4.4 between U and V with V a power function of money results in one of five possibilities for U as a function of money: a power, concave; initially convex and changing over to concave for sufficiently large amounts; convex; or initially concave changing over to convex as money increases. These forms seem to accommodate some of the behavior that has been found both in some experiments and in real-world behavior.

Finally, we closed with a cursory examination of various conditions pertaining to risk in the light of these models.

4.8   Proofs

4.8.1   Proposition 4.3.1

In the following proofs, the associativity, commutativity, and monotonicity of $\oplus$ and the transitivity of $\sim$ are used freely without comment.

Eq. (4.20): Let $k \sim f \ominus g$, then $f \sim k \oplus g \sim (f \ominus g) \oplus g$.

Eq. (4.21): Let $k = f \ominus g$ and $k' = g \ominus h$, then

$$f \sim k \oplus g \sim k \oplus (k' \oplus h) \sim k \oplus h \oplus k',$$

which by definition is equivalent to $f \ominus k' \sim k \oplus h$, which is the assertion.

Eq. (4.22): Let $f \ominus g \sim k$ and $f' \ominus g' \sim k'$, then

$$f \oplus f' \sim (g \oplus k) \oplus (g' \oplus k') \sim (g \oplus g') \oplus (k \oplus k'),$$

whence by definition of $\ominus$

$$(f \oplus f') \ominus (g \oplus g') \sim k \oplus k' \sim (f \ominus g) \oplus (f' \ominus g').$$

Eq. (4.23): Note first that setting $k = g$ and $g' = e$ in Eq. (4.22) yields $(f \oplus f') \ominus k \sim (f \ominus k) \oplus f'$. So with $k = g \ominus g'$ and using Eq. (4.21),

$$
\begin{aligned}
(f \oplus f') \ominus (g \ominus g') &\sim (f \ominus (g \ominus g')) \oplus f' \\
&\sim ((f \ominus g) \oplus g') \oplus f' \\
&\sim (f \ominus g) \oplus (g' \oplus f').
\end{aligned}
$$

Eq. (4.24): By induction on Eq. (4.22),

$$
\begin{aligned}
f(n) \ominus g(n) &\sim [f(n-1) \oplus f] \ominus [g(n-1) \oplus g] \\
&\sim [f(n-1) \ominus g(n-1)] \oplus (f \ominus g) \\
&\sim k(n-1) \oplus k
\end{aligned}
$$

$$\sim \quad k(n)$$
$$\sim \quad (f \ominus g)(n). \quad \blacksquare$$

Corollary.   Using Eq. (4.24),

$$f(n) \oplus h \sim g(n) \oplus (f \ominus g)(n) \oplus h$$
$$\succsim g(n) \oplus (h' \ominus h) \oplus h$$
$$\sim g(n) \oplus h',$$

holds if and only if

$$(f \ominus g)(n) \succsim (h' \ominus h). \quad \blacksquare$$

4.8.2   Theorem 4.4.3

Suppose that segregation and the RRDU representation with $\mu \neq 0$ both hold. Let $X = |\mu| U(x), Y = |\mu| U(y)$, and $W = W(C)$. In the following proof, we require various quantities, such as YW and XY, to be in the image of $|\mu| U$, and various denominators, such as $X, Y, XY, 1 \pm YW$, and $1 \pm XY$, to be nonzero. Because one of the conditions of the RRDU representation is $0 \leq |\mu| U \leq 1$ (see the statement of Theorem 2.2), the required conditions are satisfied provided we restrict the proof to $X, Y, W \in]0, 1[\cap \{\text{range of } |\mu| U\}$. Now let $G(X, Y) = |\mu| U(x \oplus y) = |\mu| U[U^{-1}(\frac{X}{|\mu|}) \oplus U^{-1}(\frac{Y}{|\mu|})]$. Then segregation with the RRDU representation becomes, with $\pm$ meaning use $+$ for $\mu > 0$ and $-$ for $\mu < 0$:

$$
\begin{aligned}
G(XW, Y) &= |\mu| U[U^{-1}(\frac{XW}{|\mu|}) \oplus U^{-1}(\frac{Y}{|\mu|})] \\
&= |\mu| U (U^{-1}[U(x)W(C)] \oplus y) \\
&= |\mu| U (U^{-1}[U(x, C; e)] \oplus y) \\
&= |\mu| U[(x, C; e) \oplus y] \\
&= |\mu| U[(x \oplus y, C; y] \\
&= \frac{|\mu| U(x \oplus y)W + |\mu| U(y)(1 - W) \pm \mu^2 U(x \oplus y)U(y)W}{1 \pm |\mu| U(y)W} \\
&= \frac{G(X, Y)W + Y(1 - W) \pm G(X, Y)YW}{1 \pm YW}. \quad (4.66)
\end{aligned}
$$

Rewriting,

$$
\begin{aligned}
\theta(X, Y) &= \frac{G(X, Y)(1 \pm Y)}{Y} - 1 \quad (4.67) \\
&= \frac{1}{W} \left(\frac{G(XW, Y)(1 \pm YW)}{Y} - 1 \right). \quad (4.68)
\end{aligned}
$$

So from the last equation,

$$
\begin{aligned}
G(XW,Y) &= \frac{Y[W\theta(X,Y)+1]}{1\pm YW}\\
&= G(WX,Y)\\
&= \frac{Y[X\theta(W,Y)+1]}{1\pm XY}.
\end{aligned}
$$

Cancelling Y, cross multiplying, simplifying, and dividing by WX yields

$$
\frac{1\pm XY}{X}\theta(X,Y)\mp\frac{Y}{X}=\frac{1\pm WY}{W}\theta(W,Y)\mp\frac{Y}{W}.
$$

Because X and W are independent, it follows that this expression can only depend on Y, i.e., for some function φ,

$$
\frac{1\pm XY}{X}\theta(X,Y)\mp\frac{Y}{X}=\varphi(Y),
$$

or solving

$$
\theta(X,Y)=\frac{X\varphi(Y)\pm Y}{1\pm XY}.
$$

Substituting this back into Eq. (4.67),

$$
\begin{aligned}
G(X,Y) &= \frac{Y[\theta(X,Y)+1]}{1\pm Y}\\
&= \frac{1}{1\pm XY}\left(\frac{XY}{1\pm Y}[\varphi(Y)\pm Y]+Y\right). \qquad (4.69)
\end{aligned}
$$

By the commutativity of $\oplus$, G is symmetric, so

$$
\frac{XY}{1\pm Y}[\varphi(Y)\pm Y]+Y=\frac{XY}{1\pm X}[\varphi(X)\pm X]+X.
$$

Subtracting $X+Y$ from both sides and simplifying,

$$
\frac{\varphi(Y)\pm Y}{1\pm Y}-\frac{1}{Y}=\frac{\varphi(X)\pm X}{1\pm X}-\frac{1}{X},
$$

and so for some constant ρ

$$
\frac{\varphi(Y)\pm Y}{1\pm Y}=\rho+\frac{1}{Y}.
$$

Substituting this into Eq. (4.69) yields

$$
G(X,Y)=\frac{X+Y+\rho XY}{1\pm XY}.
$$

Substituting this equation into Eq. (4.66) and carrying out the necessary algebra, we see that

$$0 = \pm XYW(1-W)(X-1)[1 \mp Y^2 + \rho Y],$$

which clearly is impossible for general X, Y, W, so $\mu \neq 0$ is impossible. ■

4.8.3   Theorem 4.4.4

(2)&(3) $\Rightarrow$ (1). We begin by showing that segregation indeed follows from RDU and the form for U given by Eq. (4.45). First, for any $f, g \in \mathcal{D}^+$ consider the left side of the segregation expression,

$$
\begin{aligned}
U[(f,C;e) \oplus g] &= U(f,C;e) + U(g) - \delta U(f,C;e)U(g) \\
&= U(f)W_E(C) + U(g) - \delta U(f)W_E(C)U(g).
\end{aligned}
$$

Next, consider the right side,

$$
\begin{aligned}
U(f \oplus g, C; g) &= U(f \oplus g)W_E(C) + U(g)[1 - W_E(C)] \\
&= [U(f) + U(g) - \delta U(f)U(g)]W_E(C) + U(g)[1 - W_E(C)] \\
&= U(f)W_E(C) + U(g) - \delta U(f)U(g)W_E(C).
\end{aligned}
$$

Thus, they are equal and, because U is order preserving, segregation holds.

(1)&(3) $\Rightarrow$ (2). Consider $f, g \in \mathcal{D}_1^+$ with $f \succsim g$. From the definition of $\ominus$ [Def. 4.3.1, Eq. (4.19)] and Eq. (4.45), it is easy to verify that

$$U(f \ominus g) = \frac{U(f) - U(g)}{1 - \delta U(g)}. \tag{4.70}$$

Because U is onto an interval, we know that $f \ominus g$ exists. Using segregation in its subtractive form, separability for the canonical experiment K, and some simple algebra, we have for any experiment E

$$
\begin{aligned}
U(f, C; g, E \backslash C) &= U[(f \ominus g, C; e, E \backslash C) \oplus g] \\
&= U[(f \ominus g, D; e, K \backslash D) \oplus g] \\
&= U(f \ominus g)W_K(D) + U(g) - \delta U(f \ominus g)W_K(D)U(g) \\
&= \left[\frac{U(f) - U(g)}{1 - \delta U(g)}\right]W_K(D) + U(g) - \delta \left[\frac{U(f) - U(g)}{1 - \delta U(g)}\right]W_K(D)U(g) \\
&= U(f)W_K(D) + U(g)[1 - W_K(D)] \\
&= U(f)W_E(C) + U(g)[1 - W_E(C)],
\end{aligned}
$$

which is the binary RDU representation with $W_E(C) = W_K(D)$. Because $\mathbb{R}_+$ is in the domain of consequences and because we assumed that money preference and inequality agree, Eq. (2.7), U has to be onto an interval including 0. By assumption W_K is onto $[0, 1]$, so the representation is onto an interval.

167

(1)&(2) $\Rightarrow$ (3). Suppose $f \succsim e, g \succsim e$. Recall that segregation asserts

$$(f, C; e) \oplus g \sim (f \oplus g, C; g).$$

Applying U to this expression and using the separability assumptions, we obtain

$$
\begin{aligned}
U\left(U^{-1}[U(f)W_{\mathbf{E}}(C)] \oplus U^{-1}U(g)\right) &= U(f \oplus g)W_{\mathbf{E}}(C) + U(g)[1 - W_{\mathbf{E}}(C)] \\
&= U[U^{-1}U(f) \oplus U^{-1}U(g)]W_{\mathbf{E}}(C) \\
&\quad + U(g)[1 - W_{\mathbf{E}}(C)].
\end{aligned}
$$

Set $X = U(f), Y = U(g), W = W_{\mathbf{E}}(C)$, and $G(X, Y) = U\left[U^{-1}(X) \oplus U^{-1}(Y)\right]$. By the weak monotonicity of $\oplus$, G is strictly increasing in each argument. The last equation becomes

$$G(XW, Y) = G(X, Y)W + Y(1 - W),$$

or

$$[G(X, Y) - Y]W = G(XW, Y) - Y.$$

Dividing by $XW > 0$, we have for some function θ

$$\theta(X, Y) = \frac{G(X, Y) - Y}{X} = \frac{G(XW, Y) - Y}{XW}.$$

Set $X = 1$ and denote $\varphi(Y) = \theta(1, Y)$, then

$$G(W, Y) = \varphi(Y)W + Y, \quad W \in \,]0, 1].$$

To extend this to $X > 1$, observe that we may choose W so that $Z = XW < 1$, whence

$$\frac{G(X, Y) - Y}{X} = \frac{\varphi(Y)Z + Y - Y}{Z} = \varphi(Y).$$

Thus,

$$G(X, Y) = \varphi(Y)X + Y, \quad X > 0. \tag{4.71}$$

By commutativity,[18] G is symmetric and so we have

$$\varphi(Y)X + Y = \varphi(X)Y + X,$$

or rewriting,

$$\frac{\varphi(X) - 1}{X} = \frac{\varphi(Y) - 1}{Y}.$$

Thus, either $\varphi \equiv 1$ or, for some δ, $\varphi(X) = -\delta X + 1$. In the former case, $G(X, Y) = X + Y$ and so $U(f \oplus g) = UF(f, g) = U(f) + U(g)$, which is Eq. (4.45) with $\delta = 0$. In the latter case $G(X, Y) = X + Y - \delta XY$, whence

$$U(f \oplus g) = UF(f, g) = U(f) + U(g) - \delta U(f)U(g),$$

which is Eq. (4.45). ■

Corollary.   For $\delta = 0$, the conclusion follows from the known uniqueness of additive representations. Rewrite Eq. (4.45) as

$$1 - \delta U(f \oplus g) = [1 - \delta U(f)][1 - \delta U(g)].$$

So for $\delta > 0$, $1 - \delta U(f) < 1$ and so $-\ln[1 - \delta U(f)]$ is an additive representation. Thus, for some constant $\kappa > 0$, $V(f) = -\frac{1}{\kappa}\ln[1 - \delta U(f)]$. The case $\delta < 0$ is similar. ■

4.8.4   Theorem 4.4.5

Choose D according to Eq. (4.51), which is possible because W_K is onto $[0, 1]$. Then, using Eq. (4.45) and separability,

$$
\begin{aligned}
1 - \delta U[(f, C; e) \oplus (g, D; e)] &= [1 - \delta U(f, C; e)][1 - \delta U(g, D; e)] \\
&= [1 - \delta U(f)W_K(C)][1 - \delta U(g)W_K(D)] \\
&= [1 - \delta U(f)W_K(C)]\left[1 - \delta U(g)W_K(C)\frac{1 - \delta U(f)}{1 - \delta U(f)W_K(C)}\right] \\
&= 1 - W_K(C)\delta[U(f) + U(g) - \delta U(f)Ug)]
\end{aligned}
$$

---

[18]   Marchant's proof using weak associativity is as follows: From Eq. (4.71) and the definition of G

$$UF(f, g) = \varphi[U(g)]U(f) + U(g).$$

So using weak associativity, one shows

$$\varphi[U(h)][\varphi[U(g)]U(f) + U(g)] = \varphi[U[F(g, h)]U(f) = \varphi[U(h)]U(g).$$

So using the commutativity of multiplication,

$$
\begin{aligned}
\varphi U[F(g, h)] &= \varphi[U(h)]\varphi[U(g) \\
&= \varphi U[F(h, g)],
\end{aligned}
$$

whence $F(g, h) = F(h, g)$.

169

$$= 1 - \delta U(f \oplus g) W_{\mathbf{K}}(C).$$

Because U is order preserving, Eq. (4.50) is satisfied. ∎

4.8.5   Theorem 4.4.6

Let $U^{(1)} = \Psi\left(U^{(2)}\right)$, $X = U^{(2)}(f)$, $Y = U^{(2)}(g)$, $Z = W_{\mathbf{K}}^{(2)}(C)$, and $P(X,Z) = W_{\mathbf{K}}^{(2)}[D(f,C)]$. Consider $U^{(1)}$ applied first to the left side of Eq. (4.50) and use the fact that $U^{(2)}$ is separable:

$$\begin{aligned}
U^{(1)}[(f \oplus g, C; e)] &= \Psi\left(U^{(2)}[(f \oplus g, C; e)]\right) \\
&= \Psi\left[U^{(2)}(f \oplus g) W_{\mathbf{K}}^{(2)}(C)\right] \\
&= \Psi\left(\Psi^{-1}[U^{(1)}(f \oplus g)] W_{\mathbf{K}}^{(2)}(C)\right) \\
&= \Psi\left(\Psi^{-1}[\Psi(X) + \Psi(Y) - \delta\Psi(X)\Psi(Y)]Z\right).
\end{aligned}$$

Next consider the right side of Eq. (4.50)

$$\begin{aligned}
U^{(1)}[(f, C; e) \oplus (g, D; e)] &= U^{(1)}(f, C; e) + U^{(1)}(g, D; e) \\
&\quad - U^{(1)}(f, C; e) U^{(1)}(g, D; e) \\
&= \Psi[U^{(2)}(f, C; e)] + \Psi[U^{(2)}(g, D; e)] \\
&\quad - \delta\Psi[U^{(2)}(f, C; e)]\Psi[U^{(2)}(g, D; e)] \\
&= \Psi(XZ) + \Psi[YP(X, Z)] \\
&\quad - \delta\Psi(XZ)\Psi[YP(X, Z)].
\end{aligned}$$

Using the assumption that joint receipt decomposition holds, these are equal. Introducing the notation

$$\Theta(X,Y) = \Psi^{-1}[\Psi(X) + \Psi(Y) - \delta\Psi(X)\Psi(Y)],$$

we have the functional equation

$$\Theta(X,Y)Z = \Theta[XZ, YP(X,Z)].$$

As noted in the text, this was solved in two stages. First, Aczél, Luce, and Maksa (1996) did it under the assumption that Ψ and Ψ^{-1} are differentiable. Next, Aczél, Maksa, and Páles (1999a) eliminated this unwanted assumption. The solution is that there exist constants $\alpha > 0$ and $\beta > 0$ such that

$$\begin{aligned}
|\delta|\Psi(X) &= 1 - (1 - X^\beta)^\alpha \\
P^\beta(X, Z) &= Z^\beta \frac{1 - X^\beta}{1 - X^\beta Z^\beta}.
\end{aligned}$$

By the fact $U^{(1)}$ has the p-additive form, we see that the following two expressions must be equal:

$$1 - \delta U^{(1)}(f \oplus g) = 1 - \delta \Psi[U^{(2)}(f \oplus g)]$$
$$= [1 - sgn(\delta)U^{(2)}(f \oplus g)^\beta]^\alpha.$$

$$[1 - \delta U^{(1)}(f)][1 - \delta U^{(1)}(g)] = \left[1 - \delta \Psi[U^{(2)}(f)]\right]\left[1 - \delta \Psi[U^{(2)}(g)]\right]$$
$$= \left[1 - \delta \Psi[U^{(2)}(f)]\right]\left[1 - \delta \Psi[U^{(2)}(g)]\right]$$
$$= \left[1 - sgn(\delta)U^{(2)}(f)^\beta\right]^\alpha \left[1 - sgn(\delta)U^{(2)}(g)^\beta\right]^\alpha.$$

Equating and taking the α root shows that $U = (U^{(2)})^\beta$ satisfies the p-additive property with $\delta = 1$ or -1, and, of course, $UW_K = (U^{(2)})^\beta \left(W_K^{(2)}\right)^\beta = \left(U^{(2)}W_K^{(2)}\right)^\beta$ is a separable representation of gambles of the form $(f, C; e)$. ∎

4.8.6   Proposition 4.5.1

By the assumptions of invariance and additivity of $\oplus$, for $r > 0$,

$$V[r(x \oplus y)] = V(rx \oplus ry) = V(rx) + V(ry).$$

Setting $V_r(x) = V(rx)$ we see that

$$V_r(x \oplus y) = V_r(x) + V_r(y).$$

So, both V and V_r are additive representations of $\oplus$, whence for some function θ,

$$V_r(x) = \theta(r)V(x) = V(rx). \tag{4.72}$$

So for $x \geq 0$, it is well known that for some $\alpha > 0$ and $\beta > 0$,

$$V(x) = \alpha x^\beta.$$

For $x < 0$, we can conclude from Eq. (4.72)

$$V(rx) = r^\beta V(x).$$

Set $x = -1$,

$$V(-r) = r^\beta V(-1) = -\alpha' r^\beta,$$

where $\alpha' = -V(-1) > 0$, establishing Eq. (4.57)

To show Eq. (4.58), simply substitute Eq. (4.57) into the additive V expression, taking into account the signs of the three terms. ∎

4.8.7   Proposition 4.6.1.

To Eq. (4.59) first apply binary RDU, then invoke the p-additivity of U, Eq. (4.45), noting that it follows, for $y \geq z$, that

$$U(y \ominus z) = \frac{U(y) - U(z)}{1 - \rho U(z)}, \tag{4.73}$$

and also take into account that both

$$U(x \oplus \varepsilon) - U(x) > 0 \quad \text{and} \quad U(y) - U(y \ominus \varepsilon) > 0.$$

A little algebra yields the result.   ■

4.8.8   Proposition 4.6.2.

Using the definition of $\ominus$ and the associativity of $\oplus$, Eq. (4.62) is equivalent to

$$
\begin{aligned}
y \oplus e \quad &\sim \quad y \\
&\sim \quad (y \oplus g) \oplus \pi(g, y) \\
&\sim \quad y \oplus (g \oplus \pi(g, y)),
\end{aligned}
$$

whence by monotonicity of $\oplus$,

$$e \sim g \oplus \pi(g, y),$$

which establishes that constant absolute risk attitude holds. So the notation can be changed to $\pi(g)$.

Further, if $g \precsim e$,

$$e \sim g \oplus \pi(g) \precsim e \oplus \pi(g) \sim \pi(g).$$

So by the fact that money preference agrees with the numerical ordering, Eq. (2.6), this is equivalent to $\pi(g) \succsim e$.   ■

Chapter 5
GENERAL GAMBLES OF GAINS

Having developed a theory of binary gambles of gains, we turn next to the general case of finite gambles of gains.

The structure of the present chapter is as follows. Section 5.1 describes the general rank-dependent utility (RDU) representation for gains (and symmetrically for losses). Using gambles with three distinct consequences, Section 5.2 resumes the discussion begun in Section 3.4 about the shape of the weighting function. Again it appears that if RDU holds, then a substantial fraction of respondents exhibit the inverse S-shape. Section 5.3 provides four axiomatic treatments, out of many possibilities, of preferences among gambles of all gains. All four lead to the same rank-dependent representation, RDU. The first axiom system is based comonotonic trade-off consistency, the second on the property of coalescing, the third on a decomposition property coupled with a very special case of coalescing, and the last uses the same decomposition property and properties of joint receipt that were presented in Section 4.4. Unhappily, as will be seen in Section 5.3.3, applying the general RDU representation to compound gambles forces a too-specific form for weighting functions, one that is decidedly not descriptive. This is the first sign that general RDU is empirically a very questionable generalization of binary RDU. Section 5.4 describes a number of experiments designed to decide if behavior exhibits rank dependence, which it seems to, and others aimed at deciding about the more specific RDU, which seems to fail descriptively. In particular, the property of coalescing seems to be too strong. Section 5.5.1 lists, more or less in historical order, the several earlier contenders for representations of general gambles. Although some of these representations have been axiomatized, I do not present any of them because I believe these models are all insufficient to account for the data. The remainder in Section 5.5.2, some of which appear to be viable empirically, have not been axiomatized. Section 5.6 points out that if one simply accepts binary RDU and the condition of gains decomposition introduced in Section 5.3.3, then a theory results that exhibits some of the anomalies discussed in Section 5.4. Section 5.7 summarizes what we have learned, and Section 5.8 provides proofs.

5.1 The General RDU Representation

Perhaps the best known generalization of subjective expected utility (SEU) is the one called rank-dependent utility (RDU). As was noted in Chapter 3, because there are many variants on rank dependence aside from the special one of RDU, a better, although appreciably longer, term might have been rank-dependent, subjective expected utility. This model has also been called "Choquet expected utility" (CEU) by, e.g., Sarin and Wakker (1994). The reason for this name is Choquet's (1953) study of the kinds of weighting functions, which he called "capacities," that later arose in utility work. Some have restricted the use of the term RDU to the risky case and use CEU for more general uncertain events. I am not convinced that this distinction is useful and will use RDU as the generic term, on a par with the use of SEU. Whatever it is called, in one variant or another it has consumed the attention of a number of theorists during the 1980s and early 1990s.

Tversky and Kahneman (1992), Wakker and Tversky (1993), and, under risk, Chatenauneuf and Wakker (1999) presented a more general model, called "cumulative prospect theory" (CPT), which was not restricted to gains. The gains portion of CPT agrees with RDU, and I will refer to the general model as rank- and sign-dependent utility (RSDU).

A great deal of the work on RDU is summarized by Quiggin (1993) and Wakker (1989). It first began for the case of known probabilities in the seminal paper of Quiggin (1982). Four authors worked on the general case of gambles, Gilboa (1987), Luce (1988), Schmeidler (1989), and Wakker (1989), but Schmeidler has clear priority in that his paper was circulated in draft form as early as 1982. Subsequent to Quiggin's book are three papers by Sarin and Wakker (1992, 1994, 1997). The former modifies the Savage (1954) approach. They generalize to uncertainty the concept of stochastic dominance and characterize their work as a "unification" of the work of Gilboa and Schmeidler. The 1997 paper on the uncertain case applies a method they used in Sarin and Wakker (1992) to derive expected utility. It is closely related to Anscombe and Aumann (1963) but avoids the use of compound gambles.

Assuming that $g_1 \succsim \cdots \succsim g_k$, we denote by $(E_1, ..., E_k)$ the partition $\{E_1, ..., E_k\}$ of E that is ordered by the consequences.

Definition 5.1.1.   Suppose that $\langle \mathcal{C}, \mathcal{E}, \mathcal{G}_1, \succsim \rangle$ is a first-order structure of gambles. A *rank-dependent utility (RDU) representation* is said to exist if there is an order-preserving utility function U over gambles (including pure consequences as a special case) and a weighting function W_E over events in $\mathcal{E}_E$, $\mathbf{E} \in \mathcal{E}$, with $W_E(\emptyset) = 0, W_E(E) = 1$, that is monotonic increasing with event inclusion such that, for $x_i \in \mathcal{C}$,

$$U(x_1, E_1; x_2, E_2; ...; x_k, E_k) = \sum_{i=1}^{k} U(x_i)W_i(E_1, ..., E_k), \qquad (5.1)$$

where, using the notation

$$E(i) = \bigcup_{j=1}^{i} E_j, \qquad E(0) = \emptyset, \qquad (5.2)$$

W_i is defined in terms of W_E as follows:

$$W_i(E_1, ..., E_k) = W_E[E(i)] - W_E[E(i-1)]. \qquad (5.3)$$

RDU is said to be *onto an interval* if the image of U is a real interval including 0 and that of W_E is onto $[0, 1]$. The representation extends to second-order gambles by replacing x_i

by $g_i \in \mathcal{G}_1$.

For $k = 2$, the weights become

$$W_1(E_1, E_2) = W_{\mathbf{E}}(E_1),$$
$$W_2(E_1, E_2) = 1 - W_1(E_1, E_2) = 1 - W_{\mathbf{E}}(E_1).$$

Thus, the binary case determines $W_{\mathbf{E}}$ and so all of the weights. If we are dealing with risky gambles where the probabilities of events are known, the Prelec form, Eq. (3.31), is probably a suitable assumption.

The RDU representation can be generalized to the second-order gambles $\langle \mathcal{C}, \mathcal{E}, \mathcal{G}_2, \succsim \rangle$ by replacing the x_i by $g_i \in \mathcal{G}_1$. It can also be limited to gambles of gains $\langle \mathcal{C}^+, e, \mathcal{E}, \mathcal{G}_1^+, \succsim \rangle$ or $\langle \mathcal{C}^+, e, \mathcal{E}, \mathcal{G}_2^+, \succsim \rangle$.

Assuming that $W_{\mathbf{E}}$ increases monotonically with event inclusion[1] guarantees that

$$W_i(E_1, ..., E_k) \geq 0, \qquad i = 1, 2, ..., k.$$

It is easy to verify that $\sum_{i=1}^{k} W_i(E_1, ..., E_k) = 1$. Observe that with $k = 2$, the model reduces to the binary RDU representation of Definition 3.1.

When we are dealing with both gains and losses, the weights have to be superscripted $W_{\mathbf{E}}^+$ and $W_{\mathbf{E}}^-$, but in this chapter, where the focus is mostly on gains, I suppress the superscripts except when they are needed for clarity. It is assumed that $W_{\mathbf{E}}(E) = 1$. But keep in mind in what follows that the underlying experiment is sometimes varied, so we must be careful about the local normalization to E implicit in Eq. (5.3).

In the case of finite additivity, i.e., where for disjoint events C and D, $W_{\mathbf{E}}(C \cup D) = W_{\mathbf{E}}(C) + W_{\mathbf{E}}(D)$, then we see immediately that $W_i(E_1, ..., E_k) = W_{\mathbf{E}}(E_i)$. This is called *subjective expected utility* (SEU) and $W_{\mathbf{E}}$ is a finitely additive probability measure. The further special case where $p_i = \Pr(E_i)$ is given and $W(E_i) = p_i$ is known as *expected utility* (EU). And finally, if $\mathcal{C} \subseteq \mathbb{R}$ = sums of money and $U(x) = x$, it is called *expected value* (EV). These special cases are discussed further in Section 5.5.

5.2   Ordinal Data on the Shape of Weighting Functions

Wu and Gonzalez (1996, 1998, 1999) devised a method for studying qualitatively the inverse S-shaped form of W without actually estimating any parameters. It is based on the following observation. Suppose $x > y$, $p < q$, $q' < q''$, and $q + q'' \leq 1$. Suppressing the 0 consequence terms, they consider the well-known *concavity condition:* If

$$R = (x, p; y, q') \sim (y, q + q') = S,$$

---

[1]   This property is assured if the utility representation is separable and monotonicity of event inclusion, Eq. (2.13), holds.

then

$$R' = (x, p; y, q'') \succsim (y, q + q'') = S'.$$

The *convexity condition* is exactly the same except that the inequality is reversed in second display.

Wu and Gonzalez (1996) proved (see their appendix):

Theorem 5.2.1.   *Suppose the RDU model holds for three consequence gambles. Then the following two conditions are equivalent:*

(i) $W(p)$ *is a concave (resp., convex) function of p in the open interval* $]\underline{r}, \overline{r}[$.

(ii)   *The concavity (resp., convexity) condition holds for* $\underline{r} < p < q < \overline{r}$.

This result was reported earlier by Segal (1987). The generalization of the result from probabilities to events was first done by Wakker (1986). Wu and Gonzalez (1999) independently uncovered necessary conditions, but did not develop a representation theorem.

The experimental idea was to construct a series of 8 pairs of gambles. The pairs were called "rungs" and each series a "ladder." A ladder began with a rung consisting of the pair $R_1 = (x, p)$ and $S_1 = (y, q)$. Each rung up the ladder involves adding an increment of the form (y, q') to each gamble. So, $R_2 = (x, p; y, q')$ and, using the coalescing property of adding two probabilities having the same consequence, $S_2 = (y, q; y, q') \sim (y, q + q')$. Each ladder began with small values of p and q for which $q - p \leq 0.05$, and the sequence of the first five values of q' was $0.10, 0.10, 0.10, 0.15, 0.15$, after which the jumps varied among the five ladders. The details are not too important for present purposes. The authors then argued, using Theorem 5.2.1, that if the weighting function is inverse S-shaped—i.e., first concave for small probabilities and then convex for large ones—then the proportion of respondents selecting R over S should rise at first and then decrease with the probability of y in the S gamble. And, indeed, this pattern is just what they found. Figure 5.1 shows the group data for one ladder. Each data point was based on responses of 105 respondents, with one set of respondents providing the data for the first four rungs and a different set for the last four. There was a total of 420 respondents in the experiment. The predicted pattern is confirmed.

But consider what one predicts if every respondent has a W that is either entirely concave or entirely convex. For the convex ones, W changes very slowly over the first few rungs where the probabilities are less than 0.30. So the probability of choosing R over S will tend not to change a great deal. But in this region, the concave ones have a rapidly changing W and so the probability of choosing R over S should increase rapidly. Assuming that these two types of respondents are both substantially represented, then averaging them would show a rising probability. By symmetry, for the top rungs, exactly the opposite pattern would be exhibited because the probabilities for respondents with concave W are changing slowly whereas those for respondents with convex W are changing rapidly. So, when averaged, the data will seem convex in that region.

The conclusion is that the data appear to be consistent with either everyone having an inverse S-shaped W or, equally well, with a mix of respondents of two types, those with purely concave W and those with purely convex W or, indeed, with a mix of all three types. Because substantial individual differences cannot be dismissed, the results are actually inconclusive without more detailed individual analysis. Other studies involving analyses of data from individuals (§ 3.4.2) suggested that inverse S-shapes are the most common, but that both concave and convex functions also exist, which they must if the simplest of reduction of compound gambles holds.

A different kind of analysis based on individual respondents will be reported in Section 7.3.5 for which 78% exhibited inverse S-shaped functions and 22% power functions.

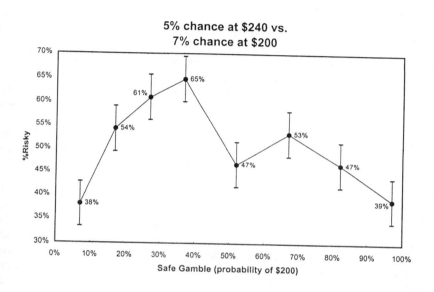

Figure 5.1. The percentage of choices of the risky gamble versus the same gamble as measured in terms of the probability of winning. This is Fig. 1 of Wu and Gonzalez (1996). Reprinted by permission, G. Wu and R. Gonzalez, Curvature of the probability weighting function, *Management Science*, 42, No. 12, December, 1996. Copyright 1996, The Institute of Management Sciences (currently INFORMS), 901 Elkridge Landing Road, Suite 400, Linthicum, Maryland 21090-2909 USA.

5.3   Four Axiomatizations of RDU

This section examines four sets of behavioral properties that give rise to the RDU representation for gains. They are all based on necessary properties of the representation, and the last one involves the concept of joint receipt. These sections are mostly theoretical except for empirical studies that bear directly on a behavioral axiom. Empirical issues concerning the rank-dependent expected utility representation itself are reserved for Section 5.4.

Throughout these sections I shall assume that $\langle \mathcal{C}, e, \mathcal{E}, \mathcal{G}_1^+, \succsim \rangle$ is a family of first-order gambles of gains with the preference order $\succsim$ and that the properties listed in Section 2.7 (and Appendix A) are satisfied. In one axiomatization, we have to go to second-order gambles.

Schmeidler (1989) first gave an axiomatization of RDU based on a generalization of the Anscombe and Aumann (1963) approach. Wakker (1989), working with what he called comonotonic gambles, developed an RDU representation, and later Wakker and Tversky (1993) provided another version and generalized it to the sign-dependent case. Tversky and Kahneman (1992) called this general model cumulative prospect theory, for which the mixed gambles are also bilinear in utility of consequences and weights of events. Recall that "bilinear" means that with the event partition held fixed, the utility of each consequence appears linearly, and with the consequences held fixed, the weight associated with each event also appears linearly. The axiomatization they gave was not in the algebraic spirit of this monograph. In following the 1993 paper I will use topological assumptions, which are quite standard, without explicitly defining them.

Wakker and Tversky began with a finite state space S and a connected topological space[2] $\mathcal{X}$ of consequences. A *gamble* (they call it a "prospect") is simply a mapping $g : S \rightarrow \mathcal{X}$. There is a preference order $\succsim$ over the set $\mathcal{G}_1$ of all first-order gambles.

5.3.1   Comonotonic trade-off consistency

5.3.1.1   Definition: Two gambles f and g are defined to be *comonotonic* if and only if their consequences do not order states in opposite ways, i.e., for any $i, j \in S$, one does not have both $f(i) \succ f(j)$ and $g(i) \prec g(j)$.

Now, consider four comonotonic gambles, f, f', g, g' where the gambles f and f' agree except at the state j, i.e., for $i \neq j$, $f(i) = f'(i)$, and where g and g' also agree except at j. Assuming an RDU representation holds, what can we say about the representation when $f \succsim g$ and $f' \prec g'$? Let ρ denote the permutation of S that agrees with the ordering of consequences of these comonotonic gambles. We see then that we have the numerical inequalities

$$\sum_{i \in S} U\left[f\left([\rho(i)]\right)\right] \left(W_{\mathbf{E}}[E(i)] - W_{\mathbf{E}}[E(i-1)]\right)$$
$$\geq \sum_{i \in S} Ug\left[\left([\rho(i)]\right)\right] \left(W_{\mathbf{E}}[E(i)] - W_{\mathbf{E}}[E(i-1)]\right),$$

$$\sum_{i \in S} U\left[f'\left([\rho(i)]\right)\right] \left(W_{\mathbf{E}}[E(i)] - W_{\mathbf{E}}[E(i-1)]\right)]$$
$$< \sum_{i \in S} U\left[g'\left([\rho(i)]\right)\right] \left(W_{\mathbf{E}}[E(i)] - W_{\mathbf{E}}[E(i-1)]\right).$$

Subtracting the latter from the former and taking into account that the pairs (f, f') and (g, g')

---

2   If the reader is unfamiliar with topological terms, it suffices to consider $\mathcal{X} = \mathbb{R}$.

agree everywhere except j, it is easy to verify that

$$U[f(j)] - U[(f'(j)] > U[g(j)] - U[g'(j)]. \tag{5.4}$$

Thus, a necessary condition for RDU is the following:

Definition 5.3.1.   Consider any eight comonotonic gambles $f, f', g, g', h, h', k, k'$ where

   (i) f agrees with f' and g with g' except at state i, and h agrees with h' and k with k' except at state $j \neq i$; and

   (ii) $f(i) = h(j)$, $f'(i) = h'(j)$, $g(i) = k(j)$, and $g'(i) = k'(j)$.

   Then *comonotonic trade-off consistency* is said to hold if and only if not both $\{f \succsim g$ and $f' \prec g'\}$ and $\{h \precsim k$ and $h' \succsim k'\}$.

The reason these cannot both hold is that, as we have seen, the former implies Eq. (5.4) whereas by the same line of argument the latter implies the contrary inequality. So, comonotonic trade-off consistency is a necessary consequence of RDU. An intuitive argument can be given for it purely in terms of preference; see Wakker (1994). Also, one can recast it as a claim that standard sequences, in the sense of conjoint measurement (Krantz et al., 1971, Ch. 6) that are constructed on two dimensions holding the other ones fixed, should be invariant relative to the choice of common elements so long as one stays in a single comonotonic class. Moreover, Wakker and Deneffe (1996) tested the idea empirically and found support for it. Given Theorem 5.3.1 below, this is tantamount to support for RDU. As we shall see in Section 5.4.2, there are several empirical studies that cast great doubt on general RDU.

Moreover, as I remarked in Section 3.7.3 in the binary case, I have never been able to convince myself that comonotonic trade-off consistency is intuitively very compelling. Nevertheless, a number of people, some closely associated with Wakker, have accepted it, and it is used in several (as I write, unpublished) papers: Abdellaoui (1998, 1999), Bleichrodt and Pinto (1998a,b), Bouzit and Gleyses (1996), Fennema and van Assen (1999), and Ghirardato and Marinacci (1997).

5.3.1.2   The result: The following result is proved by Wakker and Tversky (1993).

Theorem 5.3.1.   *Suppose $S = \{1, 2, ..., n\}$ is a finite state space, $\mathcal{X}$ is a connected topological space, $\mathcal{F} = \overbrace{\mathcal{X} \times \mathcal{X} \times \cdots \times \mathcal{X}}^{n \text{ times}}$ is the set of gambles endowed with the connected product topology, and $\succsim$ is a binary relation on $\mathcal{F}$. Then $\langle \mathcal{F}, \succsim \rangle$ has a RDU representation (Def. 5.1.1) if and only if the following three conditions are satisfied:*

   (i)   *$\succsim$ is a weak ordering;*

   (ii)   *$\succsim$ is continuous in the product topology;*

   (iii)   *comonotonic trade-off consistency holds.*

The weighting function W is unique and the utility function U is unique up to positive linear transformations (i.e., forms an interval scale).

For a proof, see Wakker and Tversky (1993).

5.3.2   Coalescing

5.3.2.1   Definition: The idea behind coalescing,[3] which we have already encountered in Chapter 3, is highly intuitive. Suppose the following consequences are assigned to the possible outcomes of a toss of a die:

$$\left(\begin{array}{cccccc} \{1\} & \{2\} & \{3\} & \{4\} & \{5\} & \{6\} \\ \$10 & \$5 & \$10 & \$5 & \$5 & \$0 \end{array} \right)$$

With a bit of thought, most of us recast it as the following gamble with only three events:

$$\left(\begin{array}{ccc} \{1,3\} & \{2,4,5\} & \{6\} \\ \$10 & \$5 & \$0 \end{array} \right)$$

This recasting is based on two elementary steps of coalescing in which the outcomes that give rise to the same consequence are treated as single events. More formally,

Definition 5.3.2.   Suppose $x_i \in C^+$ are such that for all $i = 1, ..., k-1$, $x_i \succsim x_{i+1}$.
Then the property of *coalescing* is said to hold if and only if whenever $x_{j+1} = x_j$, then

$$(x_1, E_1; ...; x_j, E_j; x_{j+1}, E_{j+1}; ...; x_k, E_k) \sim (x_1, E_1; ...; x_j, E_j \cup E_{j+1}; ...; x_k, E_k). \quad (5.5)$$

It is important to realize that coalescing applies within a single experiment **E**, not across them. The two partitions $\{E_1, ..., E_j, E_{j+1}, ..., E_k\}$ and $\{E_1, ..., E_j \cup E_{j+1}, ..., E_k\}$ are both of E, the set of possible outcomes of **E**.

Recalling the assumption that consequences and events are independent—this is essential —we see that coalescing is another example of a rational "accounting" indifference (Luce, 1990) in which the "bottom lines" of the two sides of Eq. (5.5) are identical. On each side, each x_i, except possibly for $i = j$, arises under exactly the same outcomes of the underlying chance experiment **E**. For x_j, if the experimental outcome lies in either E_j or in E_{j+1}, as on the left side, then it also lies in $E_j \cup E_{j+1}$, as on the right side. So, indeed, there is no difference.

If one begins with the right gamble and replaces it by the left one, the term "event splitting" seems the appropriate. However, substituting the right gamble for the left one, keeping in mind $x_{j+1} = x_j$, seems better described as "coalescing." And, as we shall see, it may well be the case that people coalesce better than they split events simply because the former direction has only two options—coalesce or not—whereas, in the event-splitting direction any event not a singleton can be split in as many ways as their are nontrivial partitions of the event. Currently, the common mathematical models in decision theory that are in the spirit of Savage (1954) do not seem to have room for the distinction between coalescing and event splitting, which as we shall see below probably is a behaviorally significant distinction.

---

[3]   Kahenman and Tversky (1979) called this property "combining" and Starmer and Sudgen (1993) called it "event splitting." As will become clear, "coalescing" and "event splitting" are both useful terms depending on exactly how the idea is being used.

Note that for $k = 2$ coalescing makes idempotence, Eq. (2.1), and certainty, Eq. (2.2), equivalent because by coalescing

$$(x, E_1; x, E_2) \sim (x, E),$$

and so

$$(x, E_1; x, E_2) \sim x \sim (x, E).$$

RDU implies coalescing because if $x_j = x_{j+1}$, then with the normalization $W(E) = 1$ Eq. (5.3) implies

$$W_j(E_1, ..., E_k) + W_{j+1}(E_1, ..., E_k)$$
$$= W[E(j)] - W[E(j-1)] + W[E(j+1)] - W[E(j)]$$
$$= W[E(j-1) \cup (E_j \cup E_{j+1})] - W[E(j-1)].$$

From the perspective of numerical utility theory, coalescing is a continuity property in the following sense: Suppose that the consequences are money and that utility is onto a real interval. Then in any of the utility representations that have been proposed the utility of a gamble changes continuously as x_{j+1} approaches x_j. Coalescing simply requires maintaining continuity at the limit, when $x_{j+1} = x_j$, between the utility of the gamble on the left of Eq. (5.5), which is based on a partition of k events, and the one on the right, where the partition has $k - 1$ events.

If the domain of lotteries is treated as probability distributions over the ordered set C of consequences and first-order stochastic dominance holds, then coalescing *must* be satisfied. For example, in the risky context where there are probabilities rather than events, Wakker (1994, p. 9) remarked[4]

"For example, $(\alpha, p_1; \alpha, p_2; x_3, p_3; ...; x_n, p_n)$ is identical to $(\alpha, p_1 + p_2; x_3, p_3; ...; x_n, p_n)$. This identity is not an assumption, but a logical necessity, these notations merely being two different ways of writing the same probability distribution."

This makes clear once again why I am dissatisfied with modeling lotteries as random variables. Doing so forces identities that simply may not be valid empirically. Although a distribution representation of risky alternatives forces coalescing, it really is an empirical matter whether or not these risky alternatives are actually perceived as indifferent by decision makers. So, let us turn to that issue.

5.3.2.2   Empirical studies of coalescing:

There are, as yet, only a few empirical papers on coalescing, and they all conclude that it fails.[5] In Humphrey (1995) and Starmer and

---

[4] I have changed his notation to mine.

[5] "Support theory" (Tversky & Fox, 1995; Tversky & Koehler, 1994) may at first seem to be relevant to coalescing, but that is not really the case. When an implicitly defined event is evaluated in terms of its probability of occurring and that is compared with the same event where there is at least a partial enumeration of its possible outcomes, the former (subjective) probability tends to be less than the latter. However, within the context of gambling studies the underlying chance experiment is usually completely characterized in terms of all of its possible

Sugden (1993) the focus is mostly on trying to disentangle failures of coalescing, which they call "event-splitting effects," from what they call "juxtaposition effects." Although these data have the advantage that a single group of respondents is used and so one can determine the numbers of respondents who actually are inconsistent with coalescing, they have the drawback that the coalescing condition is confounded with other changes. So I focus only on the part of their data that concerns coalescing in pure form. Unfortunately, these data from the coalesced and uncoalesced cases were from two nonoverlapping sets of respondents, so it is impossible to do a two-by-two cross tabulation on them.

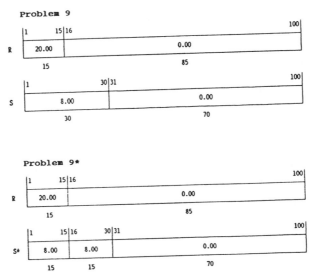

Figure 5.2. The display used by Starmer and Sugden (1993, Fig. 4) for the $(9, 9^*)$ stimulus pair. Copyright 1993 by Kluwer Academic Publishers, 101 Philip Drive, Assinippi Park, Norwell, MA 02061, USA. Reprinted by permission.

For the pure cases of coalescing, conditions $(7,7^*)$ through $(11,11^*)$ of Starmer and Sugden, the basic idea was to present pairs of the form, (R, S) and (R, S^*), where R denotes what is called the risky (higher variance) gamble and two versions of the safer one, S in coalesced form and S^* not coalesced (or split) form.[6] If coalescing holds, then $R \succ S$ if and only if $R \succ S^*$. The stimulus presentation of the $(9, 9^*)$ pair shown in Fig. 5.2 is typical, where the horizontal intervals are the number of tickets receiving the indicated amount (in British £s). The numerical values for all cases are shown in Table 5.1 along with the proportion of S and

---

outcomes. The only difference between the two listings in the coalescing property is whether or not they are also partitioned. So, I do not believe that the results of support theory bear directly on the current issue.
6   Starmer and Sugden referred to these as undivided and divided, respectively.

S^* choices made by 90 respondents for each pair. Because the proportions are significantly different (5% level) in two of the five cases, the authors conclude the evidence rejects coalescing. Given that distinct groups of respondents are being compared and we know there are substantial individual preference differences among people, I view this as a decidedly weak test of the property.

Table 5.1. Stimuli and proportions of S and S^* stimuli chosen over R in the coalescing part of the Starmer and Sugden (1993) study.

Condition	Lotteries	Proportion
7	$R = (20, \#1 - 20; 0, \#21 - 100)$	
	$S = (10, \#1 - 30; 0, \#31 - 100)$	0.400
	$S^* = (10, \#1 - 20; 10, \#21 - 30; 0, \#31 - 100)$	0.444
8	$R = (14, \#1 - 20; 0, \#21 - 100)$	
	$S = (8, \#1 - 30; 0, \#31 - 100)$	0.422
	$S^* = (8, \#1 - 15; 8, \#16 - 30; 0, \#31 - 100)$	0.711
9	$R = (20, \#1 - 15; 0, \#21 - 100)$	
	$S = (8, \#1 - 30; 0, \#21 - 100)$	0.567
	$S^* = (8, \#1 - 15; 8, \#16 - 30; 0, \#31 - 100)$	0.767
10	$R = (25, \#1 - 15; 0, \#16 - 100)$	
	$S = (10, \#1 - 30; 0, \#31 - 100)$	0.544
	$S^* = (10, \#1 - 20; 10, \#21 - 30; 0, \#31 - 100)$	0.544
11	$R = (16, \#1 - 20; 0, \#21 - 100)$	
	$S = (9, \#1 - 30; 0, \#31 - 100)$	0.500
	$S^* = (9, \#1 - 20; 0, \#21 - 90; 9, \#91 - 100)$	0.567

Subsequent papers by Humphrey (1996, 1998, 1999a,b,c) are concerned with trying to understand the relation of event-splitting effects to other phenomena, in particular what are called boundary effects. I do not try to summarize this as yet none-too-definitive work.

M. H. Birnbaum and S. Yeary (personal communication) have shown using buying and selling prices to evaluate gambles that when p is fairly small, e.g., 0.2, then for $x > y, p, r \in\ ]0, 1[$,

$$\begin{pmatrix} p & 1-p \\ x & y \end{pmatrix} \prec \begin{pmatrix} pr & p(1-r) & 1-p \\ x & x & y \end{pmatrix}$$

$$\begin{pmatrix} 1-p & p \\ x & y \end{pmatrix} \succ \begin{pmatrix} 1-p & pr & p(1-r) \\ x & y & y \end{pmatrix}.$$

The effect is quite small when $r = \frac{1}{2}$, and they conjecture that when the computation for coalescing is simple enough perhaps they do coalesce. My major reservation with this finding is the use of buying and selling prices as a measure of evaluation. As we shall see in Chapters

6 and 7, a reasonable theory of buying and selling prices does not in general give evaluations of gambles equal to their certainty equivalents and, in fact, the formulas for calculating them are fairly complex. So, as with the other studies of coalescing, I think this one is ambiguous in its meaning.

For me, the most striking data that cast possible doubt on some aspect of coalescing are taken up in Section 5.4 when we look at data rejecting general RDU.

5.3.2.3   The ranked additive representation of consequences: In Section 3.1.4.1 we encountered the binary additive representation of the rank-ordered consequences. Here again, suppose $(E_1, ..., E_k)$ is an ordered partition of events, $E_i \in \mathcal{E}_\mathbf{E}$, where the ordering agrees with the preference order among consequences: $x_1 \succsim x_2 \succsim \cdots \succsim x_k$. Let $\mathcal{P}_{k,\mathbf{E}}$ denote this family of partitions. Then, it is easy to see that the RDU representation implies the following property holds:

Definition 5.3.3.   *Rank-dependent additivity* (RDA) *is said to hold if for each k there exist functions* $U_{k,i,\mathbf{E}} : \mathcal{C}^+ \times \mathcal{P}_{k,\mathbf{E}} \xrightarrow{into} \mathbb{R}$ *that are strictly increasing in the first argument and with* $U_{k,i,\mathbf{E}}[e, (E_1, ..., E_k)] = 0$, *such that for $x_1 \succsim x_2 \succsim ... \succsim x_k$, $x_i \in \mathcal{C}^+$,*

$$U_{k,\mathbf{E}}(x_1, E_1; ...; x_k, E_k) = \sum_{i=1}^{k} U_{k,i,\mathbf{E}}[x_i, (E_1, ..., E_k)] \qquad (5.6)$$

is an order preserving representation over the gambles based on $\mathbf{E}$.

Wakker (1991a,b, 1993) has provided an axiomatization of RDA representations. I know of no directly relevant empirical studies.

5.3.2.4   The result: The following result is found in Luce (1998).

Theorem 5.3.2.   *The structure $\langle \mathcal{C}^+, e, \mathcal{E}, \mathcal{G}_1^+, \succsim \rangle$ of finite, first-order gambles of gains with a canonical experiment $\mathbf{K} \in \mathcal{E}$ has a RDU representation $(U, W_\mathbf{E})$, $\mathbf{E} \in \mathcal{E}$, that for $\mathbf{K}$ is onto an interval, Eq. (5.1), if and only if:*

(i)   *Restricted to binary gambles, $(U, W_\mathbf{K})$ forms a binary RDU representation onto an interval.*

(ii)   *Coalescing is satisfied.*

(iii)   *The consequences have a ranked additive representation of the form of Eq. (5.6).*

This provides an axiomatization in the sense that we know both how to axiomatize separately the additive representation and the binary RDU representation. Taken together, these (somewhat redundant) axioms coupled with coalescing provide an axiomatization of rank-dependent expected utility.

The proof, which is found in Section 5.8.1, uses coalescing as a principle of induction to reduce representations of gambles on partitions of size k to those of size $k - 1$ and thus inductively to the binary case.

5.3.3   Gains decomposition and status-quo coalescing

5.3.3.1   Definition of gains decomposition: Liu (1995) suggested an approach which he stated only for risky alternatives. Here I generalize it to uncertain ones in such a way that his approach is a special case. In what follows, note that

$$E = E(k) = E(k-1) \cup E_k \text{ and so } E\backslash E_k = E(k-1).$$

The key idea is to extend in a limited way to gains the idea embodied in gain-loss decomposition, Def. 2.5.1. To begin, let

$$g^{(k)} = (x_1, E_1; ...; x_{k-1}, E_{k-1}; x_k, E_k), \quad g^{(k-1)} = (x_1, E_1; ...; x_{k-1}, E_{k-1}). \quad (5.7)$$

Note that $g^{(k)} \in \mathcal{G}_1^+$ is based on the experiment $\mathbf{E}$ with the universal event $E = E(k)$ and $g^{(k-1)} \in \mathcal{G}_1^+$ is based on the subexperiment with the universal event $E(k-1)$, i.e., the restriction of $\mathbf{E}$ to outcomes in $E(k-1)$. Then:

Definition 5.3.4.   Within the domain of second-order compound gambles of gains, $\mathcal{G}_2^+$, *gains decomposition* holds if and only if for all $g^{(k)} \in \mathcal{G}_1^+$ with $x_1 \succsim \cdots \succsim x_k \succsim e$,

$$g^{(k)} \sim (g^{(k-1)}, E(k-1); x_k, E_k), \quad (5.8)$$

where $(g^{(k-1)}, E(k-1); g_k, E_k) \in \mathcal{G}_2^+$.

It is clear that this is a rational accounting indifference in the sense that on the two sides, each consequence arises under the same conditions. The difference is that the one on the left involves a single chance experiment whereas the one on the right involves two independent experiments, the first determining whether one receives x_k or goes on to the subgamble $g^{(k-1)}$ with the first $k-1$ consequences determined by independently running $\mathbf{E}$ restricted to the event $E(k-1)$.

Equation (5.8) is a necessary property if general RDU holds, as we now demonstrate. Normalizing so $W(E) = 1$ and using Eq. (5.1) we have

$$
\begin{aligned}
U[g^{(k-1)}, E(k-1); x_k, E_k)] &= U(g^{(k-1)})W[E(k-1) + U(x_k)[1 - W(E\backslash E_k)] \\
&= \sum_{i=1}^{k-1} U(x_i) \left(\frac{W[E(i)] - W[E(i-1)]}{W[E(k-1)]} \right) W[E(k-1)] \\
&\quad + U(x_k) \left(W[E(k)] - W[E(k-1)] \right) \\
&= \sum_{i=1}^{k} U(x_i) \left(W[E(i)] - W[E(i-1)] \right) \\
&= U(g^{(k)}).
\end{aligned}
$$

One has to be very careful about just how expansive one is in generalizing Eq. (5.8) to gains. Doing it for every nontrivial partition of E forces the RDU representation to become SEU. This can be seen by, for example, considering decomposing g into $(x_1, E_1; g_{\overline{E}_1}, \overline{E}_1)$.

185

Applying RDU to both sides and equating terms, it is easy to see that the $U(x_1)$ terms are identical. But for $U(x_2)$ we see that the coefficients are $W(E_1 \cup E_2) - W(E_1)$ and $W(E_2)$, respectively. Because E_1 and E_2 can be any disjoint pair of events, equating the two expressions means W is finitely additive.

5.3.3.2   Status-quo coalescing and conditionalization: To formulate the next result, it is useful first to observe the following:

Proposition 5.3.3.   *Assuming gains decomposition, the following two properties are equivalent:*

(i) **Status-Quo Coalescing:**   *For a partition $\{E_1, E_2, E_3\}$ of E,*

$$(x_1, E_1; e, E_2; e, E_3) \sim (x_1, E_1; e, E_2 \cup E_3). \tag{5.9}$$

(ii) **Conditionalization:**   *(Def. 3.2.1) For $C \subseteq D \subseteq E$,*

$$((x_1, C; e, D\backslash C), D; e, E\backslash D) \sim (x_1, C; e, E\backslash C). \tag{5.10}$$

Proof. Suppose $C \subseteq D \subseteq E$. According to gains decomposition,

$$((x_1, C; e, D\backslash C), D; e, E\backslash D) \sim (x_1, C; e, D\backslash C; e, E\backslash D).$$

Thus, status-quo coalescing is equivalent to conditionalization. ■

Status-quo coalescing, Eq. (5.9), is a special, intuitively compelling case of coalescing, Eq. (5.5), which it is difficult to believe will be widely violated. Conditionalization, Eq. (5.10), and separability say the weights act as we would expect them to if they were conditional probabilities. As was shown in Proposition 3.2.1,

$$W_{\mathbf{D}}(C) = \frac{W_{\mathbf{E}}(C)}{W_{\mathbf{E}}(D)}. \tag{5.11}$$

As was noted in Section 3.2.1, despite the plausibility of the assumptions, this result is quite strong, probably too strong. Luce (1959) studied Eq. (5.11) as an axiom, and showed among other things that it is equivalent to the existence of a ratio scale measure v over the outcomes of E such that

$$W_{\mathbf{D}}(C) = \frac{\sum\limits_{i \in C} v(i)}{\sum\limits_{i \in D} v(i)}.$$

And it is, in a sense, a generalization to uncertain alternatives that is comparable to the condition $W(pq) = W(p)W(q)$ that follows from the reduction of compound gambles, Eq. (3.17), and leads to W being a power of p. As we know, power functions describe only a fraction of the respondents. To see that this assertion is indeed true, for the case of known probabilities Eq. (5.11) becomes

$$W\left(\frac{p}{p+q}\right) = \frac{W(p)}{W(p+q)},$$

and so setting $\frac{p}{p+q} = r$ and $p + q = s$, then $p = rs$ as claimed, from which it follows that $W(p)$ is a power of p.

So, the conclusion seems to be that for a descriptive theory in which weights are not power functions, we cannot have both conditionalization and binary RDU. Or coupling that with Proposition 5.3.3, we cannot simultaneously have gains decomposition, status-quo coalescing, and binary RDU on $\mathcal{G}_2^+$. Observe that this result says nothing about the weights when the representation is limited to $\mathcal{G}_1^+$. This observation bears negatively on the following result and so on general RDU.

5.3.3.3   The result: Our third axiomatization of RDU is given as:

Theorem 5.3.4.   *Suppose $\langle \mathcal{C}, e, \mathcal{E}, \mathcal{G}_2^+ \succsim \rangle$ is a family of second-order compound gambles of gains and $\mathbf{K} \in \mathcal{E}$ is a canonical experiment. A general RDU representation $(U, W_{\mathbf{E}})$, $\mathbf{E} \in \mathcal{E}$ onto an interval, Eq. (5.1), holds if and only if the following properties hold:*

(i)   *Restricted to binary gambles, $(U, W_{\mathbf{K}})$ is a RDU representation onto an interval.*

(ii)   *Status-quo coalescing, Eq. (5.9).*

(iii)   *Gains decomposition, Eq. (5.8).*

Liu (1995) proceeded slightly differently. He did not assume consequence monotonicity of general gambles of gains (although he did for the binary case). Instead, he postulated that when all of the consequences of a gamble are perceived as gains, then the gamble itself is perceived as a gain, and instead of conditionalization he wrote what amounts to: If $x = CE(g, C; e, D \backslash C)$, then $(g, C; e, E \backslash C) \sim (x, D; e, E \backslash D)$, thereby gaining conditionalization but avoiding using compound gambles. By using status-quo coalescing instead of conditionalization I achieve the same goal.

As noted in subsection 5.3.3.2, these three conditions, which are necessary and sufficient for general RDU, do not appear to be descriptive, and so we should not expect to find RDU holding beyond the binary case. Indeed, as we shall see in Section 5.4, this expectation is correct.

5.3.4   Gains decomposition and segregation

5.3.4.1   Segregation: This fourth approach to axiomatizing general RDU rests on an inductive argument that begins the induction with the binary RDU representation. Like the third axiomatization, it assumes gains decomposition, but rather than status-quo coalescing we invoke a natural generalization of binary segregation (Def. 4.4.1) to the general case of gains. This approach was first taken in Luce and Fishburn (1991) and modified in Luce and Fishburn (1995).

Define $\ominus$ as before for $f \succsim g \succsim e$ by

$$f \ominus g \sim h \Longleftrightarrow f \sim h \oplus g.$$

Definition 5.3.5.   In the domain of gains gambles, *segregation* is said to hold if and only if for $g_1 \succsim g_2 \succsim \cdots \succsim g_k \succ e$,

$$(g_1, E_1; g_2, E_2; ...; g_k, E_k) \sim (g_1 \ominus g_k, E_1; g_2 \ominus g_k, E_2; ...; e, E_k) \oplus g_k. \qquad (5.12)$$

This includes the binary segregation of Def. 4.4.1 as a special case. Its rationality is again clear, namely, the bottom lines of the two sides are identical because $(g_i \ominus g_k) \oplus g_k \sim g_i$.

5.3.4.2   Data on shift and scale invariance: Suppose g is a lottery, then g' is said to be a *shifted* version of g if and only if for some y, $g'_i = g_i + y$, $i = 1, ..., k$. The hypothesis of *shift invariance* studied by Lopes and Oden (1999) is

$$g \succsim h \Longleftrightarrow g' \succsim h'.$$

It is easy to see that this invariance is predicted to hold if the following conditions are satisfied: transitivity, monotonicity of joint receipt, segregation, and $x \oplus y = x + y$. Assuming that transitivity and monotonicity hold, a failure of shift invariance is evidence against either segregation or the additivity of joint receipt or both.

The study involved 6 lotteries of approximately the same expected value. Each had 5 money consequences, ranging from 0 to several hundred dollars. The distributions were presented as what amounted to histograms, and they were quite varied. Each pair of lotteries was presented twice to each of 80 respondents. No payoffs were involved. The data analysis simply summed all the choices over replications and respondents to yield proportions $\widehat{P}(g, h)$. They then asked the degree to which consistency held in the sense

$$\widehat{P}(g, h) > \frac{1}{2} \quad \text{and} \quad \widehat{P}(g', h') > \frac{1}{2}.$$

Of 15 independent pairs of gains, there were 7 inconsistencies, and for losses, 3.

This result is similar to what was found in the binary case (§ 4.4.3), namely, that not both segregation and additivity of joint receipt seem to hold. Independent evidence seemed to support binary segregation and considerable doubt exists about the additivity of money joint receipts. In addition there are at least two issues concerning the data analysis. First, the simple averaging over respondents, who almost certainly had very different preference orderings over the lotteries, seems suspect. Second, the potential for misclassifications of underlying probabilities are considerable, especially for estimates near $\frac{1}{2}$. Recall the similar problem encountered with a similar, incorrect statistical analysis of transitivity (§ 2.2.3). It would be nice to see a study in which the choices between these lotteries could be studied for individual respondents.

In the same study and using the same analysis, they examined *scale invariance* (§ 4.2.3.4), i.e., for $\alpha > 0$

$$g \succsim h \Longleftrightarrow \alpha g \succsim \alpha h.$$

Using only one, quite modest value $\alpha = 1.145$, they found no violations of

$$\widehat{P}(g, h) > \frac{1}{2} \quad \text{and} \quad \widehat{P}(\alpha g, \alpha h) > \frac{1}{2}.$$

Their conclusion was that scale invariance holds, which is inconsistent with the data reported for the binary case. But recall that there the scaling factors varied over a range of 15 to 1 as compared with 1.145 to 1 here. So I think one can question whether scaling invariance was adequately challenged in this experiment.

5.3.4.3   The result: The following result is a generalization from risky to uncertain gambles of Theorem 3 of Luce and Fishburn (1995).

Theorem 5.3.5.   *Suppose* $\langle \mathcal{D}_1^+, e, \succsim, \oplus \rangle$ *forms an extensive structure with an additive representation* V *and* U *is the p-additive form of Eq. (4.45). Let* W_E *be a weighting function over events and event partitions of an experiment* **E**. *Then* (U, W_E) *forms a general RDU representation of* $\langle \mathcal{G}_1^+, \succsim \rangle$, *Eqs. (5.1)-(5.3), onto an interval if and only if:*

    (i)   *Restricted to* $\mathcal{B}_1^+$, (U, W_E) *forms a binary RDU representation onto an interval.*

    (ii)   *Segregation, Eq. (5.12), is satisfied.*

    (iii)   *Gains decomposition, Eq. (5.8), is satisfied.*

A proof is given in Section 5.8.3.

So, to the degree that general RDU is empirically invalid, that binary RDU is valid, and segregation holds, this result casts considerable doubt on the gains decomposition assumption.

5.4   Experiments on Rank Dependence

5.4.1   Evidence about rank-dependent additivity

One necessary qualitative property of RDA, Eq. (5.6), is *comonotonic independence* which says that when two gambles have the identical consequence-event pair in the same ranked position, say (x_i, E_i), then a strict preference is not reversed if E_i is held fixed and x_i is replaced by any x_i' that does not alter the rank order among the consequences. The distinction between the rank-dependent theories and those, like SEU, that are not rank dependent is whether such invariance holds for all choices of x_i', not just the comonotonic ones. When the invariance is independent of ranked positions, Birnbaum and McIntosh (1996) called it *branch independence*.

The relevant empirical studies are all based on the following natural idea. For trinary gambles, hold fixed two pairs of consequences, (x, y) and (x', y') along with the probability distribution over all three consequences. The third consequence is varied so that it falls in each of the intervals defined by the order of these two pairs. Suppose, for example, $x' \prec x \prec y \prec y'$, then the comonotonic cases are when $z \prec x'$, $x \prec z \prec y$, and $y' \prec z$.

Wakker, Erev, and Weber (1994) reported such an experiment in which there was no evidence favoring comonotonic independence over branch independence. The study was immediately criticized because the experimental implementation made dropping the common z terms a natural pre-editing step before evaluating the resulting order 2 gambles (Birnbaum & McIntosh, 1996; Weber & Kirsner, 1997; and correspondence). Avoiding that design problem, Birnbaum and Chavez (1997), Birnbaum and McIntosh (1996), and Birnbaum and Navarrete (1998) using choice procedures, Birnbaum and Beeghley (1997) and Birnbaum and Veira (1998) using judged values of gambles, Birnbaum and Yeary (manuscript) using buying and selling prices, and Weber and Kirsner (1997) using choices have all presented evidence favoring comonotonic independence and rejecting branch independence. Although Birnbaum and McIntosh commented on p. 102, "The present results are quite compatible with generic rank-dependent utility theory," they also noted they did not test other aspects of RDU, such as coalescing. However, if in addition to rank dependence one assumes the special forms of utility and weighting functions proposed by Tversky and Kahneman (1992) [power for U and Eq. (3.21) for W], then Birnbaum and McIntosh (1996) showed that this special model is rejected by their data. Also, as we shall see in Section 5.4.2, the way in which branch independence is violated appears to be inconsistent with RDU.

The Birnbaum and Chavez (1997) study also examined branch independence, replicating the above findings, and another property they called *distribution independence*. Suppose we are working with lotteries and $v > y' > y > x > x' > z$ and p, q, r, r', s, s' are probabilities such that $p + q + r + s = 1$ and $r' + s' = r + s$. Then the property asserts that

$$g = \left(\begin{array}{cccc} p & q & r & s \\ x & y & z & v \end{array} \right) \succ \left(\begin{array}{cccc} p & q & r & s \\ x' & y' & z & v \end{array} \right) = h$$

if and only if

$$g' = \left(\begin{array}{cccc} p & q & r' & s' \\ x & y & z & v \end{array} \right) \succ \left(\begin{array}{cccc} p & q & r' & s' \\ x' & y' & z & v \end{array} \right) = h'.$$

Observe that if there is no dependence on rank, then in both pairs the right two columns can be dropped and the decision should in all cases be based on the first two columns, which are the same in each comparison. Of course, in general, the rank-dependent models lead one to expect violations. A careful empirical study involving 100 undergraduate respondents was carried out in which 24 of the many choices involved provided tests of distribution independence. The authors found it was violated. However, the data tell us more than that, which we go into at the end of the next subsection.

In various ways, these and other data suggest that when respondents must choose between alternatives and they see ways to simplify the decision, such as ignoring common terms, they will. Depending upon the model in question, such editing prior to evaluation can be construed as evidence against the model as applied to unedited gambles. Kahneman and Tversky (1979) and Tversky and Kahneman (1986) emphasized the importance of such pre-editing, although subsequent theory has incorporated many of their editing steps into RDU. The cancellation of common terms, which is inconsistent with a direct application of RDU, either must not hold or must be invoked before the decision evaluation takes place. This possibility of pre-editing in certain experimental designs must to be taken into account when evaluating theories such as RDU.

My tentative conclusion is that RDA has not been rejected. Let us turn now to RDU.

5.4.2   Evidence about RDU

Had RDA or coalescing been unambiguously rejected, we would of course know that RDU is wrong. But neither has been proved wrong with sufficient clarity for us to be confident. However, there are several similar studies that place general RDU into grave doubt as a descriptive theory.

One type of study was first reported by Tversky and Kahneman (1986, problem 8) and has been elaborated by Birnbaum and Navarrete (1998), Birnbaum, Patton, and Lott (1999), and Loomes, Starmer, and Sugden (1992). The argument is as follows: By using the event-splitting direction, i.e., left to right, of coalescing,

$$\begin{pmatrix} 0.05 & 0.05 & 0.90 \\ \$12 & \$14 & \$96 \end{pmatrix} \sim \begin{pmatrix} 0.05 & 0.05 & 0.05 & 0.85 \\ \$12 & \$14 & \$96 & \$96 \end{pmatrix}$$

and

$$\begin{pmatrix} 0.10 & 0.05 & 0.85 \\ \$12 & \$90 & \$96 \end{pmatrix} \sim \begin{pmatrix} 0.05 & 0.05 & 0.05 & 0.85 \\ \$12 & \$12 & \$90 & \$96 \end{pmatrix}.$$

Clearly by consequence monotonicity the right-hand gamble of the first display dominates the right-hand one of the second display. Putting these statements together, one sees that transitivity, consequence monotonicity, and event splitting imply that the two left-hand gambles should satisfy

$$\begin{pmatrix} 0.05 & 0.05 & 0.90 \\ \$12 & \$14 & \$96 \end{pmatrix} \succ \begin{pmatrix} 0.10 & 0.05 & 0.85 \\ \$12 & \$90 & \$96 \end{pmatrix}. \tag{5.13}$$

In the Birnbaum and Navarrete experiment, the data for these and similar gamble pairs show that the dominated gamble was selected over the dominating one about 70% of the time.

Wu (1994) used a design that focuses on what he called *ordinal independence*, which combines comonotonic independence and coalescing. It is probably easiest to illustrate it by an example. Consider a choice between

$$\begin{pmatrix} 0.32 & 0.01 & 0.67 \\ \$3600 & \$3500 & 0 \end{pmatrix} \text{ and } \begin{pmatrix} 0.32 & 0.02 & 0.66 \\ \$3600 & \$2000 & 0 \end{pmatrix} \tag{5.14}$$

and another between

$$\begin{pmatrix} 0.33 & 0.67 \\ \$3500 & 0 \end{pmatrix} \text{ and } \begin{pmatrix} 0.32 & 0.02 & 0.66 \\ \$3500 & \$2000 & 0 \end{pmatrix}. \tag{5.15}$$

Using the event-splitting aspect of coalescing, we see that the first choice can be transformed

191

into

$$\left(\begin{array}{cccc} 0.32 & 0.01 & 0.01 & 0.66 \\ \$3600 & \$3500 & 0 & 0 \end{array} \right) \quad \text{vs.} \quad \left(\begin{array}{ccc} 0.32 & 0.02 & 0.66 \\ \$3600 & \$2000 & 0 \end{array} \right). \tag{5.16}$$

Then using RDA to cancel terms common to both gamble, this choice reduces to

$$\left(\begin{array}{cc} 0.01 & 0.01 \\ \$3500 & 0 \end{array} \right) \quad \text{vs.} \quad \left(\begin{array}{c} 0.02 \\ \$2000 \end{array} \right). \tag{5.17}$$

Similarly, applying event splitting to the second choice, Eq. (5.14), we obtain

$$\left(\begin{array}{cccc} 0.32 & 0.01 & 0.01 & 0.66 \\ \$3500 & \$3500 & 0 & 0 \end{array} \right) \quad \text{vs.} \quad \left(\begin{array}{ccc} 0.32 & 0.02 & 0.66 \\ \$3500 & \$2000 & 0 \end{array} \right). \tag{5.18}$$

Applying rank-dependent additivity to Display (5.18) devolves again to Display (5.17).

Given that RDU is based primarily on RDA and coalescing, it predicts that whatever choice is made in Display (5.14), the corresponding one should be made when the choice of Display (5.15) is presented. In fact, Wu found 60% of his respondents selected the left option when given the former choice whereas 78% selected the right one when given the latter choice. The experiment explored similar cases carefully, and it is unambiguous that rank-dependent additivity and the event-splitting version of coalescing do not both hold, and so general RDU does not hold.

Something is wrong with simultaneously assuming the event-splitting version of coalescing, consequence monotonicity, and transitivity—all exceedingly rational properties. Because some evidence favors consequence monotonicity for choices (von Winterfeldt, Chung, Luce, & Cho, 1997) and other data favor transitivity, perhaps the fault lies with event splitting. But before rejecting event splitting and the theories that imply it, more direct studies need to be performed. We do not yet have any adequate studies of event splitting and coalescing in isolation, as we do of transitivity and consequence monotonicity.

If, as I suspect, coalescing is sustained when studied in explicit form without simultaneously invoking other assumptions, then we must conclude that respondents simply do not carry out, implicitly or explicitly, such complex event-splitting analyses, which, after all, require a bit of creativity to recognize which splits are relevant to establishing dominance. Sometimes people simply may fail to see that it is useful to partition an event into two events to which that same consequence is attached, whereas the same respondents may have no difficulty in seeing that two subevents having the same consequence can be coalesced. This means that overall models derived from such axioms really are only normative.

One danger in experiments in which a respondent directly compares two gambles is that some respondents attempt in various ways to simplify the decision making. For example, in Display (5.13), used by Birnbaum and Navarrete, some respondents might note that the gamble on the right has two events with larger consequences whereas the one on the left has only one. If one pays little heed to the details, focusing instead on such a surface feature as the number of large consequences, choosing a dominated alternative is not surprising. Birnbaum and McIntosh (1996) called this "median theory," and showed that, by itself, it is insufficient to account for all of their data.

One experimental procedure to avoid the use of such shortcuts is to evaluate gambles in terms of choice certainty equivalents. It also has the advantage that one can check individual respondents; I fear that individual differences affect the median data in ways that we do not understand. It has the disadvantage of comparing risky with non-risky alternatives.

Returning to the several Birnbaum studies of branch independence (with Beeghley, 1997; with Chavez, 1997; with McIntosh, 1996; with Navarrete, 1998; with Véira, 1998; and with Yeary, manuscript), the two possible patterns of violations were not equally likely, and that has implications for RDU models. Looking at the distribution independence data, there were many more cases with $g \succ h$ and $g' \prec h'$ than of the opposite order. The pattern is the opposite of what RDU with an inverse S-shaped weighting function predicts. Let us see why. Consider the following gambles where $p + q + r = 1$, $z' > y' > y > x > x' > z$:

$$g = \begin{pmatrix} r & p & q \\ z & x & y \end{pmatrix}, \quad h = \begin{pmatrix} r & p & q \\ z & x' & y' \end{pmatrix},$$

$$g' = \begin{pmatrix} r & p & q \\ z' & x & y \end{pmatrix}, \quad h' = \begin{pmatrix} r & p & q \\ z' & x' & y' \end{pmatrix}.$$

From $g \succ h$ and using RDU we find that

$$[U(y) - U(y')]W(q) + [U(x) - U(x')][W(p + q) - W(q)] > 0.$$

From $g' \prec h'$, we find

$$[U(y) - U(y')][W(r + q) - W(r)] + [U(x) - U(x')][1 - W(r + q)] < 0.$$

Together, these imply

$$[U(y) - U(y')][W(r) + W(q) - W(r + q)]$$
$$+ [U(x) - U(x')][W(p + q) + W(r + q) - W(q) - 1] > 0.$$

Because we may make either utility term as small as we please, the condition implies

$$W(r) + W(q) > W(r + q) \quad \text{and} \quad W(p + q) + W(r + q) - W(q) > 1.$$

Assuming W is inverse S-shaped, select the three probabilities so that $W(q) > q$, $W(p+q) < p + q$, and $W(r + q) < r + q$. Then we see that

$$W(p + q) + W(r + q) - W(q) < (p + q) + (r + q) - q = 1.$$

Thus, we have a contradiction. So either general RDU is wrong or the weighting function is not inverse S-shaped. Because the inverse S-shaped form has been repeatedly confirmed in various ways that use only binary RDU, we are forced again to conclude general RDU is not descriptive.

Birnbaum and Chavez (1997) fit a number of fairly specific models to the data of individuals. Among the RDU models, they looked at inverse S-shaped, S-shaped, and power weighting functions. The best seemed to be the S-shaped. On average, using a power function utility was better than an exponential one. But as we have seen repeatedly, the data of individuals suggest substantial individual differences. It is unclear to me what to make of the fact they favor S-shaped weighting functions whereas all other studies favor inverse S-shape or power. Birnbaum and Chavez theorized that such contradictory results about the shape of the weighting functions based on fits using RDU simply indicate that the general RDU model is in error. Moreover, event-splitting effects, violations of stochastic dominance, and of other properties that I have not described (see various of the Birnbaum papers for results on tail independence and upper and lower cumulative independence) all suggest that RDU simply will not do.

For a full exposition of Birnbaum's views about coalescing, see Birnbaum (1999).

Humphrey (1999a) attempted to discriminate as a source of event-splitting effects between what he called a "stripped down prospect theory" and a psychological theory based on the idea of categorical number of absolute frequencies. The results were inconclusive, and so I do not report them in detail.

Another study that cast doubt on general RDU is Lopes and Oden (1999). The data, and their drawbacks, were described in Section 5.3.4.3. Fitting a variant of cumulative prospect theory plus a reference level model they call SP/A, they found the latter did better (with the same number of degrees of freedom) and that CPT failed in specific ways. Related work is Schneider and Lopes (1986).

5.5   Other Representations

I do not attempt a systematic history of the last half century of work on individual decision making (two summaries are Barberà, Hammond, and Seidl, 1998, and Fishburn, 1999). But it does seem useful to list in one place the major representations that have arisen. I will partition these into two classes: those that are very closely related to, and sometimes special cases of, the RDU representation and those that are decidedly different from RDU. For the latter, some indication is made of which behavioral properties of RDU they do and do not exhibit. The reader will notice that I have not limited the domain of these representations to gains because that has typically not been done in the literature. Of course, one can add such a limitation when that seems useful.

5.5.1   Special cases of RDU

The literature is replete with numerous axiomatizations of several the representations in this section. A recent unified approach is presented by Wakker and Zank (1999).

5.5.1.1   Expected value (EV): For lotteries—i.e., known probabilities of money outcomes —the most ancient idea is *expected value:*

$$EV(x_1, p_1; ...; x_n, p_n) = \sum_{i=1}^{n} x_i p_i, \quad p_i \geq 0, \sum_{i=1}^{n} p_i = 1, \qquad (5.19)$$

where $x_i \in \mathbb{R}$. This remains the normative criterion for decisions in situations where three conditions are met: The consequences are money, the probabilities really are known, and there are many repetitions of the same or highly similar lotteries. It is used to the extent possible by insurance companies, by companies providing warranties, and certainly by casinos and state lotteries. Indeed, it was originally developed solely to understand risks in gambling.

As Daniel Bernoulli (1738/1954) pointed out, in what has come to be called the St. Petersburg paradox, EV is not a rule many people use for one-shot lotteries. Consider tossing a fair coin until a head appears. If the first head occurs on the nth toss, then the payoff is $\$2^n$. What is the largest amount that it is reasonable to pay to play the game once? According to expected value,

$$\left(\frac{1}{2}\right) 2 + \left(\frac{1}{2}\right)^2 2^2 + \left(\frac{1}{2}\right)^3 2^3 + \cdots + \left(\frac{1}{2}\right)^n 2^n + \cdots = 1 + 1 + \cdots + 1 + \cdots.$$

So one should be willing to stake one's entire assets because the sum is unbounded. Few are willing to pay more than a few tens of dollars (or ducats, in the original example) to play the lottery just once. Indeed, according to E. U. Weber,[7] the vast majority of people pay between $4 and $8.

5.5.1.2   Expected utility (EU): Because of this observation, Bernoulli suggested that the decision is based on a "utility" of money that is not proportional to money, which for $x_i \in \mathbb{R}$ leads to an *expected utility* representation:

$$EU(x_1, p_1; ...; x_n, p_n) = \sum_{i=1}^n U(x_i) p_i, \quad p_i \geq 0, \ \sum_{i=1}^n p_i = 1. \quad (5.20)$$

Indeed, to make the sum finite, U must have a decreasing slope. Bernoulli suggested the logarithm, but that is not essential to the idea and, as is noted below, does not really avoid the paradox.

Not a great deal was done with this idea until von Neuman and Morgenstern axiomatized it in an appendix of the 1947 edition of their classic book *The Theory of Games and Economic Behavior*. Subsequently a number of alternative axiomatizations have been suggested (see Fishburn, 1970, 1988, 1989, 1999). Among the recent ones are Becker and Sarin (1987) and Sarin and Wakker (1997) whose approach is in spirit like that of Anscombe and Aumann (1963) but avoids compound gambles. For a comprehensive evaluation of the EU model as of the late 1970s see Schoemaker (1980, 1982) and a bit later Camerer (1992). For a summary of the qualitative properties implied by EU see Keller (1992). Indeed, the Edwards (1992a) volume containing her paper is a very good reference to many of the models and points of view not only about EU but also many of its generalizations. And finally, Fishburn and Wakker (1995) provide a comprehensive discussion of the early history.

Menger (1934) noted that if U is unbounded and EU describes the behavior, then the Bernoulli paradox still obtains.[8] The appropriate payoff replacing 2^i is $x_i = U^{-1}(2^i)$. So

---

[7]   Personal communication, 1998

[8]   A. A. J. Marley (personal communication, May 1998) reminded me of this observation, and P. P. Wakker

$\sum_{i=1}^{\infty} \frac{1}{2^i} U(x_i) = \sum_{i=1}^{\infty} 1$, as before. This argument rules out any convex function and un-bounded concave ones such as power and logarithmic.

5.5.1.3   Subjective expected value (SEV): Edwards (1962a) suggested an alternative to EU, namely, that maybe it is the weights that are distorted, not the money—at least not in the small amounts typical of most experimental studies. So he proposed a weighting function W over probabilities such that for $x_i \in \mathbb{R}$ the *subjective expected value* (SEV) is:

$$SEV(x_1, p_1; ...; x_n, p_n) = \sum_{i=1}^{n} x_i W(p_i), \quad W(p_i) \geq 0, \quad \sum_{i=1}^{n} W(p_i) = 1. \quad (5.21)$$

Handa (1977) attempted an axiomatization, but Fishburn (1978) showed that for sufficiently rich structures Handa's axioms reduce to EV.

One serious drawback of SEV is that if coalescing holds, it reduces to EV because by coalescing for every $p, q, p + q \in [0, 1]$,

$$(x, p; x, q; 0, 1 - p - q) \sim (x, p + q; 0, 1 - p - q),$$

whence $W(p + q) = W(p) + W(q)$. If $W(p)$ is strictly increasing with p for all $p \in [0, 1]$, it is well known that $W(p) = p$. For the binary case, the constraint does not matter except that it implies symmetry about $\frac{1}{2}$ because $W(p) + W(1 - p) = 1$, which we know is wrong empirically.

Even if the sum is not constrained to be 1, which avoids the previous difficulty, it is easy to give examples where first-order stochastic dominance is violated.

5.5.1.4   Subjective expected utility (SEU): Savage (1954) generalized the formulation in three important ways: The consequences need not be money, the chance events need not have known probabilities attached to them, and both utilities and weights play a role in evaluating a gamble. Specifically, his axiomatization, which was mentioned in Section 1.1.6.1, led to the *subjective expected utility* representation:

$$SEU(x_1, E_1; ...; x_n, E_n) = \sum_{i=1}^{n} U(x_i) W(E_i), \quad W(E_i) \geq 0, \quad \sum_{i=1}^{n} W(E_i) = 1, \quad (5.22)$$

where $x_i \in C$ and the weights are finitely additive in the sense that for all $C, D \in 2^E$ with $C \cap D = \emptyset$,

$$W(C \cup D) = W(C) + W(D). \quad (5.23)$$

It is easy to verify that finite additivity implies coalescing. It is also clear that in the case of known probabilities, it forces $W(p) = p$. Sometimes the model is generalized to second-order compound gambles by replacing the x_i by $g_i \in \mathcal{G}_1$.

Subsequently, a number of papers were published that made somewhat different assumptions about the domains and properties, but lead to the same representation (see Fishburn,

---

(personal communication, August 1998) gave me the Menger reference.

1970, 1989, 1999; Wakker, 1989). There is also a substantial empirical literature, some of it summarized earlier and some by Kahneman and Tversky (1979) and Schoemaker (1980, 1982), showing SEU is not satisfactory as a descriptive theory.

The strongest defender of SEU as a normative and—for advising clients—prescriptive theory is Howard (1992) with the strong endorsement of Edwards (1992b) in his comments in Edwards (1992a). Indeed, he remarks, "Rejection of SEU as the appropriate normative model, it seems to me, would have had dramatic implications for normative theory and practice. Acceptance has quite modest implications; it simply encourages the decision analysts to continue with the technology development that has been their main preoccupation for the last twenty years or more" (p. 256). The issue of what model is appropriate for mixed gains and losses is far more subtle, and may invite the "dramatic implications" of which Edwards speaks (Ch. 7).

The RDU theory can be seen as *the* generalization of SEU that simultaneously maintains the additivity over consequences, coalescing, and avoids the finite additivity of the weights.

5.5.2   Representations less closely related to RDU

Except for some very special cases, the following representations fail either coalescing or rank-dependent additivity.

5.5.2.1   Linear weighted utility (LWU):   Edwards (1962a) may have been the first to suggest the following generalization of SEU. *linear weighted utility* (LWU) is said to hold if there is an order-preserving utility function U over gambles and a weighting function W over events such that $W(\emptyset) = 0$ and for all $x_i \in C$ and all $E_i \in \mathcal{E}$, $E_i \cap E_j = \emptyset$, $i \neq j$,

$$U(x_1, E_1; x_2, E_2; ...; x_k, E_k) = \sum_{i=1}^{k} U(x_i)W(E_i), \quad 0 \leq W(E_i) \leq 1. \quad (5.24)$$

Note that W is not assumed to be additive over disjoint events, which is the only difference from SEU. Of course, the earlier estimates of weights on the assumption of separability, some of which were shown in Sections 3.4.1 and 3.4.2, clearly violated additivity and so, implicitly, LWU or something like it was implicated.

The original prospect theory of Kahneman and Tversky (1979) was stated explicitly only for binary lotteries and the class of trinary gambles having 0 as one of the three consequences. No explicit generalization was stated for general finite lotteries. Some authors, e.g., Starmer and Sugden (1993), have claimed that Kahneman and Tversky actually intended LWU, Eq. (5.24), to be the natural generalization for gains and losses separately. I find it difficult to justify this inference from the Kahneman-Tversky paper, in part because they simply did not write it down, and later when they did generalize they used RDU (Tversky & Kahneman, 1992).

The following result is well known (Starmer & Sugden, 1993; Luce, 1998): For gambles satisfying Eq. (5.24), coalescing holds if and only if Eq. (5.23) holds, in which case the LWU reduces to SEU. Of course, LWU satisfies additivity over consequences.

Starmer (1999) has noted that this version of the original prospect theory coupled with its editing rules of coalescing and elimination of dominated alternatives may predict intransitivities. The prediction occurs if the weights satisfy appropriate subadditivity, i.e., for probabilities p, q with $p + q < 1$,

$$W(p) + W(q) > W(p + q).$$

Using this observation, an experiment was performed on 204 respondents who selected between pairs of the following three gambles (presented in terms of 100 numbered lottery tickets) imbedded in a total of 20 choices, one of which was selected at random and run and paid off:

$$A = \left(\begin{array}{cc} \text{1-20} & \text{21-100} \\ 15.00 & 0.00 \end{array} \right)$$

$$B = \left(\begin{array}{cc} \text{1-30} & \text{31-100} \\ 8.00 & 0.00 \end{array} \right)$$

$$C = \left(\begin{array}{ccc} \text{1-15} & \text{16-30} & \text{31-100} \\ 8.00 & 7.75 & 0.00 \end{array} \right)$$

It is clear, by splitting the 1-30 event in B, that B dominates C. So Starmer focused on the non-transitive cycles: $A \succ C \succ B \succ A$ and $A \succ B \succ C \succ A$. The percentages were, respectively, 0.5% and 24.5%.

He then used a most peculiar line of reasoning to reject the hypothesis of transitivity, arguing that if noise were the source of the problem, then the probabilities of these two cycles should be equal. As is obvious, that null hypothesis was firmly rejected statistically. However, I do not think that this hypothesis makes any sense because 93.6% of the respondents recognized that B dominates C, so the percentage of cycles of the former type is bounded from above by 6.4%. Moreover, the percentage of $A \succ B$ choices was 64.7% and of $A \succ C$ choices was 48.5%. So, assuming that the corresponding proportions estimate probabilities and that the decisions are independent, the predicted percentages of intransitive cycles are, respectively, 1.1% and 31.2%. So, I conclude these data are inconclusive on the question raised. The evidence suggests that the dominance relation was perceived by most respondents, but they may have been rather uncertain about their (A, B) and (A, C) choices. To verify that conjecture would require quite a different experiment.

5.5.2.2   Weighted utility: In this subsection and the next two, I will describe the model just for the order 2 and 3 cases and I alter the notation so as to avoid subscripts. The consequences are denoted x, y, z, and the events, B, C, D.

Chew (1983) axiomatized what he called *weighted utility* in which the representation involves an order-preserving utility function U on gambles and a weighting function W from consequences (not probabilities) to $[0, 1]$ such that for $\forall x, y \in C, p, q \in [0, 1]$

$$U(x, p; y, q) = \frac{pW(x)U(x) + qW(y)U(y)}{pW(x) + qW(y)}, \quad p + q = 1.$$

$$U(x, p; y, q; z, r) = \frac{pW(x)U(x) + qW(y)U(y) + rW(z)U(z)}{pW(x) + qW(y) + rW(z)}, \quad (p + q + r = 1).$$

Hazen (1987, 1989) and Hazen and Lee (1987) presented an axiomatized generalization of Chew's model to uncertain events which they called "subjective linear weighted utility." The resulting form is the same except that p is replaced by a subjective (finitely additive) probability denoted by $\pi(C)$. They also write $\psi[U(x)]$ instead of $W(x)$, which is wise because in most other theories the weighting function is on events, not consequences.

Both versions of weighted utility satisfy coalescing but not (rank-dependent) additivity.

5.5.2.3   Quadratic utility: Chew, Epstein, and Segal (1991) axiomatized a representation they called *quadratic utility*. I state it for the trinary case (the generalization is obvious). There is an order-preserving utility function U on gambles and a symmetric function $\varphi : C \times C \to \mathbb{R}$, where C is the set of consequences, such that for $\forall x_i \in C$ and $p_i \in [0,1]$, $i = 1, 2, 3$, $p_1 + p_2 + p_3 = 1$,

$$U(x_1, p_1; x_2, p_2; x_3, , p_3) = \sum_{i,j=1}^{3} \varphi(x_i, x_j) p_i p_j.$$

It is easy to verify that quadratic utility satisfies coalescing but not rank-dependent additivity.

5.5.2.4   Configural weight models: The next approach is a family of related representations that have been proposed, starting as early as 1971, by M. H. Birnbaum and his colleagues (Birnbaum, 1992; Birnbaum & Chavez, 1997; Birnbaum, Coffey, Mellers, & Weiss, 1992; Birnbaum & McIntosh, 1996; Birnbaum, Parducci, & Gifford, 1971; Birnbaum & Stegner, 1979; Birnbaum & Sutton, 1992). They differ somewhat from one another, but in general spirit they are all similar.[9] Their common feature is that there is an underlying weighting function S on event probabilities from $[0,1]$ onto $[0,1]$ and a utility function U on consequences. The function U is independent of the configuration and point of view induced in the respondent, but S depends upon both. So the preference ranking of the consequences and whether the respondent is viewing the situation as a buyer or a seller affect S but not U. Rank dependence takes the form of different coefficients being applied to some function of the $S(p_i)$ where the coefficient depends upon the rank-order position i of the consequence. Then $U(x_i)$ is multiplied by its appropriate modified weight normalized by the sum of all the modified weights (Birnbaum, Coffey, Mellers, & Weiss, 1992). The other configural weight models lead to similar propositions. In this case there is a constant a such that in the binary and trinary cases with $x, y, z \in C$, $x \succsim y \succsim z$, $p + q = 1$,

$$U(x, p; y, q) = \frac{U(x)(1-a)[1-S(q)] + U(y)aS(q)}{(1-a)[1-S(q)] + aS(q)},$$

and for $p + q + r = 1$,

---

[9] It is somewhat frustrating to see various of the papers, including recent ones, speak of *the* configural weight model almost as if there were but one. The fact is that the models have continually been revised to deal with new empirical findings. The distinctions among them are subtle and so a reader must be cautious in trying to keep straight the taxonomy of these models. I do not attempt to lay it out here.

$$U(x, p; y, q; z, r)$$
$$= \frac{U(x)(1-a)[1 - S(1-p)] + U(y)(1-a)[1 - S(1-q)] + U(z)aS(r)}{(1-a)[2 - S(1-p) - S(1-q)] + aS(r)}.$$

Configural weight theory satisfies coalescing if and only if it is the special case of EU theory. The representation satisfies rank-dependent additivity.

Birnbaum with his various coauthors during the 1990s has shown that variants of configural weight theory predict the anomalies he has reported. The reader should approach these data and their interpretation with some caution for two reasons. They are all based on median data, and in many of the cases judgment methods (buying and selling prices being one of the more common) are used. As we shall see, some peculiarities of buying and selling prices can be explained, and the results found in Sections 6.4 and 7.4 strongly suggest that they are not closely related to certainty equivalents. So, although I think there are adequate choice data to cast great doubt on RDU, I remain very uncertain about what is an adequate theory.

5.5.2.5   Prospective reference utility: Viscusi (1989) suggested the following modification of EU: There is an order-preserving utility function U and a constant $\alpha \in [0, 1]$ such that the utility of a gamble g of order n is given by:

$$U(g) = \alpha EU(g) + (1 - \alpha)\frac{1}{n}\sum_{i=1}^{n} U(x_i).$$

For preferences satisfying prospective reference theory, coalescing holds if and only if $\alpha = 1$ and so it reduces to EU. The representation satisfies rank-dependent additivity but not coalescing when $\alpha \neq 1$.

5.6   A Less Restrictive Theory

The empirical evidence certainly invites considering theoretical alternatives to RDU for the utility of gains beyond the binary case. The remarks in Sections 5.3.3.2 and 5.3.3.3 suggest a possibility. Recall that binary RDU, status-quo coalescing, and gains decomposition imply not only general RDU but also in the case of known probabilities that $W(p)$ must be a power of p. The data estimating the form of W tell us that something is wrong. These conditions are simply too restrictive to be descriptive. Indeed, the discussion of examples suggested that coalescing is simply not descriptive.

So one possible remedy is simply to drop coalescing and retain binary RDU and gains decomposition. As is easily verified, for a partition $\{E_1, E_2, E_3\}$ of E and normalizing weights so $W(E) = 1$, this yields for trinary gambles, with $x_1 \succsim x_2 \succsim x_3$, the following form:

$$U(x_1, E_1; x_2, E_2; x_3, E_3)$$
$$= U(x_1, E_1; x_2, E_2)W(E_1 \cup E_2) + U(x_3)[1 - W(E_1 \cup E_2)] \qquad (5.25)$$

$$= (U(x_1)W_{E_1 \cup E_2}(E_1) + U(x_2)[1 - W_{E_1 \cup E_2}(E_1)]) W(E_1 \cup E_2)$$
$$+ U(x_3)[1 - W(E_1 \cup E_2)]. \tag{5.26}$$

For the case where the probabilities of events are known, this becomes

$$U(x_1, p_1; x_2, p_2; x_3, p_3)$$
$$= U(x_1, p_1; x_2, p_2)W(p_1 + p_2) + U(x_3)[1 - W(p_1 + p_2)] \tag{5.27}$$
$$= \left(U(x_1)W(\frac{p_1}{p_1 + p_2}) + U(x_2)[1 - W(\frac{p_1}{p_1 + p_2})] \right) W(p_1 + p_2)$$
$$+ U(x_3)[1 - W(p_1 + p_2)]. \tag{5.28}$$

Simple calculations can be made under various assumptions about U and W. Consider, for example, that utility of money is a power function, the exponent being less than 1, and the weighting function from the Prelec family. If we choose them to be

$$U(x) = x^{0.74} \quad \text{and} \quad W(p) = \exp[-(-\ln p)^{0.90}],$$

then, for Display (5.13), Eq. (5.28) yields

$$U \begin{pmatrix} 0.10 & 0.05 & 0.85 \\ \$12 & \$90 & \$96 \end{pmatrix} = 26.728$$

$$U \begin{pmatrix} 0.05 & 0.05 & 0.90 \\ \$12 & \$14 & \$96 \end{pmatrix} = 26.582.$$

Thus, the dominated gamble has slightly more utility than the dominating one, and so according to this theory it should be chosen, as was true of more than half the respondents. This inversion is not very sensitive to the choice of parameters. Additional parameter values for which it obtains are, for example,

β	γ	η
0.74	1	0.9
0.74	2	0.9
0.74	0.8	0.9
0.74	1	0.6
0.90	1	0.9
0.90	0.8	0.9

For the Wu situation we have for the parameters $(0.74, 1, 0.90)$

$$U \begin{pmatrix} 0.32 & 0.01 & 0.77 \\ \$3600 & \$3500 & 0 \end{pmatrix} = 142.81$$

$$U \begin{pmatrix} 0.32 & 0.02 & 0.76 \\ \$3600 & \$2000 & 0 \end{pmatrix} = 142.80$$

and

$$U\left(\begin{array}{cc} 0.33 & 0.77 \\ \$3500 & 0 \end{array}\right) = 139.99$$

$$U\left(\begin{array}{ccc} 0.32 & 0.02 & 0.76 \\ \$3500 & \$2000 & 0 \end{array}\right) = 140.00,$$

exhibiting the reversal found by Wu. Obviously for these values, the utilities are very close indeed and so the effect is not very pronounced. Moreover, numerical exploration of various combinations of plausible parameter values and also using exponential utility functions suggests that the inversion is quite rare. This casts considerable doubt on the adequacy of this explanation.

These calculations show nothing more than that gains decomposition coupled with binary RDU and plausible shapes for the utility and weighting function can exhibit nonrational failures of the sort reported in the literature. Of course, much more stringent tests of this theory are needed.

This model is readily generalized to any finite gamble. Define $E(j) = \bigcup_{i=1}^{j} E_i$ and $W_{E(k)}[E(k)] = 1$, then a simple mathematical induction generalizes Eqs. (5.26) and (5.28) to, respectively,

$$U(x_1, E_1; ...; x_k, E_k) = \sum_{j=0}^{k-1} U(x_{k-j}) \left(1 - W_{E(k-j)}[E(k-j-1)]\right)$$

$$\times \prod_{i=0}^{j-1} W_{E(k-i)}[W(k-i-1)],$$

$$U(x_1, p_1; ...; x_k, p_k) = \sum_{j=0}^{k-1} U(x_{k-j}) \left[1 - W\left(\frac{\sum_{i=1}^{k-j-1} p_i}{\sum_{i=1}^{k-j} p_i}\right)\right] \prod_{i=0}^{j-1} W\left(\frac{\sum_{m=1}^{k-i-1} p_m}{\sum_{m=1}^{k-i} p_m}\right).$$

5.7   Summary

The generalization of binary RDU to finite gambles with more than two consequences was described in Eqs. (5.1)-(5.3). Within that context, data were reported that did not require any assumptions about the form of U or W and that showed the median respondent's weighting function is inverse S-shaped. It was pointed out that this could arise as some mixture of purely concave and purely convex ones combining to look inverse S-shaped. As seen in Section 3.4.3, the form arrived at by Prelec (1998), Eq. (3.28), encompasses all three forms. Later in Section 7.3.5 estimates for individual respondents suggest that a substantial majority have inverse S-shaped weights. But truly refined tests of Prelec's weighting function have yet to be conducted.

It is fairly easy to axiomatize RDU for the canonical experiment, so it extends immediately to all experiments (see Def. 3.1.2). Indeed, four distinct axiomatizations were provided, three of which are based on very easily understood normative conditions. And there are others in the literature. Moreover, if one wants to be fully normative in the classical sense, it is simple to add conditions that force RDU to become SEU, i.e., for the weights to be finitely additive.

At a descriptive level, the evidence for some form of rank dependence being important is fairly strong, but there is considerable evidence against the specific RDU form. Coalescing, which is both a compelling and very simple normative property and a necessary condition for RDU, seems to be in doubt at least when it is used to split an event in order to carry out a dominance argument. Furthermore, the data rejecting ordinal independence make doubtful the descriptive validity of coalescing (Birnbaum & Navarrete, 1998; Wu, 1994).

Additional empirical work is clearly called for. Measurement-theoretical studies of the consequence structure with events held fixed are needed to decide if rank-dependent additivity really holds. And the evidence against RDU should be replicated but with some alteration in the experimental method such as using choice certainty equivalents.

Assuming that RDU is wrong descriptively, we need to understand what might work descriptively. One possibility is to accept binary RDU and gains decomposition. Doing so was shown in Section 5.6 possibly to accommodate the data rejecting general RDU. This model needs considerable further investigation and refinement. Of the representations described in Section 5.5.2, weighted and quadratic utility both fail RDA and satisfy coalescing, whereas linear weighted utility, configural weight theory, and prospective reference theory all satisfy RDA and fail coalescing, which is what the current data seem to suggest is needed. Among these, perhaps the most interesting are Birnbaum's several configural weight theories. None have ever been axiomatized, which seems an interesting challenge for theorists.

The apparent descriptive failure of RDU, and per force SEU, raises the question of the impact of alternative models on the development of economic theory. In fact, there has not yet been a great deal of detailed work on its impact. Frey and Eichenberger (1989) examined the issue and drew the conclusion that, indeed, economists do need to pay attention to rank dependence. The first substantive exploration of which I am aware is Camerer (1999), and he concluded that there are a number of important economic phenomena that are illuminated better by the RDU representation than the classical rank independent theories.

5.8   Proofs

5.8.1   Theorem 5.3.2

We begin with a useful subresult.

Lemma 5.8.1. *If the utilities of the binary additive model of Eq. (5.6), $U_{k,i}$, and the binary RDU model of Eq. (5.1), U, are chosen so $U_{k,i}(e) = 0 = U(e)$, and the units are such that the ranges are the same, then they are equal.*

Proof. Because both binary representations are, by definition, order preserving and the U's are onto a real interval R, there exists a strictly increasing function $\Phi : R \xrightarrow{onto} R$ such that

$$U_{2,1}[g_1, (E_1, E_2)] + U_{2,2}[g_2, (E_1, E_2)] = \Phi\left(U(g_1)W_1(E_1) + U(g_2)[1 - W(E_1)]\right).$$

Let $w = W_1(E_1)$, $u_i = U(x_i)$, where $u_1 \geq u_2$. Observe that by first setting $g_2 = e$ and then $g_1 = e$ and using the assumptions about the U's, we have

$$U_{2,1}[g_1, (E_1, E_2)] = \Phi(u_1 w), \quad u_1 \geq 0; \qquad U_{2,2}[g_2, (E_1, E_2)] = \Phi[u_2(1-w)], \quad u_2 \leq 0.$$

So for all $u_1 \geq 0 \geq u_2$ we have the functional equation

$$\Phi(u_1 w) + \Phi[u_2(1 - w)] = \Phi[u_1 w + u_2(1 - w)]. \tag{5.29}$$

We next show that Φ is symmetric about 0. Choose $u_1 w + u_2(1 - w) = 0$ and set $y = u_1 w \geq 0$, then since $\Phi(0) = 0$, we see from Eq. (5.29) that $\Phi(-y) = -\Phi(y)$. Now, for $u_1 w + u_2(1 - w) > 0$ and using symmetry we see that over the positive real numbers

$$\Phi(u_1 w) - \Phi[-u_2(1 - w)] = \Phi[u_1 w + u_2(1 - w)],$$

and letting $y = u_1 w > 0$, $z = -u_2(1 - w) > 0$,

$$\Phi(y) = \Phi(y - z) + \Phi(z), \quad y - z > 0.$$

It is well known (Aczél, 1961/1966) that the only strictly increasing solutions to this Cauchy equation for $y > 0$ are $\Phi(y) = \alpha y$, where α is a constant and > 0. Because the ranges of y and h are the same, $\alpha = 1$. For negative values of y, we have

$$\Phi(y) = -\Phi(-y) = -(-y) = y. \quad \blacksquare$$

We turn now to the theorem itself. Consider $n = 3$. By a lemma analogous to the one just proved and using coalescing, one can choose the unit of U_3 to agree with that of U_2. Assume that $g_1 \succsim g_2 \succsim g_3$, then by Eq. (5.6) we have two cases of coalescing corresponding to setting $g_1 = g_2$ and to setting $g_3 = g_2$ leading to, respectively,

$$(g_2, E_1; g_2, E_2; g_3, E_3) \sim (g_2, E_1 \cup E_2; g_3, E_3) \tag{5.30}$$

$$(g_1, E_1; g_2, E_2; g_2, E_3) \sim (g_1, E_1; g_2, E_2 \cup E_3). \tag{5.31}$$

Applying Eq. (5.6) to coalescing of gamble g of Eq. (5.30) and g' of Eq. (5.31) and using the fact that U_3 has been chosen to agree with U_2, we have:

$$\begin{aligned} U(g) &= U_{3,1}[g_2, (E_1, E_2, E_3)] + U_{3,2}[g_2, (E_1, E_2, E_3)] + U_{3,3}[g_3, (E_1, E_2, E_3)] \\ &= U_3(g_2, E_1; g_2, E_2; g_3, E_3) \\ &= U_2(g_2, E_1 \cup E_2; g_3, E_3) \\ &= U_{2,1}[g_2, (E_1 \cup E_2, E_3)] + U_{2,2}[g_3, (E_1 \cup E_2, E_3)] \\ &= U(g_2)W(E_1 \cup E_2) + U(g_3)[1 - W(E_1 \cup E_2)], \end{aligned}$$

$$
\begin{aligned}
U(g') &= U_{3,1}[g_1, (E_1, E_2, E_3)] + U_{3,2}[g_2, (E_1, E_2, E_3)] + U_{3,3}[g_2, (E_1, E_2, E_3)] \\
&= U_3(g_1, E_1; g_2, E_2; g_2, E_3) \\
&= U_2(g_1, E_1; g_2, E_2 \cup E_3) \\
&= U_{2,1}[g_1, (E_1, E_2 \cup E_3)] + U_{2,2}[g_2, (E_1, E_2 \cup E_3)] \\
&= U(g_1)W(E_1) + U(g_2)[1 - W(E_1)].
\end{aligned}
$$

Taking into account that the g_i can be chosen independently, subject to the inequalities among the g_i's being maintained, we have the following four equalities:

$$
U_{3,1}[x_2, (E_1, E_2, E_3)] + U_{3,2}[x_2, (E_1, E_2, E_3)] = U(x_2)W(E_1 \cup E_2), \tag{5.32}
$$

$$
U_{3,3}[x_3, (E_1, E_2, E_3)] = U(x_3)[1 - W(E_1 \cup E_2)], \tag{5.33}
$$

$$
U_{3,1}[x_1, (E_1, E_2, E_3)] = U(x_1)W(E_1), \tag{5.34}
$$

$$
U_{3,2}[x_2, (E_1, E_2, E_3)] + U_{3,3}[x_2, (E_1, E_2, E_3)] = U(x_3)[1 - W(E_1)]. \tag{5.35}
$$

Equations (5.33) and (5.34) yield two of the three weights. The third is obtained by substituting Eq. (5.34) into Eq. (5.32), yielding

$$
U_{3,2}[x_2, (E_1, E_2, E_3)] = U(x_2)[W(E_1 \cup E_2) - W(E_1)]. \tag{5.36}
$$

Equation (5.35) is obviously satisfied by substituting Eq. (5.33) and (5.36) into the left side. Observe that with these binary values substituted, the utilities for $n = 3$ satisfy the rank-dependent form of Eqs. (5.1) and (5.3).

The induction for $n > 3$ is routine. ∎

5.8.2 Theorem 5.3.4

Proof. We proceed by induction starting with the assumed binary RDU representation and using Propositions 5.3.3 and Eq. (5.11):

$$
\begin{aligned}
U(g^{(k)}) &= U(g^{(k-1)}, E(k-1); g_k, E_k) && \text{[Eq. (5.8)]} \\
&= U(g^{(k-1)})W_E[E(k-1)] + U(g_k)\,(1 - W_E[E(k-1)]) && \text{(binary RDU)} \\
&= \sum_{i=1}^{k-1} U(g_i)\,(W_{E(k-1)}[E(i)] - W_{E(k-1)}[E(i-1)])\,W_E[E(k-1)] \\
&\quad + U(g_k)\,(W_E[E(k)] - W_E[E(k-1)]) && \text{(induction hypothesis)} \\
&= \sum_{i=1}^{k-1} U(g_i)\,(W_E[E(i)] - W_E[E(i-1)]) \\
&\quad + U(g_k)\,(W_E[E(k)] - W_E[E(k-1)]) && \text{[Eq. (5.11)]}
\end{aligned}
$$

$$= \sum_{i=1}^{k} U(g_i) \left(W_E[E(i)] - W_E[E(i-1)] \right). \quad \blacksquare$$

5.8.3   Theorem 5.3.5

Proof. By segregation and the p-additive form of Eq. (4.45) we see

$$
\begin{aligned}
U(g^{(k)}) &= U[(g_1 \ominus g_k, E_1; \ldots; g_{k-1} \ominus g_k, E_{k-1}; e, E_k) \oplus g_k] \\
&= U(g_1 \ominus g_k, E_1; \ldots; g_{k-1} \ominus g_k, E_{k-1}; e, E_k) \\
&\quad \times [1 + \delta U(g_k)] + U(g_k).
\end{aligned}
\tag{5.37}
$$

Choosing the normalization $W_E^+(E) = 1$, by gains decomposition and the assumption of binary rank dependence,

$$
\begin{aligned}
&U(g_1 \ominus g_k, E_1; \ldots; g_{k-1} \ominus g_k, E_{k-1}; e, E_k) \\
&= U((g_1 \ominus g_k, E_1; \ldots; g_{k-1} \ominus g_k, E_{k-1}), E(k-1); e, E_k) \\
&= U(g_1 \ominus g_k, E_1; \ldots; g_{k-1} \ominus g_k, E_{k-1}) W_E[E(k-1)].
\end{aligned}
\tag{5.38}
$$

We have assumed for $k = 2$ that rank dependence holds, and the induction hypothesis is that it holds for $k - 1 \geq 2$:

$$
U(g_1 \ominus g_k, E_1; \ldots; g_{k-1} \ominus g_k, E_{k-1}) = \sum_{i=1}^{k-1} U(g_i \ominus g_k) \frac{W_E[E(i)] - W_E[E(i-1)]}{W_E[E(k-1)]}.
\tag{5.39}
$$

For $g_i \succsim g_k \succsim e$, then by Eq. (4.63),

$$
U(g_i \ominus g_k) = \frac{U(g_i) - U(g_k)}{1 - \delta U(g_k)}.
\tag{5.40}
$$

The result follows by substituting Eq. (5.40) into Eq. (5.39), that in turn into Eq. (5.38), and then into Eq. (5.37) and doing some routine algebra to prove the induction. $\blacksquare$

Chapter 6
ADDITIVE UTILITY OVER MIXED CONSEQUENCES

This and the next chapter focus on mixed joint receipts and mixed binary gambles, where "mixed" means one consequence is seen as a gain and the other as a loss. Although it is not strictly necessary to do so, I find that adopting a notation of signed subscripts sometimes helps one to recall which symbol refers to a gain and which a loss. So, for example, if $f_+ \succsim e \succsim g_-$, then the mixed joint receipt becomes $f_+ \oplus g_-$ and a typical mixed gamble becomes $(f_+, C; g_-)$. Other times, in particular in proofs when the subscripts become cumbersome, I drop them.

The situation of mixed consequences is in several ways rather more complex than are the cases of all gains or all losses. One issue centers on whether to assume that the utility function U or the value function V is simply additive over $\oplus$, i.e., either

$$U(f_+ \oplus g_-) = U(f_+) + U(g_-), \tag{6.1}$$

or

$$V(f_+ \oplus g_-) = V(f_+) + V(g_-). \tag{6.2}$$

Each assumption precludes the other except in the special case where $U = \alpha V$, $\alpha > 0$. We take up Eq. (6.1) here and Eq. (6.2) in Chapter 7. Both theories assume, as in Chapter 4, that V is additive over gains and losses separately, i.e., the structure forms an extensive one within each domain, and, for the reason given in Section 4.4.6, this means that there is a representation U that is p-additive, Eq. (4.45), in which case its relation to the additive value measure V is either proportional, negative exponential, or exponential.

Focusing now on the additive U assumption for mixed joint receipts, I call the underlying qualitative model "extensive-conjoint" because the structure is extensive in gains and losses separately and additive conjoint in the mixed case. This type of representation has a tradition, at least implicitly, back to Kahneman and Tversky (1979).

There is also a somewhat subtle question about the exact interpretation of Eq. (6.1). Does it mean what it says, namely, additivity of the dimensional measure U, or does it really mean additivity of the dimensionless ones, U_+ and U_-, Eq. (4.49)? More specifically should it be,

$$U_i(f_+ \oplus g_-) = U_+(f_+) + U_-(g_-),$$

where $i = +$ if $f_+ \oplus g_- \succsim e$ and $i = -$ if $f_+ \oplus g_- \prec e$? Some of the equations are a bit more elegant if we make this assumption, but because the literature seems to state it as written in Eq. (6.1), I will use that.

The assumption that U is additive over $\oplus$ in the mixed case tends to make things look fairly simple in terms of representations, but as we shall see it is at the price of a rather messy axiomatization that includes a behavioral assumption that is neither obviously rational nor easily tested empirically. That complication, taken up in Section 6.1, concerns how the extensive and conjoint structures are linked together.

In contrast, the assumption that V is additive over the whole structure—gains, losses, and mixed alternatives—means that $\oplus$ is associative throughout, and so it is called the "associative" axiomatization. The axiomatization in this case is simple and well understood, and it leads without further linking assumptions to the form for U over mixed joint receipts and mixed binary gambles. Although these forms are easily derived, they are more complicated than one might have anticipated in that the resulting U representation is nonlinear. Of course, the decision about which model is to be preferred, if either, has to be based on data, not on issues of which is simpler in which respect.

Clearly, in each case the major focus is not only on $U(f_+ \oplus g_-)$ but also on what follows from that about the utility of gambles, $U(f_+, C; g_-)$. To study that we are going to have to seek for mixed consequences some sort of "law-like" linkage between the joint-receipt structure and the gambling structure. Such a "law" or, better, a behavioral hypothesis will play a role analogous to that of segregation for binary gains (or losses). Two alternative proposals are explored. Thus, for each type of operation $\oplus$, extensive-conjoint and associative, the two linking hypotheses lead to different options for the form of the utility of binary gambles. Actually, the situation is richer (more complex) than that because somewhat different formulas arise depending upon whether $\delta = 0, > 0$, or < 0, which reflects itself in the way that U relates to V, i.e., proportional, negative exponential, or exponential for gains, and independently the same possibilities for losses. I work out in detail only a couple of examples. The results for the other cases are simply stated because the derivations are almost the same. An empirical comparison of the different options is ultimately presented in Section 7.3.5.

There can be no doubt that these mixed cases are, at the moment, very unsettled. So far, neither theorists nor experimentalists have devoted as much attention to them as I believe is warranted. I have two reasons for saying this. First, as will be seen in Section 6.3.3, the conventional models appear to be empirically incorrect in a fairly major way. Second, from the perspective of many real-world decision problems, the mixed case is the norm, not the exception.

6.1   The Extensive-Conjoint Axiomatization

The full extensive-conjoint representation we are concerned with in this chapter is

$$U(f \oplus g) = \begin{cases} U(f) + U(g) - \delta U(f)U(g), & f \succsim e, g \succsim e \\ U(f) + U(g), & f \succsim e \succsim g \\ U(f) + U(g) - \delta' U(f)U(g), & e \succsim f, e \succsim g \end{cases} \tag{6.3}$$

Two major problems must be addressed. The first is how to axiomatize such a representation. At first blush this may seem close to trivial: Assume the axioms JR1-6 of Chapter 4 for gains and separately for losses and the axioms C1-6 of Appendix D for additive conjoint measurement for the mixed case. The difficulty is that each axiom system provides a separate measure of utility, say U from gains and U^* from mixed consequences. Thus, over the gains domain, there are two distinct numerical representations of $\succsim$ which are not automatically the same or even proportional. A linking relation of some sort between the extensive and conjoint structures is required for that to be true. We take that up in the next subsection.

The second problem is how mixed gambles and mixed joint receipts are linked. Two hypotheses, called general segregation and duplex decomposition, are examined and their consequences are developed. This is followed by a discussion of an important empirical finding that, if sustained, rules out a huge family of models, including most of the classical ones as well as those arrived at in this chapter. Finally, a behavioral hypothesis is proposed for buying and selling prices, and the utility results are used to calculate expressions for them.

6.1.1   The approach to linking two representations

As was just noted, the extensive-conjoint axiomatization assumes a structure that is separately extensive for gains and for losses and additive conjoint for mixed joint receipt. The difficulty, however, is their separate determination.[1] Suppose U is a p-additive representation of the gains extensive structure and U^* is the additive utility function that arises from the conjoint structure. We simply do not yet have any reason to assume how U and U^* are related over gains other than that each is a strictly increasing monotonic function of the other. We want a much tighter relation than that, namely, that there is a single representation that is both p-additive for gains and additive for mixed joint receipts. Some linkage between these structures is required to draw such a conclusion. This problem was first addressed by Luce and Fishburn (1991) and revisited by Luce (1996a), who used a somewhat different approach. I follow the latter presentation fairly closely.

The basic strategy, which we have seen before, is one that can always be followed when we have two independent ways, U and U^*, of measuring the same qualitative attribute. One begins by asking what follows about the linkage between the two substructures on the assumption that $U^* = U$. Having found such a link, then we do two things. First, we attempt the reverse procedure: Assume the linking property and that $U = \Phi(U^*)$ for some strictly increasing Φ, then deduce a functional equation for Φ, and finally solve that equation. If the linking condition is sufficiently strong, then Φ is determined, and from that we may be able to find a common utility that is p-additive for gains and additive for mixed alternatives. Second, assuming success in finding a suitable linkage, we must then ask about its empirical adequacy.

---

[1] Having two measures of what purports to be one attribute is usually seen as an unresolved problem until we understand exactly how the two measures relate. This is to be sharply distinguished from have two or more methods of measuring an attribute. That is common and often necessary, e.g., measuring the size of a house with a meter stick is fine, but measuring the size of a country that way is at best tedious and error prone, and for measuring stellar distances it will not do at all.

6.1.2   Joint-receipt consistency: Linking gains and mixed joint receipts

In the present case, a likely candidate for a linking law arises by considering how associativity may fail in the mixed case. Suppose $f_+, g_+ \succsim e \succsim h_-$ are such that $f_+ \oplus h_- \succsim e$. If associativity and commutativity were both true, then we would have

$$(f_+ \oplus h_-) \oplus g_+ \sim f_+ \oplus (h_- \oplus g_+) \sim f_+ \oplus (g_+ \oplus h_-) \sim (f_+ \oplus g_+) \oplus h_-.$$

Because associativity is not being assumed in the mixed case, this equation may not hold in general. However, because e is an identity element and monotonicity holds, we have

$$f_+ \oplus g_+ \sim (f_+ \oplus e) \oplus g_+ \succsim (f_+ \oplus h_-) \oplus g_+.$$

So it is certainly plausible that there is some $k_- \precsim e$ such that

$$(f_+ \oplus h_-) \oplus g_+ \sim (f_+ \oplus g_+) \oplus k_-.$$

Now to this equivalence apply the assumptions that for gains: $U^* = U$. First, let us assume U is p-additive, with the dimensional parameter δ, U^* is additive for mixed joint receipt, and to simplify the notation the subscripts are omitted:

$$
\begin{aligned}
U[(f \oplus h) \oplus g] &= U(f \oplus h)\,[1 - \delta U(g)] + U(g) \\
&= U^*(f \oplus h)\,[1 - \delta U^*(g)] + U^*(g) \\
&= [U^*(f) + U^*(h)]\,[1 - \delta U^*(g)] + U^*(g),
\end{aligned}
$$

and

$$
\begin{aligned}
U[(f \oplus g) \oplus k] &= U^*[(f \oplus g) \oplus k] \\
&= U^*(f \oplus g) + U^*(k) \\
&= U(f \oplus g) + U(k) \\
&= U(f)\,[1 - \delta U(g)] + U(g) + U(k) \\
&= U^*(f)\,[1 - \delta U^*(g)] + U^*(g) + U^*(k).
\end{aligned}
$$

A little algebra results in (with the subscripts restored)

$$U(k_-) = U(h_-)[1 - \delta U(g_+)]. \tag{6.4}$$

Thus, k_- is a function of g_+ and h_-, but not of f_+. So we conclude that if we have a representation that is both p-additive for gains and additive for mixed cases, then the following condition must hold:

Definition 6.1.1.   A binary structure of alternatives with a joint receipt operation $\oplus$, a weak preference order $\succsim$, and identity e is said to satisfy *joint-receipt consistency* if and only if for all $f_+, f'_+, g_+ \succsim e \succsim h_-, k_-$ for which $f_+ \oplus h_-, f'_+ \oplus h_- \succsim e$,

$$(f_+ \oplus h_-) \oplus g_+ \sim (f_+ \oplus g_+) \oplus k_- \iff (f'_+ \oplus h_-) \oplus g_+ \sim (f'_+ \oplus g_+) \oplus k_-. \tag{6.5}$$

To my knowledge, no one has attempted empirically to verify joint-receipt consistency. Doing so will not be easy because it entails two estimates, first k_- and then checking the equivalence for various values of f'_+, a double source of error. Moreover, the existing empirical data of Section 6.3.3 make it very doubtful that joint-receipt consistency is worth investigating empirically.

In the following results, we shall assume that we are working with the closure of binary second-order gambles. The reason for this rather than first-order ones is, primarily, the assumption that a general gamble can be reduced by the gain-loss decomposition assumption [Def. 2.5.1, Eq. (2.17)] to the study of binary gambles whose consequences are the subgamble of all gains and the subgamble of all losses. Thus, these binary gambles are second-order.

The question to be addressed here is whether or not the property of joint-receipt consistency is sufficient to insure there is some U that is additive on mixed alternatives also p-additive over gains. The answer is *Yes* in the following sense.

Theorem 6.1.1.   *Suppose a structure $\langle \mathcal{D}_2, e, \succsim, \oplus \rangle$ generated from the binary gambles $\mathcal{B}_1$ satisfies:*

1.   *Axioms JR1-JR6 of Chapter 4 over gains, and so has a p-additive representation U onto an interval including 0.*
2.   *Axioms C1-C6 of Appendix D over mixed alternatives, and so has an additive representation U^* onto an interval including 0.*
3.   *Joint receipt consistency relating the two substructures.*

Then over gains either $U = \alpha^* U^* = \alpha V, \alpha^* > 0, \alpha > 0$, in which case $k_- \sim h_-$ in Eq. (6.5), or there is a measure U^{**} that is both p-additive over gains and additive over mixed alternative and k_- satisfies Eq. (6.4).

Clearly, a parallel theorem holds for losses.

Observe that the $U = \alpha^* U^*$ case does not degenerate into the associative model of Eq. (6.2) because the constants of proportionality for gains and losses may differ.

6.2   Linking Mixed Gambles and Mixed Joint Receipts

Assuming that Eq. (6.3) provides the correct utility function for joint receipts, the next question is how this relates to the utility of mixed consequence gambles. Again, there must be some law-like statement that links the operation $\oplus$ on mixed gambles to $\oplus$ on consequences alone. I have come up with two possibilities, but no experiments have been conducted to choose between them. One of them has been examined empirically as a null hypothesis, and it was not rejected, but that is far from conclusive. Indeed, the data analysis of Section 7.3.5 will lead us to believe that it is best to ask which is better for individual respondents, because there appear to be individual differences.

6.2.1   First linking hypothesis: General segregation

Perhaps the simplest idea for linking mixed joint receipts and binary gambles is to extend the highly rational property of segregation to mixed gambles. To do so, recall the definition of $\ominus$, namely,

$$f \ominus g \sim h \quad \text{iff} \quad f \sim h \oplus g. \tag{6.6}$$

With this definition, we can generalize Eq. (4.33) as follows:

Definition 6.2.1. (Luce, 1997) Suppose a structure of mixed binary second-order gambles with a joint receipt operation $\oplus$ satisfies the property that for all $f, g \in \mathcal{G}_1$, $f \succsim g$, $f \ominus g$ exists. Then *general segregation* is satisfied if and only if for all $f, g \in \mathcal{G}_1$, $f \succsim g$, $C \in \mathcal{E}_E$, then $f \ominus g$ and $g \ominus f$ exist and

$$(f, C; g) \sim \begin{cases} (f \ominus g, C; e) \oplus g, & \text{if } (f, C; g) \succ e \\ (e, C; g \ominus f) \oplus f, & \text{if } (f, C; g) \prec e \end{cases}. \tag{6.7}$$

Notice that if $f \succsim g \succsim e$ and $h \sim f \ominus g$, then the top line, which is the relevant one, is simply

$$(h, C; e) \oplus g \sim (h \oplus g, C; g),$$

which agrees with the concept of segregation in the gains case [Eq. (4.33) in § 4.4.1].

Observe that, as with segregation for gains, general segregation is a simple accounting indifference in which one gets the same thing on both sides: $f \sim (f \ominus g) \oplus g$ if C occurs and $g \sim e \oplus g$ otherwise.

To my knowledge, there have been no empirical studies of general segregation.

6.2.2   Second linking hypothesis: Duplex decomposition

The second—historically, the first—proposed hypothesis linking mixed gambles to joint receipt actually dates to empirical work of Slovic and Lichtenstein (1968). Their concern was whether or not variances play a controlling role in evaluating lotteries, and some of their data are described in Section 6.2.3. Their experimental method rested on comparing[2] a particular lottery $(x, p; -x)$, $x > 0$, which they called a "standard gamble," with pairs of lotteries that they called "duplex gambles." These duplex gambles were nothing more nor less than the joint receipt of two independent gambles closely related to $(x, p; -x)$. In particular, the "parallel duplex gamble" was defined to be $(x, p; 0) \oplus (0, p; -x)$, where each gamble is to be run independently. Although this pair of gambles involves exactly the same amount to win, the same amount to lose, and the same probabilities as in the standard gamble, the patterns of possible consequences are quite different on the two sides (see the discussion following Def. 6.2.2). In particular, the variance of the standard gamble is larger than that of the parallel duplex one. Their evidence seemed, nonetheless, to support the following property:

---

[2]   They also looked at the three-consequence gamble $(x, p^2; -x, (1-p)^2; 0, 2p(1-p))$ that has exactly the same distribution as the parallel duplex one, i.e., the convolution of $(x, p; 0)$ and $(0, p; -x)$. Those data were discussed in Section 4.2.4.

Definition 6.2.2.   A structure of mixed binary gambles with a joint receipt operation $\oplus$ satisfies *duplex decomposition* if and only if for all $f_+ \in \mathcal{G}_1^+$, $g_- \in \mathcal{G}_1^-$, $C \in \mathcal{E}_{\mathbf{E}}$,

$$(f_+, C; g_-) \sim (f_+, C'; e) \oplus (e, C''; g_-), \tag{6.8}$$

where C', C'' denote C occurring on independent realizations of the underlying experiment E.

This is in no way a rational assumption. It is not an accounting indifference in the sense we spoke of earlier. The reason is that the "bottom lines" on the two sides differ. On the left, one receives either f_+ or g_- but neither both nor nothing. On the right, all four of these possibilities can arise: $f_+, g_-, f_+ \oplus g_-$, or $e \sim e \oplus e$. Despite its not being rational, a number of people seem to think it is a plausible way to decompose a more complicated gamble into two simpler ones. Indeed, this idea underlies some cost-benefit analyses of risky options where the costs and benefits are linked only by chance events and are analyzed by separate teams, whose results the decision maker treats as inputs to a joint receipt that he or she evaluates.

6.2.3   Empirical studies of duplex decomposition

As was noted earlier, the first empirical study[3] of duplex decomposition was Slovic and Lichtenstein (1968). They ran three distinct experiments involving 19, 24, and 31 respondents. The first two involved a technique of having the respondents state their smallest selling price. The standard gambles were replicated and so provided a measure of reliability. The third experiment used choices between standard gambles and duplex ones, some of which were "parallel" to the standard one, i.e., the right-hand term of Eq. (6.8). Using the repeated standard gambles to estimate the noise levels involved, they concluded that in the first two experiments fewer than 20% of the respondents bid differentially on the standard and parallel duplex gambles, and in the third experiment fewer than 33% of the respondents exhibited a sufficiently strong preference to resist changing their choices when a small, 5 cent, change was made in consequences in the range of $1.40 to $1.60. Thus, it appears that a substantial majority of respondents, but not all, did not evidence a preference difference between a standard gamble from its parallel duplex form. As we shall see in Section 7.3.5, using a quite different way of estimating the quality of fit of models, we find that duplex decomposition fares better than generalized segregation for 73% of the respondents. If these results are roughly valid, then it is clear that there are respondents of both types, so it makes no sense to ask which is better using group data.

Using PEST-determined certainty equivalents, Cho, Luce, and von Winterfeldt (1994) evaluated duplex decomposition for mixed gains and losses. The experiment was mentioned in Section 4.4.1. Figure 6.1 shows the median responses of the respondents to the two sides of the duplex decomposition equation, (6.8), and we see that the correspondence is quite close.

---

[3] There were earlier studies in which the focus was on how variances affected preferences; see Edwards (1954b, 1962b).

The data were also looked at in terms of the symmetry over respondents of the differences

$$\widehat{CE}(f_+, C; g_-) - \widehat{CE}[(f_+, C'; e) \oplus (e, C''; g_-)],$$

and no reason was found to reject the hypothesis of symmetry, which was interpreted to be a necessary condition if duplex decomposition holds.

Panel a. DCMP and JRD (y=-$40, n=72)

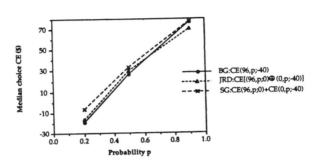

Panel b. DCMP and JRD (y=-$160, n=72)

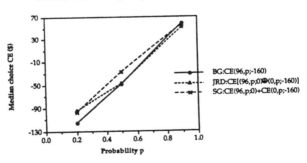

Figure 6.1. The PEST-determined CEs for the two sides of duplex decomposition, Eq. (6.8), plus the right side with $\oplus$ replaced by $+$, which, if the hypothesis $x \oplus y \succ x + y$ [§ 4.5.1, Eq. (4.52)] is correct, should lie above the terms of duplex decomposition. Although the differences are not statistically significant, this appears to be the trend in the data; however, duplex decomposition is not rejected. This is Fig. 9 of Cho, Luce, and von Winterfeldt (1994). Copyright © 1994 by the American Psychological Association. Reprinted with permission.

Of course, accepting a null hypothesis, in this case duplex decomposition, is always suspect. Comparative questions usually are better. A natural one to ask here is whether general segregation or duplex decomposition provides a better fit to the data of individual subjects. This has yet to be done.

6.3   Utility of Mixed Gambles

6.3.1   Representations of mixed binary gambles

The proof of the following result is a trivial calculation given Eqs. (6.1), (6.7), and (6.8):

Theorem 6.3.1.   *Suppose a structure of first-order, mixed binary gambles with joint receipt operation $\oplus$ has an additive representation U over $\oplus$, that (U, W_E^i), $i = +, -$, forms a separable representation over the gambles $(f_+, C; e)$ and $(e, C; g_-)$ [Def. 3.1.3, Eq. (3.6)], and that for gains and losses separately U satisfies the p-additive representation of Eq. (4.45), i.e., for all $f_+, h_+ \succsim e$*

$$U(f_+ \oplus h_+) = U(f_+) + U(h_+) - \delta U(f_+)U(h_+),$$

and a similar expression for losses with parameter δ'.

1.   *Suppose general segregation holds. Then*

$$U(f_+, C; g_-) = \begin{cases} U(f_+)W_E^+(C) + U(g_-)[1 - W_E^+(C)], & (f_+, C; g_-) \succ e \\ U(f_+)[1 - W_E^-(\overline{C})] + U(g_-)W_E^-(\overline{C}), & (f_+, C; g_-) \prec e \end{cases} . \quad (6.9)$$

2.   *Suppose duplex decomposition holds. Then*

$$U(f_+, C; g_-) = U(f_+)W_E^+(C) + U(g_-)W_E^-(\overline{C}). \quad (6.10)$$

It is curious, and possibly significant, that if general segregation holds, then unless

$$W_E^+(C) + W_E^-(\overline{C}) = 1$$

there will be a discontinuity in the utility of a mixed gamble when, by varying either f_+ or g_-, $(f_+, C; g_-)$ passes through the status quo.

The additive form for duplex decomposition was proposed in the original prospect theory of Kahneman and Tversky (1979), but only for the somewhat special case of known probabilities and assuming $W_E^+ = W_E^-$. Tversky and Kahneman (1992) assumed Eq. (6.10). Fennema and Wakker (1997) wrote a general mixed model in which there must be at least one gain and at least one loss, which they suggested may be a natural generalization of Kahneman and Tversky's (1979) model, and they compared it empirically with the present duplex decomposition model. It did not do as well.

The same representation as shown here for duplex decomposition, Eq. (6.10), was independently proposed in three papers: Luce and Fishburn (1991), Starmer and Sugden (1989, appendix), and Tversky and Kahneman (1992). Luce and Fishburn axiomatized it by using joint receipt and Wakker and Tversky (1993) by using comonotonicity axioms. Indeed, it was my desire to arrive at Eq. (6.10) using $\oplus$ that first led me (Luce, 1991) to consider duplex decomposition; only later did I become aware of Slovic and Lichtenstein's (1968) paper. Not until recently did I begin to explore general segregation and—it turns out to be important—the alternative of fully associative joint receipts.

Note that the results for segregation and duplex decomposition are substantially similar in that, holding the event fixed, the pairs of consequences have an additive conjoint representation or, put another way, the expression is linear in the utility of the consequences. The main difference among the models is what weight applies to the complementary event. Kahneman and Tversky (1979) postulated not having the weights add to 1 in the mixed case, but I do not believe they reported any data that actually forced that conclusion.

6.3.2   Framing effects

Recall that mention was made in Section 2.1 of how the framing of mixed gambles can be interpreted as undermining complementarity in that case. Note that although complementarity was used in getting the RDU representation for gains and losses separately, it played no direct role for mixed gambles in Theorem 6.3.1. If we simply assume that the impact of the framing instructions is to affect whether $(f_+, C; g_-)$ is seen as a gain or a loss and if general segregation holds, then the utility expression of Eq. (6.9) is changed according to which weighting function is applied. Nothing comparable holds for duplex decomposition under the assumption of additive U. However, as we shall see in Chapter 7 (Theorems 7.3.4-7.3.7), the utility formulas for additive V differ for both general segregation and duplex decomposition as a function of the respondent's perception of $(f_+, C; g_-)$ as a gain or a loss. So, I do not think this empirical phenomenon is especially problematic for the present theory. It is, of course, a problem for any utility theory whose calculus is unaffected by the perception of the mixed gamble relative to the status quo.

6.3.3   Event commutativity in mixed case

Recall the property of event commutativity (Def. 3.1.5). It generalizes in the mixed case to:

$$((f_+, C; g_-), D, g_-) \sim ((f_+, D; g_-), C, g_-).$$

It is not difficult to see that for the models of Theorem 6.3.1, this follows when $(f_+, C; g_-)$ and $(f_+, D; g_-)$ are both perceived as gains or both as losses, but when they are mixed the indifference is not predicted unless, of course, $W_E^+ = W_E^-$.

The experiment of Chung, von Winterfeldt, and Luce (1994), which was discussed in Section 3.1.5.2, provided the relevant data shown in Fig. 6.2. Clearly, there are substantial violations of event commutativity for the median respondent for some of these mixed gambles, especially for gamble pairs 7 and 10. These data were not reported in sufficient detail to tell if the violations are those predicted by these models.

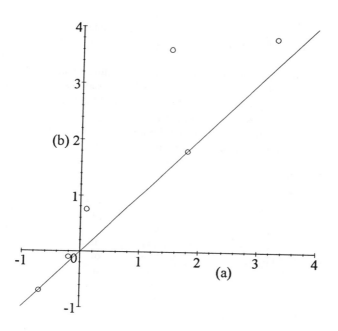

Multiply axes by 10^3.

Figure 6.2. A test of event commutativity, version (b) versus version (a), for the case of binary gambles with mixed consequences. From upper right to lower left the gambles are 5, 7, 9, 10, 11, 12. The models of this chapter do not predict that event commutativity should be satisfied. The evidence for gamble pairs 7 and 10 suggests that it is not. Adapted from Fig. 3 of Chung, von Winterfeldt, and Luce (1994). Copyright 1994 by Blackwell Publishers, Malden, MA 02148. Reprinted by permission.

6.3.4   An empirical study of mixed binary gambles

Chechile and Cooke (1997) and Chechile and Butler (1999) are the only empirical studies of which I am aware that focus in a major way on the binary mixed case. They were motivated by what Miyamoto (1988, 1992) called "generic utility,"[4] namely, in the mixed case with

---

[4]   It might better be called "generic bilinear utility." This is a different use of "generic" from that of Krzysztofowicz (1994) and Krzysztofowicz and Koch (1989).

$x, y \in \mathbb{R}_+$, $p \in [0, 1]$,

$$U(x, p; -y) = U(x)W(p) + U(-y)W^*(1 - p). \tag{6.11}$$

Note that this form, generalized so that C replaces p and $\overline{C}$ replaces $1 - p$, includes both of the forms just derived from extensive-conjoint joint receipts and either general segregation or duplex decomposition. Its main aspect is the bilinear roles of U, W, and W^*.

The most obvious way to check the empirical validity of this model is to hold the event fixed and vary the consequences systematically and ask whether the axioms–in particular, the Thomsen condition—of additive conjoint measurement hold over the consequences. I am not aware of this having been done for mixed consequences.

The two Chechile studies took a different approach that involved the respondents providing lottery-dependent, probability-equivalent judgments (§1.2.2.4). To be specific, respondents selected a probability in a comparison gamble so that it would match in preference a reference gamble. The reference gambles were of the form $g(r) = (z, r; -z)$, $z \in \mathbb{R}_+$, $r \in]0, 1[$, and the comparison ones were of the form $c(p) = (v_1, p, -v_2)$, $v_1, v_2 \in \mathbb{R}_+$, $p \in [0, 1]$. The experimenter fixed z throughout the experiment at \$50 and on each trial selected values of r, v_1, and v_2, and the task of the respondent was to select p so that

$$g(r) \sim c(p).$$

The chosen value is called a *probability equivalent*. As was discussed in Sections 1.2.2.3 and 1.2.2.4, the use of probability equivalents is controversial. Moreover, based on our experience with judged certainty equivalents, I am somewhat concerned whether judged probability equivalents are biased relative to choice determined ones. Moreover, we know from Delquié's (1993) careful examination of the biases in the lottery-dependent method using a PEST procedure that even if these Chechile studies were redone using choices, the results would still differ somewhat from what is obtained using money certainty equivalents. Despite such biases, which seem inherent in these methods, the effects described below are so enormous that it is difficult to imagine that it can be explained away by these biases. Nevertheless, because of this concern as well the importance of the empirical finding to be described, it is very desirable to verify the conclusion using other procedures.

Both the Chechile and Cooke (1997) and Chechile and Butler (1999) data analyses were based on the following observation. With r held fixed, the generic model can be thought of as having the form

$$\psi(r) = \lambda X - Y,$$

where $\psi(r)$ is proportional to the utility of the reference gamble, $X = u(v_1)W(p) > 0$, with $U(v_1) = \alpha u(v_1)$, $Y = u^*(v_2)W^*(1 - p) > 0$, with $U(-v_2) = -\alpha^*(v_2)$, and $\lambda > 0$ is the ratio of the multiplicative constants for the particular assumed models for the utility and weighting functions. The functions u and u^* are mathematical forms chosen by the experimenter that are assumed to be proportional to the unknown utility function U.

An example will make clearer what is involved. Suppose that both the utility and the weighting functions are powers, i.e.,

$$U(v_1) = \alpha v_1^\beta \quad \text{and} \quad U(-v_2) = -\alpha^* v_2^{\beta^*}$$
$$W(p) = p^\gamma \quad \text{and} \quad W^*(1-p) = (1-p)^{\gamma^*}.$$

Defining $\psi(r) = \frac{U(z,r;-z)}{\alpha^*}$, we see by substitution,

$$\begin{aligned}
\psi(r) &= \frac{U(z,r;-z)}{\alpha^*} = \frac{U(v_1,p;-v_2)}{\alpha^*} \\
&= \frac{\alpha}{\alpha^*} v_1^\beta p^\gamma - v_2^{\beta^*}(1-p)^{\gamma^*} \\
&= \lambda X - Y,
\end{aligned}$$

where $\lambda = \frac{\alpha}{\alpha^*}$, $X = v_1^\beta p^\gamma$, and $Y = v_2^{\beta^*}(1-p)^{\gamma^*}$. The point is that λ is a positive constant independent of r and, of course, z, which is held fixed throughout the experiment.

Rewriting in terms of Y and adding an error random variable, we have the regression expression

$$Y = \lambda X - \psi(r) + \epsilon. \tag{6.12}$$

The analysis entails estimating λ for each value of r under several different assumptions about the forms of the utility and weighting functions that were chosen so as to have an estimable number of parameters.

The weighting functions they used were: power, "normed" power of the form $\frac{p^s}{p^s+(1-p)^w}$ for gains and $\frac{(1-p)^w}{p^s+(1-p)^w}$ for losses, and "flexible" of the form $\frac{p^s}{p^s+(1-p)^s}$ for gains and $\frac{(1-p)^w}{p^w+(1-p)^w}$ for losses. The utility functions were: power, negative exponential, and "mixed" negative exponential for gains and exponential for losses. And the nine weight-utility combinations were: power/power; power/negative exponential; power/mixed; normed/power; normed/exponential; normed/mixed; flexible/power; flexible/negative exponential; and flexible/mixed. The later study also examined the Prelec weighting functions.

The values selected by Chechile and Cooke were

$$r \in \{0.05, 0.1, 0.3, 0.5, 0.7, 0.9, 0.95\}$$
$$v_1, v_2 \in \{\$0, \$20, \$40, \$60, \$80, \$100\}$$

Although all combinations were in fact run, it is clear that some of the combinations made no sense and basically led to a task for the respondent having no solution. For example, for all p, $(\$0, p; \$0) \sim \$0$, and almost surely $g(r) = (\$50, r; -\$50)$ is preferred to $\$0$ for all sufficiently large r. Moreover, $g(r) \succ c(p)$ may hold for all p for some triples (r, v_1, v_2). For example, consider the triple $(0.95, \$20, \$0)$. If $g(0.95) = (\$50, 0.95; -\$50) \succ \$20$, then clearly there is no p such that $g(0.95) \sim (\$20, p; 0)$.

I raised these concerns with Dr. Chechile, and he reanalyzed the data eliminating all the $(\$0, p; \$0)$ cases and all responses where p was chosen to be either 0 or 1 (Chechile & Luce, 1999). The results changed somewhat numerically from the published one, but the overall conclusions are unchanged.

More importantly, the Chechile and Butler (1999) avoided this design problem. Another significant difference between the two studies—one that proved to be most important—is that in the earlier study only group data were analyzed whereas in the later one both individual and group data were analyzed..

Based on data from 12 undergraduate respondents for whom the choices were presented as tree diagrams and also described as selections of colored balls from an opaque bag, two conclusions were unambiguous in the group analysis from Chechile and Cooke (1997):

- The estimates of λ were positive, as predicted in the bilinear model, but as r increases, λ sharply decreased by a factor of no less than 40 and sometimes as much as 700 over nine choices for utility and weighting functions. In the Chechile and Luce (1999) reanalysis, the estimated ratios of $\frac{\lambda(0.05)}{\lambda(0.95)}$ were somewhat reduced, but still remained very far from the predicted 1.
- For utility functions that could be either convex or concave, the best fits were obtained using convex gains and concave losses; for those utility models that were limited to be just concave for gains and just convex for losses, the best fits were, in effect, linear, which is as close as these functions could get to convex and concave, respectively.

The results of the Chechile and Butler (1999) study are more remarkable:

- The group data analysis is reasonably consistent with the earlier findings, but with reduced values for the ratio of λ across the extremes of r—depending on the model varying from 2.0 to 16.5, still not well approximating 1.
- The individual data are remarkable in that all estimates of λ for each model were negative, whereas the generic bilinear model requires that they be positive.
- By numerical examples, Chechile and Butler (1999) show how it is possible for both the individual estimates to be negative and the group ones to be positive—again reinforcing my strong conviction that great care must be taken not to be misled by group data.

The findings of the first experiment, although suggestive, were inconclusive because of the design flaw. Those of the second study—especially the negative regression slopes for individuals—invalidates all of the generic bilinear utility models for mixed consequences including both of the additive U ones described here and, indeed, most of the classical utility models. This is such an important—I would say sweeping—conclusion that I am sure others will attempt to find alternative ways either to reject or verify it. In Chapter 7 we will see that two nonlinear models exhibit non-constant, but positive, values of λ.

The two studies are somewhat inconsistent on the issue of the shape of utility functions. Of course, all these estimates can be dismissed as meaningless on the grounds that they arise from an invalid model. Nonetheless, let us examine what was found. In Chechile and Cooke (1997) gains had convex utility functions and losses, concave, which goes against a good deal of common belief that utility functions are on average concave for gains and convex for losses. In contrast, the Chechile and Butler (1999) study, with, of course, a different set of respondents, found concave gains and convex losses, which agrees with general wisdom.

Several observations may be relevant. First, Fishburn and Kochenberger (1979) assembled results from a number of studies in which utility functions for gains and losses had been separately estimated using expected utility $[W(p) = p]$. Hershey, Kunreuther, and Schoemaker (1982, p. 940) noted that, over studies, the pattern of concavity and convexity found depended upon the method of estimation, certainty equivalents or probability equivalents:

Gain/Loss	CE	PE
Concave/Convex	12	1
Convex/Concave	0	7

(The entries are numbers of studies in each category..) The interaction is striking and, of course, agrees with what Chechile and Cooke found.

Using the same data base of studies, they also observed (p. 945) that the conclusion one draws depends on whether the utility estimates are from pure cases–all gains or all losses–or from mixed ones:

Gamble type	Losses		Gains	
	Convex	Concave	Convex	Concave
Pure	14	1	4	11
Mixed	4	9	8	5

There are not sufficient cases to partition simultaneously by elicitation type and gamble type.

The second observation is that the amounts of money involved usually are not very large, and it may be that in these regions some people reverse how they would behave for substantially larger amounts. Recall that in Section 4.5.3 we showed the following. Suppose that the value function V of money is a power of money. If U for gains is concave in V, then for suitable values of the power-function exponent U can be initially convex and then concave as a function of money. The reverse—first concave and then convex—can hold for money losses. The study may simply have tapped only the convex/concave portions. Moreover, Krzysztofowicz and Koch (1989) reported estimates for a few respondents with such mixed convex-concave forms (see Fig. 4.2).

And the third observation, which will be detailed in Section 7.3.5 where data from 144 respondents fitted to a number of models are reported, is that although the modal respondent is concave/convex, a substantial number are also convex/concave. Different small samples of respondents may vary considerably in their mix of each.

6.3.5   Rank- and sign-dependent utility (RSDU)

The gain-loss decomposition assumption [Def. 2.5, Eq. (2.17)] states that a general gamble can be written

$$g \sim (g_+, E_+; g_-, E_-),$$

where E_+ is the union of all events giving rise to a gain or the status quo, g_+ is the restriction of g to E_+, and similarly for the losses. Thus,

$$U(g) = U(g_+, E_+; g_-, E_-).$$

The right side, depending upon which form we assume for U as a function of V, can be expressed in terms of $U(g_+)$, $W_E^+(E_+)$, $U(g_-)$, and $W_E^-(E_-)$.

Further, if one assumes that the representations over gains and over losses separately are rank dependent, then each of these is a species of rank- and sign-dependent utility. In the literature, that term is most closely associated with the assumption that the representation is bilinear, in particular the duplex decomposition one, but in principle it could apply to non-bilinear cases of the type we will encounter in the next chapter as well.

6.4   Buying and Selling Prices

6.4.1   Definitions

By a (maximum) buying price, b, I mean the largest sum of money that one is willing to pay to gain the gamble $(f, C; g)$, and by a (minimum) selling price, s, the smallest amount one will accept to forego the gamble. So, in the former case one gets the gamble less b and in the latter case one gets s at the expense of no longer having the gamble.

The initial temptation is to define these as, respectively,

$$(f, C; g) \ominus b \sim e \quad \text{and} \quad s \ominus (f, C; g) \sim e. \tag{6.13}$$

However, given the definition of $\ominus$ in terms of $\oplus$ we see that

$$b \sim b \oplus e \sim (f, C; g) \sim (f, C; g) \oplus e \sim s.$$

Perhaps this makes sense in that we are defining the maximum buying price and the minimum selling price and presumably these are each bounded by the certainty equivalent of the gamble. It is, however, widely believed that actual maximum buying and minimum selling prices satisfy

$$s \succ (f, C; g) \succ b.$$

Evidence for $s \succ (f, C; g)$ is provided by Tversky, Slovic, and Kahneman (1990) and for $s > b$ is provided by Kahneman, Knetsch, and Thaler (1990, 1991). Quite detailed parametric data on buying and selling prices have been reported by Birnbaum and Yeary (manuscript) and Birnbaum and Zimmermann (1998).

So, something a bit more subtle must be involved. One can think of the entire situation after the exchange is completed as still being a gamble. The reason is that if one has bought the gamble, then when it is run the outcomes for the buyer are either $f \ominus b$ if C occurs or $g \ominus b$ otherwise. If the gamble is sold, then the consequence to the seller is either $s \ominus f$ if C occurs or $s \ominus g$ otherwise. Summarizing,

Definition 6.4.1.   (Hazen & Lee, 1991; Luce, 1991) For any binary gamble $(f, C; g)$ the *(maximum) buying price* b and the *(minimum) selling price* s are the solutions to the following indifferences:

$$(f \ominus b, C; g \ominus b) \sim e \sim (s \ominus f, C; s \ominus g). \tag{6.14}$$

The generalization to general gambles is obvious.

The distinction between this definition and Eq. (6.13) is important. For $f \succ b \succ g$, it rests upon the fact that $f \ominus b$ is a gain whereas $g \ominus b$ is a loss independent of whether g itself is either a gain or a loss. Similarly, $s \ominus f$ is always a loss and $s \ominus g$ is a gain. Thus, even if we begin in the domain of gains, establishing buying and selling prices automatically takes us into the domain of mixed gambles. And to the degree that the utility models for the mixed case are different from and perhaps more complex than for gains, the results may have unexpected features.

Proposition 6.4.1.   *Suppose weak order, idempotence, and consequence monotonicity and satisfied and that b, s are defined as in Eq. (6.14). If $f \succsim g$, then $f \succsim b, s \succsim g$.*

Proof. Suppose, on the contrary, $b \succ f$, then $e \succ f \ominus b \succsim g \ominus b$ and so by idempotence and consequence monotonicity

$$(f \ominus b, C; g \ominus b) \sim e \sim (e, C; e) \succ (f \ominus b, C; g \ominus b),$$

which by transitivity is a contradiction. The other three cases are similar. ■

6.4.2   Formulas for buying and selling prices

This subsection calculates $U(b)$ and $U(s)$ from the extensive-conjoint models applied to the above definition of buying and selling prices. According to Theorem 6.3.1 and since $f_+ \succsim b, s \succsim g_-$, we see that if general segregation holds,

$$
\begin{aligned}
0 &= U(f_+ \ominus b)W^+(C) + U(g_- \ominus b)[1 - W^+(C)], \\
0 &= U(s \ominus f_+)[1 - W^+(\overline{C})] + U(s \ominus g_-)W^+(\overline{C}).
\end{aligned} \tag{6.15}
$$

When duplex decomposition holds, this changes to

$$
\begin{aligned}
0 &= U(f_+ \ominus b)W^+(C) + U(g_- \ominus b)W^-(\overline{C})], \\
0 &= U(s \ominus f_+)W^-(C)] + U(s \ominus g_-)W^+(\overline{C}).
\end{aligned} \tag{6.16}
$$

The result depends upon how the utilities of the several differences work out. To that end we use the following:

Proposition 6.4.2.   *Suppose U is additive in the sense of Eq. (6.1) and p-additive for gains in the sense of Eq. (4.45).*

1. *If* $f \succsim e \succsim g$, *then*

$$U(f \ominus g) = U(f) - U(g),$$
$$U(g \ominus f) = U(g) - U(f).$$

2. *If* $f \succsim g \succsim e$, *then*

$$U(f \ominus g) = \frac{U(f) - U(g)}{1 - \delta U(g)},$$
$$U(g \ominus f) = U(g) - U(f).$$

Proof. In each case, one rewrites the difference $\ominus$ in terms of $\oplus$ and then applies Eq. (4.45) or Eq. (6.1) as appropriate. ■

Using Proposition 6.4.2 in Eqs. (6.15) and (6.16) and a bit of algebra yields:

Theorem 6.4.3. *Suppose the structure is extensive-conjoint with a representation U that is additive over mixed gambles, Eq. (6.1), p-additive over gains, and separable. Suppose $(f_+, C; g_-) \succsim e$ and b and s are defined by Eq. (6.14) with b approaching from below and s from above.*

(1) *If general segregation, Eq. (6.7), holds, then*

$$
\begin{aligned}
0 = {} & \delta U(b)^2 [1 - W_{\mathbf{E}}^+(C)] - U(b)\left(1 - \delta U(g)[1 - W_{\mathbf{E}}^+(C)]\right) \\
& + U(f) W_{\mathbf{E}}^+(C) + U(g)[1 - W_{\mathbf{E}}^+(C)],
\end{aligned}
\tag{6.17}
$$
$$U(s) = U(f)[1 - W_{\mathbf{E}}^+(\overline{C})] + U(g) W_{\mathbf{E}}^+(\overline{C}). \tag{6.18}$$

(2) *If duplex decomposition, Eq. (6.8), holds, then*

$$
\begin{aligned}
0 = {} & \delta U(b)^2 W_{\mathbf{E}}^-(\overline{C}) - U(b)[W_{\mathbf{E}}^+(C) + W_{\mathbf{E}}^-(\overline{C}) - \delta U(g) W_{\mathbf{E}}^-(\overline{C})] \\
& + U(f) W_{\mathbf{E}}^+(C) + U(g) W_{\mathbf{E}}^-(\overline{C})
\end{aligned}
\tag{6.19}
$$
$$U(s) = \frac{U(f) W_{\mathbf{E}}^-(C) + U(g) W_{\mathbf{E}}^+(\overline{C})}{W_{\mathbf{E}}^-(C) + W_{\mathbf{E}}^+(\overline{C})}. \tag{6.20}$$

6.4.2.1 Computation formulas: In actually making computations, it is useful to recast these formulas in terms of the dimensionless measures

$$U_+(f) = \begin{cases} 1 - e^{-\kappa V(f)}, & \delta > 0 \\ \alpha V(f), & \delta = 0, \\ e^{\kappa V(f)} - 1, & \delta < 0 \end{cases} \quad f \succsim e, \tag{6.21}$$

$$U_-(f) = \begin{cases} 1 - e^{-\kappa' V'(f)}, & \delta' > 0 \\ \alpha' V(f) & \delta' = 0, \\ e^{\kappa' V'(f)} - 1, & \delta' < 0 \end{cases} \quad f \prec e. \tag{6.22}$$

In converting into this form we take into careful account the values of δ, δ' and whether $g \succsim e$

or $g \prec e$. To that end, we define

$$sgn(\delta) = \begin{cases} +, & \delta > 0 \\ 0, & \delta = 0 \\ -, & \delta < 0 \end{cases} . \tag{6.23}$$

So, for example, Eq. (6.19) becomes, for $g \succsim e$,

$$\begin{aligned} 0 = \ & sgn(\delta)U_+(b)^2 W_{\mathbf{E}}^-(\overline{C}) - U_+(b)[W_{\mathbf{E}}^+(C) + W_{\mathbf{E}}^-(\overline{C}) - sgn(\delta)U_+(g)W_{\mathbf{E}}^-(\overline{C})] \\ & + U_+(f)W_{\mathbf{E}}^+(C) + U_+(g)W_{\mathbf{E}}^-(\overline{C}), \end{aligned}$$

whereas for $g \prec e$ and $\delta' \neq 0$, if we set $\Lambda = \left|\frac{\delta}{\delta'}\right|$ we have

$$\begin{aligned} 0 = \ & sgn(\delta)U_+(b)^2 W_{\mathbf{E}}^-(\overline{C}) - U_+(b)[W_{\mathbf{E}}^+(C) + W_{\mathbf{E}}^-(\overline{C}) - sgn(\delta)\Lambda U_-(g)W_{\mathbf{E}}^-(\overline{C})] \\ & + U_+(f)W_{\mathbf{E}}^+(C) + \Lambda U_-(g)W_{\mathbf{E}}^-(\overline{C}). \end{aligned}$$

And, similarly,

$$U_+(s) = \begin{cases} \dfrac{U_+(f)W_{\mathbf{E}}^-(C) + U_+(g)W_{\mathbf{E}}^+(\overline{C})}{W_{\mathbf{E}}^-(C) + W_{\mathbf{E}}^+(\overline{C})}, & g \succsim e \\[2ex] \dfrac{U_+(f)W_{\mathbf{E}}^-(C) + \Lambda U_+(g)W_{\mathbf{E}}^+(\overline{C})}{W_{\mathbf{E}}^-(C) + W_{\mathbf{E}}^+(\overline{C})}, & g \prec e \end{cases} .$$

6.4.2.2   Remarks on the relations among $g, b(g)$, and $s(g)$: I do not see any general inequalities holding among these quantities.

In the case where $\delta > 0$, i.e., gains are concave in V, there is no assurance that real solutions occur, whereas in the case where $\delta < 0$ we can be sure that the terms within the square root expression for the solutions are positive.

A numerical example may be useful. The following numbers are vaguely plausible on the assumption that C is appreciably more likely to occur than not and that the weighting function for negative consequences is larger than that for positive ones:

$$\begin{aligned} U_+(f) &= 0.60, \ U_+(g) = -0.20 \\ W_{\mathbf{E}}^+(C) &= 0.70, \ W_{\mathbf{E}}^-(\overline{C}) = 0.40 \\ W_{\mathbf{E}}^-(C) &= 0.80, \ W_{\mathbf{E}}^+(\overline{C}) = 0.25 \\ \Lambda &= 1 \text{ and } 1.5. \end{aligned}$$

Using the abbreviations C = concave, i.e., $\delta > 0$, V = convex, i.e., $\delta' < 0$, GS = general segregation, and DD = duplex decomposition, then the following numbers arise (I omit all solutions that fall outside the possible range for positive values):

		$\Delta = 1$			$\Lambda = 1.5$		
		$U_+(b)$	$U_+(f,C;g)$	$U_+(s)$	$U_+(b)$	$U_+(f,C;g)$	$U_+(s)$
C/V	GS	0.447	0.360	0.400	0.421	0.330	0.375
	DD	0.395	0.340	0.410	0.359	0.300	0.386
V/C	GS	0.312	0.360	0.400	0.281	0.330	0.375
	DD	0.264	0.340	0.410	0.229	0.300	0.386

The fact that in all four of the concave/convex, denoted C/V, cases $U(b) > U(s)$ certainly makes that model suspect. Kahneman, Knetsch, and Thaler (1990, 1991) report, as seems most reasonable, that for their respondents $U(b) < U(s)$. For the convex/concave case we do have $U(b) < U(f,C;g) < U(s)$ for general segregation and $U(b) < U(s) < U(f,C;g)$ for duplex decomposition. I not aware of any data in which certainty equivalents have been compared with carefully elicited buying and selling prices, so I do not know whether empirically one always finds the certainty equivalent bounded by the buying and selling prices or whether it can, in fact, fall outside the interval $[U(b), U(s)]$.

6.4.3   Consequence monotonicity of buying and selling prices

The simplest aspects of the hypothesis that buying and selling prices satisfy consequence monotonicity are the assertions that, for $x > y > 0$,

$$b(x,p;y) > b(x,p;0) \text{ and } s(x,p;y) > s(x,p;0). \tag{6.24}$$

Recall that much data, summarized in Birnbaum (1997), has established violations of Eq. (6.24) for both buying and selling prices when p is fairly close to 1. We will see more of this in Section 7.4.3.

In the present model, it is clear that the sale prices are predicted to be monotonic because of their linear character in $U(f)$ and $U(g)$, which argues against the additive U model. The argument for buying prices is more complex. It will suffice to give it for duplex decomposition because the general segregation case is the same but with $W^-(\overline{C})$ replaced by $1 - W^+(C)$. Let $b_0 = b(x,p;e)$ and $b = b(x,p;y)$. From Eq. (6.19) we compute each, and subtracting the former expression from the latter get

$$U(b) - U(b_0) = \frac{U(y)[1 + \delta U(b)]W^-(1-p)}{W^+(p) + W^-(1-p) - \delta[U(b) + U(b_0)]W^-(1-p)}.$$

So, assuming that $1 + \delta U(b) > 0$,

$$U(b) - U(b_0) > 0 \iff W^+(p) + W^-(1-p) > \delta[U(b) + U(b_0)]W^-(1-p).$$

For $p \to 1$, we know that $W^+(p) \to 1$ and $W^-(1-p) \to 0$, so no violation of monotonicity is predicted in the region where it has been found. Thus, the theory of this chapter does not account for the empirical findings about the nonmonotonicity of buying and selling prices for large p.

This failure of prediction suggests one of two things: Either the models arrived at in this chapter are wrong or the definitions of buying and selling prices are inappropriate. On the assumption that it is the former, for which other evidence has accumulated, we turn to an alternative model in the next chapter.

6.5   Summary

The underlying hypothesis of the chapter is that the utility function U that has arisen in the study of gains and losses separately is also additive over the joint receipt of mixed gains and losses. Thus, the joint receipt structure for mixed consequences has to satisfy the necessary axioms of additive conjoint measurement, but these have not been directly checked empirically. To do so carefully is a fairly major task. Even if these axioms are found to hold and the usual structural axioms are invoked, the resulting additive representation need be no more than monotonically related to the p-additive representation from gains and losses. A necessary and sufficient condition for them to be the same, namely, joint-receipt consistency (Def. 6.1.1), was developed. This too has not been studied empirically.

Next we addressed the question: Given that U is additive over mixed joint receipts, what form does U have over gambles with mixed consequences? This requires some linking relation between the joint receipt structure and the gambling one, something analogous to segregation in the case of gains. Two linking hypotheses were considered. One actually generalizes the concept of segregation. Although that assumption was supported empirically for gains, it has yet to be studied empirically in the mixed case. The other linking hypothesis, duplex decomposition, which to some people seems plausible despite its being decidedly nonrational, has received some empirical support. Both linking relations were shown to lead to bilinear forms for the utility of a binary mixed gamble. The representation derived from duplex decomposition is exactly the same as the one proposed by Tversky and Kahneman (1992) in their cumulative prospect theory. In particular, the weight assigned to the event C leading to a gain was $W_E^+(C)$ and that, $\overline{C}$, leading to a loss was $W_E^-(\overline{C})$. In general, these do not sum to 1. The bilinear representation derived from general segregation differs from the duplex decomposition case only to the extent that the weights do add to 1.

An experiment of Chechile and Cooke (1997), although flawed, and an improved one, avoiding the flaw, by Chechile and Butler (1999) strongly suggests that no bilinear model comes close to accounting for their data. So an alternative approach seems needed, and one is described in the next chapter.

Finally, plausible hypotheses were proposed for buying and selling prices, and expressions for them were derived for both the general segregation and duplex decomposition models. One prediction of these models is that the buying and selling prices should exhibit consequence monotonicity, whereas we know empirically that for large probabilities they do not.

This suggests that either the bilinear models of this chapter simply are not correct descriptively or the definitions of buying and selling prices are inappropriate. The topic requires considerable further investigation.

6.6   Proofs

6.6.1   Theorem 6.1.1

Proof. Suppose U is a p-additive representation for gains and that U^* is additive for mixed joint receipts. For simplicity I omit the sign subscripts on the symbols for gambles. Because U and U^* both preserve $\succsim$ over gains, there is a strictly increasing function Φ such that $U = \Phi(U^*)$. Consider the left side of joint-receipt consistency, Eq. (6.5),

$$
\begin{aligned}
U[(f \oplus h) \oplus g] &= U(f \oplus h)\,[1 - \delta U(g)] + U(g) \\
&= \Phi[U^*(f \oplus h)]\,[1 - \delta \Phi[U^*(g)]] + \Phi[U^*(g)] \\
&= \Phi[U^*(f) + U^*(h)]\,(1 - \delta \Phi[U^*(g)]) + \Phi[U^*(g)].
\end{aligned}
$$

Next, consider the right side of Eq. (6.5),

$$
\begin{aligned}
U[(f \oplus g) \oplus k] &= \Phi\left(U^*[(f \oplus g) \oplus k]\right) \\
&= \Phi\left[U^*(f \oplus g) + U^*(k)\right] \\
&= \Phi\left(\Phi^{-1}[U(f \oplus g)] + U^*(k)\right) \\
&= \Phi\left[\Phi^{-1}\left(U(f)\,[1 - \delta U(g)] + U(g)\right) + U^*(k)\right] \\
&= \Phi\left(\Phi^{-1}\left[\Phi[U^*(f)]\,(1 - \delta \Phi[U^*(g)]) + \Phi[U^*(g)]\right] + U(k)\right).
\end{aligned}
$$

Writing $X = U^*(f), Y = U^*(g), Z = -U^*(h), K = -U^*(k)$ and equating these two expressions yields the functional equation

$$
\Phi(X - Z)\,[1 - \delta\Phi(Y)] + \Phi(Y) = \Phi\left[\Phi^{-1}\left(\Phi(X)\,[1 - \delta\Phi(Y)] + \Phi(Y)\right) - K\right]. \tag{6.25}
$$

This can be placed in a simpler looking form by defining

$$
\begin{aligned}
H(X, Y) &= \Phi^{-1}\left(\Phi(X)\,[1 - \delta\Phi(Y)] + \Phi(Y)\right) \\
&= \Phi^{-1}\left(\Phi(X) + \Phi(Y) - \delta\Phi(X)\Phi(Y)\right), \tag{6.26}
\end{aligned}
$$

in which case Eq. (6.25) becomes

$$
H(X - Z, Y) = H(X, Y) - K. \tag{6.27}
$$

The following solution to Eq. (6.27) is adapted from Aczél, Luce, and Maksa (1996). With no loss of generality we may assume that the variables lie in a half open interval I that includes $[0, 1[$. Since $\Phi(0) = 0$, $H(0, Y) = Y$. Because by assumption $f \oplus h \succsim e$, we see $X \geq Z$.

Because f can be varied subject to this constraint, we may set $X = Z$ in Eq. (6.27), from which we obtain $K = H(Z, Y) - Y$. So, defining $\phi(X, Y) = H(X, Y) - Y$, Eq. (6.27) becomes

$$\phi(X - Z, Y) = \phi(X, Y) - \phi(Z, Y),$$

or setting $W = X - Z$ it becomes

$$\phi(W + Z, Y) = \phi(W, Y) + \phi(Z, Y), \quad W, Z, W + Z, Y \in I.$$

With Y fixed, this Cauchy equation can be extended to $\mathbb{R}_+$ as is done in, e.g., Aczél (1987, p. 82). Thus, $\phi(X, Y) = \psi(Y)X$ and so

$$H(X, Y) = \psi(Y)X + Y. \tag{6.28}$$

Although f and g, and so $X = U^*(f)$ and $Y = U^*(Y)$, play different roles in the statement of joint-receipt consistency, their only constraints are $X \geq 0$, $Y \geq 0$, and $X \geq Z$. But the equation holds for all choices of $Z \geq 0$, the numerical values of X and Y can be interchanged. Thus, because the right side is symmetric in X and Y, we have

$$\psi(Y)X + Y = \psi(X)Y + X,$$

or, rewriting,

$$\frac{\psi(X) - 1}{X} = \frac{\psi(Y) - 1}{Y}.$$

So, for some real γ,

$$\psi(Y) = 1 - \gamma Y. \tag{6.29}$$

Substituting Eq. (6.29) into Eq. (6.28) and that into Eq. (6.26) yields the functional equation

$$\Phi[X + Y - \gamma XY] = \Phi(X) + \Phi(Y) - \delta\Phi(X)\Phi(Y). \tag{6.30}$$

We solve this in four distinct cases.

Case 1: $\gamma = 0, \delta = 0$. It follows immediately that

$$\Phi(X) = \alpha X, \ \alpha > 0.$$

Thus $U = \alpha U^*$ and it is routine in this case to verify that $k \sim h$.

Case 2: $\gamma = 0, \delta \neq 0$. It follows immediately from Eq. (6.30) that

$$1 - \delta\Phi(X + Y) = [1 - \delta\Phi(X)][1 - \delta\Phi(Y)]. \tag{6.31}$$

Setting $\Theta(X) = 1 - \delta\Phi(X)$, we have a Cauchy equation with solution $\Theta(X) = e^{\kappa X}$, and so

$$\delta\Phi(X) = 1 - e^{\kappa X},$$

whence

$$\delta U(f) = 1 - e^{\kappa U^*(f)}.$$

Observe that from this follows

$$
\begin{aligned}
\delta U(f, C; e) &= 1 - e^{\kappa U^*(f, C; e)} \\
&= 1 - e^{\kappa U^*(f) W^+(C)} \\
&= 1 - \left(e^{\kappa U^*(f)}\right)^{W^+(C)} \\
&= 1 - (1 - \delta U(f))^{W^+(C)}.
\end{aligned}
$$

So,

$$\ln\left(1 - \delta U(f, C; e)\right) = \ln\left(1 - \delta U(f)\right) W^+(C)$$

is a separable representation and from Eq. (6.31) we see that

$$\ln\left(1 - \delta U(f \oplus g)\right) = \ln\left(1 - \delta U(f)\right) + \ln\left(1 - \delta U(g)\right)$$

is additive, and so p-additive.

Case 3: $\gamma \neq 0$, $\delta = 0$. For these assumptions, we may rewrite Eq. (6.30) as

$$\Phi\left(\frac{1 - (1 - \gamma X)(1 - \gamma Y)}{\gamma}\right) = \Phi\left(\frac{1 - (1 - \gamma X)}{\gamma}\right) + \Phi\left(\frac{1 - (1 - \gamma Y)}{\gamma}\right).$$

Setting $\Theta(Z) = \Phi\left(\frac{1-Z}{\gamma}\right)$ and $X^* = 1 - \gamma X, Y^* = 1 - \gamma Y$, we have the Cauchy equation

$$\Theta(X^* Y^*) = \Theta(X^*) + \Theta(Y^*),$$

whence

$$\Theta(X^*) = \alpha \ln X^*,$$

and so

$$\Phi(X) = \alpha \ln(1 - \gamma X).$$

Therefore

$$U(f) = \Phi[U^*(f)] = \alpha \ln[1 - \gamma U^*(f)],$$

or rewriting,

$$\gamma U^*(f) = 1 - e^{U(f)/\alpha}.$$

Thus, using the fact that U is additive ($\delta = 0$),

$$
\begin{aligned}
\gamma U^*(f \oplus g) &= 1 - e^{U(f \oplus g)/\alpha} \\
&= 1 - e^{U(f)/\alpha} e^{U(g)/\alpha}
\end{aligned}
$$

$$= 1 - [1 - \gamma U^*(f)] [1 - \gamma U^*(g)],$$

proving that γU^* is both separable and p-additive.

Case 4: $\gamma \neq 0, \delta \neq 0$. Rewrite Eq. (6.30) as

$$1 - \delta\Phi \left(\frac{1 - (1 - \gamma X)(1 - \gamma Y)}{\gamma} \right)$$
$$= [1 - \delta\Phi(X)][1 - \delta\Phi(Y)]$$
$$= \left[1 - \delta\Phi \left(\frac{1 - (1 - \gamma X)}{\gamma} \right) \right] \left[1 - \delta\Phi \left(\frac{1 - (1 - \gamma Y)}{\gamma} \right) \right].$$

Defining $\Theta(Z) = 1 - \delta\Phi \left(\frac{1-Z}{\gamma} \right)$ and $X^* = 1 - \gamma X$ yields

$$\Theta(X^* Y^*) = \Theta(X^*) \Theta(Y^*),$$

whence for some β

$$\Theta(X^*) = (X^*)^{\beta},$$

and so

$$\delta\Phi(X) = 1 - \Theta(1 - \gamma X) = 1 - (1 - \gamma X)^{\beta},$$

whence

$$\delta U(f) = \Phi[U^*(f)] = 1 - (1 - \gamma U^*(f))^{\beta}$$

or

$$\gamma U^*(f) = 1 - (1 - \delta U(f))^{1/\beta}$$
$$= 1 - e^{-\kappa V(f)/\beta},$$

which establishes that U^* also has a negative exponential form.   ∎

Chapter 7
ADDITIVE VALUE OVER MIXED CONSEQUENCES

This chapter continues the discussion of binary mixed joint receipts and gambles begun in the last one. The difference is that we now assume it is the value function V, not the utility function U, that is additive over mixed joint receipts—indeed, over the entire structure of gambles and their joint receipt. Of course, we continue to assume that the structure is sufficiently rich so that V and U are onto intervals that include 0. Much of the chapter is an expansion of Luce (1997) plus some subsequent experimental studies.

7.1 Associative Joint Receipts

The basic idea of the additive value model of joint receipts is, perhaps, the simplest possible model. The joint receipt operation is assumed to be associative independent of where the alternatives stand relative to the status quo. The grouping simply does not matter independent of whether the entities are gains, losses, or mixtures. I will also assume that the alternatives are confined to those such that for each f, whether seen as a gain or a loss, there exists a perfectly compensating alternative, denoted f^{-1}, such that $f \oplus f^{-1} \sim e$. For some people, this assumption may exclude some gambles from the scope of the theory, e.g., those for which death is a possible consequence, because no gain is sufficiently compensating. On the other hand, judging by the numbers of people who regularly risk their lives in somewhat dangerous activities—driving, skiing, and mountain climbing come to mind—the assumption of inverses may not be totally unrealistic. Finally, retaining the several axioms of a joint-receipt preference structure, Def. 4.2.1, plus the existence of an inverse, then the more traditional form of the Archimedean axiom can be assumed.

7.1.1 Archimedean, weakly ordered group

Summarizing (and retaining the names from Def. 4.2.1),

Definition 7.1.1. $\langle \mathcal{D}, e, \succsim, \oplus \rangle$, where $e \in \mathcal{D}$, $\succsim$ is a binary relation and $\oplus$ is a (closed) binary operation on $\mathcal{D}$, is said to form a *joint-receipt, Archimedean, weakly ordered group* if and only if for all $f, g, h \in \mathcal{D}$:

Axiom JR1. Weak Order:

$\succsim$ is transitive and connected.

Axiom JR2. Weak Commutativity:

$$f \oplus g \sim g \oplus f.$$

Axiom JR3. Weak Associativity:

$$f \oplus (g \oplus h) \sim (f \oplus g) \oplus h.$$

Axiom JR4. Weak Monotonicity:

$$f \succsim g \Longleftrightarrow f \oplus h \succsim g \oplus h \Longleftrightarrow h \oplus f \succsim h \oplus g.$$

Axiom JR5. Weak Identity:

$$f \oplus e \sim e \oplus f \sim f.$$

Axiom JR6'. Archimedean: For any $f \succ e$ and any g, there exists an integer n such that

$$f(n) \succ g.$$

Axiom JR7. Weak Inverse: For each f there exists $f^{-1} \in \mathcal{D}$ such that

$$f \oplus f^{-1} \sim f^{-1} \oplus f \sim e.$$

In applying this concept to gambles, we take $\mathcal{D}$ to be the closure under $\oplus$ of the set $\mathcal{B}_2$ of binary second-order gambles, in which case we denote it $\mathcal{D}_2$. The reason for formulating theory in terms of the closure of $\mathcal{B}_2$ under $\oplus$ rather than the closure of $\mathcal{B}_1$ is that we assume general gambles are reduced according to the gain-loss decomposition assumption of Eq. (2.17) into a binary gamble composed of the gains subgamble and the loss subgamble.

As stated, the axioms are redundant (but consistent). In each of JR4, JR5, and JR7 one of the forms can be omitted on the grounds that it follows from weak commutativity, JR2. On the other hand, one can simply omit JR2 entirely because it can be shown—although not in a simple way—to follow from the other six axioms (see, e.g., Fuchs, 1963; Krantz, Luce, Suppes, & Tversky, 1971, pp. 77-78). Working with the equivalence classes under $\sim$, the axioms JR3, JR5, and JR7 define what is technically called a mathematical *group*. Adding JR1 and JR4 makes it an *ordered group* on the equivalence classes or what can be called a *weakly ordered group* on the entire domain $\mathcal{D}$. And finally adding JR6' makes it an *Archimedean, weakly ordered group*.

An important and well-known mathematical result due to Hölder (1901), which is the basis of a great deal of the representational theory of measurement, is that any Archimedean ordered group is isomorphic to a subgroup of the ordered additive real numbers. [For an English translation of the first part of paper see Michell and Ernst (1996).] The result may be formulated as follows:

Theorem 7.1.1.   (Hölder, 1901) *The following two assertions are equivalent:*
1. $\langle \mathcal{D}, e, \succsim, \oplus \rangle$ *forms a joint-receipt, Archimedean, weakly ordered group.*
2.   *There exists a function V from $\mathcal{D}$ into a subset of the real numbers closed under addition such that for all $f, g \in \mathcal{D}$,*

$$
\begin{aligned}
f \succsim g &\Leftrightarrow V(f) \geq V(g); \\
V(f \oplus g) &= V(f) + V(g); \\
V(e) &= 0.
\end{aligned}
$$

Note that by Axiom JR7 and parts (ii) and (iii),

$$V(f^{-1}) = -V(f). \tag{7.1}$$

Associativity of a binary operation is, of course, a very strong property. It means that one need not say anything about the pairwise grouping of the entities. In terms of our interpretation, it says that we do not need to worry at all about the theory of joint receipt of three or more goods—it simply follows from the binary case. If this holds, it is a valuable property. The empirical question is whether or not it holds for at least some people.

7.1.2   Experimental results on associativity

To realize an experiment on associativity entails two major, somewhat interlocked decisions. One is the types of stimuli to use in a laboratory setting. The other is how to interpret the parentheses in an expression such as $(x \oplus y) \oplus z$. There is nothing automatic about what the pairing means, and almost independent of how one realizes the parentheses there always seems to be the potential for misunderstanding on the part of respondents. G. Fisher attempted such a study in his dissertation (Fisher, 1999). His stimuli were of two types: money and pictorial images of commonly valued equipment, e.g., computer system, phone-answering machine, copier, etc. Examples are shown in Fig. 7.1, which shows a typical display used in the experiment.

For the money, gains were interpreted as checks, losses as bills, and the parentheses as envelopes. Thus, one was to think of $(x \oplus y)$ as an envelope containing x and y and to think of z as really an envelope (z) containing z. The joint receipt $(x \oplus y) \oplus z = (x \oplus y) \oplus (z)$ was to be interpreted as receiving both envelopes. For the equipment, the parentheses were to be interpreted as cartons containing one or two of pieces of equipment, as the case may be.

The problem of what constitutes a negative with respect to the equipment is not automatic. Fisher interpreted it to mean when the carton was opened the equipment was "damaged" or "defective" to the point of requiring repair or replacement. The respondents were instructed to say merely in terms of their preferences for the objects which packaging was preferred or if they were indifferent between the two ways of grouping the objects. For money, the negative

235

of a check for $x was interpreted as a bill for $x.

A major concern is whether or not the instructions kept the respondents from basing their decisions on something other than the goods themselves. For example, suppose one is comparing $(x_- \oplus y) \oplus z$ to $x_- \oplus (y \oplus z)$, where x_- means the defective or damaged object x. Many of us would almost automatically prefer the right-hand formulation because then all we need do is close up the carton containing x_- and return it, whereas in the left-hand formulation the carton containing both x_- and y would be far too large for just x_-, and so it would entail the inconvenience of either finding a more suitable carton or introducing a lot of filler material. As we shall see, I fear the instructions may not have precluded this kind of reasoning by a few respondents.

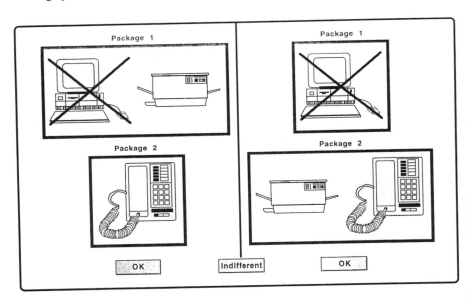

Figure 7.1. A typical display used by Fisher in testing the associativity of joint receipt.

The study involved 36 potentially associative pairs $x \oplus (y \oplus z)$, $(x \oplus y) \oplus z$. They arose from six basic types: There could be either one gain and two losses or two gains and one loss. And the singleton, gain or loss, could either be the "isolated"[1] term in one of the two alternatives or it could always be "grouped" with one of the other items in the triple. This makes for four types: GI, GG, LI, and LG, where GI means the singleton is a gain that is "isolated" and GG means the gain is "grouped" with either of the other two objects on both sides of

---

[1] For "isolated" and "grouped," Fisher used "segregated" and "integrated." As we shall see in Section 7.2.3, the latter terms had been used earlier for a rather different distinction. Also, we have earlier used the term "segregated" to define an important behavioral property. So, new terms seem appropriate.

the indifference. In addition, each isolated case has two variants depending on whether the isolated element lies to the right or left of the pair. Using x_- as the loss version of x, these six cases are summarized as Table 7.1. Because the three symbols can be permuted in 6 ways, there is a total of 36 stimulus pairs. There were 10 variants on each combination involving different stimuli.

These 36 stimuli could also be grouped into 18 pairs that differed only by commutative changes. For example, the pair $x \oplus (y_- \oplus z_-)$, $(x \oplus y_-) \oplus z_-$ and the pair $(z_- \oplus y_-) \oplus x$, $z_- \oplus (y_- \oplus x)$ differ only as the result of two commutative changes for each member of the pair. So, one can ask the degree to which the violations of associativity are maintained under commutative changes.

Table 7.1. The six variants on associativity used in Fisher's (1999) experiment.

Type	Left	Right
GI	$x \oplus (y_- \oplus z_-)$	$(x \oplus y_-) \oplus z_-$
GI	$x_- \oplus (y_- \oplus z)$	$(x_- \oplus y_-) \oplus z$
GG	$x_- \oplus (y \oplus z_-)$	$(x_- \oplus y) \oplus z_-$
LI	$x_- \oplus (y \oplus z)$	$(x_- \oplus y) \oplus z$
LI	$x \oplus (y \oplus z_-)$	$(x \oplus y) \oplus z_-$
LG	$x \oplus (y_- \oplus z)$	$(x \oplus y_-) \oplus z$

In addition, the experiment included 180 cases of associativity combined with consequence monotonicity.[2] For example, if $x \succ w$, then assuming that associativity and monotonicity both hold, one predicts $(x \oplus y) \oplus z \succ w \oplus (y \oplus z)$. So, one can check the degree to which this is true.

For each pair presented, the respondents indicated either indifference or preference for one or the other. The data from the 16 respondents for purely associative pairs are shown in the first column of Table 7.2 ordered by decreasing percentage of indifference responses. For the responses that were not indifferent, the responses are partitioned into the four types—GI, GG, LI, and LG—and the numerical data are shown. The next to last column is the percentage of consistent responses to the pairs that differed only by commutative changes. And the last column shows the percentage of cases where monotonicity is preserved despite an associative change. In this case, the preference order between x and w was determined to be those cases where, out of 8 presentations, 5 or more agreed.

It is clear that six respondents are fully associative, two more are associative in 80% of the cases, and the remaining do not seem to exhibit associativity. No left-right bias was evident. For the nonassociative responses, the 7th through 10th respondents seem to favor the isolated response when it is possible, and the 16th favors the grouped package. The remaining five

---

2   The original plan was for 360 such comparisons, but an error of design rendered all of the loss cases involving x_-, y_- or z_- meaningless.

distribute their non-associative responses with no obvious pattern. One concern in such an experiment is the fact that, in order to evidence associativity, a very large fraction of responses must be indifference ones, and some respondents may resist doing this.

Mixing monotonicity with associativity leads to a fairly high percentage of consistent responses for all of the respondents, with an average of 79%. Because for the (x, w) comparisons, in 75% of the cases either 7 or 8 out of 8 presentations agreed, we see that the monotonicity results are no less consistent. The correlation over respondents between the percentage figures for the (x, w) choice and the corresponding monotonicity one was 0.77. This suggests that when the decision makes a difference, associativity seems to hold, in which case, the low correlation of 0.37 between the first and last columns is not surprising.

Table 7.2. For each of 16 respondents, the percentages of 360 presentations of associative pairs in which the respondent was indifferent between the two ways of grouping the stimuli. The nonassociative responses are partitioned by those having just one gain or just one loss that is segregated, with the number (#) of isolated and number of grouped responses, as well as the number where the single gain or loss is always grouped with one of the other two consequences. Column 6 is the percentage of consistent choices among the 180 pairs of presentations that differed only by commutative changes. Column 7 is the percentage of presentations for which monotonicity combined with associativity was sustained when the preference order of the (x, w) pair was determined by the choice being the same for 5 or more presentations.

% Assoc.	GI #I	GI #G	LI #I	LI #G	GG #	LG #	% Agree Comm.	% Mono.
100							100	92
100							100	88
99						2	99	90
99	1				2	1	98	68
98	3	1	1		1		97	87
96	1	1	3	4		4	93	72
80	36		35		1		99	91
80	16	5	23	6	10	13	70	82
73	43	1	46		1	8	91	84
53	56	6	34	29	20	26	53	67
51	35	23	24	37	32	27	61	72
49	17	42	71	13	17	25	53	77
40	47	23	46	27	36	36	76	81
26	47	37	50	49	40	44	37	56
19	69	24	75	34	36	55	56	63
18	8	89	19	96	42	42	78	98

Column 8 shows the degree of consistency in responses when only commutative changes are made. For the six highly associative subjects, this percentage is necessarily high. For the remaining 10 no necessary pattern exists, and although a correlation in such a situation involving the same data analyzed in two ways is necessarily suspect, it is 0.55. Restricted to the last 8, it dropped to 0.37.

The conclusion seems to be that associativity is clearly a good descriptive assumption for about half of these respondents; however, 16 is a small sample on which to infer an accurate proportion. Later we shall see a data analysis that leads us to think associativity may be adequate for 84% of 144 respondents (§ 7.3.5). Further, in situations where associativity must be invoked to apply monotonicity, all of the respondents exhibited fairly similar levels of consistency, suggesting that associativity may in fact hold better than suggested by the first column. In any event, associativity holds for a sufficiently large fraction of people that it is surely worth further investigation.

7.2   Utility of Mixed Joint Receipts

Given that binary gambles of gains have an RDU representation U, that $\oplus$ is commutative, and that segregation holds, we know how U and V are related, namely, either proportionally, exponentially, or negative exponentially (§4.4.6). If, in addition, V is not just additive over gains but throughout the structure and assuming segregation, then as we shall see U for the mixed case follows almost automatically. This contrasts sharply with the extensive-conjoint case for which a linking hypothesis, joint receipt consistency (Def. 6.1.1), was required to relate the additive representation of the extensive structures over gains and the conjoint one over mixed joint receipt.

Although simple to derive, the results in the present case are somewhat complex to state because there are several options to consider. First, there is the issue of whether $f_+ \oplus g_-$ is perceived as a gain or a loss, and second there is the question of whether the p-additive U has the parameter $\delta \gtreqless 0$ and, so, of whether U is a concave, proportional, or convex function of V, Eqs. (4.46)-(4.48), for gains. And, independently, the same question holds for losses with parameter δ'. A total of 6 cases are considered explicitly out of the $18 = 2 \times 3 \times 3$ possible. This reduction is achieved by the device of stating things in terms of inverses of elements so that the expressions are stated entirely in terms of either gains or entirely in terms of losses. This will be remarked on again after Proposition 7.2.1 is stated.

7.2.1   A representation of the utility of mixed joint receipts

Our first result focuses on one way to represent $U(f_+ \oplus g_-)$. I will work out in detail only the proofs for the proportional and the negative exponential cases of a gain (§ 7.6.1). This gives the reader an opportunity to see what drives the results. In a word, the key to the exponential cases is its defining property $e^{x+y} = e^x e^y$. This coupled with V being additive means $e^{\kappa V(f_+ \oplus g_-)} = e^{\kappa V(f_+) + \kappa V(g_-)} = e^{\kappa V(f_+)} e^{\kappa V(g_-)} = e^{\kappa V(f_+)} e^{-\kappa V(g_-^{-1})}$. These exponential terms can then all be reexpressed in terms of U. The somewhat unanticipated result is nonlinear expressions for U over $\oplus$. These nonlinearities pervade the chapter and, if models of this type correctly describe behavior, then it is clear why attempts to apply purely bilinear models were doomed to fail for mixed gambles.

It should be noted that these and the other results in Propositions 7.2.1 and 7.2.2 are stated not in terms of $g_- \precsim e$ when $f_+ \oplus g_- \succsim e$, but in terms of $g_-^{-1} \succsim e$, thus keeping the entire expression in the domain of gains. Similarly, when $f_+ \oplus g_- \precsim e$, it is stated in terms of f_+^{-1} rather than f_+, thereby staying entirely in the domain of losses. To get either expression back into the mixed case depends on what assumption—concave, linear, or convex—is made for the opposite domain. Under a special assumption concerning the relation of the gains to loss forms, Theorem 7.2.3 works out the various exponential and negative exponential cases.

Conventions: For the case where U is said to be proportional to V, corresponding to $\delta = 0, \delta' = 0$ we mean that, for some $\alpha, \alpha' > 0$,

$$U(f) = V(f) \begin{cases} \alpha, & \text{if } f \succsim e \\ \alpha', & \text{if } f \prec e. \end{cases} \tag{7.2}$$

For the case of U a negative exponential (concave) function of V, corresponding to $\delta > 0$, we mean that for gains

$$U_+(f) = \delta U(f) = 1 - e^{-\kappa V(f)}, \quad f \succsim e, \tag{7.3}$$

and for the exponential (convex) function, corresponding to $\delta < 0$,

$$U_+(f) = |\delta| U(f) = e^{\delta V(f)} - 1, \quad f \succsim e. \tag{7.4}$$

For losses, replace δ by δ' and κ by κ'.

Proposition 7.2.1.   *Suppose V is additive in $\oplus$ and U is p-additive with parameter δ. Let $\lambda = \frac{\alpha}{\alpha'}$.*

(i)   *Suppose $\delta = 0, \delta' = 0$, i.e., U is proportional to V for gains. Then*

$$U(f^{-1}) = -U(f) \begin{cases} \frac{1}{\lambda}, & \text{if } f \succsim e \\ \lambda, & \text{if } f \prec e \end{cases} \tag{7.5}$$

and

$$U(f_+ \oplus g_-) = \begin{cases} U(f_+) + \lambda U(g_-), & f_+ \oplus g_- \succ e \\ \frac{1}{\lambda} U(f_+) + U(g_-), & f_+ \oplus g_- \prec e \end{cases} . \tag{7.6}$$

(ii)   *Suppose $\delta \neq 0$, i.e., U is either concave or convex relative to V for gains, then for $f_+ \oplus g_- \succ e$,*

$$\begin{aligned} U_+(f_+ \oplus g_-) &= \frac{U_+(f_+) - U_+(g_-^{-1})}{1 - sgn(\delta) U_+(g_-^{-1})} \\ &= [U_+(f_+) - U_+(g_-^{-1})] \begin{cases} \frac{1}{1 - U_+(g_-^{-1})}, & \delta > 0 \\ \frac{1}{1 + U_+(g_-^{-1})}, & \delta < 0 \end{cases} . \end{aligned} \tag{7.7}$$

240

(iii)   *Suppose $\delta' \neq 0$, then for $f_+ \oplus g_- \prec e$*

$$U_-(f_+ \oplus g_-) = \frac{U_-(g_-) - U_-(f_+^{-1})}{1 - sgn(\delta')U_-(f_+^{-1})}$$

$$= [U_-(g_-) - U_-(f_+^{-1})] \begin{cases} \frac{1}{1-U_-(f_+^{-1})}, & \delta' > 0 \\ \frac{1}{1+U_-(f_+^{-1})}, & \delta' < 0 \end{cases} . \qquad (7.8)$$

Observe that the $\delta \neq 0$ and $\delta' \neq 0$ cases differ only in the sign of the U term in the denominator. The proof of this proposition is given in Section 7.6.1.

7.2.2   The special case of $\kappa = \kappa'$

Because the equations for the utility of gambles become very complex indeed in the general case, Luce (1997) made the special assumption that the parameters for gains and losses are the same, $\kappa = \kappa'$, in the concave and convex cases. Without this assumption, the resulting expressions will have some of the utility terms appearing to powers, making for considerable complexity. Because this simpler case is already quite complicated, I do not think we should try the more complex $\kappa \neq \kappa'$ case until data reject the simpler one.

Making this simplifying assumption permits one to rewrite the expressions in Proposition 7.2.1 in somewhat different form. To do so, we have to examine how $f \succsim e$ is related to f^{-1} under the various combinations of shape. For example, if for gains $\delta > 0$, i.e., U is concave in V, and for losses $\delta' < 0$, which means U convex, then using Eqs. (7.1), (7.7), and (7.8), we see that for a gain

$$\delta'U(f^{-1}) = e^{\kappa'V(f^{-1})} - 1 = e^{-\kappa V(f)} - 1 = -\delta U(f), \quad f \succsim e. \qquad (7.9)$$

This same expression also holds for the convex-concave case. In the concave-concave case we obtain

$$|\delta'|U(f^{-1}) = \frac{-\delta U(f)}{1 - \delta U(f)}, \quad f \succsim e. \qquad (7.10)$$

And in the convex-convex case the $-$ sign in the denominator is changed to $+$.

To abbreviate the resulting equations somewhat, define the following identifier variable

$$\sigma = \begin{cases} + & \text{if } f_+ \oplus g_- \succ e \\ - & \text{if } f_+ \oplus g_- \prec e \end{cases} . \qquad (7.11)$$

And to simplify further, we will simply exclude all cases of proportionality and concentrate on paired cases of concavity and convexity.

Theorem 7.2.2.   *Suppose U is p-additive in $\oplus$ with parameter δ, V is the corresponding additive representation, and $\kappa = \kappa'$.*

(i)   If $\delta > 0 > \delta'$, i.e., U in terms of V is concave for gains and convex for losses, then for σ defined by Eq. (7.11)

$$U_\sigma(f_+ \oplus g_-) = \left\{ \begin{array}{ll} \frac{U_+(f_+)+U_-(g_-)}{1+U_-(g_-)}, & \sigma = + \\ \frac{U_+(f_+)+U_-(g_-)}{1-U_+(f_+)}, & \sigma = - \end{array} \right. \tag{7.12}$$

(ii)   If $\delta < 0 < \delta'$, i.e., U is convex for gains and concave for losses, then the signs in the denominators of Eq. (7.12) are reversed.

(iii)   If $\delta > 0$ and $\delta' > 0$, i.e., U is concave for both gains and losses, then

$$U_\sigma(f_+ \oplus g_-) = U_+(f_+) + U_-(g_-) - U_+(f_+)U_-(g_-). \tag{7.13}$$

(iv)   If $\delta < 0$ and $\delta' < 0$, i.e., U is convex for both gains and losses, then the $-$ before the last term changes to $+$.

The proof of (i) involves substituting Eqs. (7.9) and (7.11) into Eq. (7.7) or (7.8). The other cases are similar.

7.2.3   "Integrate" or "segregate" joint receipt of money?

Recall (§ 4.5.1) that Thaler (1985) raised the following issue. When talking about money, does one prefer to segregate[3] alternatives in the sense of getting and evaluating the two alternatives separately or does one prefer to integrate them into a single alternative? If the two amounts are x and y, does one prefer to think of each individually or as lumped together as $x + y$? He approached the question by describing to respondents scenarios in which person A received the two amounts segregated and person B received them integrated. Each respondent stated which person, A or B, he or she believed would be happier.

As summarized[4] by Thaler and Johnson (1990, p. 647), the average result of Thaler's 87 respondents were:

"1. Segregate gains.
"2. Integrate losses.
"3. Segregate small gains from larger losses (the 'silver lining' principle).
"4. Integrate (cancel) smaller losses with larger gains."

Treating the two separate consequences as $x \oplus y$, we see that his data tell us

$$x \oplus y \succ x + y, \quad \text{for gains}$$
$$x \oplus y \prec x + y, \quad \text{for losses}.$$

---

[3]   This use of the word "segregate" differs both from the one introduced in Chapter 4, which was first used by Kahneman and Tversky (1979). The meanings, although somewhat similar, are distinct, and the reader will have to distinguish them by context.
[4]   As Fishburn and Luce (1995) pointed out, the actual inferences justified by their assumptions and data are rather more complex than they thought. As we will see, the present theory is much more limited in the possible inferences.

As was pointed out in Section 4.5.1, Thaler assumed the segregated evaluation to be $U(x) + U(y)$ and the integrated one, $U(x + y)$, and that a person's decision is based on the sign of $U(x + y) - U(x) - U(y)$, negative for gains and positive for losses. These two observations combine as:

$$U(x) + U(y) \; > \; U(x \oplus y) \; > \; U(x + y), \text{ for gains,}$$
$$U(x) + U(y) \; < \; U(x \oplus y) \; < \; U(x + y), \text{ for losses.}$$

Observe that within the context of exponential and negative exponential relations between U and V, we must have the negative exponential (concave) case for gains and the exponential (convex) one for losses.

Within the present additive V theory for the mixed cases we can examine the sign of $U(x \oplus y) - U(x) - U(y)$ to see the degree of agreement with Thaler's observations.

Proposition 7.2.3.   *For associative joint receipts, if $\delta > 0 > \delta'$, i.e., U is concave for gains and convex for losses, and so Eq. (7.12) holds in the mixed case $x > 0 > y$, then*

$$U(x \oplus y) - U(x) - U(y) \gtreqless 0 \Longleftrightarrow U(x) \gtreqless \frac{1}{\delta} - \frac{1}{|\delta'|} - U(y), \tag{7.14}$$

$$U(x \oplus y) \gtreqless 0 \Longleftrightarrow U(x) \gtreqless - \left| \frac{\delta'}{\delta} \right| U(y) = U(y^{-1}). \tag{7.15}$$

Figure 7.2 puts these results together graphically, and we see that the model is reasonably consistent with Thaler's findings for the case $|\delta'| < \delta$.

7.3   Utility of Mixed Gambles

Depending upon which combination of concavity and convexity holds, different expressions arise for $U(f_+, C; g_-)$. I work out in detail only the simpler cases for which $\kappa = \kappa'$ because, otherwise, the mathematical expressions become extremely cumbersome. Also I will work out in detail only the modal case of concave gains and convex losses, and simply state the other cases. Recall that there is substantial evidence of considerable individual differences in this respect, and so some data analyses will explore the several combinations.

Recall that the defining equation of general segregation, Eq. (6.7), is: For $f, g \in \mathcal{G}_1$, $f \succsim g, C \in \mathcal{E}_E$,

$$(f, C; g) \sim \begin{cases} (f \ominus g, C; e) \oplus g, & \text{if } (f, C; g) \succ e \\ (e, C; g \ominus f) \oplus f, & \text{if } (f, C; g) \prec e \end{cases}. \tag{7.16}$$

And duplex decomposition, Eq. (6.8), is that for all $f_+ \in \mathcal{G}_1^+, g_- \in \mathcal{G}_1^-, C \in \mathcal{E}_E$,

$$(f_+, C; g_-) \sim (f_+, C'; e) \oplus (e, C''; g_-), \tag{7.17}$$

where C', C'' denote C occurring on two independent realizations of the underlying experiment E.

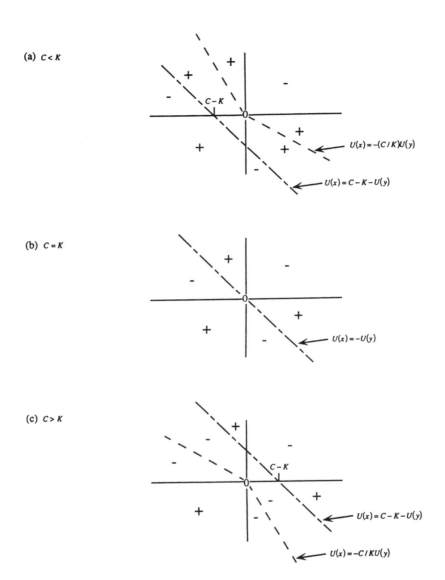

Figure 7.2. The sign of $U(x \oplus y) - U(x) - U(y)$ for the additive V model. The notation of the figure relates to that of the text as follows: $C = 1/\delta$ and $K = 1/\delta'$. Reprinted from *Mathematical Social Sciences*, 34, R. D. Luce, "Associative joint receipts." Pp. 51-74, Fig. 1, Copyright 1997, with permission from Elsevier Science.

7.3.1   Under general segregation

The results for the two cases, U is proportional to V and U is exponential with V, are just enough different to require separate theorems. As a preliminary we need:

Proposition 7.3.1.   *Suppose V is additive and U is the corresponding p-additive representation with parameters δ. If $\delta = 0, \delta' = 0$ and so U proportional to V, and $f \succsim g, f \succsim e$, then with $\lambda = \frac{\alpha}{\alpha'}$,*

$$U(f \ominus g) = \begin{cases} U(f) - U(g), & g \succsim e \\ U(f) - \lambda U(g), & g \prec e \end{cases}$$

$$U(g \ominus f) = \begin{cases} \frac{1}{\lambda}[U(g) - U(f)], & g \succsim e \\ U(g) - \frac{1}{\lambda} U(f), & g \prec e \end{cases}.$$

Proof. Suppose $g \succsim e$, then taking into account that V is everywhere additive and noting $f \ominus g \succsim e \succsim g \ominus f$,

$$U(f \ominus g) = \alpha V(f \ominus g) = \alpha V(f) - \alpha V(g) = U(f) - U(g),$$
$$U(g \ominus f) = \alpha' V(g \ominus f) = \alpha'[V(g) - V(f)]$$
$$= \frac{1}{\lambda}\alpha[V(g) - V(f)] = \frac{1}{\lambda}[U(f) - U(g)].$$

The case $g \prec e$ is similar.   ∎

Using this one can show the following (§ 7.6.3):

Theorem 7.3.2.   *Suppose $\langle \mathcal{D}_2, e, \succsim, \oplus \rangle$ forms a joint receipt, Archimedean, weakly ordered group generated from $\mathcal{B}_2$ with additive representation V onto an interval. Suppose U is proportional to V, Eq. (7.2). Let $\lambda = \frac{\alpha}{\alpha'}$. Then any two of the following statements imply the third:*

1.   *General segregation, Eq. (7.16), is satisfied.*
2.   *There exist $W_E^i : \mathcal{E}_E \to [0,1], i = +, -,$ such that for $(f_+, C; g_-) \succ e$,*

$$U(f_+, C; g_-) = U(f_+)W_E^+(C) + \lambda U(g_-)[1 - W_E^+(C)]; \tag{7.18}$$

and for $(f_+, C; g_-) \prec e$,

$$U(f_+, C; g_-) = \frac{1}{\lambda}U(f_+)[1 - W_E^-(\overline{C})] + U(g_-)W_E^-(\overline{C}). \tag{7.19}$$

3.   *There exist $W_E^i : \mathcal{E}_E \to [0,1], i = +, -,$ such that the pair (U, W_E^+) forms a separable representation of the binary gambles $(f_+, C; e)$ and (U, W_E^-) a separable representation of gambles of the form $(e, C; g_-)$.*

For the next result the following proposition is useful. Recall that $sgn(\delta) = +, 0, -$ according to $\delta \gtreqless 0$ [Eq. (6.23)].

Proposition 7.3.3. *Suppose V is additive and U is the corresponding p-additive representation with parameters δ, δ' and $f \oplus g \succsim e$.*

1. *Suppose $f \succsim g \succsim e$, then:*

   (i) *If $\delta > 0 \ (< 0)$,*

   $$U_+(f \ominus g) = \frac{U_+(f) - U_+(g)}{1 - sgn(\delta)U_+(g)}.$$

   (ii) *If $\delta\delta' < 0$*

   $$U_-(g \ominus f) = \frac{U_+(g) - U_+(f)}{1 - sgn(\delta)U_+(g)}.$$

   (iii) *If $\delta\delta' > 0$*

   $$U_-(g \ominus f) = \frac{U_+(g) - U_+(f)}{1 - sgn(\delta)U_+(f)}$$

2. *Suppose $f \succsim e \succsim g$, then:*

   (i) *If $\delta\delta' < 0$,*

   $$U_+(f \ominus g) = U_+(f) - U_-(g) + sgn(\delta)U_+(f)U_-(g),$$
   $$U_-(f \ominus g) = U_-(g) - U_+(f) - sgn(\delta)U_+(f)U_-(g).$$

   (ii) *If $\delta\delta' > 0$,*

   $$U_+(f \ominus g) = \frac{U_+(f) - U_-(g)}{1 - sgn(\delta)U_-(g)}$$
   $$U_-(f \ominus g) = \frac{U_-(g) - U_+(f)}{1 - sgn(\delta)U_+(f)}$$

Proof. The basic line of argument is based on the following observations. If $f \succsim g \succsim e$, then $f \ominus g \sim h \succsim e \Longleftrightarrow f \sim g \oplus h$, and if $f \succsim e \succsim g$, then $f \ominus g \sim k \prec e \Longleftrightarrow f \sim g \oplus k$. To these one applies in the first case the Corollary to Theorem 4.4.4 and in the second Theorem 7.2.2 in order to arrive at $U(h)$ and $U(k)$ under the several assumptions of concavity and convexity. The details are left to the reader. ∎

This proposition is used to show the following:

Theorem 7.3.4. (Luce, 1997, Theorem 3) *Suppose $\langle \mathcal{D}_2, e, \succsim, \oplus \rangle$ forms a joint receipt, Archimedean, weakly ordered group generated from $\mathcal{B}_2$ with an overall additive representation V that has a corresponding p-additive representation U for gains with parameter δ and a similar one for losses with parameter δ'. Suppose that $\delta\delta' < 0$, i.e., U in terms of V is either concave for gains and convex for losses or convex for gains and concave losses. Then for $f_+ \succsim e \succsim g_-$, any two of the following statements implies the third:*

1. *General segregation, Eq. (7.16), is satisfied.*

2. *There exist* $W_{\mathbf{E}}^i : \mathcal{E}_{\mathbf{E}} \to [0,1]$, $i = +, -$, *such that for* $(f_+, C; g_-) \succ e$,

$$U_+(f_+, C; g_-) = U_+(f_+)W_{\mathbf{E}}^+(C) + \frac{U_-(g_-)}{1 + sgn(\delta)U_-(g_-)}[1 - W_{\mathbf{E}}^+(C)]; \qquad (7.20)$$

and for $(f_+, C; g_-) \prec e$,

$$U_-(f_+, C; g_-) = \frac{U_+(f_+)}{1 - sgn(\delta)U_+(f_+)}[1 - W_{\mathbf{E}}^-(\overline{C})] + U_-(g_-)W_{\mathbf{E}}^-(\overline{C}). \qquad (7.21)$$

3. *There exist* $W_{\mathbf{E}}^i : \mathcal{E}_{\mathbf{E}} \to [0,1]$, $i = +, -$, *such that* $(U, W_{\mathbf{E}}^+)$ *forms a separable representation of the binary gambles* $(f_+, C; e)$ *and* $(U, W_{\mathbf{E}}^-)$ *of those of the form* $(e, C; g_-)$.

Note that, as compared to the all gains or all losses cases and also to the case where U is proportional to V, the representation of binary gambles in the concave-convex case[5] has the feature that the less dominant consequence is somewhat "overrepresented" in the sense that the usual value of that consequence is divided by, respectively, $1 + U_-(g_-) < 1$ or $1 - U_+(f_+) < 1$. Likewise, it is "underrepresented" in the convex-concave case. Other than that it is exactly the same as the gains and loss representations found earlier for gains and losses separately. Note, however, that as one moves $(f_+, C; g_-)$ from a perceived gain to a perceived loss there is a discontinuous change in its utility. This seems suspect.

Recall that we have earlier dealt with the question of when U is both p-additive over $\oplus$ and with $W_{\mathbf{E}}^+$ forms a separable representation (Theorems 4.4.5 and 4.4.6). So the property of joint receipt decomposability, Eq. (4.50), must also be assumed in order for statement (1), general segregation, and statement (3), the existence of a separable representation involving the same U, to imply the gamble representation of statement (2). As was noted earlier, joint receipt decomposability has not been investigated experimentally.

The following example makes clear that were one to estimate the utility and weighting functions from just gains and just losses, then what one predicts in the mixed case differs between the classical theories and the one given in Eq. (7.20). Suppose the gambles are $(f_+, C; g_-) \succ e$ and $(f'_+, C'; g'_-) \succ e$ and the utility for gains is concave and for losses is convex. Consider the special case where $U_+(f_+)W_{\mathbf{E}}^+(C) = U_+(f'_+)W_{\mathbf{E}}^+(C') = 0.20$. Choose $g_-, g'_- C$, and C', so that $U_-(g_-) = -0.50$, $U_-(g'_-) = -0.20$, and $1 - W_{\mathbf{E}}^+(C) = 0.10$, $1 - W_{\mathbf{E}}^+(C') = 0.35$. Then within the classical model one has

$$U(f_+, C; g_-) = 0.20 - 0.05 = 0.15 > 0.13 = 0.20 - 0.07 = U(f'_+, C'; g'_-),$$

whereas under Eq. (7.20) one has

$$U(f_+, C; g_-) = 0.20 - \frac{0.05}{0.5} = 0.10 < 0.1125 = 0.20 - \frac{0.07}{0.8} = U(f'_+, C'; g'_-).$$

---

[5] Recall the convention made just before Proposition 7.2.1 that concave is equivalent to $\delta > 0$, which in turn is equivalent to negative exponential, Eq. (7.3), whereas convex means $\delta < 0$, which is equivalent to exponential, Eq. (7.4).

Thus, the predicted preference order between these gambles is opposite under the two models.

When we change the assumption about how U relates to V, it is not difficult to show what happens to $U(f_+, C; g_-)$. In the other opposite case, convex-concave, Eqs. (7.20) and (7.21) are changed only to the extent that in the terms in the denominator the sign of $U_-(g_-)$ and $U_+(f_+)$, respectively, are changed.

For the concave-concave and convex-convex cases, the form of $U(f_+ \oplus g_-)$ is different, namely Eq. (7.13), and using that and general segregation we easily obtain the following form:

Theorem 7.3.5.   *Suppose $\langle \mathcal{D}_2, e, \succsim, \oplus \rangle$ forms a joint receipt, Archimedean, weakly ordered group generated from $\mathcal{B}_2$ with an additive representation V onto an interval. Suppose that $\delta\delta' > 0$, i.e., U (in terms of V) is concave for both gains and losses or convex for both. Then under general segregation for $(f_+, C; g_-) \succ e$,*

$$U_+(f_+, C; g_-) = U_+(f_+)W_{\mathbf{E}}^+(C) + U_-(g_-)[1 - W_{\mathbf{E}}^+(C)]; \qquad (7.22)$$

and for $(f_+, C; g_-) \prec e$,

$$U_-(f_+, C; g_-) = U_+(f_+)[1 - W_{\mathbf{E}}^-(\overline{C})] + U_-(g_-)W_{\mathbf{E}}^-(\overline{C}). \qquad (7.23)$$

Observe that these equations are simply the extensions of the gains (and loss) form, derived in Theorem 4.4.4 under the assumption of general segregation, Eq. (6.7)≡Eq. (7.16).

7.3.2   Under duplex decomposition

Again, we have separate theorems for the proportional, $\delta = 0$, and exponential cases, $\delta \neq 0$.

Theorem 7.3.6.   *Suppose $\langle \mathcal{D}_2, e, \succsim, \oplus \rangle$ forms a joint receipt, Archimedean, weakly ordered group with additive representation V onto an interval and the corresponding p-additive representation U. Suppose $\delta = 0, \delta' = 0$, i.e., U is proportional to V, Eq. (7.2). Then, with $\lambda = \frac{\alpha}{\alpha'}$, any two of the following statements imply the third:*

1.   *Duplex decomposition, Eq. (7.17), is satisfied.*
2.   *There exist $W_{\mathbf{E}}^i : \mathcal{E}_{\mathbf{E}} \to [0, 1]$, $i = +, -$, such that for $(f_+, C; g_-) \succ e$,*

$$U(f_+, C; g_-) = U(f_+)W_{\mathbf{E}}^+(C) + \lambda U(g_-)W_{\mathbf{E}}^-(\overline{C}); \qquad (7.24)$$

and for $(f_+, C; g_-) \prec e$,

$$U(f_+, C; g_-) = \frac{1}{\lambda}U(f_+)W_{\mathbf{E}}^+(C) + U(g_-)W_{\mathbf{E}}^-(\overline{C}). \qquad (7.25)$$

3.   *There exist $W_{\mathbf{E}}^i : \mathcal{E}_{\mathbf{E}} \to [0, 1]$, $i = +, -$, such that $(U, W_{\mathbf{E}}^+)$ forms a separable representation of the binary gambles $(f_+, C; e)$ and $(U, W_{\mathbf{E}}^-)$ of those of the form $(e, C; g_-)$.*

The proof of this result closely parallels that of Theorem 7.3.2 using duplex decomposition instead of general segregation.

Theorem 7.3.7.   (Luce, 1997, Theorem 2) *Suppose* $\langle \mathcal{D}_2, e, \succsim, \oplus \rangle$ *forms a joint receipt, Archimedean, weakly ordered group with additive representation* V *onto an interval. Suppose* U *in terms of* V *is p-additive for both gains and losses and* $\delta\delta' < 0$. *Then for* $f_+ \succsim e \succsim g_-$, *any two of the following statements implies the third:*

1. *Duplex decomposition, Eq. (7.17), is satisfied.*
2. *There exist* $W_{\mathbf{E}}^i : \mathcal{E}_{\mathbf{E}} \to [0,1]$, $i = +, -$, *such that*

$$U_+(f_+, C; g_-) = \frac{U_+(f_+)W_{\mathbf{E}}^+(C) + U_-(g_-)W_{\mathbf{E}}^-(\overline{C})}{1 + sgn(\delta)U_-(g_-)W_{\mathbf{E}}^-(\overline{C})}, \ (f_+, C; g_-) \succ e$$

$$(7.26)$$

$$U_-(f_+, C; g_-) = \frac{U_+(f_+)W_{\mathbf{E}}^+(C) + U_-(g_-)W_{\mathbf{E}}^-(\overline{C})}{1 - sgn(\delta)U_+(f_+)W_{\mathbf{E}}^+(C)}, \ (f_+, C; g_-) \prec e.$$

3. *There exist* $W_{\mathbf{E}}^i : \mathcal{E}_{\mathbf{E}} \to [0,1]$, $i = +, -$, *such that* $(U, W_{\mathbf{E}}^+)$ *forms a separable representation of the binary gambles* $(f_+, C; e)$ *and* $(U, W_{\mathbf{E}}^-)$ *of those of the form* $(e, C; g_-)$.

The remark made after Theorem 7.3.2 about the need to assume joint receipt decomposability to insure the existence of a function U that is both p-additive and separable applies here if one wishes to use the assumptions of statements (1) and (3) as an axiomatic justification for statement (2), Eq. (7.26).

Let us compare the expressions in Eqs. (7.20) and (7.21) for general segregation with those of Eq. (7.26) for duplex decomposition. Both involve division by a factor less than 1, but in the general segregation case the factor differentially affects one of the consequences whereas for duplex decomposition it affects the whole expression $U_+(f_+)W_{\mathbf{E}}^+(C) + U_-(g_-)W_{\mathbf{E}}^-(\overline{C})$. Of course, this last expression is close to the one assumed by Kahneman and Tversky (1979) and the same as the one of Tversky and Kahneman (1992) in their prospect theory and which appeared in Chapter 6. Also note that the nonlinear factor in the general segregation case depends on either $U_-(g_-)$ or $U_+(f_+)$ whereas in the duplex decomposition case the nonlinear factor depends on either $U_-(g_-)W_{\mathbf{E}}^-(\overline{C})$ or $U_+(f_+)W_{\mathbf{E}}^+(C)$.

Again, I provide an example where the classical theory and this one make different predictions. Choose gambles such that with concave gains and convex losses $U_+(f_+)W_{\mathbf{E}}^+(C) = 0.32$, $U_-(g_-)W_{\mathbf{E}}^-(\overline{C}) = -0.20$, $U_+(f'_+)W_{\mathbf{E}}^+(C') = 0.50$, and $U_-(g'_-)W_{\mathbf{E}}^-(\overline{C}') = -0.40$. Then, according to the classical bilinear model,

$$U_+(f_+, C; g_-) = 0.32 - 0.20 = 0.12 > 0.10 = 0.50 - 0.40 = U_+(f'_+, C'; g'_-),$$

whereas, according to Eq. (7.26),

$$U_+(f_+, C; g_-) = \frac{0.32 - 0.20}{0.80} = 0.15 < 0.167 = \frac{0.50 - 0.40}{0.60} = U_+(f'_+, C'; g'_-).$$

Thus, the models make opposite predictions.

Finally, we turn to the cases where $\delta\delta' > 0$. A simple calculation using Eq. (7.13) and using Eq. (7.11) yields:

Theorem 7.3.8.   *Suppose* $\langle \mathcal{D}_2, e, \succsim, \oplus \rangle$ *forms a joint receipt, Archimedean, weakly ordered group generated from* $\mathcal{B}_2$ *with an additive representation* V *onto an interval and the corresponding p-additive* U with parameters δ for gains and δ' for losses. *Suppose* $\delta\delta' > 0$, i.e., U is concave for both gains and losses or convex for both. *Then under duplex decomposition,*

$$
\begin{aligned}
U_\sigma(f_+, C; g_-) \;=\; & U_+(f_+)W_{\mathbf{E}}^+(C) + U_-(g_-)W_{\mathbf{E}}^-(\overline{C}) \\
& - sgn(\delta)U_+(f_+)W_{\mathbf{E}}^+(C)U_-(g_-)W_{\mathbf{E}}^-(\overline{C}).
\end{aligned} \tag{7.27}
$$

7.3.3   Event commutativity and consequence monotonicity

It is easy to verify that assuming general segregation, Eqs. (7.20) and (7.21) yield event commutativity when $(f_+, C; g_-)$ and $(f_+, D; g_-)$ are both perceived as gains or both as losses, but not in the mixed case. For duplex decomposition, simple calculations verify that event commutativity always fails in the mixed case. The data reported in Fig. 6.2 are probably not sufficiently refined to tell the difference between these predictions.

The issue of consequence monotonicity is a bit more complex. Observe, first, that there is nothing about the calculations that we have carried out that guarantees that it holds for the utility of gambles. Second, the problem has two distinct aspects: Does it hold within the domain of mixed gambles, and does it hold between purely gains gambles and mixed gambles and purely loss gambles and mixed gambles? One has to go through each of the models separately. It is not very difficult to establish for each one that it holds within the domain of mixed gambles. It is trivial for the bilinear forms, and simple differentiation establishes it in the nonlinear cases.

What is somewhat more subtle is the relation between domains. Consider, for example, the cases of mixed gambles and losses, i.e., cases where $(f_+, C; g_-) \prec e$ is being compared with $(f, C; g)$ and $f_+ \succ e \succ f$ and $e \succ g_- \succsim g$. In any of the cases where $U(g_-)W_{\mathbf{E}}^-(\overline{C})$ stands alone, there is no problem because, whatever the utility term is involving f_+, it is ≥ 0 whereas $U(f)[1 - W_{\mathbf{E}}^-(\overline{C})] < 0$. This remark includes the case of Theorem 7.3.8 by rewriting the representation as

$$
U_-(f_+, C; g_-) = U_+(f_+)W_{\mathbf{E}}^+(C)[1 - sgn(\delta)U(g_-)W_{\mathbf{E}}^-(\overline{C})] + U(g_-)W_{\mathbf{E}}^-(\overline{C}),
$$

and noting that $1 - sgn(\delta)U(g_-)W_{\mathbf{E}}^-(\overline{C}) > 0$.

So, the only case requiring further attention is Theorem 7.3.7. A bit of algebra using Eqs. (7.26) and the RDU expression for losses establishes that

$$
\begin{aligned}
& U_-(f_+, C; g_-) > U_-(f, C; g) \\
\Longleftrightarrow \; & U_+(f_+)W_{\mathbf{E}}^+(C)[1 + sgn(\delta)U(g_-)W_{\mathbf{E}}^-(\overline{C})] > 0,
\end{aligned}
$$

which is clearly true.

7.3.4   Chechile and Cooke and Chechile and Butler data

Of the several forms for the utility of a binary mixed gamble derived in Theorems 7.3.2 and 7.3.4-7.3.8, three are bilinear in form, and so they are rejected by the Chechile and Cooke (1997) data. They are:

- Theorem 7.3.2 with general segregation and U proportional to V, Eqs. (7.18) and (7.19).
- Theorem 7.3.5 with general segregation and the concave-concave or convex-convex relation of U to V, Eqs. (7.22) and (7.23).
- Theorem 7.3.6 with duplex decomposition and proportional U to V, Eqs. (7.24) and (7.25)

The following two cases are not bilinear:

- Theorem 7.3.4, general segregation and concave-convex or convex-concave, Eqs. (7.20) and (7.21).
- Theorem 7.3.7, duplex decomposition with either concave-convex or convex-concave relations between U and V, Eq. (7.26)
- Theorem 7.3.8, duplex decomposition and concave-concave or convex-convex, Eq. (7.27).

The latter cannot be put in the form of Eq. (6.12) because in their notation it has the form $\psi(r) = \lambda_r X + Y \pm \mu_r XY$, which of course is not a *linear* regression.

For the analyses of Theorems 7.3.4 and 7.3.7, we set $X = U_+(f_+)W^+(C)$, $Y = -U_-(g_-)W^-(\overline{C})$, and $\psi_\sigma(r) = U_\sigma(g_r)$, where σ is defined in Eq. (7.11) applied to the gamble $(z, r; -z)$. For the former, general segregation with $\delta\delta' < 0$, using Eqs. (7.20) and (7.21),

$$\psi_\sigma(r) = \begin{cases} X - \frac{Y}{1+sgn(\delta)U_-(g_-)}, & \sigma = + \\ \frac{X}{1-sgn(\delta)U_+(f_+)} - Y, & \sigma = - \end{cases}.$$

Rewriting this as a regression of Y on X,

$$Y = \begin{cases} [1 + sgn(\delta)U_-(g_-)][X - \psi_+(r)], & \sigma = + \\ \frac{X}{1-sgn(\delta)U_+(f_+)} - \psi_-(r), & \sigma = - \end{cases}.$$

So, we have for the slopes using the appropriate exponential or negative exponential forms, which is determined by the sign of δ and δ',

$$\lambda_r = \begin{cases} e^{\kappa V(g_-)}, & \sigma = + \\ e^{\kappa V(f_+)}, & \sigma = - \end{cases}, \delta > 0$$

$$\lambda_r = \begin{cases} e^{-\kappa V(g_-)}, & \sigma = + \\ e^{-\kappa V(f_+)}, & \sigma = - \end{cases}, \delta < 0.$$

Notice that these slopes are all positive, which is not in accord with the Chechile and Butler (1999) finding of everywhere negative slopes in an analysis of individual respondents. Also notice that for fixed f_+ and g_- and for the reference gamble being seen as a gain all the slopes are the same independent of r. The same is true for the reference gamble seen as a loss, but with a different slope. However, the data analysis mixed various values of the gain and loss consequences, so it is difficult to say what the pattern of slope ratios is predicted to be.

For Theorem 7.3.7, covering duplex decomposition with $\delta\delta' < 0$, the calculations are similar leading to:

$$\psi_\sigma(r) = \begin{cases} \frac{X-Y}{1-sgn(\delta)Y}, & \sigma = + \\ \frac{X-Y}{1-sgn(\delta)X}, & \sigma = - \end{cases},$$

$$Y = \begin{cases} \frac{X-\psi_+(r)}{1-sgn(\delta)\psi_+(r)}, & \sigma = + \\ X[1 + sgn(\delta)\psi_-(r)] - \psi_-(r), & \sigma = - \end{cases},$$

$$\lambda_r = \begin{cases} e^{\kappa V(g_r)}, & \delta > 0 \\ e^{-\kappa V(g_r)}, & \delta < 0 \end{cases},$$

$$\frac{\lambda_{0.05}}{\lambda_{0.95}} = \begin{cases} e^{\kappa[V(g_{0.05})-V(g_{0.95})]} < 1, & \delta > 0 \\ e^{-\kappa[V(g_{0.05})-V(g_{0.95})]} > 1, & \delta < 0 \end{cases}.$$

Again, the slopes are all positive, which does not agree with the Chechile and Butler (1999) finding. Unlike the general segregation case, however, the slope ratio varies in the correct direction for $\delta < 0$ and, although not very restrictive, it certainly includes all of the values calculated by Chechile and Cooke (1997) and Chechile and Butler (1999) from their data and various models based on generic bilinear utility theory.

Chechile and I plan to do a more detailed appraisal of these two nonlinear models.

7.3.5   Reanalysis of PEST CE data

In our laboratory much PEST-determined certainty equivalent data has been collected by Y. Cho with several collaborators to test various properties, and some of those results were described earlier. It turned out that the Cho, Luce, and von Winterfeldt (1994) study included sufficient PEST data from 144 respondents for Sneddon and Luce (1999) to carry out the following detailed model fitting.

All of the models of this and the previous chapter rest on a common theory for gains and separately for losses, which was described in Chapter 4. For the mixed case, this led to four major types of theories: extensive-conjoint (additive U) or associative (additive V) crossed with general segregation or duplex decomposition. We abbreviate the possibilities AGS, ADD, ECGS, and ECDD. The experimental data were such that we could treat the weights as parameters to be estimated. For the utility functions three possible relations exist between U and V: proportional, negative exponential, and exponential. We considered, however, only the four gain-loss pairings of negative exponential and exponential in which we assumed $V(x) = x$ and the one gain-loss pairing of proportionality. In the former case we identify the cases by concave (C) and convex (V). So, for example, C/V means concave (negative exponential) gains and convex (exponential) losses. In the proportional case we assumed $V(x) = x^\beta$, and so the value of $\beta \gtrless 1$ determines the C and V combinations. Note that restricting V in the exponential cases to be linear puts those models at a disadvantage compared to the proportional ones. In total, therefore, $4 \times 5 = 20$ models were fit to each respondent's data. This was done by minimizing a least-squares form corrected for different degrees of freedom. Then the best fitting model was selected. Table 7.2 shows the number of respondents whose best fitting model is each of the 20 types.

Table 7.2. Classification of respondents by the best fitting of the 20 models. The entries are the numbers of respondents best fit by that model (with fractions meaning two or more models fit equally well).

Gain	C	V	C	V	Power	Total
Loss	V	C	C	V		
ADD	40.5	23	17.5	6	8.25	95.25
AGS	6	4	3	4	7.25	25.25
ECDD	2	1	1	1	4.25	9.25
ECGS	3	4	1	1	6.25	15.25
Total	51.5	32	22.5	12	26	144

For those respondents for which the proportional power function did best, the distribution of concave-convex pairs are determined by the estimates of β and β'. In the same order as Table 7.2, the distribution was: 3, 7, 5, 11.

Certain things are noteworthy.

- The associative models are better than the extensive-conjoint ones for about 84% of the respondents.
- The duplex decomposition models are better than the general segregation ones about 73% of the respondents.
- The nonlinear models are better than bilinear ones for 67% of the respondents.
- The pattern of concavity and convexity overall has the following percentages: $(38, 28, 19, 16)$. This pattern is fairly consistent with other data reported in Section 3.3.1. Once again, although concave gains/convex losses is clearly the mode, all three of the other possibilities also occur.

As noted above, the weights were treated as parameters. These were then fit by various functions that have been proposed: power [Eq. (3.27)], Tversky-Kahneman [Eq. (3.30)], Karmarkar [Eq. (3.28) with $\eta = 1$], and Gonzalez-Wu [Eq. (3.28)]-Prelec [Eq. (3.31)].[6] The percentages are 22, 9, 8, and 61, respectively. When one considers that the power ones are special cases of the Prelec function, its percentage (but not that of the Gonzalez-Wu one) rises to 83%.

---

[6]   Recall that except for power function cases, it is very difficult to distinguish the Gonzalez-Wu function from the Prelec one using estimated weights.

Several observations about the theory suggest what would be a more ideal experiment and analysis.

- Over gains and losses separately, all of the models agree up to the type of utility function (Ch. 4), whereas for the mixed case there are four quite different models.
- Whatever the relation of U to V, we really should assume in all cases that V is a power function of money. Thus, each piece of the utility function has for the proportional case one parameter and for the exponential cases, two parameters. In addition, there is one parameter, either $\lambda = \frac{\alpha}{\alpha'}$ in the proportional case or $\Lambda = \frac{\delta}{\delta'}$ in the exponential ones, that cannot be estimated from gains and losses separately.
- Although W^+ and W^- can be treated as parameters, as Sneddon and Luce did, it is probably better to assume the Prelec form of Eq. (3.31), which means estimating two parameters for gains and two for losses.
- Once these estimates are made for each respondent from gains data alone and loss data alone, then one predicts his or her data for the mixed case with either no degrees of freedom in the exponential cases or one degree of freedom in the proportional ones.

Thus, one should collect sufficient data on gains and losses separately so as to estimate the parameters of U, W^+, and W^- for the models of Chapter 4, as described above, and sufficient data on mixed gambles to be able to estimate the, at most, one parameter needed and to compare the quality of the fit of the several models. The most perplexing aspect of doing this, which otherwise should increase the sensitivity of the analysis, is how to deal with the differing degrees of freedom. This is clearly an important, but major, study to do.

7.3.6   On problems of inconsistent estimates of U

Over quite a number of years of trying to apply utility ideas in practical decision-making situations, including certain business decisions and medical diagnosis and treatment, frustration has been expressed about the inconsistencies that arise in attempting to estimate utilities (Fishburn & Kochenberger, 1979; Hershey, Kunreuther, & Schoemaker, 1982; von Winterfeldt & Edwards, 1986). This is especially true when both pure and mixed gambles are used. Without exception, so far as I know, these attempts have been based on one version or another of a bilinear weighting of utilities of the components, such as the models of Chapters 4 and 6. But suppose one or another of the nonlinear associative models of this chapter is descriptive. Then trying to fit the behavior with either the prospect theory formula or, as was true in the early studies, with the very special case of expected utility, is a recipe for trouble: The U estimated from mixed gambles cannot possibly agree in general with U estimated from pure gains or pure losses. The Chechile and Cooke (1997) study established in a laboratory setting that bilinearity fails for mixed gambles (see § 6.3.3), and Sneddon's and Luce's reanalysis of existing certainty equivalent data favor the nonlinear models (i.e., exponential utility and associative joint receipts) for some 73% of the respondents. Thus, the inconsistency of the estimates using bilinear models is not too surprising.

Given the apparently greater accuracy of associative model, new attempts using the resulting nonlinear representations seem warranted to see if estimates of U that are consistent between gains, losses, and mixed gambles can be achieved. In particular, additional laboratory research is needed to confirm that nonlinear models are needed in, at least, these artificial settings. Should that be sustained, then attempts to apply them in more serious situations, such as medical decision making, will be warranted. A major theoretical concern is the extension of the model beyond the binary case because, as we have seen in Chapter 5, there is considerable uncertainty about how to extend the binary models to more consequences.

7.4   Buying and Selling Prices

Recall the hypothesis that, for any binary gamble $(f, C; g)$ based on some experiment **E**, the (maximum) *buying price* $b = b(f, C; g)$ and the (minimum) *selling price* $s = s(f, C; g)$ are given by the solutions to the following indifferences:

$$(f \ominus b, C; g \ominus b) \sim e \sim (s \ominus f, C; s \ominus g). \tag{7.28}$$

The explicit dependence of b and s on the gamble is omitted for simplicity. Because of the potential discontinuity in U when $(f_+, C; g_-) \sim e$ for general segregation, we will assume that buying prices approach the limit b from below. Thus, if $b' \prec b$, we have $(f \ominus b', C; g \ominus b') \succ e$. For selling prices, we assume the approach is from above and if $s' \succ s$, then $(s' \ominus f, C; s' \ominus g) \succ e$. So in both cases we must use the appropriate equation.

Recall from Section 6.4 that, under the basic assumptions of Chapter 2, if $f \succsim g$, then $f \succsim b, s \succsim g$. We assume the case where $f \succsim b, s \succsim e$. We consider separately whether $g \succsim e$ or $g \prec e$.

Throughout this section we will draw on various properties of $\oplus$ and $\ominus$ which are summarized as:

Proposition 7.4.1.   *If $\sim$ is transitive and $\oplus$ is associative, commutative, and monotonic relative to $\sim$, then*

(1) $f \ominus f \sim e.$
(2) $f \oplus (g \ominus h) \sim (f \oplus g) \ominus h.$
(3) $(f \ominus g) \ominus h \sim f \ominus (g \oplus h).$
(4) $(f \oplus g) \ominus g \sim f.$
(5) $(f \ominus g) \oplus g \sim f.$
(6) $(f \ominus h) \ominus (g \ominus h) \sim f \ominus g.$
(7) $(h \ominus f) \ominus (h \ominus g) \sim g \ominus f.$

7.4.1   Under associative joint receipt and general segregation

7.4.1.1   Buying price = CE: The following simple result holds for buying prices.

Proposition 7.4.2.   *If a joint receipt structure is associative and general segregation holds, then $b \sim (f, C; g)$.*

There is a sense in which this proposition seems trivial. And, indeed, it would be trivial if we knew $(f \ominus b, C; g \ominus b) \oplus b \sim (f, C; g)$. However, this statement is not an immediate consequence of general segregation, so the result needs to be proved.[7] This result makes sense in one interpretation, namely, that the price one will pay for a gamble is limited from above by one's certainty equivalent of the gamble. However, no similar result seems to hold for the selling price, where the result varies depending upon what is assumed about the relation of U to V.

7.4.1.2   Selling price for U proportional to V: For the next result it is convenient to use the following

$$\tau = \begin{cases} 0, & g \succsim e \\ 1, & g \prec e \end{cases}. \tag{7.29}$$

Recall that $\lambda = \frac{\alpha}{\alpha'}$.

Proposition 7.4.3. *Suppose the structure is associative with additive representation V with the corresponding p-additive representation U, that $\delta = 0 = \delta'$, i.e., U is proportional to V, and that general segregation, Eq. (7.16), holds. Then*

$$U(s) = U(f)[1 - W_{\mathbf{E}}^+(\overline{C})] + \lambda^\tau U(g) W_{\mathbf{E}}^+(\overline{C}). \tag{7.30}$$

7.4.1.3   Positive prices for U nonlinear in V: In this and successive sections, we will develop formulas for buying and selling prices where we assume that gambles are such that the prices are seen as gains. An example of a selling price that is negative is taken up in Section 7.4.4.

By nonlinear one means, of course, $\delta\delta' \neq 0$. In these cases, the expressions are sufficiently complex that the following abbreviations are useful:

$$B = U_+(b), S = U_+(s), F = U_+(f), G = U_\sigma(g). \tag{7.31}$$

Proposition 7.4.4. *Suppose the structure is associative with additive representation V and corresponding p-additive representation U, that general segregation, Eq. (7.16), holds, and that U is nonlinear with V.*

(i)   *If $\delta\delta' < 0$, then*

$$S = \frac{F[1 - W^+(\overline{C})] + GW^+(\overline{C}) - sgn(\delta)FG}{1 - sgn(\delta)(F - G)W^+(\overline{C}) - sgn(\delta)G}, \quad g \succsim e \tag{7.32}$$

$$S = \frac{F[1 - W^+(\overline{C})] + GW^+(\overline{C}) - sgn(\delta)FGW^+(\overline{C})}{1 - sgn(\delta)(F - G)W^+(\overline{C}) - FGW^+(\overline{C})}, \quad g \prec e. \tag{7.33}$$

---

[7]   Recall that earlier we noted a discontinuity in $U(f_+, C; g_-)$ as the gamble changes from a gain to a loss. This will not affect our calculations because I am assuming the gamble is perceived as a gain.

(ii)   *If* $\delta\delta' > 0$, *then*

$$S = \frac{F[1 - W^+(\overline{C})] + GW^+(\overline{C}) - sgn(\delta)FG}{1 - sgn(\delta)(F - G)W^+(\overline{C}) - sgn(\delta)G}. \tag{7.34}$$

7.4.1.4   Monotonicity of buying and selling prices: It follows immediately from Proposition 7.4.1 that buying prices under general segregation are monotonic in the sense that for $f \succsim g \succ e$,

$$b(f, C; g) \succ b(f, C; e). \tag{7.35}$$

Because this is not descriptively true in aggregated data (Birnbaum, 1997), it suggests that either general segregation does not hold for many respondents or that our hypothesis for the definition of these prices is wrong.

Selling prices are also monotonic, as we now show. For Proposition 7.4.2, the linearity in $U_+(f)$ and $U_\sigma(g)$ insures it. For Proposition 7.4.3 one must calculate $U_+(s) - U_+(s_0)$, where the s corresponds to $g \succ e$ and s_0 to $g \sim e$. It is routine to show that $U_+(s) - U_+(s_0) > 0$ is equivalent to $U_+(g)W^+(\overline{C})[1 - U_+(f)]^2 > 0$, which of course is always the case.

7.4.2   Under associative joint receipt and duplex decomposition

As with general segregation, we state separately the results for the case where U is proportional to V and when they are exponentially related.

7.4.2.1 U proportional to V: With buying and selling prices as defined in Eq. (7.28) we have the following:

Proposition 7.4.5.   *Suppose the structure is associative with additive representation V, that duplex decomposition, Eq. (7.17), holds, and that U is proportional to V. Recall τ is defined by Eq. (7.29). Then*

$$U(b) = \frac{U(f)W_{\mathbf{E}}^+(C) + \lambda^\tau U(g)W_{\mathbf{E}}^-(\overline{C})}{W_{\mathbf{E}}^+(C) + W_{\mathbf{E}}^-(\overline{C})} \tag{7.36}$$

$$U(s) = \frac{U(f)W_{\mathbf{E}}^-(C) + \lambda^\tau U(g)W_{\mathbf{E}}^+(\overline{C})}{W_{\mathbf{E}}^-(C) + W_{\mathbf{E}}^+(\overline{C})}. \tag{7.37}$$

Observe that in the case where, for all C, $W_{\mathbf{E}}^-(C) = 1 - W_{\mathbf{E}}^+(\overline{C})$ these expressions reduce to those of general segregation. And the proof closely parallels that of Proposition 7.4.2.

These expressions are linear in $U(f)$ and $U(g)$, and so this model again predicts monotonicity. Our only remaining hope to explain this phenomenon is the more complex exponential cases.

7.4.2.2 U is nonlinearly related to V: In these cases we again use the abbreviations of Eq. (7.31).

Proposition 7.4.6.   *Suppose the structure is associative with additive representation V and corresponding p-additive U, and suppose duplex decomposition, Eq. (7.17), holds. Let b and s be defined by Eq. (7.28).*

(i)   *If $\delta\delta' < 0$ and $f \succsim g \succsim e$,*

$$
\begin{aligned}
0 =\ & sgn(\delta)B^2 W_E^-(\overline{C}) \\
& - B\left(W_E^+(C) + W_E^-(\overline{C}) - sgn(\delta)G[W_E^+(C) - W_E^-(\overline{C})]\right) \\
& + FW_E^+(C) + GW_E^-(\overline{C}) - sgn(\delta)FGW_E^+(C),
\end{aligned}
\tag{7.38}
$$

$$
\begin{aligned}
0 =\ & sgn(\delta)S^2 W_E^+(\overline{C}) \\
& - S\left(W_E^+(\overline{C}) + W_E^-(C) + sgn(\delta)G[W_E^+(\overline{C}) - W_E^-(C)]\right) \\
& + FW_E^-(C) + GW_E^+(\overline{C}) - sgn(\delta)FGW_E^-(C).
\end{aligned}
\tag{7.39}
$$

If $f \succsim e \succsim g$

$$
\begin{aligned}
0 =\ & sgn(\delta)B^2[1 - sgn(\delta)G]W_E^-(\overline{C}) \\
& - B[W_E^+(C) + W_E^-(\overline{C})] \\
& + FW_E^+(C) + GW_E^-(\overline{C}),
\end{aligned}
\tag{7.40}
$$

$$
\begin{aligned}
0 =\ & sgn(\delta)S^2[1 + sgn(\delta)G]W_E^+(\overline{C}) \\
& - S[W_E^-(C) + W_E^+(\overline{C}) + sgn(\delta)2GW_E^+(\overline{C})] \\
& + FW_E^-(C) + GW_E^+(\overline{C}).
\end{aligned}
\tag{7.41}
$$

(ii)   *Suppose $\delta\delta' > 0$. If $f \succsim g \succsim e$,*

$$
\begin{aligned}
0 =\ & sgn(\delta)B^2\left(W_E^+(\overline{C}) + W_E^-(C) - W_E^+(\overline{C})W_E^-(C)\right) \\
& - B\{[1 + sgn(\delta)F]W_E^+(\overline{C})W_E^-(C) \\
& + [1 + sgn(\delta)G]W_E^-(C) + sgn(\delta)(F + G)W_E^+(\overline{C})\} \\
& + FW_E^+(\overline{C}) + GW_E^-(C) - sgn(\delta)FGW_E^+(\overline{C})W_E^-(C).
\end{aligned}
\tag{7.42}
$$

If $f \succsim e \succsim g$,

$$
0 = B^2 GW_E^-(C) - B[W_E^+(\overline{C}) + W_E^-(C)] + FW_E^+(\overline{C}) + GW_E^-(C).
\tag{7.43}
$$

In both cases,

$$
S = \frac{F[1 - sgn(\delta)G]W_E^-(C) + G[1 - sgn(\delta)F]W_E^+(\overline{C})}{[1 - sgn(\delta)G]W_E^-(C) + [1 - sgn(\delta)F]W_E^+(\overline{C})}.
\tag{7.44}
$$

7.4.2.3   Issues of the relation of buying and selling prices: I do not see how B and S relate to one another in these exponential cases. In general the difficulty in establishing anything is that although B and S are both functions of F and G, the former is also a function of $W_E^+(C)$ and $W_E^-(\overline{C})$ whereas the latter is of $W_E^+(\overline{C})$ and $W_E^-(C)$.

Returning to the example of Section 6.4.2.2, we have the following:

		B	$U_+(f_+,C;g_-)$	S
C/V	DD	0.368	0.586	0.507
V/C	DD	0.285	0.239	0.329
C/C	DD	0.302	0.306	0.525
V/V	DD	0.302	0.374	0.385

Here $B < S$ in all four cases. But in both the C/V and V/C cases $U_+(f_+,C;g_-)$ falls outside the $[B,S]$ interval, in the former case above it and in the latter below it. I am not sure what, if anything, to conclude from this fact. In the C/C and V/V cases it is in the interval, near the B value in the former and near the S value in the latter.

7.4.2.4   Nonmonotonicity of buying and selling prices for large p: Let us consider the question of the monotonicity of B and S in the case of concave gains and convex losses (C/V). As before, let B_0 and S_0 denote the buying and selling prices of $(f,C;e)$. From Eq. (7.38) we see that subtracting the expression for B_0 (obtained by setting $G = 0$) from that for B and abbreviating $W^- = W_E^-(\overline{C})$ and $W^+ = W_E^+(C)$ we find that:

$$0 = (B - B_0)[(B + B_0)W^- - (W^+ + W^-)] - GW^+(F - B) + W^-G(1 - B).$$

Observe that as $p = \Pr(C) \to 1$, $W^+ \to 1$ and $W^- \to 0$, so the right two terms approach $-G(F - B) < 0$. Thus, for the sum to be 0 the left-hand term must be positive. However, for large p the term $(B + B_0)W^- - (W^+ + W^-) \to -1$, and so the left-hand term is positive only if $B < B_0$, which is the kind of nonmonotonicity seen in the data.

Similar arguments show that the sale prices for this model also violate monotonicity and that for the V/C case the same conclusions hold.

For the C/C case, one shows using the same method that for $W^+ = W^+(\overline{C})$ and $W^- = W^-(C)$,

$$0 = (B-B_0)[(B+B_0)W^- - (W^+ + W^-) - FW^+(1 + W^-)] - GW^+[1 - B - W^-(F + B)].$$

As $\Pr(C) \to 1$, $W^+ \to 0$ and $W^- \to 1$, so we have

$$0 = (B - B_0)(B + B_0 - 1) + G(1 - B).$$

Because $G(1 - B) > 0$, the left term must be negative. Thus, for $B + B_0 > 1$, we see that $B < B_0$. Although the condition $B + B_0 > 1$ is possible, it is unlikely because that means both buying prices must be large in utility relative to the full range of possibilities.

It is routine to show that $S - S_0 > 0$ if and only if $G(1 - F)^2 W^+(W^+ + W^-) > 0$, which is necessarily true.

For the V/V case, the same line of argument yields, for large p,

$$0 = -(B - B_0)(B + B_0 + 1) + G(1 + B).$$

Thus, $B > B_0$. And $S - S_0 > 0$ if and only if $G(1 + F)^2 W^+(W^+ + W^-) > 0$, which is necessarily true.

So, in summary, for large probabilities, a violation of monotonicity of buying and selling prices occurs with associative joint receipts, duplex decomposition, and either C/V or V/C. In addition, in the C/C case a violation may occur in buying prices if $B + B_0 > 1$; otherwise no violations are predicted.

At the time of writing, these equations have not been fitted to any data, in particular, not to those of Birnbaum and Yeary (manuscript). It is hoped that this will be done sometime in early 2000.

7.4.3   An example of insurance premiums

Insurance purchases amount to selling a negative gamble $(-x, p; 0)$, $-x < 0$, for a negative sum $-I < 0$, the insurance premium. So, in particular, we assume

$$0 \sim (-I \ominus -x, p; -I). \tag{7.45}$$

The easiest, if not most realistic, case to deal with is where U is proportional to V and is a power function of money. And given that duplex decomposition seems the most common assumption, we examine that case. We cannot use the formulas already calculated, for they were done on the assumption that the sale price of a gamble was a gain, where that is clearly not so for insurance. The seller of the gamble—buyer of insurance—pays to be rid of the gamble. So we must recalculate for this case.

By duplex decomposition and Proposition 7.2.1(i) we see

$$0 = U(-I \ominus -x)W^+(p) + \lambda U(-I)W^-(1 - p).$$

From another application of the same proposition,

$$U(-I \ominus -x) = \lambda[U(-I) - U(-x)],$$

whence

$$U(-I) = \frac{U(-x)W^+(p)}{W^+(p) + W^-(1 - p)}. \tag{7.46}$$

Assuming U is a power function with exponent β', this can be put in the following very convenient form:

$$\frac{I}{EV} = \frac{1}{p} \left(\frac{W^+(p)}{W^+(p) + W^-(1 - p)} \right)^{\frac{1}{\beta'}}. \tag{7.47}$$

We use plausible weighting parameters in the Prelec function of Eq. (3.31) and three different values of β'. The results are shown in Fig. 7.3.

We see from this plot that for sufficiently small probabilities, such a person is willing to pay considerably more than the expected value. The crossover point where $I^* = \frac{I}{EV} = 1$ is about 0.4 for $\beta' = 1.2$, which characterizes a highly risk-averse person, and about 0.1 for

$\beta' = 0.8$, someone who is not especially averse to losses. These differences no doubt relate to the apparently surprisingly successful business practice of selling extended warranties on appliances. But for almost everyone, for some sufficiently small p and with a correspondingly high x, such as the loss of a house to fire, one is willing to pay considerably in excess of the expected value to be rid of the gamble.

The case just described, although simple to analyze, is probably not very realistic. So we look at the cases of $\delta\delta' \neq 0$. For the case $\delta\delta' < 0$, a calculation similar to that underlying Proposition 7.4.6(i), but assuming the selling price is negative, results in

$$0 = U_-(-I)^2W^-(1-p) + sgn(\delta)U_-(-I)[W^-(1-p) + W^+(p)] - sgn(\delta)W^+(p).$$

Once we have estimates for parameters for U_- and W^i, $i = +, -$, from buying and selling prices, plots of $U_-(-I)$ can be developed.

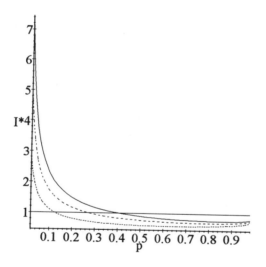

Figure 7.3. Insurance prediction for the additive V, $\delta = 0$, duplex decomposition model with the values $\gamma = 1.15, \eta = 0.50, \gamma' = 0.60, \eta' = 0.55$, and $\beta' = 1.2$ (solid), 1 (dashed), and 0.8 (dotted) in Eq. (7.47).

7.5   Summary

The main thrust of this chapter is based on what is, after all, the simplest and, perhaps, the most rational assumption about joint receipt, namely, that it has an additive value representation V throughout. Coupling this with the exponential and negative exponential forms derived in Chapter 4 for the relation of U to V over gains and over losses separately yields tolerably complex formulas for U of mixed joint receipts (Proposition 7.2.1 and Theorem 7.2.2). Using either general segregation or duplex decomposition, this complexity is carried over to the U of mixed binary gambles (Theorems 7.3.2 and 7.3.4-7.3.8). In particular, half of these forms are not of the traditional bilinear form. Of course, this is exactly what is called for by the data of Chechile and Cooke (1997) reported in Chapter 6. Indeed, we were able to show that the model based on duplex decomposition and the nonlinear utility functions derived in Chapter 4 is not rejected by the Chechile and Cooke findings of a certain slope ratio being different from 1, but its prediction of positive slopes is inconsistent with the Chechile and Butler (1999) finding of negative slopes. This last finding is perplexing, and it will be interesting to see if it stands up to changes in experimental procedure.

Given these complexities for binary mixed gains and losses, it is reasonably clear that had one attempted to begin with general gambles of mixed gains and losses, as has been traditional in the field, one would have either gotten mired down or been led to gross oversimplifications. Thus, there seems to be merit in partitioning the theory into the subparts I have used in this monograph.

Fitting the several models to certainty equivalence data obtained for other purposes provided evidence that the associative joint receipt models of this chapter fare appreciably better than the extensive-conjoint ones of Chapter 6. Moreover, the duplex decomposition assumption for the associative case was clearly better than the general segregation one. In addition, of the several proposed weighting functions, the Prelec one is by far the most satisfactory.

One application was to the largest buying and smallest selling prices. Under general segregation, which is a rational condition, the prediction is that the buying price should equal the certainty equivalent. The selling price was more involved. For U proportional to V and applied to the special case of $(x, p; 0)$ the predictions are the same as those of Chapter 6. Under the various exponential assumptions, quadratic equations arise and examples were given where various odd things happen such as the certainty equivalent lying outside the buy-sell interval. Looking at the buying and selling prices of $(x, p; 0)$ and $(x, p; y)$, $y > 0$, we found that the models predict monotonicity except in two cases: when both buying and selling prices under the duplex decomposition model with $\delta\delta' < 0$, i.e., either concave gains and convex losses or convex gains and concave losses. For these cases, we showed that as p approaches 1, buying and selling violations of consequence monotonicity are forced by the model. Because such nonmonotonicities have been extensively demonstrated by Birnbaum (1997), their prediction is a vote in favor of associative, duplex decomposition models.

Thus, three types of data seem to favor the model based on associative joint receipts, duplex decomposition, and exponential utilities: It is not rejected by the Chechile and Cooke findings; it gave the best fit of the several models to certainty equivalence data; and it predicts for large p nonmonotonic buying and selling prices which has been reported empirically by Birnbaum (1997). The one serious failure is that these models predict positive slopes rather than the negative ones estimated by Chechile and Butler (1999).

What is needed now is some additional serious testing of these forms using detailed data, such as those on buying and selling prices, and attempts to see whether they work better in practice than have the bilinear forms. This promises to be a substantial effort.

7.6   Proofs

7.6.1   Proposition 7.2.1

(i) Using Eq. (7.1), Eq. (7.5) follows by substituting the appropriate terms from Eq. (7.2). Observe that by the additivity of V,

$$U(f_+ \oplus g_-) = \alpha V(f_+ \oplus g_-) = \alpha V(f_+) + \alpha V(g_-) = U(f_+) + \lambda U(g_-).$$

(ii) Assume $f_+ \oplus g_- \succ e$. Because $V(g_-^{-1}) = -V(g_-)$ and V is additive over $\oplus$, we see that for $\delta > 0$,

$$
\begin{aligned}
U_+(f_+ \oplus g_-) &= \delta U(f_+ \oplus g_-) \\
&= 1 - e^{-\kappa V(f_+ \oplus g_-)} \\
&= 1 - e^{-\kappa V(f_+) - \kappa V(g_-)} \\
&= 1 - \frac{e^{-\kappa V(f_+)}}{e^{\kappa V(g_-)}} \\
&= 1 - \frac{e^{-\kappa V(f_+)}}{e^{-\kappa V(g_-^{-1})}} \\
&= 1 - \frac{1 - U_+(f_+)}{1 - U_+(g_-^{-1})} \\
&= \frac{U_+(f_+) - U_+(g_-^{-1})}{1 - U_+(g_-^{-1})}.
\end{aligned}
$$

The case of $\delta < 0$ is similar as is that of (iii) with $f_+ \oplus g_- \prec e$. ∎

7.6.2   Proposition 7.2.3

Suppose $x > 0 > y$, $x \oplus y \succ 0, \delta > 0 > \delta'$. Taking into account that $1 + |\delta'| U(y) = 1 + U_-(y) > 0$ and $U_-(y) < 0$ and setting $\Lambda = \left| \frac{\delta'}{\delta} \right|$,

$$
\begin{aligned}
U(x \oplus y) &= \frac{1}{\delta} \frac{U_+(x) + U_-(y)}{1 + U_-(y)} \\
&= \frac{U(x) + \Lambda U_-(y)}{1 + |\delta'| U(y)} \\
&\gtreqless U(x) + U(y)
\end{aligned}
$$

if and only if

$$U(x) + \Lambda U(y) \gtreqless [U(x) + U(y)][1 + |\delta'| U(y)]$$

263

if and only if

$$\frac{1}{\delta} \lessgtr \frac{1}{|\delta'|} + U(x) + U(y),$$

which is Eq. (7.14). The proof of Eq. (7.15) is similar. ∎

7.6.3   Theorem 7.3.2

The general background assumption is proportionality between U and V, so Eq. (7.2) holds.

1 & 3 → 2. Suppose $(f_+, C; g_-) \succsim e$, then applying U to general segregation and using assumption 3 and Proposition 7.2.1 we have

$$\begin{aligned}
U(f_+, C; g_-) &= U[(f_+ \ominus g_-, C; e) \oplus g_-] \\
&= U(f_+ \ominus g_-)W_+(C) + \lambda U(g_-).
\end{aligned}$$

Evaluate $U(f_+ \ominus g_-)$ by Proposition 7.3.1 and substitute in the former expression to obtain the first part of 2. The other case is similar.

2 & 3 → 1. Simply calculate the two sides of the general segregation expression and show they equate.

1 & 2 → 3. Trivial. ∎

7.6.4   Theorem 7.3.4

To simply notation, I omit the $+$ and $-$ subscripts on f and g.

Assuming that (3) holds, we first show the equivalence of (1) and (2). First, suppose $(f, C; g) \succsim e$, then by general segregation, Eq. (7.16), and Proposition 7.6.3

$$\begin{aligned}
U_+(f, C; g) &= U_+[(f \ominus g, C; e) \oplus g] \\
&= \frac{U_+(f \ominus g, C; e) + U_-(g)}{1 + sgn(\delta)U_-(g)} \\
&= \frac{U_+(f \ominus g)W_{\mathbf{E}}^+(C) + U_-(g)}{1 + sgn(\delta)U_-(g)} \\
&= U_+(f)W_{\mathbf{E}}^+(C) + \frac{U_-(g)}{1 + sgn(\delta)U_-(g)}[1 - W_{\mathbf{E}}^+(C)].
\end{aligned}$$

The case $(f, C; g) \precsim e$ is similar.

(3) follows trivially from (2). ∎

Comment: As is shown in Luce (1997), one can formulate the theorem with less assumed structure on $\oplus$ and derive from (1) and (2) that it must be associative and U is negative exponential in V. The proof is basically that of Theorem 4.4.4.

7.6.5   Theorem 7.3.7.

(1) and (2) → (3). Trivial.

(1) and (3) → (2). Consider the case where $(f_+, C; g_-) \succsim e$. From (1) and Eq. (7.12)

$$
\begin{aligned}
U_+(f_+, C; g_-) &= U_+[(f_+, C'; e) \oplus (e, C''; g_-) \\
&= \frac{U_+(f_+, C'; e) + U_-(e, C''; g_-)}{1 + sgn(\delta)U_-(e, C''; g_-)} \\
&= \frac{U_+(f_+)W_{\mathbf{E}}^+(C) + U_-(g_-)W_{\mathbf{E}}^-(\overline{C})}{1 + sgn(\delta)U_-(g_-)W_{\mathbf{E}}^-(\overline{C})},
\end{aligned}
$$

which is Eq. (7.17) for gains. The proof for losses is similar.
(2) and (3) → (1). Just invert the above argument. ∎

7.6.6   Proposition 7.4.1

(1) Let $u = f \ominus f$, so by definition of $\ominus$ and commutativity, $f \oplus e \sim f \sim u \oplus f \sim f \oplus u$, whence by monotonicity $u \sim e$.

(2) Let $u = g \ominus h$, so $g \sim u \oplus h$. So, using associativity, $f \oplus g \sim f \oplus u \oplus h$, whence $f \oplus (g \ominus h) \sim f \oplus u \sim (f \oplus g) \ominus h$.

(3) Let $u = f \ominus g$, $v = u \ominus h$, $v' = f \ominus (g \oplus h)$. Then using associativity,

$$
g \oplus h \oplus v' \sim f \sim u \oplus g \sim v \oplus h \oplus g.
$$

So, by commutativity and monotonicity, $v' \sim v$, which is the assertion.

(4) and (5) are immediate from (1) and (2).

(6) Let $w = f \ominus h$, $u = g \ominus h$, $v = w \ominus u$, and $v' = f \ominus g$. Thus, using monotonicity $w \oplus h \sim f \sim v' \oplus g \sim v' \oplus u \oplus h$, and so by transitivity and monotonicity, $v \oplus u \sim w \sim v' \oplus u$. Using monotonicity again, $v = v'$, which proves the result.

(7) The proof is analogous to (6). ∎

7.6.7   Proposition 7.4.2

Consider the buying price first. Recall that $f \succsim b \succsim g$, so $f \ominus b \succsim e \succsim g \ominus b$. Then,

$$
\begin{aligned}
e &\sim (f \ominus b, C; g \ominus b) & \text{definition of } b \\
&\sim ((f \ominus b) \ominus (g \ominus b), C; e) \oplus (g \ominus b) & \text{general segregation} \\
&\sim (f \ominus g, C; e) \oplus (g \ominus b) & \text{Prop. 7.4.1(6)} \\
&\sim [(f \ominus g, C; e) \oplus g] \ominus b & \text{Prop. 7.4.1(2)} \\
&\sim ((f \ominus g) \oplus g, C; g) \ominus b & \text{general segregation} \\
&\sim (f, C; g) \ominus b & \text{Prop. 7.4.1(5).}
\end{aligned}
$$

Thus, by Proposition 7.4.1(1),

$$
b \sim (f, C; g).
$$

∎

7.6.8   Proposition 7.4.3

By definition of s, $e \sim (s \ominus f, C; s \ominus g)$, so by Eq. (7.18) we have

$$0 = U(s) = U(s \ominus g)W^+(\overline{C}) + \lambda U(s \ominus f)[1 - W^+(\overline{C})].$$

Substituting from Proposition 7.4.1 and solving yields the results.   ∎

7.6.9   Proposition 7.4.4

(i) Applying Eq. (7.20) and the definition of s, Eq. (7.28), we see

$$0 = U_+(s \ominus g)W^+(\overline{C}) + \frac{U_-(s \ominus f)}{1 + sgn(\delta)U_-(s \ominus f)}[1 - W^+(\overline{C})].$$

Then using Proposition 7.4.3, for $g \succsim e$ and the abbreviations of Eq. (7.31),

$$
\begin{aligned}
0 &= \frac{S - G}{1 - sgn(\delta)G}W^+ \\
&\quad + \left(\frac{S - F}{1 - sgn(\delta)S}\right)\left(\frac{1}{1 + sgn(\delta)\frac{S - F}{1 - sgn(\delta)S}}\right)(1 - W^+) \\
&= \frac{S - G}{1 - sgn(\delta)G}W^+ + \frac{S - F}{1 - sgn(\delta)F}(1 - W^+).
\end{aligned}
$$

Solving yields result. For $g \prec e$, again using Proposition 7.4.3,

$$
\begin{aligned}
0 &= [S - G + sgn(\delta)SG]W^+ \\
&\quad + \left(\frac{S - F}{1 - sgn(\delta)S}\right)\left(\frac{1}{1 + sgn(\delta)\frac{S - F}{1 - sgn(\delta)S}}\right)(1 - W^+) \\
&= S[1 + sgn(\delta)G][1 - sgn(\delta)F]W^+ \\
&\quad - G[1 - sgn(\delta)F]W^+ + S(1 - W^+) - F(1 - W^+).
\end{aligned}
$$

Solving yields the result.

(ii) By Proposition 7.4.3, we see that the expression is exactly the same for both $g \succsim e$ and $g \prec e$, namely,

$$0 = \frac{S - G}{1 - sgn(\delta)G}W^+ + \frac{S - F}{1 - sgn(\delta)F}(1 - W^+).$$

Solving yields the result.

7.6.10   Proposition 7.4.6

(i) Assuming duplex decomposition, Eq. (7.17), and the definitions of buying and selling prices, Eq. (7.28),

$$e \sim (f \ominus b, C; g \ominus b) \sim (f \ominus b, C; e) \oplus (e, C; g \ominus b).$$

Then by Eq. (7.26), this is equivalent to

$$0 = U_+(f \ominus b)W_E^+(C) + U_-(g \ominus b)W_E^-(\overline{C}).$$

Using the fact that $f \succsim b \succsim g \succsim e$, Proposition 7.4.3, and the abbreviations we see

$$0 = \frac{F - B}{1 - sgn(\delta)B}W_E^+(C) + \frac{G - B}{1 - sgn(\delta)G}W_E^-(\overline{C}).$$

Simplifying yields the quadratic in B asserted. For the case $f_+ \succsim b \succsim e \succsim g_-$, we obtain

$$0 = \frac{F - B}{1 - sgn(\delta)B}W_E^+(C) + [G - B - sgn(\delta)GB]W_E^-(\overline{C}).$$

Again, simplifying yields the quadratic in B asserted.

Applying duplex decomposition to the sale equation

$$e \sim (s \ominus f, C; s \ominus g) \sim (s \ominus g, \overline{C}; e) \oplus (e, \overline{C}'; s \ominus g),$$

and using Eq. (7.26) and replacing the primed values by the unprimed ones, this is equivalent to

$$0 = U_+(s \ominus g)W_E^+(\overline{C}) + U_-(s \ominus f)W_E^-(C).$$

Again, using Lemma 7.4.3 and the abbreviations, this is equivalent in the case of all gains to

$$0 = \frac{S - G}{1 - sgn(\delta)G}W_E^+(\overline{C}) + \frac{S - F}{1 - sgn(\delta)S}W_E^-(C)$$

and in the case of mixed consequences to

$$0 = [S - G + sgn(\delta)SG]W_E^+(\overline{C}) + \frac{S - F}{1 - sgn(\delta)S}W_E^-(C).$$

Simplifying these leads to the quadratics asserted.

(ii) Applying Theorem 7.3.8 to

$$0 \sim (f \ominus b, C; g \ominus b)$$

and using Proposition 7.4.1 for $g \succsim e$ yields

$$
\begin{aligned}
0 \ = \ & \frac{F - B}{1 - sgn(\delta)B}W_E^+(\overline{C}) + \frac{G - B}{1 - sgn(\delta)B}W_E^-(C) \\
& - sgn(\delta)\frac{F - B}{1 - sgn(\delta)B}W_E^+(\overline{C})\frac{G - B}{1 - sgn(\delta)B}W_E^-(C).
\end{aligned}
$$

Some algebra yields the result. For $g \prec e$,

$$0 = \frac{F - B}{1 - sgn(\delta)B} W_{\mathbf{E}}^{+}(\overline{C}) + [G - B - sgn(\delta)GB]W_{\mathbf{E}}^{-}(C),$$

and again algebra yields the result.

For sales, we obtain the same equation for $g \succsim e$ and $g \prec e$, namely,

$$0 = \frac{S - G}{1 - sgn(\delta)G} W_{\mathbf{E}}^{+}(\overline{C}) + \frac{S - F}{1 - sgn(\delta)F} W_{\mathbf{E}}^{-}(C),$$

and the conclusion again follows for algebra.   ■

Chapter 8
CONCLUDING COMMENTS

This final chapter attempts to summarize briefly the main ideas we have encountered and to list some of the major empirical and conceptual problems that are not yet adequately addressed.

8.1 Main Ideas

The five main ideas that we have encountered were:

- The formulation of the domain of choice;
- The decomposition of the problem into subproblems;
- Utility representations of gambles and their major behavioral properties;
- The interplay of gambles and joint receipt and how that impacts the utility representation; and
- Restrictions on the forms of utility and weighting functions.

8.1.1 Formulation of the domain of choice

A somewhat underrated issue in the study of individual decision making is how best to formulate mathematically the domain of choice. This was discussed at some length in Chapter 1, and I ended up using an algebraic structure having two major features. It allows one to distinguish easily between gains and losses, and it treats each alternative as being based on its own underlying chance experiment that is independent of other chance experiments. Not only does this accord closely with experimental practice, but also with the way that most people structure explicit choice situations such as, for example, when deciding on a mode of travel, e.g., car, bus, or airplane, or a choice by a patient among alternative therapies, e.g., do nothing, surgery, radiation, or chemotherapy. The impact that the domain formulation has on the resulting theories can be considerable, as is elaborated in Section 8.3.6.

8.1.2 Decomposing the problem into subproblems

At the onset we assumed a number of elementary behavioral properties, which are summarized both in Section 2.7 and Appendix B. The most basic of these, in the sense of determining the nature of the resulting theory, were grouped as an "elementary rational binary structure" (Def. 2.5.1): $\succsim$ is a weak order that satisfies consequence monotonicity, idempotence, certainty, complementarity, and order independence of events. Beyond those, we introduced the following important additional behavioral assumption:

- *Gain-loss decomposition, Eq. (2.17)*. The idea is that any general gamble is recast by the decision maker into a binary gamble whose consequences are the gains and loss subgambles of the original gamble. Formally, if g is a general, first-order gamble, let $E(+)$ denote the union of all events whose consequences are either the status quo or a gain, $E(-)$ the union of all events whose consequences are a loss, g^+ the restriction of g to $E(+)$, and g^- the restriction to $E(-)$. The property called *gain-loss decomposition* asserts:

$$g \sim (g^+, E(+); g^-, E(-)). \tag{8.1}$$

If this property holds, then the theory of utility representation can be divided into three simpler pieces: the representation of binary gambles of mixed gain-loss consequences, the representation of general gambles all of whose consequences are gains or the status quo, and the representation of general gambles all of whose consequences are losses. Because the latter two are basically the same theory, there are just two parts to develop: gains and binary mixed gambles. I took them up in that order. Further, the case of all gains was divided first into the binary one and then those involving three or more consequences.

8.1.3   Representations and their behavioral properties

For general gambles, the following property was assumed throughout:

- *General monotonicity of consequences, Eq. (2.9)*. This is the assumption that the ordering that the preference order induces on a single component of a gamble, holding the others fixed, does not depend in any way on those fixed components. In the conjoint measurement literature this invariance is called "independence," but I avoided using that term in this context because it is widely used in the utility literature for a related but much stronger property that follows by combining consequence monotonicity with a reduction of compound gambles.

Except for binary gambles, the condition of consequence monotonicity together with other necessary and structural conditions imply the existence of an additive numerical representation of the consequences

$$U_k(g_1, E_1; ...; g_k, E_k) = \sum_{i=1}^{k} U_{k,i}[g_i, (E_1, ..., E_k)]. \tag{8.2}$$

The representation of Eq. (5.6) or (8.2) is said to be *additive over consequences* when there is no constraint on the ordering of consequence-event pairs, and it is called *rank-dependent additive* (RDA) representation when the consequences are constrained to the preference order

$g_1 \succsim \cdots \succsim g_k$. Such an additive representation is common to all of the theories that were discussed for gains and for losses separately, but was notably absent in some of the models in Chapter 7 for binary mixed gains and losses.

This additive form was first seen in the binary case (§ 3.5.3) and as Eq. (5.6) in the general case. To get the additive representation for binary gambles one needs something in addition to monotonicity to insure that the terms $U_{k,i}$ break into one that depends only on g_i and another that depends only on $(E_1, ..., E_k)$ and that these impact each other multiplicatively. This representational property is called separability, Eq. (3.6), i.e., there is a function U on gambles and consequences and a weighting function W_E^+ on events such that for $x \succsim e$,

$$U(x, p; e) = U(x) W_E^+(p). \tag{8.3}$$

The relevant qualitative property is the Thomsen condition or some form of triple cancellation (Appendix D). For binary gambles satisfying the elementary assumptions, the Thomsen condition is equivalent to the following property: In two independent realizations of the same experiment, suppose that a valued consequence x occurs when the event C occurs in one realization and the event D occurs in the other independent realization, and otherwise the consequence is the status quo e. *Status-quo event commutativity* is the assertion that the order in which the two events are realized is immaterial to the decision maker (Def. 3.1.5). This property is the main driving force behind separability.

Formulating this property is one of two places where second-order, compound gambles really played a role in the present development. The other was, of course, the gain-loss decomposition, Eq. (2.17) $\equiv$ Eq. (8.1).

In Sections 3.6, 3.7, and 4.4, several different set of conditions were provided to characterize the *binary rank-dependent utility* representation, Eq. (3.4), i.e., for $f \succsim e, g \succsim e$,

$$U(g, C; h, \overline{C}) = \begin{cases} U(g) W_E^+(C) + U(h)[1 - W_E^+(C)], & g \succ h \\ U(g), & g \sim h \\ U(g)[1 - W_E^+(\overline{C})] + U(h) W_E^+(\overline{C}), & g \prec h \end{cases}. \tag{8.4}$$

Chapter 5 took up the question of generalizing this representation. The main focus was on the general rank-dependent utility (RDU) model, Eqs. (5.1)-(5.3):

$$U(g_1, E_1; g_2, E_2; ...; g_k, E_k) = \sum_{i=1}^{k} U(g_i) W_i(E_1, ..., E_k). \tag{8.5}$$

In this expression W_i is defined in terms of W_E^+, where $W_E^+(E) = 1$, as follows. Let

$$E(i) = \bigcup_{j=1}^{i} E_j, \tag{8.6}$$

then

$$W_i(E_1, ..., E_k) = W_E^+[E(i)] - W_E^+[E(i-1)]. \tag{8.7}$$

- *Coalescing, Eq. (5.5).* A major property of this representation is coalescing (or event splitting): Consider a gamble with an event partition into k subevents, and suppose that two of the consequences are identical. The assertion is that the decision maker is indifferent between the original gamble and the one, with $k - 1$ events, that is formed by replacing the pair of events having the same consequence by a single event consisting of the union of the two. Coalescing is transparently rational in the sense of being a very simple accounting indifference. Theorem 5.3.2 showed that the additive representation over consequences, Eq. (8.2), plus coalescing, Eq. (5.5), and binary rank RDU, Eq. (8.4), are necessary and sufficient for the general RDU representation.
- *Data and coalescing.* The data appear, however, to reject the general RDU model despite the reasonableness of its assumptions. Indeed, the work of Birnbaum and his students strongly suggests that coalescing, no matter how compelling it may be in isolation, can when coupled with other simple conditions lead to predictions not in accord with empirical data. The apparent difficulty lies not in the direction of putting together two events with a common consequence, which presents the decision maker with the simple choice of coalescing or not, but rather it is in going the opposite direction, event splitting, where the options for splitting are numerous and only very special ones permit one to see dominance relations among certain pairs of gambles or lotteries. The mathematics of the representation does not distinguish these two forms of coalescing. It says that the behavior should be *as if* respondents are capable of the equivalent of event splitting. Apparently this is not the case—at least for data averaged over respondents.
- *SEU and universal accounting indifferences.* The special case of binary RDU in which the ordering of the consequences does not, in fact, matter is equivalent to the additivity of W_E^+ over complementary events, which we called rank-independent utility, RIU. If we have the added property that W_E^+ is finitely additive, then the resulting general representation is called subjective expected utility, SEU. The remarkable fact is that SEU entails all possible accounting indifferences of compound gambles that differ only in the order in which experiments are conducted, whereas all of the other RDU models fail to entail any accounting indifferences beyond event commutativity and trivial variants of it. This clear partitioning of the models is notable and it explicitly formulates one aspect of "bounded rationality."

8.1.4   Behavioral properties and representations of joint receipt and gambles

The remaining basic concepts invoked a binary operation, $\oplus$, of joint receipt over the preference structure of consequences and gambles. The preference relation is extended to preferences of jointly received gambles. Although this operation is not a part of the traditional decision-theory framework, it is intuitively quite natural. We daily experience the joint receipt of valued things. And, as we saw, it is a powerful mathematical aid in formulating theory.

- *Joint receipt preference structure for gains (Def. 4.2.1).* The structure $\langle \mathcal{D}_2^+, \succsim, \oplus \rangle$ of gambles of gains under joint receipt typically takes $\mathcal{D}_2^+$ to be the closure of second-order, compound gambles from $\mathcal{G}_2^+$ under the operation $\oplus$. By far the simplest assumption about this structure is that it is extensive, i.e., the positive quadrant of an Archimedean weakly ordered group, and so in particular it is commutative, associative, monotonic, and Archimedean. Put in another, more intuitive way, preference over joint receipt of gains acts formally like the ordering of masses concatenated on a pan balance. This means that it has an additive representation V which I call a *value function* to distinguish it from the utility function U obtained from the properties of gambles (discussed in § 8.1.5). The relation of U to V for gains turned out to be one of three types (see below).

- *The basis of the additive representation of joint receipt (Theorems 4.4.4 and 7.1.1).* Two basic behavioral properties are involved: monotonicity and associativity of $\oplus$ (Def. 7.1.1). Monotonicity has been sustained using choice procedures. Associativity has been examined for mixed gains and losses, and was found to hold in a clear-cut fashion for about half of the respondents. We do not understand what, if any, pattern holds for the other half of the respondents. However, when associativity is coupled with consequence monotonicity, all of the respondents seemed to be behaving fairly rationally—up to the noise level of the experiment.

- *General segregation, Eq. (6.7).* This is the simple idea that for any binary gamble that is perceived as a gain, one can "subtract" off the worst consequence from each of the other consequences, so it is replaced by the status quo, and then recombine it with the modified gamble. For a gamble perceived as a loss, one subtracts off the best outcome (which may be the least loss). Formally, in the binary case for $f \succsim g$,

$$(f, C; g) \sim \begin{cases} (f \ominus g, C; e) \oplus g, & \text{if } (f, C; g) \succ e \\ (e, C; g \ominus f) \oplus f, & \text{if } (f, C; g) \prec e \end{cases} \tag{8.8}$$

where

$$f \ominus g \sim h \iff f \sim h \oplus g. \tag{8.9}$$

In the special case of a gamble of all gains, or of all losses, this is simply called *segregation*. Some data support segregation, but general segregation has not yet been explored empirically in the case of mixed gambles.

- *The relation of U and V (Theorem 4.4.4).* Binary rank dependence of Eq. (8.4) plus segregation for gains imply that for some real δ, having the dimension of $1/U$,

$$U(f \oplus g) = U(f) + U(g) - \delta U(f)U(g), \quad f \succsim e, g \succsim e. \tag{8.10}$$

This is called a *p-additive* form. Indeed, assuming Eq. (8.10), then binary rank dependence forces segregation and it, together with separability, Eq. (8.3), imply binary rank dependence. Under any of these conditions, U is related to V in one of three ways:

1.   *If $\delta = 0$, then for some $\alpha > 0$,*

$$U = \alpha V. \tag{8.11}$$

2.   *If $\delta > 0$, then U is subadditive, i.e., $U(f \oplus g) < U(f) + U(g)$, is bounded by $1/\delta$, and for some $\kappa > 0$*

$$U_+(f) = |\delta| U(f) = 1 - e^{-\kappa V(f)}, \quad \delta > 0, \kappa > 0. \tag{8.12}$$

3.   *If $\delta < 0$, then U is superadditive, unbounded, and for some $\kappa > 0$*

$$U_+(f) = |\delta| U(f) = e^{\kappa V(f)} - 1, \quad \delta < 0, \kappa > 0. \tag{8.13}$$

- *General segregation and U of mixed binary gambles (Theorems 6.3.1, 7.3.2, 7.3.4, and 7.3.5).* Two basic assumptions about mixed binary gambles were explored. Chapter 6 assumed U to be additive in the mixed case. This was shown to be rather more problematic than it first seemed. In particular, it leads to bilinear forms rejected by data of Chechile and Cooke (1997) and Chechile and Butler (1999). Chapter 7 assumed instead that V is everywhere additive. This assumption led to a simpler axiomatic theory in the sense that no special assumptions were needed to link the utility of gains and of losses to the mixed case. Except when $U = kV$, it resulted in a somewhat more complex representation for U over mixed consequences and gambles than did the postulate of additive U. For example, assuming the negative exponential of Eq. (8.12) and general segregation one derives (Theorem 7.3.4) that for $(f_+, C; g_-) \succ e$,

$$U_+(f_+, C; g_-) = U_+(f_+) W_{\mathbf{E}}^+(C) + \frac{U_-(g_-)}{1 + U_-(g_-)}[1 - W_{\mathbf{E}}^+(C)]; \tag{8.14}$$

and for $(f_+, C; g_-) \prec e$,

$$U_-(f_+, C; g_-) = \frac{U_+(f_+)}{1 - U_+(f_+)}[1 - W_{\mathbf{E}}^-(\overline{C})] + U_-(g_-) W_{\mathbf{E}}^-(\overline{C}), \tag{8.15}$$

where the signs in the denominator are for the case of concave gains and convex losses. These signs for the convex-concave case interchange those above. In the case of proportionality, Eq. (8.11), the form is (Theorem 7.3.2): for $(f_+, C; g_-) \succ e$ and $\lambda = \frac{\alpha}{\alpha'}$

$$U(f_+, C; g_-) = U(f_+) W_{\mathbf{E}}^+(C) + \lambda U(g_-)[1 - W_{\mathbf{E}}^+(C)]; \tag{8.16}$$

and for $(f_+, C; g_-) \prec e$,

$$U(f_+, C; g_-) = \frac{1}{\lambda} U(f_+)[1 - W_{\mathbf{E}}^-(\overline{C})] + U(g_-) W_{\mathbf{E}}^-(\overline{C}). \tag{8.17}$$

- *Duplex decomposition and U of mixed binary gambles (Theorems 6.3.1, 7.3.6, 7.3.7, and 7.3.8).* An alternative, nonrational assumption was considered. It is *duplex decomposition*, i.e.,

$$(f_+, C; g_-) \sim (f_+, C'; e) \oplus (e, C''; g_-), \tag{8.18}$$

where C', C'' are the event C on independent realizations of the underlying experiment. The resulting form under additive U is that postulated by Kahneman and Tversky (1979) in their prospect theory,

$$U(f_+, C; g_-) = U(f_+)W_E^+(C) + U(g_-)W_E^-(\overline{C}). \tag{8.19}$$

Note that it is bilinear. In contrast, for the case of concave gains and convex losses under additive V and with $(f_+, C; g_-) \succsim e$,

$$U_+(f_+, C; g_-) = \frac{U_+(f_+)W_E^+(C) + U_-(g_-)W_E^-(\overline{C})}{1 + U_-(g_-)W_E^-(\overline{C})}; \tag{8.20}$$

and with $(f_+, C; g_-) \prec e$,

$$U_-(f_+, C; g_-) = \frac{U_+(f_+)W_E^+(C) + U_-(g_-)W_E^-(\overline{C})}{1 - U_+(f_+)W_E^+(C)}. \tag{8.21}$$

The signs in the denominator are changed for the convex-concave case (Theorem 7.3.7). The concave-concave and convex-convex cases are given by (Theorem 7.3.8),

$$\begin{aligned} U_\rho(f_+, C; g_-) &= U_+(f_+)W_E^+(C) + U_-(g_-)W_E^-(\overline{C}) \\ &\quad - sgn(\rho)U_+(f_+)W_E^+(C)U_-(g_-)W_E^-(\overline{C}). \end{aligned} \tag{8.22}$$

None of these is bilinear.

- *Relation to data.* The representation arising from duplex decomposition in the convex-concave case, which is not bilinear, is not refuted by the data of Chechile and Cooke (1997) but it appears to be by those of Chechile and Butler (1999). This needs more careful appraisal. An analysis of CE data collected by Cho et al. (1994), in which the several models, which all agree over gains and over losses but differ in the mixed case, showed the following: The additive V models were better for 84% of the respondents than the additive U ones, and the duplex decomposition assumption was better than general segregation for 73% of the respondents.

- *An application to buying and selling prices (§§ 6.4 and 7.4).* How are the maximum buying price b and the minimum selling price s of a gamble characterized? One possibility is that they are the same as the certainty equivalent of the gamble. But behavioral observation suggests that probably this is incorrect. Instead, the assumption that they are given by

$$(f \ominus b, C; g \ominus b) \sim e \sim (s \ominus f, C; s \ominus g) \tag{8.23}$$

was explored. These were calculated for the several theories—additive U and additive V crossed with the three possibilities of U relative to V, namely, proportional, negative exponential, and exponential. The results for additive U proportional to additive V and general segregation were that b is simply the certainty equivalent and $U(s)$ is linear in $U(f)$ and $U(g)$. In the other cases, the solutions involved quadratic equations. There do

275

not seem to be simple relations among buying and selling prices as defined and certainty equivalents, and by example some odd things were shown to happen. For some of these cases, particularly in Chapter 7, we saw that the sort of observed non-monotonicity of buying and selling prices that has been demonstrated by Birnbaum (1997) is predicted by the non-bilinear models. The conceptual issues of buying and selling prices within the context of these theories is not at all well understood and so bears additional study, and the models have yet to be confronted seriously by data.

8.1.5   Restrictions on the forms of utility and weighting functions

In practice, these kinds of utility theories can be difficult to work with because tradition-ally the functions U, $W_E^+(p)$, and $W_E^-(p)$ were subject to very few constraints, mainly, strict monotonicity of U with money and of $W_E^{(i)}$ with probability. So, some interest attaches to finding constraints on the functions.

- *Empirical utility functions (§3.3)*. From early on, attempts have been made to estimate the utility functions of money, usually using separability, and then compare the data with various ad hoc mathematical forms. Power functions and exponential ones seem to do rather well, certainly better than linear or logarithmic. However, some individual data exhibited more complex forms, such as S-shaped and inverse S-shaped.
- *Theoretical utility functions (§§ 4.4.6 and 4.5.3)*. The theoretical relations between U and V are highly constrained (see above), but that leaves open how V depends on money. As was shown in Proposition 4.5.1, if $\oplus$ is invariant in the sense that for $r > 0$,

$$r(x \oplus y) \sim rx \oplus ry,$$

and if V is additive over $\oplus$, then V must be a power function of money and $x \oplus y$ is given by Eq. (4.58). In particular, for $x > 0, y > 0$, for some $\beta > 0$,

$$x \oplus y = (x^\beta + y^\beta)^{1/\beta}.$$

So under this assumption U is either a power function, a negative exponential of a power of money, or an exponential of a power of money. These appear to accommodate all of the empirical estimates.

- *Empirical weighting functions (§§ 3.4.1 and 3.4.2)*. A good deal of attention has been paid over the years to the form of the weighting functions $W_E^+(p)$ and $W_E^-(p)$ where the probabilities of the underlying events are known. Relatively little is known about the weights for uncertain events. The empirical studies have rested primarily on applying separability to binary gambles $(x, p; 0)$. The upshot seems to be that when we look at individual respondents we see some who are concave, $W(p) > p$ for all $p \in]0, 1[$, a few who are convex, $W(p) < p$ for all p, and a plurality who are inverse S-shaped in the following sense: There is some $p_0 \in]0.25, 0.50[$ such that (i) $W(p_0) = p_0$; (ii) for $p < p_0$, $W(p) > p$; (iii) for $p > p_0$, $W(p) < p$; and (iv) W is initially concave and switches to convex. Sometimes we see only a central piece of the inverse S-type which looks linear with slope less than 1 and intersects the $W(p) = p$ diagonal at p_0. Data averaged over groups of respondents seem to look inverse S-shaped. This is presumably due to the fact that the average of a concave and convex function typically is inverse S-shaped, and so combining those cases with some truly inverse S-shaped ones results only in that form. However, the average result, being a mixture of several forms, almost certainly is not of the same mathematical form as any of its components.

- *Theoretical weighting functions ($\S$ 3.4.3).* Although several ad hoc formulas have been proposed that fit the inverse S-shaped data reasonably well, the only axiomatic theory is due to Prelec (1998) with some improvements by Luce (1999). Two assumptions, *N-compound invariance* [Eqs. (3.36)-(3.37)], and *N-reduction invariance* [Eqs.(3.38)-(3.39)], both for $N = 2, 3$, are each equivalent under reasonable conditions to Eq. (3.31), i.e., for gains

$$W(p) = \exp\left[-\gamma(-\ln p)^{\eta}\right], \tag{8.24}$$

where $\gamma > 0, \eta > 0$. (For losses, different parameters, γ', η', arise.) Note that when $\eta = 1$, $W(p)$ is a power function of p, and so is concave if $\gamma < 1$ and convex if $\gamma > 1$. Otherwise it has an inverse S-shape. So this theory includes all three types seen empirically. It is trivial to see that averages over distributions of the parameters γ and η are not of this form, and so testing the model using group data is clearly inappropriate. Gonzalez and Wu (1999) have successfully fit data for individual respondents to an empirical function different from, but practically indistinguishable from, Eq. (8.24). And Sneddon and Luce (1999) found the Prelec function did best compared to several other alternatives for 83% of their respondents. No direct empirical test of either invariance condition has yet been reported.

8.2   Open Empirical Problems

As we proceeded, we saw that some but by no means all of the fundamental properties have been explored experimentally in a direct fashion. I list here those that are most conspicuously untested or inadequately tested.

8.2.1   Behavioral properties of gambles

- *Certainty and probability equivalents.* A number of issues about these simplifying equivalents were discussed in Section 1.2.2, and questions about them kept arising. We know that judged and choice-estimated CEs are not the same. We also have some reasons to suspect that the PEST-estimated choice ones from several papers may be slightly biased. We also know that judged certainty and probability equivalents are not fully consistent. So far as I know, there are no data about the relation of CE to PE choice-based estimates. Although these discrepancies may be of little inherent interest, the fact that the estimates are not exactly what we want, namely, CEs and

PEs as defined, is very frustrating. More work needs to be done to straighten out this methodological point so that we have reliable ways of determining accurate CEs and PEs.

- *Consequence monotonicity, Eq. (2.9).* For binary gambles, this property is well studied. It appears to be sustained in choice experiments, but not when judged CEs are used. Little work has been done on testing it for more elaborate gambles.

- *Event inclusion, Eq. (2.13), and order independence of events, Eq.(2.14).* These are both highly rational properties and seem likely to be correct, but neither has been studied empirically in isolation.

- *Gain-loss decomposition, Eq. (2.17).* To my knowledge, this basic assumption has not been tested at all empirically. Should it fail, then the strategy of decomposing the general problem into two simpler subproblems is not descriptively viable, although it is fine normatively because it is a simple accounting indifference.

- *N-compound invariance, Eqs. (3.36)-(3.37), and N-reduction invariance, Eqs. (3.38)-(3.39).* Basically, each of these properties holding for $N = 2, 3$ is equivalent to Eq. (8.24) for the weighting function. Probably most attempts to evaluate this model will use separability to estimate the weighting function empirically, and then test the fit of the Prelec function to these estimates, but it would also be interesting to see if direct violations of these invariance properties can be devised. As was noted, N-reduction invariance should be simpler to test and less prone to the impact of cumulative error.

- *Coalescing, Eq. (5.5).* Examples exist where the event-splitting variant of coalescing together with consequence monotonicity and transitivity permit one to show that one alternative indirectly dominates another, but nonetheless respondents, on average, prefer the dominated one. Such examples, clear as they are, involve some creative argument based on selective uses of event splitting. Apparently, such reasoning or what amounts to its behavioral equivalence is beyond the capacity of many untutored respondents. We need to understand more fully the nature of such failures if, as I expect, coalescing turns out to be sustained in direct studies. In particular, we must be concerned about the depth of deductive reasoning within which it may be invoked. The evidence seems to suggest that the general RDU model is pushing the deductions too far to describe the respondents. Of course, normatively coalescing should hold because it is a simple accounting indifference.

8.2.2 Behavioral properties of joint receipt and gambles

- *Joint-receipt decomposition, Eq. (4.50).* Although it will probably be difficult to test joint-receipt decomposition in a sensitive way, it would be desirable to do so because of its importance. This property is exactly what is needed to guarantee, from the existence of a separable representation of binary gambles and a distinct p-additive representation of joint receipt, $\oplus$, that a single representation (U, W) exists that is both separable and U has a p-additive form. Thus, the property is key if one chooses to axiomatize binary RDU by assuming separability, p-additivity, and segregation relates joint receipt to gambles.

- *The relation of $x \oplus y$ to money amounts x and y (§ 4.5).* The data concerning this relationship are far from firm. Some direct and some indirect studies suggest $x \oplus y \succ x + y$ for gains and $\prec$ for losses. But the results do not seem definitive at this point. Additional empirical work is clearly needed. Moreover, we do have a prediction about the form of $x \oplus y$ if an invariance condition holds. It is important to check how well such a function fits the data. A major experimental issue is how best to gain information about $x \oplus y$. If one tries to determine $CE(x \oplus y)$ directly one seems to find it is equal to $x + y$ (although the existing PEST estimates may be slightly biased), whereas if one imbeds the question in a scenario, as Thaler (1985) did, the findings are much more complex. Additional work is called for.

- *Joint-receipt consistency, Eq.(6.5).* Suppose U is additive over mixed joint receipts. Then, joint-receipt consistency is necessary and sufficient to tie together the gains and mixed joint-receipt structures so that U is either exponential or negative exponential in V for gains as well as additive in the mixed case. No empirical tests of the property have been reported, and I think it should have a low priority among the other empirical needs because the resulting bilinear models of Chapter 6 probably are not descriptively correct (Chechile & Butler, 1999; Chechile & Cooke, 1997; Chechile & Luce, 1999).

- *General segregation, Eq. (6.7)* $\equiv$ *Eq. (8.8).* When general segregation is restricted to binary gambles with both consequences gains, Eq. (4.33), it has been tested and sustained. But it has not yet been studied for mixed gambles, where it is one of two possible ways to arrive at forms for the utility of mixed gambles. It has also not been tested for gambles with three or more distinct consequences.

- *Comparing general segregation, Eq. (6.7), and duplex decomposition, Eq. (6.8)* $\equiv$*Eq. (8.18).* There are data supporting duplex decomposition in the mixed case but none, one way or the other, about general segregation in that case. An obvious experimental strategy is to collect data suitable to decide for each individual which assumption appears to be more accurate. In general, choosing between two alternative properties is easier and more convincing than accepting or rejecting either as a null hypothesis. Judging by the data analysis by Sneddon and Luce (1999), we expect that a substantial majority of respondents will be better described by duplex decomposition than by the rational general segregation.

8.2.3   Global fitting of representations

- *Utility of binary gambles and joint receipt.* The situation described in Chapters 4, 6, and 7 has the feature that a single model for binary gambles of gains (and, separately, losses) is arrived at in Chapter 4. Moreover, except for a few parameters, the utility function is determined: On the assumption that for money $V(x) = \alpha x^\beta$, $x \geq 0$, which follows from the invariance principle $r(x \oplus y) \sim rx \oplus ry$, then one of three representations holds for

$x \geq 0$,

$$U_+(x) = \begin{cases} 1 - e^{-\kappa x^\beta}, & \delta > 0 \\ x^\beta, & \delta = 0 \\ e^{\kappa x^\beta} - 1, & \delta < 0 \end{cases}.$$ (8.25)

For losses, the same expressions exist with, of course, different primed parameters. If one works with a small (10 or fewer), fixed set of m probabilities, varies the consequences, and finds the corresponding certainty equivalents, it should not be difficult to estimate for each respondent the $m + 2$ parameters, i.e., the m weights plus κ and β. Fitting the losses is similar. Then each of the models of Chapters 6 and 7 predicts what to expect in the mixed case. The prediction is parameter free for the additive U models and entails estimating one additional parameter, $\lambda = \frac{\alpha}{\alpha'}$, for the additive V ones. Thus, the models can be compared for each respondent separately.

- *Weighting functions.* An alternative to estimating the m weights is to assume the weighting function is Prelec's Eq. (3.31) [i.e., Eq. (8.24)]. This adds two more parameters for gains and two for losses. So, there are a total of four estimable parameters for gains, four for losses, and at most one additional parameter, λ, in the mixed case with additive V. The form of the weights can also be explored reasonably thoroughly using separability. The case where U is assumed to be a power function exists in the literature, but is reported only for average data. No attempt has been made to examine individual respondents using all three possibilities in Eq. (8.25).

8.3   Open Conceptual Problems

Theories of individual decision making can be viewed from at least three perspectives. One is descriptive: Does the theory account for the behavior of people? To a considerable degree that has been the focus of the monograph, but subject to the constraint that the descriptive theory should include the prescriptive and normative theories as special cases. The, admittedly improbable, "rational" person should not in my opinion be ruled out by the descriptive theory. The issue of normative and prescriptive theories is discussed in Section 8.3.6.

8.3.1   Descriptive theory

To the extent that we are attempting to devise descriptive theories, something appears to be wrong about the general rank-dependent form, Eqs. (5.1)-(5.3) [i.e., (8.5)-(8.7)], for gambles of three or more gains (and presumably of losses, as well). Recall that the RDU theory can be constructed from three major assumptions: ranked additive consequences (events fixed), coalescing, and binary rank dependence. Depending upon which property appears empirically to be the most suspect, one must consider modifying it to something more descriptive. If coalescing is the culprit, as is suggested by several experiments, then it is reasonable to try, for example, to derive, at least for gains, a qualitative property from Birnbaum's configural weight models that together with binary rank dependence and additive consequences leads to his representation or something very similar to it. At present I do not know of such a property. If binary rank dependence is the trouble, then the only suggestion I can think of is to explore what happens by considering the most general binary form that maintains U as a ratio scale (Luce & Narens, 1985). That means for a family of functions F_C, where C ranges over the events,

$$U(x,C;y) = U(y)F_C\left[\frac{U(x)}{U(y)}\right], \quad x \succsim y \succsim e.$$

The question is to work out the relation of this form to V. This assumption may be too restrictive in that it does not accommodate the possibility of dimensional constants. If the trouble lies in the additivity over consequences, then I am not sure what to suggest.

8.3.2   Probabilistic choice

One of the least descriptive aspects of any of the theories discussed here is their algebraic nature. Repeatedly, we have found that the data suggest respondents do not necessarily make the same choice when a gamble pair is repeated. Various more-or-less ad hoc approaches have been taken in trying to fit the algebraic models to the data. The natural question to raise is: Why not start with choice probabilities $P_G(f)$ of selecting alternative f from a choice set G of gambles? A fairly substantial theory exists for unstructured alternatives, but gambles are structured, as are their joint receipts. We are not very skilled at this point in putting together the algebraic structure of the stimuli with the probabilistic structure of choice. The reader is invited to attempt to write down, for example, a probabilistic version of segregation.

One attempt to develop a probabilistic version of decision theory has been proposed by Busemeyer and Townsend (1993). I do not attempt to describe it in detail. In their paper they mention the fact that Busemeyer found in his 1979 dissertation empirical failures of monotonicity of the form

$$P(f,h) > P(g,h) \quad \text{and} \quad P(f,h') < P(g,h'),$$

which violates a monotonicity property often assumed in probabilistic theories. A quite different approach was taken by Marley (1997a).

Progress on this front would be most welcome.

8.3.3   What restricts the weights?

In addition to the overall form of the theory, there are questions about the form of the two functions involved, utility and weights. As we have seen, there was little difficulty, using joint receipts together with the locally rational property of segregation, in tying down the possible utility functions to proportionality, negative exponential, and exponential in V, Eqs. (8.11)-(8.13). For the weighting functions there is one theoretical suggestion that seems very appealing. The difficulty is that its basic qualitative properties, N-compound invariance or N-reduction invariance, $N = 2,3$, do not seem as normatively compelling as some other properties such as segregation. This invites additional research to see whether it can be arrived at in another way involving more compelling properties or whether some alternative form can be derived from such properties.

Because the joint receipt operation is defined over consequences and not over events, it does not appear to be a feasible way to get at the weights. An alternative is to consider an operation on events, the most obvious one being the union of disjoint events. The usual axioms (see Ch. 5 of Krantz et al., 1971) typically lead to a (finitely) additive probability representation. Some weakening would be needed for a descriptive theory.

Moreover, there is no theory at all about the weights when the underlying events do not have associated probabilities. We do not know, for example, of conditions that would allow us to construct a probability measure over the events in terms of which the weights could be described by a Prelec function.

8.3.4   Context effects

The conceptual problem of context effects strikes me as so important that I devote a separate subsection to it. The problem is easily described. Is it really feasible to assign utilities to alternatives that are independent of the context within which a decision is being made and in such a way that choices correspond to comparing utility values? Put a bit more formally, can the choice between f and g and between f and h be reflected numerically with an invariant number, $U(f)$, playing a comparable role in representing both decisions? Most of the theories of the past half century have accepted that it makes sense to assume so, but much data strongly suggests it is a serious idealization. The simplest and, to me, most convincing demonstration was by MacCrimmon, Stanbury, and Wehrung (1980) (§1.2.1.3).

Perhaps the classical approach is wrong. On that assumption, three theoretical approaches have been suggested.

The first supposes that each choice situation somehow gives rise to a local "status quo" or, as it is more commonly called, an "aspiration" or "reference" level. In some fashion, this amount is "subtracted" from each consequence and the resulting mixed gambles are evaluated in terms of some classical choice theory. So, the approach says that the classical model is correct provided the given alternatives are "modified" to take into account the reference level generated by the context. To date, all of the evaluations have been in terms of one or another of the bilinear forms, in part no doubt because the non-bilinear models of Chapter 7 became available only recently. Clearly, the predictions under the nonlinear models will be quite different from anything in the literature.

A key unresolved issue of this approach is how the local status quo is determined. Several more or less ad hoc suggestions have been made, but there is little by way of principled theory about the local status quo. No one has suggested any direct way to determine or estimate it empirically; indeed, it has been studied empirically only quite indirectly. Among the relevant papers are: Bell (1982, 1983); Birnbaum (1974); Leland (1994); Lopes (1996, and references there to her earlier work); Lopes and Oden (1999); Luce (1996b); Luce, Mellers, and Chang (1993); Payne, Laughhunn, & Crum (1981); and Schneider (1992).

A second approach assumes that in some sense each pair of uncertain alternatives f and

g is evaluated jointly as a pair, i.e., that there is some function $\phi : \mathcal{G} \times \mathcal{G} \to \mathbb{R}$ such that

$$f \succsim g \iff \phi(f,g) \geq 0.$$

It is easy to see that except for very special cases of ϕ, e.g., $\phi(f,g) = U(f) - U(g)$, such a representation corresponds to an intransitive preference order $\succsim$. Fishburn (1982, 1988, 1991), who summarized much of the work in the area, to which he has contributed greatly, attempted to make the case that transitivity should not be imposed even normatively. In the 1991 paper he lists and debates the many arguments that have been provided for transitivity. Unlike him, I find the arguments given for transitivity rather more persuasive than those he mounts against it, except, of course, when context effects exist in which case intransitivities are likely to occur.

Much of the theoretical literature (Fishburn, 1988, 1991, van Acker, 1990, and references therein) concerns specializations and corresponding axiomatizations of the functional ϕ. Perhaps the most relevant version to decision making under uncertainty is the skew-symmetric, bilinear form where if C_f and C_g denote the (finite) sets of consequences that can arise from f and g, respectively, then there is a weighting function W such that

$$\phi(f,g) = \sum_{x \in C_f} \sum_{y \in C_g} W[f^{-1}(x)]W[g^{-1}(y)]\phi(x,y),$$

where $f^{-1}(x) = \{\varepsilon \in E : f(\varepsilon) = x\}$ and ϕ on $C \times C$ is skew symmetric in the sense

$$\phi(x,y) + \phi(y,x) = 0.$$

I do not go into the many details of these mathematical forms, which Fishburn summarizes better than I could do. Marley (1997a) developed a class of aspiration-level models that yield some of Fishburn's models as special cases.

The person who has most fully pursued this class of models empirically, under the title of "regret theory," is G. Loomes with several collaborators (Loomes, 1988; Loomes, Starmer, & Sugden, 1991, 1992; Loomes & Sugden, 1982, 1986, 1987a,b, 1995; Loomes & Taylor, 1992). They have repeatedly provided group evidence concerning violations of monotonicity and transitivity that accords with specialized assumptions about the skew-symmetric functional. Because of my general uneasiness about group data in situations involving nonlinearities, I hope that future empirical designs will admit data analysis of individual respondents.

A third approach taken by several authors, including Leland (1994) and Mellers and Biagini (1994), is to assume that respondents make judgments about the similarity between elements of the set of events or of the set of consequences, and when one of these two sets is sufficiently similar, then the choice is based primarily on the dissimilar set. This, too, provides an explanation of the reported context effects.

Perhaps it is worth noting that the second and third approaches, but not the first, have been stated only for choices between pairs of gambles. It is far from clear how best to generalize these approaches to three or more alternatives.

Little has yet been done to try to select among these alternative approaches or to unify them into a single approach.

8.3.5   The relation of choices and judgments

Beyond a doubt, choices and judgments yield somewhat different behavioral properties. We need theories for each because the naïve assumption that judgments correspond to indifference in choice theories is thoroughly discredited. Nonetheless, few decision scientists would claim that the two response modes are unrelated. The question is: How?

Chapters 6 and 7 show how one can arrive at a nontrivial theory of buying and selling prices, which are common forms of judgment, from a theory of choices. Moreover, in some cases in Chapter 7, the anomalous but observed property of consequence nonmonotonicity in prices is predicted. So we have at least one nontrivial example of how to go from choices to judgments.

Other researchers appear to believe that judgments are more basic and that choices should be understood in terms of them. The most common hypothesis is that some judged evalua- tion is used to order the gambles and so to predict the choices. Such an approach has two drawbacks. First, a theory of judgments that builds in at the start violations of consequence monotonicity is unlikely to be very intuitively compelling, and yet that property is necessary if buying and selling prices are empirical candidates for evaluating gambles. Second, given that there are at least two, and probably more, kinds of judgments, which one is basic? It is certainly the case that different ones will lead to different theories of choice. For example, if one chooses on the basis of comparing judged prices, then the predictions from buying and selling prices will not necessarily agree. Perhaps we can assume that different people in dif- ferent contexts use one or the other. Then the problem will be to figure out how to classify people and contexts. On reflection, this approach strikes me as moderately unappealing.

8.3.6   Normative and prescriptive theories

The intuitive concept of a normative theory is what one "should" do under some accepted definition of "should." The traditional normative theories are, of course, the logic(s) that we use in mathematical reasoning and, closer to decision making, the strictures of axiomatic probability theory. Within the decision making area, normativeness rests upon some concepts of rational behavior.

The notion of a prescriptive theory is related to a normative one but typically is less formal. It seems to refer either to attempts to convince a client to accept the tenets of some normative theory, such as SEU, or to relax the normative theory somewhat, such as by trying to adapt SEU to talk about gains and losses rather than states of total assets. As Fishburn (1991, p. 115) put it, "Normative theory used as the basis for decision making in practice, and with the cognizance of human limitations, gives rise to prescriptive decision theory (Brown, 1989) and decision analysis (Raiffa, 1968)." Among many others, Luce and von Winterfeldt (1994) discuss these distinctions.

What principles of rationality should we invoke? Often this seems to be left somewhat implicit, but as well as I have been able to make out from reading the literature, three principles are widely accepted:

- *Preference rationality:* Consider a set S of valued entities with none preferred to $g \in S$.

If g' is created by replacing some aspect of g by something at least as preferred, all else fixed, then no entity in S is preferred to g'. This is often called "dominance."

- *Likelihood rationality:* If the chance of receiving something that is valued is made more likely at the expense of something less valued, then the modified alternative is preferred to the original one.

- *Accounting rationality:* Suppose two alternatives, without regard to how they are described, have the same bottom lines in the sense of giving rise to the same consequences when the same event pattern occurs except, possibly, for the order in which the events are realized. Then one should be indifferent between these two alternatives. A somewhat more general formulation is that two distinct framings of a gamble should be perceived as equivalent and so the decision maker should be indifferent between them.

Not touched by these principles are two issues: the timing of the resolution of uncertainty in compound gambles and the inherent utility of seeing the chance experiment realized. No attempt has been made to study these in the present monograph.

Since Savage (1954), whose basic assumptions were of these three types plus some structural ones, SEU has been accepted as *the* resulting normative preference representation. This view, which is reinforced by the fact it exhibits other, more complex conditions of rationality, was strongly attested to by the participants in Ward Edwards' 1989 Santa Cruz conference, summarized as Edwards (1992a). (Of course, all participants were fully aware of its descriptive failings.) And, indeed, SEU has been the theory that decision analysts have attempted to use when advising clients. Some difficulty has been reported in these applications in the form of inconsistent estimates of utility from gains alone, losses alone, and from mixed gains and losses.

This monograph makes clear that the concept of normativeness is actually more complex than this traditional view because the resulting representation depends not only upon the three principles of rationality but also upon the initial formulation of the decision situation. If one includes the concept of a status quo and adds the operation of joint receipt to the primitives, then equally rational behavioral assumptions—monotonicity and associativity of joint receipt, binary rank dependence for gains and losses separately (of which gain/loss SEU is a special case), and general segregation—give rise to non-bilinear representations of gambles of mixed gains and losses that are quite different from SEU. Of course, such a model fails some of the properties of SEU and, in a precise sense, can be said to make precise a form of bounded rationality. Introducing the decidedly nonrational duplex decomposition instead of general segregation yields additional representations that seem better, on the whole, descriptively.

To my knowledge, no one has provided a rational argument for choosing between a total assets and a gain-loss formulation of the decision situation. To be sure, those who accept SEU as *the* normative theory claim it is irrational to succumb to the widespread tendency to distinguish gains from losses. To the contrary, I think it perverse, in the face of an almost universal tendency to make the distinction, to develop theories that omit it altogether. But neither claim is the same as showing how a principle of rationality has been violated by either building the distinction in from the start or avoiding it all together. No rational argument has been offered telling us which to do.

Thus, I do not think that we yet have a clear understanding of the status of domain formulation in our concepts of rationality. But given what has been shown about locally rational arguments leading to nonlinear utility forms in the case of mixed gains and losses, decision analysts may want to reconsider the advice they provide decision makers about how to appraise mixed gambles, which, after all, are what mostly concern them.

8.4   Final Comment

Over the past 50 years, interesting progress has been made on the topic of individual decision making under risk and uncertainty. The effort has turned out to be rather more complex than many of us anticipated when we first encountered von Neumann and Morgenstern's (1947) axiomatization of expected utility theory. Despite progress, it is clear that much remains to be done. The whole issue of nonlinear forms for mixed gambles needs considerable further investigation and, perhaps, attempts at application until we get a firm idea of what really is descriptive. And the issue of a suitable descriptive theory for gambles with three or more consequences is very much up in the air. It is clear that coalescing leads to a suitable normative theory (RDU) for gains and losses separately, but it is also clear that it is not descriptive. There are ad hoc representations that seem to work better, but they lack a clear behavioral (axiomatic) basis. Much remains for the next generation of researchers in this area.

Appendices

Appendix   A
Summary of Notations

Basic Sets (§ 1.1.1-6):
C : Certain alternatives

e : Status quo, $e \in C$.

$\mathbb{R}$: Real numbers, often interpreted as money in the decision context.

$\mathcal{R}$: a subset of $\mathbb{R} \cap C$.

$\mathcal{E}$: Set of "experiments."

$\mathbf{E}$: an experiment, i.e., $\mathbf{E} \in \mathcal{E}$.
$\Omega_{\mathbf{E}}$: the set of possible outcomes of $\mathbf{E}$.
$\mathcal{E}_{\mathbf{E}}$: an algebra of subsets of E; closed under union and complementation.
For a single experiment, the subscript $\mathbf{E}$ is suppressed and set $E = \Omega_{\mathbf{E}}$.
$\overline{C} = \Omega_{\mathbf{E}} \backslash C = E \backslash C$, where $C \in \mathcal{E}_{\mathbf{E}}$
$\mathbf{K}$: a canonical experiment

Gambles (§ 1.1.6):
$\mathcal{G}_0 = C$
$\mathcal{G}_k = \mathcal{G}_{k-1} \cup$ {all mappings from finite, ordered partitions of $\Omega_{\mathbf{E}}$, where $\mathbf{E} \in \mathcal{E}$, into $\mathcal{G}_{k-1}$}; elements of $\mathcal{G}_k \backslash \mathcal{G}_{k-1}$ are called k^{th}−order compound gambles. Mostly, we use $k = 2$.
$\mathcal{G}_\infty = \bigcup_{k=0}^{\infty} \mathcal{G}_k$
$\mathcal{B}_k =$ gambles involving only binary partitions.

Preference (§ 1.2.1):
$\succsim$: Weak preference, a connected, binary relation over a set of gambles such as $\mathcal{G}_2$.

$\sim$: Indifference, i.e., both $\succsim$ and $\precsim$.
$\succ$: Preference, i.e., both $\succsim$ and not $\precsim$.

Matching Indifferences (§ 1.2.2)
$CE(g)$: The certainty equivalent defined to be $x \in C$ such that $x \sim g$.

$JCE(g)$: The $CE(g)$ as judged by the respondent.
$CCE(g)$: The $CE(g)$ as determined by some choice procedure such as PEST.

$PE(x,y)$: Given $x, y \in C$, $x \succ y$, the probability equivalent such that $y \sim (x, PE; 0)$

JPE : The $PE(g)$ as judged by the respondent.
CPE : The $PE(g)$ as determined by a choice procedure.

288

Joint Receipt (§ 1.3)

$\oplus$: A binary operation on $\mathcal{G}_2$.

$\mathcal{D}_2$: The closure of $\mathcal{G}_2$ under $\oplus$.

$\mathcal{D}_\infty$: The closure of $\mathcal{G}_\infty$ under $\oplus$.

Appendix B
Basic Behavioral Assumptions

In the following, the universal quatifiers are suppressed.   **Idempotence, Eq. (2.1):**

$$(g, C; g) \sim g.$$

Certainty, Eq. (2.2):

$$(g, E; h) \sim g.$$

Complementarity, Eq. (2.3):

$$(g, C; h) \sim (h, \overline{C}; g).$$

Transitivity, Eq. (2.4):

$$f \succsim g \text{ and } g \succsim h \Longrightarrow f \succsim h.$$

Money Preference, Eq. (2.6): For $\alpha, \beta \in \mathbb{R} \cap C$,

$$\alpha \succsim \beta \Longleftrightarrow \alpha \geq \beta.$$

Consequence Monotonicity, Eq. (2.9): For $E_i \neq \emptyset$,

$$g_j' \succsim g_j \Longleftrightarrow$$
$$(g_1, E_1; ....; g_j', E_j; ...; g_n, E_n) \succsim (g_1, E_1; ....; g_j, E_j; ...; g_n, E_n).$$

Monotonicity of Event Inclusion, Eq. (2.13):

$$g \succ h \text{ and } C \supset D \Longrightarrow (g, C; h) \succ (g, D; h).$$

Order-Independence of Events, Eq. (2.14): For $g, h \succ e$,

$$(g, C; e) \succsim (g, D; e) \Longleftrightarrow (h, C; e) \succsim (h, D; e).$$

Gain-Loss Decomposition, Eq. (2.17): For $g \in \mathcal{G}_1$,

$$g \sim (g_+, E(+); g_-, E(-)).$$

Note that although event monotonicity, Eq. (2.12), was discussed, it is definitely is not assumed.

Appendix C
PEST Procedure

A *psychometric function* is the probability of choosing x over y, $\Pr(x, y)$, as a function of x when the reference stimulus y is held fixed. For any designated probability level π, the idea of a PEST (parameter estimation by sequential testing) procedure is to locate the stimulus $x(y, \pi)$ for which $\Pr[x(y, \pi), y] = \pi$. This method first arose in psychophysics where the concern was to estimate the slope and mean of the psychometric function by establishing points close to $\pi = 0.25$ and $\pi = 0.75$ and interpolating linearly between them. Initially a simple up-down method was used, but to increase experimental efficiency Taylor and Creelman (1967) introduced the PEST procedure, and Pollack (1968) investigated some of its properties. In the context of estimating certainty equivalents, one wishes to establish which stimulus corresponds to the median response value, i.e., $\pi = 0.50$. Bostic, Herrnstein, and Luce (1990) suggested an adaptation that was based on the following reasoning. In the general neighborhood of the 0.50 point, empirical psychometric functions appear to be approximately linear and so can be treated as if they are symmetric. Thus, if CE is the median of a lottery g and ε is a perturbation on it, then approximately $\Pr(CE+\varepsilon, g) = 1 - \Pr(CE-\varepsilon, g)$. This suggested that, unlike the original PEST algorithms, we should use a perfectly symmetric algorithm to converge on the CE.

The basic structure of the PEST algorithm used in several studies is that various pairs (x, g) are presented where x is a sum of money and g is a lottery, and the respondent chooses between them. Depending upon which choice is made,[1] the value of x is either increased or decreased by some amount for the next presentation of the same lottery g, which typically is not repeated until after quite a few intervening trials involving different lotteries have occurred. So, the following rules need to be specified: (1) the initial value of x; (2) the conditions under which an increment or decrement is made; (3) the size of the changes; (4) the conditions under which a particular lottery is no longer presented; (5) the estimate of CE; and (6) how to maintain a constant mean number of trials between successive presentations of the same gamble. We describe these rules in order:

1.   *The initial value* of x is chosen from a uniform distribution over the range of possible consequences of g rounded to whatever unit, dollars, 5 cents, or 1 cent, that is appropriate to the lotteries being used.

2.   *The direction of change* is a decrement when the respondent selects x over g and an increment when the respondent selects g over x. This rule reflects the symmetry anticipated in the psychometric function.

3.   *The size of change*, ε, has four aspects:

   (a)   *Initial step size:* The value of ε used at the first presentation of g is a constant multiple of the criterion used in the exit rule, item 4 below.

---

[1]   In the psychophysical procedure, some of the recent history of choices to the same reference stimulus, g in our case, also plays a role in order to deal with the fact one is trying to estimate something other than the median.

(b)   *Halving rule:* Each time the choice changes from the previous choice, the step size ε is reduced by a factor of 2.

(c)   *Doubling rule:* If two successive choices are the same, then ε is doubled except for the initial presentation of g, in which case doubling does not occur until there are three in the same direction.

(d)   *Boundary rule:* If following rules 2 (a)-(c) ever leads to a value of x that exceeds the best consequence in g, then x is limited to that value; and if it goes below the worst consequence, then it is limited to that value.

4.   *The exit rule* is that g is no longer presented once the change dictated by (3) is less than a fixed fraction of the range of the consequences. Often $\frac{1}{50}$ was used for that fraction.

5.   *The estimate of CE* is the mean of the terminating x value and the preceding one.

6.   *Trial separation between successive presentations* is maintained at a constant average value by introducing a filler lottery each time a lottery, whether experimental or filler, is terminated. These filler lotteries are similar to those whose CEs are being estimated, but they do not play any role in the experimental design beyond maintaining a fixed expected separation of successive presentations of the same lottery.

The boundary rule, (3d), was introduced because it did not seem reasonable to go beyond the range of the consequences of the lottery. However, invoking this rule may have been a mistake because it introduces an asymmetry into the procedure when the gambles are skewed. Sneddon (1999) has shown by simulation that small biases occur in the estimate of CE when the lottery itself is seriously skewed, e.g., ($\$100, 0.9; 0$). Sections 4.2.3, 4.4.3, and 4.4.4 discuss some evidence that this, or other biases, may have affected some results. Note that I said "may have" because a subsequent attempt to estimate certainty equivalents without invoking the boundary rule has led to quite chaotic results.[2] So one may be better off living with the small bias that is introduced by the rule.

---

[2]   Younghee Cho, personal communication, September, 1999.

Appendix D
Additive Conjoint Measurement

Consider a structure $\langle A_1 \times A_2, \succsim \rangle$, where the A_i are in general distinct sets and $\succsim$ is a binary ordering of $A_1 \times A_2$. Some axioms of additive conjoint measurement, C1-C4 below, are necessary in the sense that if one assumes an additive representation $\phi_1 + \phi_2$ exists, then the properties must hold. In all cases, the necessity is easily shown.

Axiom C1. Weak ordering:
$\succsim$ weakly orders $A_1 \times A_2$ in the sense that $\succsim$ is transitive and connected.

Axiom C2. Order Independence:
For all $x, y \in A_1$ and $u, v \in A_2$:

$$(x, u) \succsim (y, u) \iff (x, v) \succsim (y, v)$$
$$(x, u) \succsim (x, v) \iff (y, u) \succsim (y, v).$$

Note that by order independence[3] a weak order is induced on each component by the following definitions:

$$x \succsim_1 y \iff (x, u) \succsim (y, u),$$
$$u \succsim_2 v \iff (x, u) \succsim (x, v).$$

Axiom C2 asserts that the choice of the fixed value from A_i is immaterial in defining these induced orders.

Axiom C3. Thomsen Condition:
For all $x, y, z \in A_1$ and $u, v, w \in A_2$:

$$(x, w) \sim (z, v) \text{ and } (z, u) \sim (y, w) \implies (x, u) \sim (y, v). \tag{D.1}$$

The Thomsen condition is a form of cancellation property that must hold if there is an additive representation. Note that w and z, which each appears once on opposite sides in the suppositions, are, in effect, canceled.

To state the next condition, we need the concept of a standard sequence. The idea is that the elements of such a sequence, like the marks on a meter stick, are all equally spaced in the attribute being measured.

Definition D.1. A set of elements $\{x_i\}$, $x_i \in A_1$ is said to form a *standard sequence* if for some u_0, u_1, with $u_0 \prec_2 u_1$, $(x_{i+1}, u_0) \sim (x_i, u_1)$. If for some $y, z \in A_1$ and all x_i in a standard sequence, it is the case $y \precsim_1 x_i \precsim_1 z$, then the sequence is said to be *bounded*. The definitions on the second component are similar.

---

[3] In the measurement literature, this property has been called just "independence." As noted earlier, this word has multiple meanings and so the adjective has been introduced. It could also have been called monotonicity, for that is really what it is, but to be consistent with the measurement literature, where proofs can be found, I retain the "independence" language.

Note that in a certain sense, the elements of a standard sequence are chosen so that the "increment" from x_i to x_{i+1} on $\mathcal{A}_1$ is "equivalent" to the fixed "increment" from u_0 to u_1 on $\mathcal{A}_2$. Thus, they are all "equivalent" to each other.

Axiom C4. Archimedean:
Every bounded standard sequence is finite.

The next two axioms are not necessary properties of the representation, but the first is satisfied in any nontrivial situation and the second is a form of continuity that is often satisfied at least approximately.

Axiom C5. Essentialness:
There exist $x, y \in \mathcal{A}_1$ and $u, v \in \mathcal{A}_2$ such that $x \succ_1 y$ and $u \succ_2 v$.

Axiom C6. Restricted Solvability:
If there exist $\bar{y}, y, x \in \mathcal{A}_1$ and $u, v \in \mathcal{A}_2$ such that $(\bar{y}, v) \succsim (x, u) \succsim (\underline{y}, v)$, then there exists $y \in \mathcal{A}_1$ such that $(y, v) \sim (x, u)$. The parallel condition on $\mathcal{A}_2$ also holds.

Theorem D.1.   *If a conjoint structure satisfies Axioms C1-C6, then it has a numerical, additive, order-preserving representation. Moreover, the representation is unique up to positive affine transformations, i.e., $\phi_1 + \phi_2$ and $\phi_1' + \phi_2'$ are both additive representations if and only if there are real constants $\alpha > 0$, β_i, $i = 1, 2$, such that $\phi_i' = \alpha\,\phi_i + \beta_i$, $i = 1, 2$. If the representation is restricted so that the value 0 is a specified element in each set, then the uniqueness is up to positive multiplicative transformations, i.e., the β_i are 0.*

A proof of this theorem can be found in various places including Krantz et al. (1971) and Wakker (1989). Michell (1990) discusses with care some of its uses in psychology, and in his 1999 book places it in a general setting of scientific quantification.

The generalization to n components, $n > 2$, is actually a simpler theorem to state. One omits C3, the Thomsen condition, and generalizes order independence to apply to every subset of indices in $\{1, ..., n\}$ when the values of the components with the complementary set are held fixed. All of the other assumptions generalize in the obvious way. From these assumptions one can show that for every pair of indices the Thomsen condition holds on those components. The result is an additive representation with uniqueness up to affine transformations with a common unit $\alpha > 0$.

Appendix E
Major Definitions

Additive Utility, Rank-Dependent: See rank-dependent additive utility.

Archimedean (Def. 3.5.4): Every bounded standard sequence is finite.

Autodistributivity (Right) (Def. 3.2.2): for each $E \in \mathcal{E}$, $C \subseteq E$, and $x, y, z \in C^+$,

$$((x, C'; y), C; z) \sim ((x, C'; z), C; (y, C''; z)), \tag{E.1}$$

where C', C'' are cases of C occurring on independent realizations of the underlying experiment E.

Canonical Experiment (Def. 3.1.2): An experiment K that for any $E \in \mathcal{E}$ and $C \subseteq E$, there exists $D = D(C, E) \subseteq K$ such that for all $x, y \in C^+$ with $x \succsim y$,

$$(x, C; y, E \backslash C) \sim (x, D; y, K \backslash D).$$

Coalescing (Def. 5.3.2): Suppose $g^{(k)}$ is a gamble of gains with $x_i \succsim x_{i+1}$. *Coalescing* is said to hold if whenever $x_{j+1} = x_j$, then

$$(x_1, E_1; ...; x_j, E_j; x_{j+1}, E_{j+1}; ...; x_k, E_k) \sim (x_1, E_1; ...; x_j, E_j \cup E_{j+1}; ...; x_k, E_k).$$

Status-quo coalescing (Proposition 5.3.3) holds if for a partition $\{E_1, E_2, E_3\}$ of E,

$$(x_1, E_1; e, E_2; e, E_3) \sim (x_1, E_1; e, E_2 \cup E_3).$$

Comonotonic gambles (§ 5.3.1.1): Suppose f and g are gambles. They are *comonotonic* if and only for any $i, j \in S$, not both $f(i) \succ f(j)$ and $g(i) \prec g(j)$.

Comonotonic (trade-off) consistency (Def. 5.3.1): Consider any eight comonotonic gambles $f, f', g, g', h, h', k, k'$ where

(i) f agrees with f' and g with g' except at state i, and h agrees with h' and k with k' except at state $j \neq i$; and

(ii) $f(i) = h(j), f'(i) = h'(j), g(i) = k(j)$, and $g'(i) = k'(j)$.

Then *comonotonic (trade-off) consistency* is said to hold if and only if not both $\{f \succsim g$ and $f' \prec g'\}$ and $\{h \precsim k$ and $h' \succsim k'\}$.

Compound Invariance: See N-compound invariance.

Conditionalization (Def. 3.2.1): For $C \subseteq D \subseteq E$,

$$((x_1, C; e, D \backslash C), D; e, E \backslash D) \sim (x_1, C; e, E \backslash C).$$

Decomposition: See gains, gain-loss, or duplex decomposition

Dense Ordering (Def. 3.5.1): Whenever $x \succ y$, there exists z in the domain such that $x \succ z \succ y$.

Duplex Decomposition (Def. 6.2.2): For all $f_+ \in \mathcal{G}_1^+$, $g_- \in \mathcal{G}_1^-$, $C \in \mathcal{E}_{\mathbf{E}}$,

$$(f_+, C; g_-) \sim (f_+, C'; e) \oplus (e, C''; g_-),$$

where C', C'' denote C occurring on independent realizations of the underlying experiment **E**.

Elementary Rational Structure (Def. 2.5.1): A structure of binary gambles $\langle \mathcal{B}_2, \succsim \rangle$ that satisfies the following conditions: $\succsim$ is a weak order (transitive and connected), idempotence, certainty, complementarity, consequence monotonicity, monotonicity of event inclusion, and order-independence of events.

Event commutativity (Def. 3.1.5): For all $x, y \in \mathcal{C}^+$, $x, y \succ e$, $\mathbf{E}, \mathbf{F} \in \mathcal{E}$, $C \subseteq E$, and $D \subseteq F$,

$$((x, C; y, E \backslash C), D; y, F \backslash D) \sim ((x, D; y, F \backslash D), C; y, E \backslash C).$$

When this holds just for $y = e$, i.e., restricted to $\mathbb{C}^+ = \langle \mathcal{B}_1^+ \times \mathcal{E}_{\mathbf{E}}, \succsim \rangle$, we say that *status-quo event commutativity* holds.

Gain-Loss Decomposition (Def. 2.6.1): For every $\mathbf{E} \in \mathcal{E}$ and $g \in \mathcal{G}_1$ with at least one gain and at least one loss consequence

$$g \sim (g_+, E(+); g_-, E(-)).$$

Note that $g \in \mathcal{G}_1$ whereas $(g_+, E(+); g_-, E(-)) \in \mathcal{G}_2$.

Gains Decomposition (Def. 5.3.4): Within $\mathcal{G}_2^+$, for each integer k and for each $g^{(k)} \in \mathcal{G}_1^+$ with $x_1 \succsim \cdots \succsim x_k \succsim e$,

$$g^{(k)} \sim (g^{(k-1)}, E(k-1); x_k, E_k),$$

where $(g^{(k-1)}, E(k-1); g_k, E_k) \in \mathcal{G}_2^+$.

Gains Partition (Def. 3.6.1): There exists a 1-1 function $M : \mathcal{E} \xrightarrow{onto} \mathcal{E}$ that inverts the order $\succsim_{\mathcal{E}}$ such that for $x, x', y, y' \in \mathcal{B}_0$, with $x \succsim y$, $x' \succsim y'$, and $C, C' \in \mathcal{E}$, if

$$(x, C; e) \sim (x', C'; e) \quad \text{and} \quad (y, M(C); e) \sim (y', M(C'); e),$$

then

$$(x, C; y) \sim (x', C'; y').$$

General Segregation (Def. 6.2.1): For all $f, g \in \mathcal{G}_1$, $f \succsim g$, $C \in \mathcal{E}_{\mathbf{E}}$,

$$(f, C; g) \sim \begin{cases} (f \ominus g, C; e) \oplus g, & \text{if } (f, C; g) \succ e \\ (e, C; g \ominus f) \oplus f, & \text{if } (f, C; g) \prec e \end{cases}.$$

Invariance: See compound, money, or reduction invariance

Joint-Receipt Consistency (Def. 6.1.1): For all $f_+, f'_+, g_+ \succsim e \succsim h_-, k_-$ for which $f_+ \oplus h_-, f'_+ \oplus h_- \succsim e$,

$$(f_+ \oplus h_-) \oplus g_+ \sim (f_+ \oplus g_+) \oplus k_- \iff (f'_+ \oplus h_-) \oplus g_+ \sim (f'_+ \oplus g_+) \oplus k_-.$$

Joint-Receipt Decomposable Structure (Def. 4.4.2): For each $f \in \mathcal{D}_1^+$ and $C \in \mathcal{E}_{\mathbf{K}}$, there exists an event $D = D(f, C) \in \mathcal{E}_{\mathbf{K}}$ such that for all $g \in \mathcal{D}_1^+$,

$$(f \oplus g, C; e) \sim (f, C; e) \oplus (g, D; e).$$

Joint-Receipt Preference Structure (Def. 4.2.1): $\langle \mathcal{D}, e, \succsim, \oplus \rangle$ such that for all $f, g, h \in \mathcal{D}$:

Axiom JR1. Weak Order:

$$\succsim \text{ is transitive and connected.}$$

Axiom JR2. Weak Commutativity:

$$f \oplus g \sim g \oplus f.$$

Axiom JR3. Weak Associativity:

$$f \oplus (g \oplus h) \sim (f \oplus g) \oplus h.$$

Axiom JR4. Weak Monotonicity:

$$f \succsim g \iff f \oplus h \succsim g \oplus h.$$

Axiom JR5. Weak Identity:

$$f \oplus e \sim f.$$

It is called *Archimedean* if

Axiom JR6. Archimedean: For all $f, g, h, h' \in \mathcal{D}^+$ such that $f \succ g$, there exists an integer n such that

$$f(n) \oplus h \succsim g(n) \oplus h'.$$

Money Invariance (§ 4.5.2):

$$rx \oplus ry = r(x \oplus y), \quad r > 0.$$

N-Compound Invariance (Def. 3.4.1): Suppose $x, y, x', y' \in C^i$ and $p, q, r, s \in]0, 1[$, with $q < p, r < s$, and N is a natural number. If

$$(x, p) \sim (y, q), \quad (x, r) \sim (y, s), \text{ and } (x', p^N) \sim (y', q^N)$$

then

$$(x', r^N) \sim (y', s^N).$$

Compound invariance means N-compound invariance for all natural numbers N. φ-compound invariance: see Def. 3.4.5.

N-Reduction Invariance (Def. 3.4.2): Suppose N is a natural number, $x \in C^i$, and $p, q, r \in]0, 1[$. If

$$((x, p), q) \sim (x, r)$$

then

$$((x, p^N), q^N) \sim (x, r^N)$$

Reduction invariance means N-reduction invariance for all natural numbers N. φ-reduction invariance: see Def. 3.4.6.

Nontrivial Ordering (Def. 3.5.1): An ordering $\succsim$ for which there exist elements x, y in the domain such that $x \succ y$.

Permutable Family (Def. 3.4.4): Suppose that for an open interval I of real numbers $\varphi :]0, 1[\times I \xrightarrow{onto}]0, 1[$ is a function that is strictly increasing in the first variable and strictly monotonic in the second. Then for all $p \in]0, 1[$ and $\lambda, \mu \in I$,

$$\varphi[\varphi(p, \lambda), \mu] = \varphi[\varphi(p, \mu), \lambda].$$

Rank-Dependent Additive (RDA) (Def. 3.1.4 for binary and Def. 5.3.3 for the general case): For each k there exist functions $U_{k,i,\mathbf{E}} : C^+ \times \mathcal{P}_{k,\mathbf{E}} \xrightarrow{into} \mathbb{R}$ that are strictly increasing in the first argument and with $U_{k,i,\mathbf{E}}[e, (E_1, ..., E_k)] = 0$, such that for $x_1 \succsim x_2 \succsim \cdots \succsim x_k$, $x_i \in C^+$,

$$U_{k,\mathbf{E}}(x_1, E_1; ...; x_k, E_k) = \sum_{i=1}^{k} U_{k,i,\mathbf{E}}[x_i, (E_1, ..., E_k)]$$

is an order preserving representation over the gambles based on $\mathbf{E}$.

Rank-Dependent Utility (Binary) (Def. 3.1.1): A mapping $U : \mathcal{B}_2^+ \to \mathbb{R}^+ = \{\alpha : \alpha \in \mathbb{R} \text{ and } \alpha \geq 0\}$ and, for each $\mathbf{E} \in \mathcal{E}$, a mapping $W_{\mathbf{E}} : \mathcal{E}_{\mathbf{E}} \to [0, 1]$ with $W_{\mathbf{E}}(\emptyset) = 0, W_{\mathbf{E}}(E) = 1$ and that is monotonic increasing with event inclusion such that, for $g, h \in \mathcal{B}_2^+$,

$$g \succsim h \iff U(g) \geq U(h),$$
$$U(e) = 0,$$

and for $g, h \in \mathcal{B}_1^+$,

$$U(g, C; h, \overline{C}) = \begin{cases} U(g)W_{\mathbf{E}}(C) + U(h)[1 - W_{\mathbf{E}}(C)], & g \succ h \\ U(g), & g \sim h \\ U(g)[1 - W_{\mathbf{E}}(\overline{C})] + U(h)W_{\mathbf{E}}(\overline{C}), & g \prec h \end{cases}.$$

Rank-Dependent Utility (general) (Def. 5.1.1): There is an order-preserving utility function $U : \mathcal{G}_1 \to \mathbb{R}$ and, for each $\mathbf{E} \in \mathcal{E}$, a mapping $W_{\mathbf{E}} : \mathcal{E}_{\mathbf{E}} \to [0,1]$ with $W_{\mathbf{E}}(\emptyset) = 0$, $W_{\mathbf{E}}(E) = 1$ and that is monotonic increasing with event inclusion such that, for $x_i \in \mathcal{C}$,

$$U(x_1, E_1; x_2, E_2; ...; x_k, E_k) = \sum_{i=1}^{k} U(x_i)W_i(E_1, ..., E_k),$$

where, using the notation

$$E(i) = \bigcup_{j=1}^{i} E_j, \qquad E(0) = \emptyset,$$

W_i is defined in terms of $W_{\mathbf{E}}$ as follows:

$$W_i(E_1, ..., E_k) = W_{\mathbf{E}}[E(i)] - W_{\mathbf{E}}[E(i-1)].$$

Reduction Invariance: See N-reduction invariance.

Reidemeister condition: See triple cancellation.

Restricted Solvability (Def. 3.5.2, Appendix D): For all $x, x^*, x_*, y, z \in \mathcal{B}_1^+$ and $C, C^*, C_*, D \in \mathcal{E}$,

    If $(x^*, C; y) \succsim (z, D; y) \succsim (x_*, C; y)$,

          then there exists $x \in \mathcal{B}_0$ such that $(x, C; y) \sim (z, D; y)$;

    If $(x, C^*; y) \succsim (z, D; y) \succsim (x, C_*; y)$,

          then there exists $C \in \mathcal{E}$ such that $(x, C; y) \sim (z, D; y)$.

Segregation (of gains) (Def. 4.4.1 for the binary case and 5.3.5 for the general case): For $g_1 \succsim g_2 \succsim \cdots \succsim g_k \succ e$,

$$(g_1, E_1; g_2, E_2; ...; g_k, E_k) \sim (g_1 \ominus g_k, E_1; g_2 \ominus g_k, E_2; ...; e, E_k) \oplus g_k.$$

See also General Segregation.

Separable Representation (Def. 3.1.3): For each $\mathbf{E} \in \mathcal{E}$, there exist $U^* : \mathcal{C}^+ \to \mathbb{R}^+$ and $W_{\mathbf{E}}^* : \mathcal{E}_{\mathbf{E}} \to [0,1]$ such that the product $U^* W_{\mathbf{E}}^*$ is order preserving of the conjoint substructure $\mathbb{C}^+ = \langle (\mathcal{B}_1^+ \backslash \{e\}) \times (\mathcal{E}_{\mathbf{E}} \backslash \{\emptyset\}), \succsim \rangle$, i.e.,

$$(x, C; e, E \backslash \overline{C}) \succsim (y, D; e, E \backslash D) \iff U^*(x)W_{\mathbf{E}}^*(C) \geq U^*(y)W_{\mathbf{E}}^*(D)$$

299

and $W_{\mathrm{E}}^*(E) = 1$. The representation is said to be *onto* (or *dense in*) an *interval* if in addition U^* is onto (dense in) a real interval containing 0 and W_{E}^* is onto (dense in) $[0, 1]$.

Standard Sequences (Def. 3.5.3, Appendix D) Sequences $\{x_i\}$ from $\mathcal{B}_1^+$ and $\{E_j\}$ such that

$$(x_i, E; z) \sim (x_{i+1}, D; z), \quad E \succ_{\mathcal{E}} D$$
$$(x, E_i; z) \sim (y, E_{i+1}; z), \quad x \succ y.$$

Status-Quo Coalescing: See coalescing.

Status-Quo Event Commutativity: See event commutativity.

Subproportionality (Def. 3.4.3): Suppose $p, q, r \in]0, 1[$, $p \neq q$, and for some $x, y \in \mathcal{C}$, $(x, p) \sim (y, q)$. Then for $y > x > 0$, $(y, rq) \succ (x, rp)$, and for $0 > x > y$, $(y, rq) \prec (x, rp)$.

Subtraction (Def. 4.3.1): For $f, g \in \mathcal{D}$ with $f \succsim g$, define

$$f \ominus g \sim k \quad \text{iff} \quad f \sim k \oplus g.$$

Transitive Family (Def. 3.4.4): Suppose that for an open interval I of real numbers $\varphi :]0, 1[\times I \xrightarrow{onto}]0, 1[$ is a function that is strictly increasing in the first variable and strictly monotonic in the second. Then for each $p, q \in]0, 1[$ there is some $\lambda \in I$ such that

$$\varphi(p, \lambda) = q.$$

Triple Cancellation (Def. 3.5.5): Suppose each pair of elements lies in $\mathcal{A}^+$.

$$(x, r) \succsim (y, s), (t, s) \succsim (w, r), \text{ and } (w, u) \succsim (t, v) \implies (x, u) \succsim (y, v).$$

When it holds for $\sim$ rather than $\succsim$, it is called the Reidemeister condition.

REFERENCES

[1] Abdellaoui, M. (1998). Eliciting utilities and decision weights under cumulative prospect theory. Manuscript.

[2] Abdellaoui, M. (1999). Parameter-free elicitation of utilities and probability weighting functions. Manuscript.

[3] Aczél, J. (1955). A solution of some problems of K. Borsuk and L. Jánossy. *Acta Phys. Acad. Sci. Hung., 4,* 351-362.

[4] Aczél, J. (1966). *Lectures on Functional Equations and Their Applications.* New York: Academic Press. This was a translation and updating of the 1961 German edition.

[5] Aczél, J. (1987). *A Short Course on Functional Equations Based on Applications to the Social and Behavioral Sciences.* Dordrecht-Boston-Lancaster-Tokyo: Reidel-Kluwer.

[6] Aczél, J., Ger, R., & Járai, A. (1999). Solution of a functional equation arising from utility that is both separable and additive. *Proceedings of the American Mathematical Society.* In press.

[7] Aczél, J., Luce, R. D., & Maksa, G. (1996). Solutions to three functional equations arising from different ways of measuring utility. *Journal of Mathematical Analysis and Applications, 204,* 451-471.

[8] Aczél, J., Maksa, G. (1999). A functional equation generated by event commutativity in separable and additive utility theory. Submitted.

[9] Aczél, J., Maksa, G., Ng, C. T., & Páles, Z. (1999). A functional equation arising from ranked additive and separable utility. Submitted.

[10] Aczél, J., Maksa, G., & Páles, Z. (1999a). Solution of a functional equation arising from different ways of measuring utility. *Journal of Mathematical Analysis and Applications.* In press.

[11] Aczél, J., Maksa, G., & Páles, Z. (1999b). Solution of a functional equation arising in an axiomatization of the utility of binary gambles. *Proceedings of the American Mathematical Society.* In press.

[12] Adams, E. W., & Fagot, R. F. (1959). A model of riskless choice. *Behavioral Science, 4,* 1-10.

[13] Allais, M. (1953). Le comportement de l'homme rationnel devant le risque: Critique des postulats et axiomes de l'école Americaine. *Econometrica, 21,* 503-546.

[14] Allais, M. (1988). The general theory of random choice in telation to the invariant cardinal utility function and the specific probability function. In B. Munier (Ed.). *Risk, Decision and Rationality.* Bordrecht: Reidel. Pp. 233-289.

[15] Allais, M., & Hagen, O. (Eds.) (1979). *Expected Utility Hypothesis and the Allais Paradox.* Dordrecht: Reidel.

[16] Alt, F. (1936/1971). Über die Messbarkeit des Nutzens. *Zeitschrift für Nationalökonomie, 7,* 161-216. Translated into English by S. Schach. On the measurement of utility. In J. S.

Chipman, L. Hurwicz, M. K. Richter, & H. F. Sommenschein (Eds.). *Preferences, Utility, and Demand.* New York: Harcourt Brace Jovanovich. Pp. 424-431.

[17] Anand, P. (1987). Are the preference axioms really rational? *Theory and Decision, 23,* 189-214.

[18] Anderson, N. (1970). Functional measurement and psychophysical judgment. *Psychological Review, 77,* 153-170.

[19] Anderson, N. (1981). *Foundations of Information Integration Theory.* New York: Academic Press.

[20] Anderson, N. (1982). *Methods of Information Integration Theory.* New York: Academic Press.

[21] Anderson, N. (1991a,b,c). *Contributions to Information Integration Theory: Vol. 1, Cognition; Vol. 2, Social; Vol. 3 Developmental.* Hillsdale, NJ: Lawrence Erlbaum Associates.

[22] Anderson, N. (1996). *A Functional Theory of Cognition.* Mahwah, NJ: Lawrence Erlbaum Associates.

[23] Anscombe, F. J., & Aumann, R. J. (1963). A definition of subjective probability. *Annals of Mathematical Statistics, 34,* 199-205.

[24] Arrow, K. J. (1951). Alternative approaches to the theory of choice in risk-taking situations. *Econometrica, 19,* 404-437.

[25] Arrow, K. J. (1971). The theory of risk aversion. In K. J. Arrow. *Essays in the Theory of Risk Bearing.* Chicago: Markham Publishing Co. Pp. 90-120.

[26] Barberà, S., Hammond, P. J., & Seidl, C. (Eds.) (1998). *Handbook of Utility Theory, Vol. I: Principles.* Dordrecht: Kluwer Academic Publishers.

[27] Barron, F. H., von Winterfeldt, D., & Fischer, G. W. (1984). Empirical and theoretical relationships between value and utility functions. *Acta Psychologica, 56,* 233-244.

[28] Batchelder, W. H., & Reifer, D. M. (1990). Multinomial processing models of source monitoring. *Psychological Review, 97,* 548-564.

[29] Becker, J. L., & Sarin, R. K. (1987). Lottery dependent utility. *Management Science, 33,* 1367-1382.

[30] Bell, D. E. (1982). Regret in decision making under uncertainty. *Operations Research, 30,* 961-981.

[31] Bell, D. E. (1983). Risk premiums for decision regret. *Management Science, 29,* 1156-1166.

[32] Bell, D. E., & Fishburn, P. C. (1999). Utility functions for wealth. *Journal of Risk and Uncertainty.* In press.

[33] Bernoulli, D. (1738/1954). Specimen theoriae novae de mensura sortis. *Commentarii Academiae Scientiarum Imperialis Petropolitanae, 5,* 175-192. English translation by L. Sommer. Exposition of a new theory on the measurement of risk. *Econometrica, 22,* 23-36.

[34] Birnbaum, M. H. (1972). *The Nonadditivity of Impressions.* Ph.D. Thesis, University of California, Los Angeles.

[35] Birnbaum, M. H. (1974). Using contextual effects to derive psychophysical scales. *Perception & Psychophysics, 15,* 89-96.

[36] Birnbaum, M. H. (1992). Violations of monotonicity and contextual effects in choice-based

certainty equivalents. *Psychological Science, 3,* 310-314.

[37] Birnbaum, M. H. (1997). Violations of monotonicity in judgment and decision making. In A. A. J. Marley (Ed). *Choice, Decision, and Measurement: Essays in Honor of R. Duncan Luce.* Mahwah, NJ: Lawrence Erlbaum Associates. Pp. 73-100.

[38] Birnbaum, M. H. (1999). The paradoxes of Allais, stochastic dominance, and decision weights. In J. Shanteau, B. A. Mellers, & D. A. Schum (Eds.) *Decision Science and Technology: Reflections on the Contributions of Ward Edwards.* Boston: Kluwer Academic Publishers. Pp. 27-52.

[39] Birnbaum, M. H., Beeghley, D. (1997). Violations of branch independence in judgments of the value of gambles. *Psychological Science, 8,* 87-94.

[40] Birnbaum, M. H., & Chavez, A. (1997). Tests of theories of decision making: Violations of branch independence and distribution independence. *Organizational Behavior and Human Decision Processes, 71,* 161-194.

[41] Birnbaum, M. H., Coffey, G., Mellers, B. A., & Weiss, R. (1992). Utility measurement: Configural-weight theory and the judge's point of view. *Journal of Experimental Psychology: Human Perception and Performance, 18,* 331-346.

[42] Birnbaum, M. H., & McIntosh, W. R. (1996). Violations of branch independence in choices between gambles. *Organizational Behavior and Human Decision Processes, 67,* 91-110.

[43] Birnbaum, M. H., & Navarrete, J. (1998). Testing descriptive utility theories: Violations of stochastic dominance and cumulative independence. *Journal of Risk and Uncertainty, 17,* 49-78.

[44] Birnbaum, M. H., Parducci, A., & Gifford, R. K. (1971). Contextual effects in information integration. *Journal of Experimental Psychology, 88,* 158-170.

[45] Birnbaum, M. H., Patton, J. N., & Lott, M. K. (1999). Evidence against rank-dependent utility theories: Violations of cumulative independence, interval independence, stochastic dominance, and transitivity. *Organizational Behavior and Human Decision Processes.* In press.

[46] Birnbaum, M. H., & Stegner, S. E. (1979). Source credibility in social judgment: Bias, expertise, and the judge's point of view. *Journal of Personality and Social Psychology, 37,* 48-74.

[47] Birnbaum, M. H., & Sutton, S. E. (1992). Scale convergence and utility measurement. *Organizational Behavior and Human Decision Processes, 52,* 183-215.

[48] Birnbaum, M. H., & Veira, R. (1998). Configural weighting in judgments of two- and four-outcome gambles. *Journal of Experimental Psychology: Human Perception and Performances, 24,* 216-226.

[49] Birnbaum, M. H., & Yeary, S. Tests of stochastic dominance, cumulative independence, branch independence, coalescing, event-splitting independence, and asymptotic independence in buying and selling prices. Manuscript.

[50] Birnbaum, M. H., & Zimmermann, J. M. (1998). Buying and selling prices of investments: Configural weight model of interactions predicts violations of joint independence. *Organizational Behavior and Human Decision Processes, 74,* 145-187.

[51] Bleichrodt, H., & Pinto, J. L. (1998a). The validity of QALYs when expected utility theory no longer holds. Manuscript.

[52] Bleichrodt, H., & Pinto, J. L. (1998b). A parameter-free elicitation of the probability weighting function in medical decision analysis. Manuscript.

[53] Bock, R. D., & Jones, L. V. (1968). *The Measurement and Prediction of Judgment and Choice.* San Francisco, CA: Holden-Day.

[54] Bostic, R., Herrnstein, R. J., & Luce, R. D. (1990). The effect on the preference-reversal phenomenon of using choice indifferences. *Journal of Economic Behavior and Organization 13,* 193-212.

[55] Bouyssou, D., & Vansnick, J.-C. (1988). A note on the relationships between utility and value functions. In B. R. Munier (Ed.). *Risk, Decision, and Rationality.* Dordrecht: Reidel. Pp. 103-114.

[56] Bouzit, A. M., & Gleyses, G. (1996). Empirical estimation of RDEU preference functional in agricultural production. Manuscript.

[57] Brachinger, H. W., & Weber, M. (1997). Risk as a primitive: A survey of measures of perceived risk. *OR Spektrum, 19,* 235-250.

[58] Broome, J. (1991). *Weighing Goods: Equality, Uncertainty, and Time.* Cambridge, MA: Basil Blackwell.

[59] Brothers, A. (1990). *An Empirical Investigation of Some Properties that are Relevant to Generalized Expected-Utility Theory.* Unpublished doctoral dissertation, University of California, Irvine.

[60] Brown, R. V. (1989). Toward a prescriptive science and technology of decision aiding. *Annals of Operations Research, 19,* 467-483.

[61] Busemeyer, J. R., & Townsend, J. T. (1993). Decision field theory: A dynamic-cognitive approach to decision making. *Psychological Review, 100,* 432-459.

[62] Camerer, C. F. (1989). An experimental test of several generalized utility theories. *Journal of Risk and Uncertainty, 2,* 61-104.

[63] Camerer, C. F. (1992). Recent tests of generalizations of expected utility theory. In W. Edwards (Ed.). *Utility Theories: Measurement and Applications.* Boston: Kluwer Academic Publishers. Pp. 207-251.

[64] Camerer, C. F. (1999). Prospect theory in the wild: Evidence from the field. In D. Kahneman & A. Tversky (Eds.). *Choices, Values and Frames.* New York: Cambridge University Press. In press.

[65] Camerer, C. F., & Ho, R.-H. (1994). Violations of the betweenness axiom and nonlinearity in probability. *Journal of Risk and Uncertainty, 8,* 167-196.

[66] Camerer, C. F., & Weber, M. (1992). Recent developments in modeling preferences: Uncertainty and ambiguity. *Journal of Risk and Uncertainty, 5,* 325-370.

[67] Carbone, E. (1997). Investigation of stochastic preference theory using experimental data. Manuscript.

[68] Carbone, E., & Hey, J. D. (1994). Discriminating between preference functionals—A preliminary Monte Carlo study. *Journal of Risk and Uncertainty, 8,* 223-242.

[69] Carbone, E., & Hey, J. D. (1995). A comparison of the estimates of EU and non-EU preference functionals using data from pairwise choice and complete ranking experiments. *Geneva Papers on Risk and Insurance Theory, 2,* 111-133.

[70] Carlin, P. S. (1990). Is the Allais paradox robust to a seemingly trivial change of frame?

Economic Letters, 34, 241-244.

[1] Chateauneuf, A., & Wakker, P. (1999). An axiomatizaton of cumulative prospect theory for decision under risk. *Journal of Risk and Uncertainty, 18,* 137-145.

[2] Chechile, R. A., & Butler, S. F. (1999). Is "generic utility theory" a suitable theory of choice behavior for gambles with mixed gains and losses? Submitted.

[3] Chechile, R. A., & Cooke, A. D. J. (1997). An experimental test of a general class of utility models: Evidence for context dependency. *Journal of Risk and Uncertainty, 14,* 75-93.

[4] Chechile, R. A., & Luce, R. D. (1999). Reanalysis of the Chechile-Cooke experiment: Correcting for mismatched gambles. *Journal of Risk and Uncertainty,* submitted.

[5] Chew, S. H. (1983). A generalization of the quasilinear mean with applications to the measurement of income inequality and decision theory resolving the Allais paradox. *Econometrica, 51,* 1065-1092.

[6] Chew, S. H., & Epstein, L. G. (1989). Axiomatic rank-dependent means. *Annals of Operations Research, 19,* 299-309.

[7] Chew, S. H., Epstein, L. G. & Segal, U. (1991). Mixture symmetry and quadratic utility. *Econometrica, 59,* 139-163.

[8] Chew, S. H., & Ho, J. L. (1994). Hope: An empirical study of attitude toward the timing of uncertainty resolution. *Journal of Risk and Uncertainty, 8,* 267-288.

[9] Chew, S. H., & Tan, G. (1999). The market for sweepstakes. Manuscript.

[0] Cho, Y., & Fisher, G. (1999). Receiving two consequences: Tests of monotonicity and scale invariance. Submitted.

[1] Cho, Y., & Luce, R. D. (1995). Tests of hypotheses about certainty equivalents and joint receipt of gambles. *Organization Behavior and Human Decision Processes, 64,* 229-248.

[2] Cho, Y., Luce, R. D., & von Winterfeldt, D. (1994). Tests of assumptions about the joint receipt of gambles in rank- and sign-dependent utility theory. *Journal of Experimental Psychology: Human Perception and Performance, 20,* 931-943.

[3] Choquet, G. (1953). Theory of capacities. *Annales Institut Fourier, 5,* 131-295.

[4] Chung, N.-K., von Winterfeldt, D., & Luce, R. D. (1994). An experimental test of event commutativity in decision making under uncertainty. *Psychological Science, 5,* 394-400.

[5] Conlisk, J. (1989). Three variants on the Allais example. *The American Economic Review, 79,* 392-407.

[6] Coombs, C. H. (1964). *A Theory of Data.* New York: Wiley.

[7] Coombs, C. H. (1975). Portfolio theory and the measurement of risk. In M. F. Kaplan & S. Schwartz (Eds.). *Human Judgment and Decision Processes.* New York: Academic Press. Pp. 63-86.

[8] Coombs, C. H., Bezenbinder, T. G., & Good, F. M. (1967). Testing expectation theories of decision making without measuring utility or subjective probability. *Journal of Mathematical Psychology, 4,* 72-103.

[9] Coombs, C. H., & Komorita, S. S. (1958). Measuring utility of money through decisions. *American Journal of Psychology, 71,* 383-389.

[0] Curley, S. P., Yates, J. F., & Abrams, R. D. (1986). Psychological sources of ambiguity avoidance. *Organizational Behavior and Human Decision Making, 38,* 230-256.

[1] Currim, I. S., & Sarin, R. K. (1989). Prospect versus utility. *Management Science, 35,* 22-41.

305

[92] Daniels, R. L., & Keller, R. L. (1990). An experimental evaluation of the descriptive valid of lottery dependent utility theory. *Journal of Risk and Uncertainty, 3,* 115-134.

[93] Daniels, R. L., & Keller, R. L. (1992). Choice-based assessment of utility functions. *Organizational Behavior and Human Decision Processes, 52,* 524-543.

[94] Davison, M., & McCarthy, D. (1988). *The Matching Law. A Research Review.* Hillsdale, I Lawrence Erlbaum Associates.

[95] de Finetti, B. (1931). Sul Significato Soggettivo della Probabilità, *Fundamenta Mathemati 17,* 298-329. Translated into English in P. Monari and D. Cocchi (Eds.). (1993). On the Subjective Meaning of Probability, *Probabilitá e Induzione,* Bologna: Clueb. Pp. 291-321

[96] De Leeuw, J., Young, F. W., & Takane, Y. (1976). Additive structure in qualitative data: A alternating least squares method with optimal scaling features. *Psychometrika, 41,* 471-5(

[97] Delquié, P. (1993). Inconsistent trade-offs between attributes: New evidence in preferenc assessment biases. *Management Science, 39,* 1382-1395.

[98] Diederich, A., & Busemeyer, J. R. (1999). Conflict and the stochastic-dominance princip of decision making. *Psychological Science, 10,* 353-359.

[99] Dyer, J. S., & Sarin, R. K. (1982). Relative risk aversion. *Management Science, 28,* 875-8

[100] Edwards, W. (1954a). The theory of decision making. *Psychological Bulletin, 41,* 380-41

[101] Edwards, W. (1954b). Variance preferences in gambling. *The American Journal of Psychology, 67,* 441-452.

[102] Edwards, W. (1955). The prediction of decisions among bets. *Journal of Experimental Psychology, 50,* 201-214.

[103] Edwards, W. (1962a). Subjective probabilities inferred from decisions. *Psychological Revi 69,* 109-135.

[104] Edwards, W. (1962b). Utility, subjective probability, their interaction, and variance preferences. *The Journal of Conflict Resolution, 6,* 42-51.

[105] Edwards, W. (Ed.). (1992a). *Utility Theories: Measurements and Applications.* Boston: Kluwer.

[106] Edwards, W. (1992b). Toward the demise of economic man and woman; bottom lines fro Santa Cruz. In W. Edwards (1992a). Pp. 253-267.

[107] Ellsberg, D. (1961). Risk, ambiguity and the Savage axioms. *Quarterly Journal of Economics, 75,* 643-669.

[108] Farquhar, P. (1984). Utility assessment methods. *Management Science, 30,* 1283-1300.

[109] Fennema, H., & van Assen, M. A. L. M. (1999). Measuring the utility of losses by means the tradeoff method. *Journal of Risk and Uncertainty, 17,* 277-295.

[110] Fennema, H., & Wakker, P. P. (1997). Original and new prospect theory: A discussion of empirical differences. *Journal of Behavioral Decision Making, 10,* 53-64.

[111] Fine, T. (1973). *Theories of Probability: An Examination of Foundations.* New York: Academic Press.

[112] Fishburn, P. C. (1970). *Utility Theory for Decision Making.* New York: John Wiley & Son

[113] Fishburn, P. C. (1978). On Handa's "New theory of cardinal utility" and the maximization expected return. *Journal of Political Economy, 86,* 321-324.

[114] Fishburn, P. C. (1982). Non-transitive measurable utility. *Journal of Mathematical Psychology, 26,* 31-67.

[5] Fishburn, P. C. (1985). *Interval Orders and Interval Graphs*. New York: John Wiley & Son.

[6] Fishburn, P. C. (1986). The axioms of subjective probability. *Statistical Science, 1,* 335-358.

[7] Fishburn, P. C. (1988). *Nonlinear Preference and Utility Theory.* Baltimore, MD: Johns Hopkins Press.

[8] Fishburn, P. C. (1989). Retrospective on the utility theory of von Neumann and Morgenstern. *Journal of Risk and Uncertainty, 2,* 127-158.

[9] Fishburn, P. C. (1991). Nontransitive preferences in decision theory. *Journal of Risk and Uncertainty, 4,* 113-134.

[0] Fishburn, P. C. (1999). Preference structures and their representations. *Theoretical Computer Science, 217,* 359-383.

[1] Fishburn, P. C., & Keeney, R. L. (1974). Seven independence concepts and continuous multiattribute utility functions. *Journal of Mathematical Psychology, 11,* 294-327.

[2] Fishburn, P. C., & Kochenberger, G. A. (1979). Two-piece von Neumann-Morgenstern utility functions. *Decision Sciences, 10,* 503-518.

[3] Fishburn, P. C., & Luce, R. D. (1995). Joint receipt and Thaler's hedonic editing rule. *Mathematical Social Sciences, 29,* 33-76.

[4] Fishburn, P. C., & Wakker, P. P. (1995). The invention of the independence condition. *Management Science, 41,* 1130-1144.

[5] Fisher, G. (1999). *Empirical Investigation of Three Properties of Binary Joint Receipt.* Ph. D. dissertation. University of California, Irvine.

[6] Fox, C. R., & Tversky, A. (1995). Ambiguity aversion and comparative ignorance. *Quarterly Journal of Economics, 110,* 585-603.

[7] Fox, C. R., & Tversky, A. (1997). A belief-based account of decision making under uncertainty. *Management Science,* in press.

[8] Frey, B. S., & Eichenberger, R. (1989). Should social scientists care about choice anomalies? *Rationality and Society, 1,* 101-122.

[9] Fuchs, L. (1963). *Partially Ordered Algebraic Systems.* Reading, MA: Addison-Wesley.

[0] Ghirardato, P., & Marinacci, M. (1997). Ambiguity made precise: A comparative foundation and some implications. Manuscript.

[1] Gilboa, I. (1987). Expected utility with purely subjective non-additive probabilities. *Journal of Mathematical Economics, 16,* 65-88.

[2] Gonzalez, R., & Wu, G. (1999). On the shape of the probability weighting function. *Cognitive Psychology, 38,* 129-166.

[3] Grether, D. M., & Plott, C. R. (1979). Economic theory of choice and the preference reversal phenomena. *American Economic Review, 69,* 623-638.

[4] Gulliksen, H. (1956a). A least squares solution for paired comparisons with incomplete data. *Psychometrika, 21,* 125-134.

[5] Gulliksen, H. (1956b). Measurement of subjective values. *Psychometrika, 21,* 229-244.

[6] Hammond, P. J. (1988). Consequentialist foundations of expected utility. *Theory and Decision, 25,* 25-78.

[7] Hammond, P. J. (1998a). Consequentialism and Baysian rationality in normal form games. In W. Leinfellner and E. Köhler (Eds.) *Game Theory, Experience, Rationality.* Dordrecht: Kluwer Academic Publishers. Pp. 187-196.

[138] Hammond, P. J. (1998b). Objective expected utility: A consequentialist perspective. In S. Barberà, P. J. Hammond, and C. Seidl (Eds.) *Handbook of Utility Theory. Vol. 1 Principle* Dordrecht: Kluwer Academic Publishers. Pp. 143-211.

[139] Hammond, P. J. (1998c). Subjective expected utility. In S. Barberà, P. J. Hammond, and C. Seidl (Eds.) *Handbook of Utility Theory. Vol. 1 Principles.* Dordrecht: Kluwer Academi Publishers. Pp. 213-271.

[140] Handa, J. (1977). Risk, probabilities, and a new theory of cardinal utility. *Journal of Politic Economy, 85,* 97-122.

[141] Harless, D., & Camerer, C. F. (1994). The predictive utility of generalized expected utility theories. *Econometrica, 62,* 1251-1290.

[142] Hazen, G. B. (1987). Subjectively weighted linear utility. *Theory and Decision, 23,* 261-28

[143] Hazen, G. B. (1989). Ambiguity aversion and ambiguity content in decision making unde uncertainty. *Annals of Operations Research, 19,* 415-434.

[144] Hazen, G. B., & Lee, J.-S. (1991). Ambiguity aversion in the small and in the large for weighted linear utility. *Journal of Risk and Uncertainty, 4,* 177-212.

[145] Heath, C., & Tversky, A. (1991). Preference and belief: Ambiguity and competence in choice under uncertainty. *Journal of Risk and Uncertainty, 4,* 5-28.

[146] Herrnstein, R. J. (H. Rachlin & D. I. Laibson, Eds.). (1997). *The Matching Law. Papers in Psychology and Economics.* Cambridge, MA: Russell Sage Foundation and Harvard University Press.

[147] Hershey, J., Kunreuther, H. C., & Schoemaker, P. J. H. (1982). Sources of bias in assessmer procedures for utility functions. *Management Science, 28,* 936-954.

[148] Hershey, J., & Schoemaker, P. J. H. (1985). Probability versus certainty equivalence metho in utility measurement: Are they equivalent? *Management Science, 31,* 1213-1231.

[149] Herstein, I. N., & Milnor, J. (1953). An axiomatic approach to measurable utility. *Econometrica, 21,* 291-297.

[150] Hey, J. D. (1995). Experimental investigations of errors in decision-making under risk. *European Economic Review, 39,* 633-640.

[151] Hey, J. D. (1997a). An application of Selten's measure of predictive success. Manuscript.

[152] Hey, J. D. (1997b). Experiments and the economics of individual decision making. In D. M. Kreps & K. F. Wallis (Eds.). *Advances in Economics and Econometrics.* Cambridge: Cambridge University Press. Pp. 171-205.

[153] Hey, J. D. (1997c). Comparing theories: What are we looking for? Manuscript.

[154] Hey, J. D., & Carbone, E. (1995). Stochastic choice with deterministic preferences: An experimental investigation. *Economic Letters, 47,* 161-167.

[155] Hey, J. D., & Orme, C. D. (1994). Investigating generalizations of expected utility theory using experimental data. *Econometrica, 62.* 1291-1326.

[156] Hirsch, M. (1978). Desegregated probabilistic accounting information: The effect of sequential events on expected value maximization decisions. *Journal of Accounting Research, 16,* 254-269.

[157] Hölder, O. (1901). Die Axiome der Quantität und die Lehre vom Mass. *Ber. Verh. Kgl. Sächsis Ges. Wiss. Leipzig, Math.-Phys. Classe, 53,* 1-64. For an English translation of Part see Michell and Ernst (1996).

158] Howard, R. A. (1992). In praise of the old time religion. In W. Edwards (Ed.). *Utility Theories: Measurements and Applications.* Boston: Kluwer. Pp. 27-56.

159] Hsee, C. K., & Weber, E. U. (1999). Cross-national differences in risk preference and lay predictions. *Journal of Behavioral Decision Making, 12,* 165-179.

160] Hsee, C. K., Loewenstein, G. F., Blount, S., & Bazerman, M. H. (1999). Preference reversals between joint and separate evaluations of options: A review and theoretical analysis. *Psychological Bulletin, 125,* 576-590.

161] Humphrey, S. J. (1995). Regret aversion and event-splitting effects? More evidence under risk and uncertainty. *Journal of Risk and Uncertainty, 11,* 263-274.

162] Humphrey, S. J. (1996). Do anchoring effects underlie event-splitting effects? An experimental test. *Economic Letters, 51,* 303-308.

163] Humphrey, S. J. (1998). More mixed results on boundary effects. *Economic Letters, 61,* 79-84.

164] Humphrey, S. J. (1999a). Probability learning, event-splitting effects and the economic theory of choice. *Theory and Decision, 46,* 51-78.

165] Humphrey, S. J. (1999b). The common consequence effect: Testing a unified explanation of recent mixed evidence. *Journal of Economic Behavior and Organization.* In press.

166] Humphrey, S. J. (1999c). Are event-splitting effects actually boundary effects? Unpublished manuscript.

167] Iverson, G., & Falmagne, J.-C. (1985). Statistical issues in measurement. *Mathematical Social Sciences, 10,* 131-153.

168] Johnson, E., & Schkade, D. (1989). Bias in utility assessments: Further evidence and explanations. *Management Science, 35,* 406-424.

169] Kachelmeier, S. J., & Shehata, M. (1992). Examining risk preferences under high monetary incentives: Experimental evidence from the People's Republic of China. *American Economic Review, 82,* 1120-1141.

170] Kahneman, D., Knetsch, J., & Thaler, R. H. (1990). Experimental tests of the endowment effect and the Coase theorem. *Journal of Political Economy, 98,* 1325-1348.

171] Kahneman, D., Knetsch, J., & Thaler, R. H. (1991). The endowment effect, loss aversion, and status quo bias. *Journal of Economic Perspectives, 5,* 193-206.

172] Kahneman, D., & Tversky, A. (1979). Prospect theory: An analysis of decision under risk. *Econometrica, 47,* 263-291.

173] Kahneman, D., & Tversky, A. (1984). Choices, values, and frames. *American Psychologist, 39,* 341-350.

174] Karmarkar, U. S. (1978). Subjectively weighted utility: A descriptive extension of expected utility model. *Organizational Behavior and Human Performance, 21,* 61-72.

175] Karmarkar, U. S. (1979). Subjectively weighted utility and the Allais paradox. *Organizational Behavior and Human Performance, 24,* 67-72.

176] Keeney, R. L. (1973). Risk independence and multiattributed utility functions. *Econometrica, 41,* 27-34.

177] Keeney, R. L., & Raiffa, H. (1976). *Decisions with Multiple Objectives.* New York: Wiley.

178] Keller, L. R. (1985a). The effects of problem representation on the sure-thing and substitution principles. *Management Science, 31,* 738-751.

309

[179] Keller, L. R. (1985b). Testing of the 'reduction of compound alternatives' principle. *OMEC The International Journal of Management Science, 13,* 349-358.

[180] Keller, L. R. (1985c). An empirical investigation of relative risk aversion. *IEEE Transactic on Systems, Man, and Cybernetics, 15,* 475-482.

[181] Keller, L. R. (1992). Properties of utility theories and related empirical phenomena. In W. Edwards (Ed.). *Utility Theories: Measurements and Applications.* Norwell, MA: Kluw Academic Publishers. Pp. 3-23.

[182] Kilka, M., & Weber, M. (1998). What determines the shape of the probability weighting function under uncertainty? Manuscript.

[183] Knight, F. H. (1921). *Risk, Uncertainty and Profit.* Boston: Houghton Mifflin.

[184] Komorita, S. S. (1964). A model for decision-making under risk. *American Journal of Psychology, 77,* 429-436.

[185] Krantz, D. H., Luce, R. D., Suppes, P., & Tversky, A. (1971). *Foundations of Measuremer Vol. I.* New York: Academic Press.

[186] Kreps, D. M. (1990). *A Course in Microeconomic Theory.* Princeton, NJ: Princeton University Press.

[187] Krzysztofowicz, R. (1994). Generic utility theory: Explanatory model, behavioral hypotheses, empirical evidence. In M. Allais & O. Hagen (Eds.). *Cardinalism.* Boston: Kluwer Academic Publishers. Pp. 249-288.

[188] Krzysztofowicz, R., & Koch, J. D. (1989). Estimation of cardinal utility based on a nonlin theory. *Annals of Operations Research, 19,* 181-204.

[189] Lattimore, P. K., Baker, J. R., & Witte, A. D. (1992). The influence of probability on risky choice: A parametric examination. *Journal of Economic Behavior and Organization, 17,* 377-400.

[190] Leland, J. W. (1994). Generalized similarity judgments: An alternative explanation for choice anomalies. *Journal of Risk and Uncertainty, 9,* 151-172.

[191] Lewis, B., & Bell, J. (1985). Decisions involving sequential events: Replications and extensions. *Journal of Accounting Research, 23,* 228-239.

[192] Li, S. (1994). Is there a problem with preference reversals? *Psychological Reports, 74,* 675-679.

[193] Lichtenstein, S., & Slovic, P. (1971). Reversal of preferences between bids and choices ir gambling decisions. *Journal of Experimental Psychology, 89,* 46-55.

[194] Lichtenstein, S., & Slovic, P. (1973). Response-induced reversals of preference in gamblir An extended replication in Las Vegas. *Journal of Experimental Psychology, 101,* 16-20.

[195] Lindman, H. R. (1971). Inconsistent preferences among gambles. *Journal of Experimenta Psychology, 89,* 390-397.

[196] Lindman, H. R., & Lyons, J. (1978). Stimulus complexity and choice inconsistency amon, gambles. *Organizational Behavior and Human Performance, 21,* 146-159.

[197] Link, S. W. (1992). *The Wave Theory of Difference and Similarity.* Hillsdale, NJ: Lawrenc Erlbaum Associates.

[198] Linville, P. W., & Fischer, G. W. (1991). Preferences for separating or combining events. *Journal of Personality and Social Psychology, 60,* 5-23.

[199] Liu, L. (1995). *A Theory of Coarse Utility and its Application to Portfolio Analysis.*

Ph.D. Dissertation, University of Kansas.

0] Loewenstein, G., & Elster, J. (Eds.). (1992). *Choice over time*. New York: Russell Sage Foundation.

1] Loomes, G. (1988). Further evidence on the impact of regret and disappointment in choice under uncertainty. *Economica, 55,* 47-62.

2] Loomes, G., Starmer, C., & Sugden, R. (1991). Observing violations of transitivity by experimental methods. *Econometrica, 59,* 425-439.

3] Loomes, G., Starmer, C., & Sugden, R. (1992). Are preferences monotonic? Testing some predictions of regret theory. *Economica, 59,* 17-33.

4] Loomes, G., & Sugden, R. (1982). Regret theory: An alternative theory of rational choice under uncertainty. *The Economic Journal, 92,* 805-824.

5] Loomes, G., & Sugden, R. (1986). Disappointment and dynamic consistency in choice under uncertainty. *Review of Economic Studies, 53,* 271-282.

6] Loomes, G., & Sugden, R. (1987a). Some implications of a more general form of regret theory. *Journal of Economic Theory, 41,* 270-287.

7] Loomes, G., & Sugden, R. (1987b). Testing for regret and disappointment in choice under uncertainty. *Economic Journal, 97,* 118-129.

8] Loomes, G., & Sugden, R. (1995). Incorporating a stochastic element into decision theories. *European Economic Review, 39,* 641-648.

9] Loomes, G., & Taylor, C. (1992). Non-transitive preferences over gains and losses. *The Economic Journal, 102,* 357-365.

0] Lopes, L. L. (1984). Risk and distributional inequality. *Journal of Experimental Psychology: Human Perception and Performance, 10,* 456-485.

1] Lopes, L. L. (1987). Between hope and fear: The psychology of risk. In L. Berkowitz (Ed.). *Advances in Experimental Social Psychology, Vol. 20.* New York: Academic Press. Pp. 255-295.

2] Lopes, L. L. (1990). Re-modeling risk aversion. In G. M. Furstenberg (Ed.). *Acting Under Uncertainty: Multidisciplinary Conceptions.* Boston: Kluwer Academic Press. Pp. 267-299.

3] Lopes, L. L. (1996). When time is of the essence: Averaging, aspiration, and the short run. *Organizational Behavior and Human Decision Processes, 65,* 179-189.

4] Lopes, L. L., & Oden, G. C. (1999). The role of aspiration level in risky choice: A comparision of cumulative prospect theory and SP/A theory. *Journal of Mathematical Psychology, 43,* 286-313.

5] Luce, R. D. (1956). Semiorders and a theory of utility discrimination. *Econometrica, 24,* 178-191.

6] Luce, R. D. (1959). *Individual Choice Behavior.* New York: John Wiley & Sons.

7] Luce, R. D. (1964). Some one-parameter families of commutative learning operators. In R. C. Atkinson (Ed.). *Studies in Mathematical Psychology.* Stanford, CA: Stanford University Press. Pp. 380-398.

8] Luce, R. D. (1986). *Response Times: Their Role in Inferring Elementary Mental Organization.* New York: Oxford University Press.

9] Luce, R. D. (1988). Rank- and sign-dependent linear utility models for finite first-order gambles. *Journal of Risk and Uncertainty, 4,* 29-59.

[220] Luce, R. D. (1990). Rational versus plausible accounting equivalences in preference judgments. *Psychological Science, 1, 225*-234. Reprinted in 1992 with minor changes in W. Edwards (Ed.). *Utility Theories: Measurements and Applications*. Boston, MA: Kluwer Academic Publishers. Pp. 187-206.

[221] Luce, R. D. (1991). Rank- and sign-dependent linear utility models for binary gambles. *Journal of Economic Theory, 53,* 75-100.

[222] Luce, R. D. (1992). Where does subjective expected utility fail descriptively? *Journal of Risk and Uncertainty, 5,* 5-27.

[223] Luce, R. D. (1995). Joint receipt and certainty equivalents of gambles. *Journal of Mathematical Psychology, 39,* 73-81.

[224] Luce, R. D. (1996a). When four distinct ways to measure utility are the same. *Journal of Mathematical Psychology, 40,* 297-317.

[225] Luce, R. D. (1996b). Commentary on aspects of Lola Lopes paper. *Organizational Behavior and Human Decision Processes, 65,* 190-193.

[226] Luce, R. D. (1997). Associative joint receipts. *Mathematical Social Sciences, 34,* 51-74.

[227] Luce, R. D. (1998). Coalescing, event commutativity, and theories of utility. *Journal of Risk and Uncertainty, 16,* 87-114.

[228] Luce, R. D. (1999). Reduction invariance and Prelec's weighting functions. *Journal of Mathematical Psychology.* In press.

[229] Luce, R. D., & Fishburn, P. C. (1991). Rank- and sign-dependent linear utility models for finite first-order gambles. *Journal of Risk and Uncertainty, 4,* 29-59.

[230] Luce, R. D., & Fishburn, P. C. (1995). A note on deriving rank-dependent utility using additive joint receipts. *Journal of Risk and Uncertainty, 11,* 5-16.

[231] Luce, R. D., Krantz, D. H., Suppes, P., & Tversky, A. (1990). *Foundations of Measurement, Vol. III.* San Diego: Academic Press.

[232] Luce, R. D., & Marley, A. A. J. (1999a). Separable and additive representations of binary gambles of gains. Submitted.

[233] Luce, R. D., & Marley, A. A. J. (1999b). On elements of chance. Submitted.

[234] Luce, R. D., Mellers, B., & Chang, S.-J. (1993). Is choice the correct primitive? On using certainty equivalents and reference levels to predict choices among gambles. *Journal of Risk and Uncertainty, 6,* 115-143.

[235] Luce, R. D., & Narens, L. (1985). Classification of concatenation measurement structures according to scale type. *Journal of Mathematical Psychology, 29,* 1-72.

[236] Luce, R. D., & Narens, L. (1992). Intrinsic Archimedeanness and the continuum. In C. W. Savage & P. Erlich (Eds.). *Philosophical and Foundational Issues in Measurement Theory.* Hillsdale, NJ: Lawrence Erlbaum Associates. Pp. 15-38.

[237] Luce, R. D., & Weber, E. U. (1986). An axiomatic theory of conjoint, expected risk. *Journal of Mathematical Psychology, 30,* 188-205.

[238] Luce, R. D., & von Winterfeldt, D. (1994). What common ground exists for descriptive, prescriptive, and normative utility theories? *Management Science, 40,* 263-279.

[239] MacCrimmon, K. R. (1968). Descriptive and normative implications of the decision-theory postulates. In K. Borch & J. Mossin (Eds.). *Risk and Uncertainty.* New York: St. Martin's Press. Pp. 3-23.

240] MacCrimmon, K.R., & Larsson, S. (1979). Utility theory: Axioms versus paradoxes. In M. Allais and O. Hagen (Eds.). *Expected Utility and the Allais Paradox.* Dordrecht, Holland: D. Reidel. Pp. 333-409.

241] MacCrimmon, K. R., Stanbury, W. T., & Wehrung, D. A. (1980). Real money lotteries: A study of ideal risk, context effects, and simple processes. In T. S. Wallsten (Ed.). *Cognitive Process in Choice and Decision Behavior.* Hillsdale, NJ: Lawrence Erlbaum Associates. Pp. 155-177.

242] Machina, M. (1987a). Decision-making in the presence of risk. *Science, 236,* 537-543.

243] Machina, M. (1987b). Choice under uncertainty: Problems solved and unsolved. *Journal of Economic Perspectives, 1,* 121-154.

244] Machina, M. (1989). Dynamic consistency and non-expected utililty models of choice under uncertainty. *Journal of Economic Literature, 27,* 1622-1688.

245] Markowitz, H. (1952). The utility of wealth. *The Journal of Political Economy, 60,* 151-158.

246] Marley, A. A. J. (1967). Abstract one-parameter families of commutative learning operators. *Journal of Mathematical Psychology, 4,* 414-429.

247] Marley, A. A. J. (1997a). Probabilistic choice as a consequence of nonlinear (sub) optimization. *Journal of Mathematical Psychology, 41,* 382-391.

248] Marley, A. A. J. (Ed.). (1997b). *Choice, decision, and measurement: Essays in honor of R. Duncan Luce.* Mahwah, NJ: Lawrence Erlbaum Associates.

249] Marley, A. A. J. , & Luce, R. D. (1999). A simple axiomatization of binary rank-dependent expected utility of gains (losses). Submitted.

250] McClennen, E. F. (1990). *Rationality and Dynamic Choice.* Cambridge, England: Cambridge University Press.

251] McCord, M., & de Neufville, R. (1986). "Lottery equivalents": Reduction of the certainty effect problem in utility assessment. *Management Science, 32,* 56-60.

252] Mellers, B. A., & Biagini, K. (1994). Similarity and choice. *Psychological Review, 101,* 505-518.

253] Mellers, B. A., Chang, S.-J., Birnbaum, M. H., & Ordóñez, L. D. (1992). Preferences, prices, and rating in risky decision making. *Journal of Experimental Psychology: Human Perception and Performances, 18,* 347-361.

254] Mellers, B. A., Schwartz, A., & Cooke, A. D. J. (1998). Judgment and decision making. *Annual Review of Psychology.* Palo Alto, CA: Annual Reviews, Inc. Pp. 447-477.

255] Mellers, B.A., Weiss, R., & Birnbaum, M. H. (1992). Violations of dominance in pricing judgments. *Journal of Risk and Uncertainty, 5,* 73-90.

256] Menger, K. (1934). Das Unsichrheitsmoment in der Wertlehre. *Zeitschrift für National-ökonomie, 51,* 459-485. Translated into English by W. Schoellkopf as "The role of uncertainty in economics," in M. Shubik (Ed.). (1967). *Essays in Mathematical Economics in Honor of Oskar Morgenstern.* Princeton, NJ: Princeton University Press. Pp. 211-231.

257] Michell, J. (1990). *An Introduction to the Logic of Psychological Measurement.* Hillsdale, NJ: Lawrence Erlbaum Associates.

258] Michell, J. (1999). *Measurement in Psychology: Critical History of a Methodological Concept.* Cambridge: Cambridge University Press.

259] Michell, J., & Ernst, C. (1996). The axioms of quantity and the theory of measurement.

Translated from Part I of Otto Hölder's German text "Die Axiome der Quantität und die Lehre vom Mass." *Journal of Mathematical Psychology, 40,* 235-252.

[260] Miyamoto, J. M. (1988). Generic utility theory: Measurement foundations and applications in multiattribute utility theory. *Journal of Mathematical Psychology, 32,* 357-404.

[261] Miyamoto, J. M. (1992). Generic analysis of utility models. In W. Edwards (Ed.). *Utility Theories: Measurements and Applications.* Norwell, MA: Kluwer Academic Publishers. Pp. 73-106.

[262] Montgomery, H. (1977). A study of intransitive preferences using a think aloud procedure. In J. Jungermann & G. de Zeeuw (Eds.). *Decision Making and Change in Human Affairs.* Dordrecht: D. Reidel Publishing. Pp. 347-362.

[263] Moser, D. V., Birnberg, J. G., & Do, S. (1994). A similarity strategy for decisions involving sequential events. *Accounting, Organizations and Society, 19,* 439-458.

[264] Moskowitz, H. (1974). Effects of problem presentation and feedback on rational behavior in Allais and Morlat type problems. *Decision Sciences, 5,* 225-242.

[265] Nakamura, Y. (1990). Subjective expected utility with non-additive probabilities on finite state spaces. *Journal of Economic Theory, 51,* 346-366.

[266] Nakamura, Y. (1992). Multi-symmetric structures and non-expected utility. *Journal of Mathematical Psychology, 36,* 375-395.

[267] Nakamura, Y. (1995). Rank dependent utility for arbitrary consequence spaces. *Mathematical Social Sciences, 29,* 103-129.

[268] Newell, A. (1990). *Unified Theories of Cognition.* Cambridge, MA: Harvard University Press.

[269] O'Neill, B. (1999). Risk aversion in international relations theory. Discussion paper B445, Sonderforschungbereich 3003, University of Bonn.

[270] Payne, J. W., & Braunstein, M. L. (1971). Preferences among gambles with equal underlying distributions. *Journal of Experimental Psychology, 87,* 13-18.

[271] Payne, J. W., Laughhunn, D. J., & Crum, R. (1980). Translation of gambles and aspiration level effects in risky choice behavior. *Management Science, 26,* 1039-1060. *Management Science, 27,* 953-958.

[272] Payne, J. W., Laughhunn, D. J., & Crum, R. (1981). Further tests of aspiration level effects in risky choice behavior. *Management Science, 27,* 953-957.

[273] Pfanzagl, J. (1959). A general theory of measurement—Applications to utility. *Naval Research Logistics Quarterly, 6,* 283-294.

[274] Pollack, I. (1968). Methodological examination of the pest (parametric estimation by sequential testing) procedure. *Perception & Psychophysics, 3,* 285-289.

[275] Pope, R. E. (1983). The pre-outcome period and the utility of gambling. In B. P. Stigum & E. Wenstøp (Eds.). *Foundations of Utility and Risk Theory with Applications.* Dordrecht, Reidel. Pp. 137-177.

[276] Pope, R. E. (1985). Timing contradictions in von Neumann and Morgenster's axioms and in Savage's 'sure-thing' proof. *Theory and Decision, 18,* 229-261.

[277] Pope, R. E. (1991). The delusion of certainty in Savage's sure-thing principle. *Journal of Economic Psychology, 12,* 209-241.

[278] Pope, R. E. (1995). Towards a more precise decision framwork: A separation of the negative

utility of chance from diminishing marginal utility and the preference for safety. *Theory and Decision, 39,* 241-265.

[279] Pope, R. E. (1996/97). Debates on the utility of risk, A look back to move forward. *Journal for Science of Research, 11/12,* 43-92.

[280] Pope, R. E. (1998). Attractions to and repulsions from chance. In W. Leinfellner & E. Köhler (Eds.). *Game Theory, Experience, Rationality.* Netherlands: Kluwer Academic Publishers. Pp. 95-107.

[281] Pratt, J. W. (1964). Risk aversion in the small and in the large. *Econometrica, 32,* 122-136.

[282] Prelec, D. (1998). The probability weighting function. *Econometrica, 66,* 497-527.

[283] Preston, M. G., & Baratta, P. (1948). An experimental study of the auction-value of an uncertain outcome. *American Journal of Psychology, 61,* 183-193.

[284] Quiggin, J. (1982). A theory of anticipated utility. *Journal of Economic Behavior and Organization, 3,* 323-343.

[285] Quiggin, J. (1993). *Generalized Expected Utility Theory: The Rank-Dependent Model.* Boston: Kluwer Academic Publishers.

[286] Raiffa, H. (1968). *Decision Analysis: Introductory Lectures on Choice under Uncertainty.* Reading, MA: Addison-Wesley.

[287] Ranyard, R. H. (1976). An algorithm for maximum likelihood ranking and Slater's i from paired comparisons. *British Journal of Mathematical and Statistical Psychology, 29,* 242-248.

[288] Ranyard, R. H. (1977). Risky decisions which violate transitivity and double cancellation. *Acta Psychologica, 41,* 449-459.

[289] Rényi, A. (1970). *Foundations of Probability.* San Francisco: Holden-Day, Inc.

[290] Roberts, F. S., & Luce, R. D. (1968). Axiomatic thermodynamics and extensive measurement. *Synthese, 18,* 311-326.

[291] Ronen, J. (1971). Some effects of sequential aggregation in accounting on decision making. *Journal of Accounting Research, 9,* 307-332.

[292] Ronen, J. (1973). Effects of some probability displays on choices. *Organizational Behavior and Human Performances, 9,* 1-15.

[293] Rothschild, M., & Stiglitz, J. E. (1970). Increasing risk I: A definition. *Journal of Economic Theory, 2,* 225-243.

[294] Rubinstein, A. (1988). Similarity and decision-making under risk (Is there a utility theory resolution to the Allais paradox?). *Journal of Economic Thought, 46,* 145-153.

[295] Samuelson, P. A. (1948). Consumption theory in terms of revealed preference. *Economica, 15,* 243-253.

[296] Samuelson, P. A. (1963). Risk and uncertainty: A fallacy of large numbers. *Scienta, 98,* 108-113.

[297] Samuelson, W., & Zeckhauser, R. (1988). Status quo bias in decision making. *Journal of Risk and Uncertainty, 1,* 7-59.

[298] Sarin, R., & Wakker, P. P. (1992). A simple axiomatization of nonadditive expected utility. *Econometrica, 60,* 1255-1272.

[299] Sarin, R., & Wakker, P. P. (1994). Gains and losses in nonadditive expected utility. In B. Munier & M. L. Machina (Eds.). *Models and Experiments in Risk and Rationality.*

Netherlands: Kluwer. Pp. 157-172.

[300] Sarin, R., & Wakker, P. P. (1997). A single-stage approach to Anscombe and Aumann's expected utility. *Review of Economic Studies, 64*, 399-409.

[301] Savage, L. J. (1954). *The Foundations of Statistics*. New York: Wiley.

[302] Schmeidler, D. (1989). Subjective probability and expected utility without additivity, *Econometrica, 57*, 571-587.

[303] Schneider, S. L. (1992). Framing and conflict: Aspiration level contingency, the status-quo, and current theories of risky choice. *Journal of Experimental Psychology: Learning, Memory, and Cognition, 18*, 1040-1057.

[304] Schneider, S. L., & Lopes, L. L. (1986). Reflection of preferences under risk: Who and when may suggest why. *Journal of Experimental Psychology: Human Perception and Performance, 12*, 535-548.

[305] Schoemaker, P. J. H. (1980). *Experiment on Decisions under Risk: The Expected Utility Hypothesis*. Boston: Nijhoff Publishing Co.

[306] Schoemaker, P. J. H. (1982). The expected utility model: Its variants, purposes, evidence, an limitations. *Journal of Economic Literature, 20*, 529-563.

[307] Segal, U. (1987). Some remarks on Quiggin's anticipated utility. *Journal of Economic Behavior and Organization, 8*, 145-154.

[308] Segal, U. (1988). Does the preference reversal phenomenon necessarily contradict the independence axiom? *American Economic Review, 78*, 233-236.

[309] Segal, U. (1990). Two-stage lotteries without the reduction axiom. *Econometrica, 58*, 349-377.

[310] Segal, U. (1992). The independence axiom versus the reduction axiom: Must we have both? In W. Edwards (Ed.). *Utility Theories: Measurements and Applications*. Boston, MA: Kluwer Academic Publishers. Pp. 165-183.

[311] Selten, R. (1991). Properties of a measure of predictive success. *Mathematical Social Sciences, 21*, 153-167.

[312] Shanteau, J. (1974). Component processes in risky decision making. *Journal of Experimenta Psychology, 103*, 680-691.

[313] Shanteau, J. (1975). An information-integration analysis of risky decision making. In M. F. Kaplan & S. Schwartz (Eds.). *Human Judgment and Decision Processes*. New York: Academic Press. Pp. 109-137.

[314] Simon, H. A. (1956). Rational choice and the structure of the environment. *Psychological Review, 63*, 129-138.

[315] Slovic, P., & Lichtenstein, S. (1968). Importance of variance preferences in gambling decisions. *Journal of Experimental Psychology, 78*, 646-654.

[316] Slovic, P., & Tversky, A. (1974). Who accepts Savage's axiom? *Behavioral Science, 19*, 368-373.

[317] Sneddon, R. (1999a). Bias in a PEST procedure. *Psychological Methods*. Under revision.

[318] Sneddon, R. (1999b). Testing monotonicity with a fixed preference strength. Submitted.

[319] Sneddon, R., Cho, Y., & Fisher, G. (in preparation). Testing the substitution property of certainty equivalents.

[320] Sneddon, R., & Luce, R. D. (1999). Empirical comparisons of bilinear and non-linear utility

theories. Submitted

321] Snowball, D., & Brown, C. (1979). Decision making involving sequential events: Some effects of disaggregated data and dispositions toward risk. *Decision Sciences, 10,* 527-546.

322] Starmer, C. (1999). Cycling with rule of thumb: an experimental test for a new form of non-transitive behavior. *Theory and Decision, 46,* 141-158.

323] Starmer, C., & Sugden, R. (1989). Violations of the independence axiom in common ratio problems: An experimental test of some competing hypotheses, *Annals of Operations Research, 19,* 79-101.

324] Starmer, C., & Sugden, R. (1991). Does the random-lottery incentive system elicit true preferences? An experimental investigation. *The American Economic Review, 81,* 971-978.

325] Starmer, C., & Sugden, R. (1993). Testing for juxtaposition and event-splitting effects. *Journal of Risk and Uncertainty, 6,* 235-254.

326] Stevenson, M. K., Busemeyer, J. R., & Naylor, J. C. (1991). Judgment and decision-making theory. In M. Dunnette & L. M. Hough (Eds.). *New Handbook of Industrial-Organizational Psychology.* Palo Alto, CA: Consulting Psychologist Press. Pp. 283-374

327] Suppes, P., Krantz, D. H., Luce, R. D., & Tversky, A. (1989). *Foundations of measurement, Vol. II.* San Diego: Academic Press.

328] Taylor, M., & Creelman, C. D. (1967). Pest: Efficient estimates on probability functions. *Journal of the Acoustical Society of America, 41,* 782-787.

329] Thaler, R. H. (1985). Mental accounting and consumer choice. *Marketing Science, 36,* 199-214.

330] Thaler, R. H., & Johnson, E. (1990). Gambling with the house money or trying to break even: The effects of prior outcomes on risky choice. *Management Science, 36,* 643-660.

331] Thurstone, L. L. (1927). A law of comparative judgment. *Psychological Review, 34,* 273-286.

332] Thurstone, L. L. (1959). *The Measurement of Value.* Chicago: University of Chicago Press.

333] Torgerson, W. S. (1958). *Theory of Methods of Scaling.* New York: John Wiley & Sons.

334] Townsend, J. T., & Ashby, F. G. (1983). *Stochastic modeling of elementary psychological processes.* Cambridge, UK: Cambridge University Press.

335] Tversky, A. (1967a). Additivity, utility, and subjective probability. *Journal of Mathematical Psychology, 4,* 175-201.

336] Tversky, A. (1967b). Utility theory and additivity analysis of risky choices. *Journal of Experimental Psychology, 75,* 27-36.

337] Tversky, A. (1969). Intransitivity of preferences. *Psychological Review, 76,* 31-48.

338] Tversky, A., & Fox, C. R. (1995). Weighing risk and uncertainty. *Psychological Review, 102,* 269-283.

339] Tversky, A., & Kahneman, D. (1981). The framing of decisions and the rationality of choice. *Science, 221,* 453-458.

340] Tversky, A., & Kahneman, D. (1986). Rational choice and framing of decisions, *Journal of Business,* 59, S251-S278. Also in R. M. Hogarth & M. W. Reder (Eds.). (1987). *Rational Choice. The Contrast between Economics and Psychology.* Chicago and London: University of Chicago Press. Pp. 67-94

341] Tversky, A., & Kahneman, D. (1992). Advances in prospect theory: Cumulative representation of uncertainty. *Journal of Risk and Uncertainty, 5,* 297-323.

[342] Tversky, A., & Koehler, D. K. (1994). Support theory: A nonextensional representation of uncertainty. *Psychological Review*, 101, 547-567.

[343] Tversky, A., Sattath, S., & Slovic, P. (1988). Contingent weighting in judgment and choice *Psychological Review*, 95, 371-384.

[344] Tversky, A., Slovic, P., & Kahneman, D. (1990). The causes of preference reversal. *The American Economic Review*, 80, 204-217.

[345] Tversky, A., & Thaler, R. H. (1990). Anomalies: Preference reversals. *Journal of Economic Perspectives*, 4, 201-211.

[346] Tversky, A., & Wakker, P. P. (1995). Risk attitudes and decision weights. *Econometrica*, 63, 1255-1280.

[347] van Acker, P. (1990). Transitivity revisited. *Annals of Operations Research*, 23, 1-35.

[348] van der Meer, H. C. (1963). Decision-making: The influence of probability preference, variance preference and expected value on strategy in gambling. *Acta Psychologica*, 21, 231-259.

[349] Viscusi, W. K. (1989). Prospective reference theory: Toward an explanation of the paradoxe *Journal of Risk and Uncertainty*, 2, 235-264.

[350] von Neumann, J., & Morgenstern, O. (1947). *The Theory of Games and Economic Behavic* Princeton, NJ: Princeton University Press.

[351] von Winterfeldt, D., Chung, N.-K., Luce, R. D., & Cho, Y. (1997). Tests of consequence monotonicity in decision making under uncertainty. *Journal of Experimental Psychology: Learning, Memory, and Cognition*, 23. 406-426.

[352] von Winterfeldt, D., & Edwards, W. (1986). *Decision Analysis and Behavioral Research.* Cambridge: Cambridge University Press.

[353] Wakker, P. P. (1986). *Representations of Choice Situations.* Ph.D. dissertation, University of Brabant, Tilburg, The Netherlands.

[354] Wakker, P. P. (1988). The algebraic versus the topological approach to additive representation *Journal of Mathematical Psychology*, 32, 421-435.

[355] Wakker, P. P. (1989). *Additive Representations of Preferences: A New Foundation of Decisic Analysis.* Dordrecht, The Netherlands: Kluwer Academic Publishers.

[356] Wakker, P. P. (1990). Characterizing optimism and pessimism directly through comonotonicit *Journal of Economic Theory*, 52, 453-463.

[357] Wakker, P. P. (1991a). Additive representations on rank-ordered sets. I. The algebraic approach. *Journal of Mathematical Psychology*, 35, 501-531.

[358] Wakker, P. P. (1991b). Additive representations of preferences, a new foundation of decisior analysis; the algebraic approach. In J.-P. Doignon and J.-C. Falmagne (Eds.). *Mathematical Psychology Current Developments.* New York: Springer-Verlag. Pp. 71-87.

[359] Wakker, P. P. (1993). Additive representations on rank-ordered sets. II. The topological approach. *Journal of Mathematical Economics*, 22, 1-26.

[360] Wakker, P. P. (1994). Separating marginal utility and probabilistic risk aversion. *Theory and Decision*, 36, 1-44.

[361] Wakker, P. P., & Deneffe, D. (1996). Eliciting von Neumann-Morgenstern utilities when probabilities are distorted or unknown. *Management Science*, 42, 1131-1150.

[362] Wakker, P. P., Erev, I., & Weber, E. U. (1994). Comonotonic independence: The critical test

between classical and rank-dependent utility theories. *Journal of Risk and Uncertainty, 9,* 195-230.

63] Wakker, P. P., & Tversky, A. (1993). An axiomatization of cumulative prospect theory. *Journal of Risk and Uncertainty, 7,* 147-175.

64] Wakker, P. P., & Zank, H. (1999). A unified derivation of classical subjective expected utility models through cardinal utility. *Journal of Mathematical Economics, 38,* 1-19.

65] Weber, E. U. (1994). From subjective probabilities to decision weights: The effects of asymmetric loss functions on the evaluation of uncertain outcomes and events. *Psychological Bulletin, 115,* 228-242.

66] Weber, E. U. (1997). The utility of measuring and modeling perceived risk. In A. A. J. Marley (Ed). *Choice, Decision, and Measurement: Essays in Honor of R. Duncan Luce.* Mahwah, NJ: Lawrence Erlbaum Associates. Pp. 45-56.

67] Weber, E. U., & Hsee, C. R. (1998). Cross-cultural differences in risk perception, but cross-cultural similarities in attitudes toward perceived risk. *Management Science, 44,* 1205-1217.

68] Weber, E. U., & Kirsner, B. (1997). Reasons for rank dependent utility evaluation. *Journal of Risk and Uncertainty, 14,* 41-61.

69] Weber, E. U., & Milliman, R. A. (1997). Perceived risk attitudes: Relating risk perception to risky choice. *Management Science, 43,* 123-144.

70] Weber, M., & Camerer, C. F. (1987). Recent developments in modelling preferences under risk. *OR Spektrum, 9,* 129-151.

71] Wu, G. (1994). An empirical test of ordinal independence, *Journal of Risk and Uncertainty, 9,* 39-60

72] Wu, G., & Gonzalez, R. (1996). Curvature of the probability weighting function. *Management Science, 42,* 1676-1690.

73] Wu, G., & Gonzalez, R. (1998). Common consequence conditions in decision making under risk. *Journal of Risk and Uncertainty, 16,* 115-139.

74] Wu, G., & Gonzalez, R. (1999). Nonlinear decision weights in choice under uncertainty. *Management Science, 45,* 74-85.

75] Yaari, M. E. (1987). The dual theory of choice under risk. *Econometrica, 55,* 95-115.

Author Index

321

Author Index

324

Author Index

Y
Yaari, M.E., 72
Yates, J.F., 4
Yeary, S., 183, 190, 222, 260
Young, F.W., 100

Z
Zank, H., 194
Zeckhauser, R., 2
Zimmermann, J.M., 222

Subject Index

327

Subject Index